RUMPELSTILTSKIN'S SECRET

Everyone knows Rumpelstiltskin's story—or thinks they do. We heard it as children. We might affectionately remember the adult voices reciting the tale or recall the light in the room and the time of day when we enjoyed hearing this scripted performance. A grown-up's voice added roughness and pitch to mimic the characters, to murmur tension-filled passages, to pause drawing out the suspense between the Queen's guesses. Maybe the storyteller's voice finally rose to exult when shouting the discovered name or, drawing close, whispered it malevolently. Those long-ago readers intended to enchant us, sometimes to put us to sleep, and for a while we delighted in this magical performance. Then we grew up: obligated to attend to an adult's endless travails, we forgot little Rumpelstiltskin. But he eventually returned. Years later we told this story to our children, joining a parade of generations stretching back—no one knows how far. We voluntarily enrolled in a long procession that greys toward the back of the line, blurred, nameless, and wispy before the figures pale translucent and finally become invisible. We became merely the foremost reciters of a tale whose narration enrolled us in a club whose rules we think we know, but don't really. This tale may count among the world's oldest dirty jokes. The punchline misplaced, over time its wickedly funny insights about adult life passed for childish nonsense.

Harry Rand is a senior curator of cultural history at the Smithsonian Institution.

RUMPELSTILTSKIN'S SECRET

What Women Didn't Tell the Grimms

Harry Rand

Routledge
Taylor & Francis Group

NEW YORK AND LONDON

First published 2020
by Routledge
52 Vanderbilt Avenue, New York, NY 10017

and by Routledge
2 Park Square, Milton Park, Abingdon, Oxon, OX14 4RN

Routledge is an imprint of the Taylor & Francis Group, an informa business

© 2020 Taylor & Francis

The right of Harry Rand to be identified as author of this work has been asserted by him in accordance with sections 77 and 78 of the Copyright, Designs and Patents Act 1988.

Library of Congress Cataloging-in-Publication Data
A catalog record for this book has been requested

ISBN: 978-0-8153-8456-4 (hbk)
ISBN: 978-0-8153-8458-8 (pbk)
ISBN: 978-1-3512-0415-6 (ebk)

Typeset in Bembo
by Apex CoVantage, LLC
Printed and bound by CPI Group (UK) Ltd, Croydon, CR0 4YY

Dedicated to
Jaguar and Lozenger

Who Was Rumpelstiltskin?

FIGURE 0.1 Fourteenth-century English. This woman is our story's heroine: she's trying to get some spinning done when this leering fellow grabs her bottom. An early example of workplace sexual harassment, she frowns; he, smirking, thinks he's God's gift to women.

A woman like her composed the fairytale.

Source: © The British Library Board.

CONTENTS

ILLUSTRATIONS

INTRODUCTION

Everyone knows Rumpelstiltskin's story—or thinks they do. We heard it as children. We might affectionately remember the adult voices reciting the tale or recall the light in the room and the time of day when we enjoyed hearing this scripted performance. A grown-up's voice added roughness and pitch to mimic the characters, to murmur tension-filled passages, and to pause drawing out the suspense between the Queen's guesses. Maybe the storyteller's voice finally rose to exult when shouting the discovered name or, drawing close, whispered it malevolently. Those long-ago readers intended to enchant us, sometimes to put us to sleep, and for a while we delighted in this magical performance. Then we grew up: obligated to attend to an adult's endless travails, we forgot little Rumpelstiltskin. But he eventually returned. Years later we told this story to our children, joining a parade of generations stretching back—no one knows how far. We voluntarily enrolled in a long procession that greys toward the back of the line, blurred, nameless, and wispy before the figures pale translucent and finally become invisible. We became merely the foremost reciters of a tale whose narration enrolled us in a club whose rules we think we know, but don't really. This tale may count among the world's oldest dirty jokes. The punchline misplaced, over time, its wickedly funny insights about adult life, passed for childish nonsense.

Memories of Bedtime Stories

There's something different and a bit disturbing about Rumpelstiltskin. Disney never released a charming Rumpelstiltskin cartoon and probably won't. No other film producer ventured a successful movie about him either, knowing full well that there'd be no audience for this brooding tale of various forms of unpleasantness. The late-medieval belief system that Rumpelstiltskin hails from doesn't easily translate to modern movie sensibilities. No popular musical sings Rumpelstiltskin's tale; the story befits the scale and intensity of opera, a form that rarely entertains children. Yet, while its troubling plot may distress youngsters, the tale remains a feature of childhood.

Rumpelstiltskin is unlikely to be confused with other characters, while simpering interchangeable princesses are routinely rescued and their names and bland attributes easily blend.[1] Rumpelstiltskin's story survives in several scarcely different variants, and in none does Rumpelstiltskin offer an attractive figure to befriend; other cherished stories engender loyalty, but Rumpelstiltskin evokes only misgivings about the world and foreboding about parents' loyalties.[2] Children intuit that much. Unpleasant little Rumpelstiltskin inhibited marketing possibilities for dolls, toys, board games, a regularly syndicated newspaper cartoon, video games, action figures, fast-food dishes, and so on. In contrast, the audience that cherished *Snow White*, *Cinderella*, or *Sleeping Beauty* never outgrew such romantic tales.

Rumpelstiltskin remains un-saleable because neither he nor any of the story's characters command devotion or admiration—as we shall see, for good reason. No one in the story could be embraced with fondness, which demoted the tale to second-tier status in children's affections. No young girl wants to grow up as the victimized maiden or the story's avenging Queen. No little boy plays at being Rumpelstiltskin or dresses up like him for parties or trick or treat. Rumpelstiltskin is ignored despite his otherwise-appealing magic powers: a kind of mini-Superman who can fly and possesses super-hearing and other powers. Even in the throes of a drunken Mardi Gras or other carnival, grown-ups do not pretend to be the stupid, boasting Miller or the murderously greedy King. The story attracts neither boys nor girls nor adults.

Rumpelstiltskin persists in being un-marketable but lurks as an unbeloved feature of childhood's suspicions. That love-hate contradiction flows from an adult situation: the tale was created as a lewdly funny story by and for grown-ups. Unsuspecting parents relate the fairytale to youngsters as an almost obligatory part of child-rearing although this tale offers neither comfort nor coping skills to negotiate childhood. It neither proposes a useful guide to conduct (as a lesson to be taught and learned) nor concludes with a sage adage. Rumpelstiltskin presents a troubling anomaly that deviates from what we expect from fairytales—with good reason.

Rumpelstiltskin wanders a landscape changed more in the last few centuries than in all recorded time. It's no wonder we don't recognize him. We greet him as a visiting foreigner from a harshly alien world. Or he's fleetingly espied in modernity like a supposedly extinct creature that no one expects to see. Rumpelstiltskin seems an unanticipated ghost. He's all the more remarkable for surviving unassisted by contemporary popular electronic media. Now Rumpelstiltskin mostly prowls the pages of a story primarily read at bedtime. But even that activity seems old-fashioned.

No American any longer evades the vast commercial, and highly profitable, competition for children's attention.[3] Parental dollars purchase novel diversions, amusements that never existed during childhood's vast history. The sad results of this shift to passive entertainment are well known and devastating to olden culture that we've inherited from countless generations but have ceased to convey to the future as decent heirs. Yet, after the great die-off of authentic folk culture somehow, resisting the immense flow of hostile commercial pap, an irreplaceable and inexplicably riveting character, Rumpelstiltskin endures. Perhaps because, however unlikely for a dwarfish misfit from fairyland, we unconsciously sense his truth, Rumpelstiltskin preserves a precious nub of acute psychological accuracy.

Although he did not begin as a genuine historical character, as we will see, Rumpelstiltskin was real enough. His tale addresses a problem that lives on universally, unfortunately timeless, in a story that skillfully camouflaged its purpose. Finally, besides learning to understand a particular salacious story, there's a much larger reward to studying this fairytale's details and organization.

If we plunge into history's deepest murky waters and the psyche's abyss, we return with treasure: assurances that long ago people expressed themselves strangely (to us) but in a way that confirms our ancestors perceived the world—and they commented upon their condition—using terms that remain wholly understandable and essentially accurate. The Tale of Rumpelstiltskin improbably confirms human contact across epochs; as Ezra Pound reminded us, "Art is news that stays news".[4] This old tale notifies us that our foremothers long ago understood present-day conceptions of male-female relations. In guarded forms intended for a specific and knowing audience that was in on the joke, this tale discreetly hid from unintended observers its slyly observed nuances of gender's emotional transactions.

Two questions drive the following inquiry.

First, why was this story told? Why would anybody find this tale amusing or interesting or sensible? This tale lingers at the edges of the corpus of fairytales as among the most bizarre and unusual. It's just about unique among the stories recorded by the Brothers Grimm. If we arrive at a plausible answer to the question of "why", the second question will almost solve itself: Who first told the story?

Notes

1. While Rumpelstiltskin's irreplaceable cultural artifacts replace themselves, they molt, dramatically transforming to match succeeding users' expectations. Modernized versions that clash with the original material cancel from memory the ancestor when a new language floods out the speakers of an old tongue. A former hero may require renaming, or a secondary character becomes central to yield really startling replacements—as Noah, a biblical star, had been a Sumerian supporting player. Here's one of my favorite series of replacements; it began with a real-life event.

    The Shogun (military leader of the Japanese empire) Minamoto no Yoritomo (1147–1199) defeated his half-brother Minamoto no Yoshitsune (1159–1189). Yoshitsune was among the most famous samurai warriors and a revered general of their clan. The brothers' fight for the control of the throne formed a central part of the great epic *Heike Monogatari* (the tale of the Heike), a performance piece about a military struggle intended for recitation—like Homer's *Iliad*. And in Japanese culture the tale towered every bit as important and popular as the *Iliad* in the West. The legend developed to center the story on how Yoshitsune fled across the country with his loyal retainers disguised as wandering mountain priests. This tale supplied the basis for the highly formal Japanese Noh drama (written in 1465 by Kanze Nobomitsu) *Ataka*, which is the name of the checkpoint through which the party had to pass the interrogation of Yoritomo's suspicious soldiers. The drama spawned the most famous and beloved of all Kabuki plays (a more accessible and public form than Noh), *Kanjincho*, a word that means subscription book, the document that the fleeing general pretends to read in order to convince officers who detain him and his lord to let his party pass. In 1945 Akira Kurosawa's film version, *The Men Who Tread on the Tiger's Tail*, little altered the basic story of the general who succeeds not so much by strength as by cunning and force of will. Made at the end of World War II, Japanese censors thought the movie defeatist and delayed release while subsequent American occupation authorities considered the movie too mired in ideals of feudal loyalty, so they too banned it. Kurosawa's film was not released until 1952 and, like most of the director's movies, was not a financial success in its homeland. To counter his generally poor Japanese box office, Kurosawa decided to remake the story as an over-the-top comic-book style movie intended to please the fickle Japanese public, which then rewarded him with commercial success; in 1958 Kurosawa made *The Hidden Fortress*, essentially the same story with flipped genders: a defeated prince(ss) masquerades as a menial in service to her disguised general. Kurosawa reset the story in the sixteenth century and added two Samuel Beckett-like tragicomic characters (who first appear bickering in a blasted landscape reminiscent of *Waiting for Godot*, the movie's contemporary). The same subterfuge played out when the unarmed travelers try to pass a barrier station manned by enemy soldiers. The sex change of the defeated aristocrat from male to female was noted by the young George Lucas, who in 1977 remade the story yet again, calling it *Star Wars*. In his homage movie—dressed up as a Flash Gordon piece set in the distant past as a winking nod to the source material's legendary historicity—Lucas changed the two nattering sidekicks to robots; retained the female gender of the escaping princess borrowed from *The Hidden Fortress*; and, most importantly, to the flow of the story, featured the disguised defeated general who escapes his confrontation at the armed barrier by force of character (called "The Force"). As a replacement, in all these variations the basic story did not change.

2. Well-beloved tales became feature-length animated movies, or even an opera—like *Hansel and Gretel*, whose father recants his wife's wicked advice—or a TV series (however remotely related to the namesake personality). In the fall lineup of 2011, Disney's ABC television network presented *Once Upon a Time*. This weekly show featured Snow White, Prince Charming, the wicked queen, the dwarfs, and diverse fairytale characters, now all amnesiacs with scant recollection of their enchanted history but entangled by a magical spell to dwell in a town in modern-day Maine. Fairytales deliver spin-off characters, more or less whole easily introduced into other stories, characters who appear as known entities with costumes, physique, dislikes, and desires.

3. In the early 1960s George Oppen (1908–1984) posted fairytales' death date when the poet noted (1963, p. 33) that "I belong to a generation that grew more American—literarily at least . . . we grew up on English writing—and German fairy tales—as I think no American any longer does". He was right about Germanic fairytales, genuine folk music, and authentic lullabies—all mostly gone from the average electronic childhood.

4. The original line is "Literature is news that STAYS news" Ezra Pound (1960, p. 29).

THE TALE OF RUMPELSTILTSKIN

Here is the story in modern English. It is not the Grimms' last interpretation but a standard one. Recorded versions differ slightly; some vary Rumpelstiltskin's song, his means of exit, or include a helpfully eavesdropping nursemaid or woodsman.

Once upon a time there was a poor miller. He had in this world only a beautiful daughter.

One day the king and his court came riding by and stopped before the home of the miller who dutifully greeted the king. Almost immediately the miller began boasting about his daughter. In this company the miller felt he had to make himself feel important. "Your majesty" bragged the miller "I have a daughter who is more beautiful than all the girls in this region and can spin excellently, both quickly and fine". But the king was not impressed. The miller continued, hoping to interest the king, and before he knew what he was saying the miller blurted out, "My daughter can spin straw into gold".

Now this claim stopped the king cold and got his attention. Like all kings he was greedy, but this king really loved gold. He could not imagine a finer skill than making as much gold as he wanted and he pictured the girl turning out rooms full of gold for him. But what if the miller were lying? He would put her to the test. "The spinning of straw into gold is an art that pleases me well". So he ordered the miller to send his daughter to the castle the very next day.

As he had ordered, the next day the terrified girl was brought before him. The king led her through the palace to a little room that was filled with straw. In the room were spools and a spinning wheel. The king said, "If by the next morning you have not spun this straw into gold you will have to die". Then he locked the door, and the girl was left inside, alone.

There sat the poor miller's daughter. She had no idea how to spin straw into gold. She did not know what to do. She tried spinning the straw but it just got tangled in the wheel. The straw certainly did not turn into gold. Time passed and she tried time and again to spin the straw and as time passed and the night came on she grew more and more frightened. At last, helpless amid all the straw, she began to lament and weep.

Suddenly the door opened and a tiny man walked into the room.

"Good evening, Mistress Miller" he said. "Why are you sobbing so?"

"Oh" the girl cried, "I must spin this straw into gold and I don't know how".

"What will you give me if I spin it for you?" the little man asked.

The miller's daughter was dumbfounded to think that anybody could spin straw into gold but, presently, gaining her wits she answered, "My necklace". And she offered the necklace she was wearing.

The little man took her necklace and sat down at the spinning wheel. He pulled three times—whirl! whirl! whirl!—and the spool was wound full of gold thread. She was amazed. He fitted another spool on, and—whirl! whirl! whirl!—three pulls and that one too was full. And so it went until morning, when all the straw was spun and all the spools were full of gold.

Early in the morning the curious king eagerly came to the girl's room. He was amazed and delighted, but seeing all that shining gold only made him greedier. So he led the miller's daughter to a larger room filled with straw. "If you value your life" he commanded "spin this straw into gold before dawn". Then he left and locked her into the room filled with straw.

The girl did not know what to do. She began to weep. But, as on the night before, into her room the same little man appeared. "What will you give me if I spin this straw into gold for you?" he asked.

Now she looked at him carefully and answered, "The ring on my finger". And the little man took her ring. Then he set the spinning wheel turning, and before the night was over, he had spun all the straw into gleaming gold.

Early in the morning the impatient king opened the door to her room, entered and gazed in happy amazement. Everywhere were piles of golden spools glittering in the morning light. The king rejoiced at the sight of so much gold, but still he was not satisfied.

He led the miller's daughter to a third, even bigger room that was piled high with straw. "Tonight you must spin this straw too" ordered the king. "And if you succeed, you shall become my wife". Because, he thought, "Even though she is only a miller's daughter, I could not find a richer wife in all the world".

When the king had left, the little man appeared for the third time. "What will you give me if I spin for you yet once more?" he asked.

"I have nothing left that I could give to you" the girl replied.

"Then promise that when you become queen, your first child will belong to me".

The miller's daughter gasped. How could she promise such a thing? Then she thought, But who knows whether that will ever happen? But she could think of no other way to save herself, so she promised. Once more the little man spun all the straw into gold.

When the king opened the door at sunrise and found the entire room full of gold he did as he promised. He married the pretty miller's daughter, and she became a queen.

A year passed. The queen brought a handsome baby boy into the world. She hardly ever thought of the little man. But one day he appeared suddenly in her room. "Now give me what you promised me" he demanded. The queen was horrified.

The queen pleaded with the little man: He could take all the riches in her kingdom if he would only let her keep her child. But her pleading was in vain. "No" he replied "something alive is dearer to me than all the world's treasures". Then she began to weep so piteously that at last the little man was moved.

"I will give you three days time" he said. "If by the end of that time you know my name, you may keep your child".

All through the night the queen sat thinking, and through the next day she paced and thought, recalling all the names she had ever heard.

That evening the little man returned. Beginning with Caspar, Melchior, and Balthazar, the queer recited every name she knew, one after another. But to each one the little man replied, "That is not my name".

The second day the queen had inquiries made in town of all the people there, searching for new names. And when the little man came that evening, she posed the strangest and most unusual ones to him. She tried Shortribs, Sheepshanks, and Laceleg, but he would only reply, "That is not my name".

Now the queen grew truly frightened. The third day was coming and the bargain would be sealed. She sent her most faithful handmaid throughout the countryside to discover the little man's name. When the servant returned she told of searching through thickets and over clearings, deep into the forest, but she could not discover the name. At last, near the top of a high hill, she spied a little house and in front of it burned a bright fire and around the fire flew a little man riding his cooking spoon, and as he rode he sang:

> Today I bake, tomorrow brew,
> The next I'll have the young Queen's child.
> O glad am I, For no one knows
> That Rumpelstiltskin I am called!

After witnessing this scene the servant made her way back as fast as she could manage. At midday she reached the castle. You can imagine how glad the queen was when she heard the name.

Late that evening the little man arrived. "Now, Mistress Queen" he said, "what is my name?"

So the queen asked him, "Is your name Konrad?"

"No".

"Is your name Paul?"

"No".

"Then, perhaps your name is Rumpelstiltskin?"

"The Devil told you that! The Devil told you that!" shrieked Rumpelstiltskin. And in a fury he [jumped on his cooking spoon and flew out the window] disappeared.

And he never was heard from again.

1

THE STORY'S HISTORY

Of the best known Grimm tales, this one is perhaps the most obscure and puzzling.
James M. McGlathery

The Life and Times of Rumpelstiltskin:
Foreword from Eden

Despite their durability ancient stories float insubstantial in the air. They're easily destroyed artifacts until nailed down to the page, pinned like butterflies. Granted incarnation in a body of ink and paper, stories traded their free-ranging immortality for a fixed written form. Formerly sovereign wanderers, once rounded up, paralyzed as exhibits, stared at like caged animals, fairytales endured poking here and there by scholarly gawkers. Most prominently by the Brothers Grimm.

The famous brothers gathered, classified, sometimes extensively edited, then published quaintly outlandish materials. Their German expeditions resembled explorations that combed the countryside of France, Russia, England, and Scandinavia. The far-ranging explorers of different countries and languages harvested collections variously named Mother Goose or the Arabian Nights. As part of this collecting effort the Grimms created one tale's fixed pattern. That form, called the Tale of Rumpelstiltskin, endures like a classic recipe that only a fool would alter for knowledgeable consumers. The story lives in the reveries of every modern child who hears it recited or who silently reads the fairytale.[i] It has stopped evolving.

---

i. Folklorists strictly define the terms "story", "tale", "variant", "version", "type", and "fable". This book is intended for the rest of us who make no such distinctions. I cannot argue with professionals who

Frozen in form, ancient Rumpelstiltskin, though apparently unsuited to our era, tenants imaginations constructed in post–Industrial Age childhoods. He faced unprecedented competition for childhood's fond attention. This latest generation saw folk music drained of authenticity and replaced with commercial popular sounds. The same assault swept every branch of authentic folk traditions. Now drenched in visual and aural kitsch childhood must work to reclaim its original culture. In addition, as if things weren't bad enough for taletelling as amusement, for three generations movies foamed inanity to blunt lived experience. Adolescents and adults undergo pop culture's vapid moralizing, perhaps intended to dissuade proletarian reflection by substituting anger or sentimentality for shrewd observation. With scant exceptions, throw-away novels, so-called airport reading, dilute critical awareness to change standards for concentration on the storytelling art. Background (elevator) music taught us how not to pay attention; indeed, this aural wallpaper forced the captive listener to disregard surroundings or go mad. Music had never been intended to be ignored but was formerly regarded as precious. The fairytale largely succumbed to kitsch.

Industrial modernity's harsh winds evaporated oceans of vital folklore when steam-driven machines doomed an essential and age-old home craft. Industrialization and mechanization on an enormous scale began in the early nineteenth century with automated devices for pumping out mines and for thread-spinning. The latter is especially pertinent. Hellish workshops of unprecedented size cloistered factory workers away from hand-spinning, and such industrialization decisively changed Rumpelstiltskin's world. As poorly as male factory workers were served when sweating near puffing, noisy, and lethal machines that whirled indifferent to lopping off an arm or head to fill a spindle with thread, women's self-confidence fared worse. Knowledge formerly essential to womanhood, the crafts of fiber arts became the first automated victims of alienated labor. Along with society's titanic upheaval and the huge migration from farm to factory, industrialization demoted the womanly crafts that supplied the key to understanding the Tale of Rumpelstiltskin. By divorcing a population from its formerly proud handiwork in just two generations, employment in maddeningly loud and dangerous cotton or wool mills expunged the specific knowledge listeners needed to understand this strange story. Rumpelstiltskin emerges from the twin background of industry's encroachments on folklife and the Grimms' editing.

Who Owns This Story?

More than a season spanning a few years, childhood proposes a way of doing, a biologically driven process of seeing and reacting while under the protection of grown-ups. Sheltered in the care of adult guardians who exercise more or less trustworthy oversight,

---

discriminate niceties of the folklorists' trade, but the various terms for stories will be used informally. To the vexation of diploma-bearing specialists I intend to be easy going with such fine points of their livelihood. If you belong to the scholarly ilk of professional folklorists, you might feel less lenient than merely irritated but the rest of us won't notice the difference if the usage slides from calling Rumpelstiltskin a fairytale or a story.

life's first years feature almost daily "ah-ha!" moments of learning, of discovery. That sensation rouses or quenches appetites to last a lifetime. As part of childhood experience, those sometimes-dependable adults recited Rumpelstiltskin's story. Or they introduced us to the library where we found it ourselves. Rumpelstiltskin names a sanctioned activity. But why?

What act do we commit when telling his story? Folklorists assign Rumpelstiltskin to Aarne and Thompson's folklore type 500, a "guess the [helper's] name" or "The Name of the Helper" story.[1] In addition to the Secret Name, some of the other fairytale themes in the Tale of Rumpelstiltskin are the Impossible Task, the Hard Bargain, and the Changeling Child.[2] To some, this story exemplifies a so-called Rise fairy tale that opens "with a dirt-poor girl or boy who suffers the effect of grinding poverty and whose story continues with tests, tasks, and trials until magic brings about a marriage to royalty and a happy accession to great wealth".[3] Chafing at the standard classification, a prominent commentator suggested that Rumpelstiltskin's function in the story "has always been presented in a misleading way. . . . Rumpelstiltskin is categorized as a helper, while he is obviously a blackmailer and oppressor".[4] Much depends on assessing his moral stature.

While enthralling children, Rumpelstiltskin perplexed adult readers. One of the story's most knowledgeable commentators flatly stated that "[o]f the best known Grimm tales, this one is perhaps the most obscure and puzzling".[5] The enigma has not impeded this story's acceptance. Despite its unique status—a story that belongs to a class with only one constituent—Rumpelstiltskin entered our culture. Not only "part of" our culture, Rumpelstiltskin contributes a small but irreplaceable parcel to the great sum of occidental literature, a story recalled by nearly everyone. The story's title entered English as a word now found in the dictionary. But it's a strange word in that everyone knows it—most use it without hesitation or fear of seeming esoteric or being misunderstood—yet the word apparently lacks any meaning: this everyday reference lacks a referent. We mention the name knowingly but understand not what it means. That was not always the case.

An Unlovely Story About Unpleasant People

Generations embraced this tale of an unlovable character who seems neither admirable nor approachable. But that's also true for *all* the story's characters.

Rumpelstiltskin's harsh story offers no moral or spiritual uplift. Other fairytales shine definitive "happy endings", but Rumpelstiltskin's story suggests nothing superior to everyday life's often grubby choices. The contrasts emerge obvious and striking.

Sleeping Beauty wakes to the kiss of a prince—not bad—while the Miller's Daughter essentially submits to being raped by the King following a frenzy of cupidity.

Snow White's hopeful tale condemns villainy. Wickedness sets the tale in motion balanced by the ending's bracing uplift. After her crisis, good-willed rescuers flock to assist Snow White. Her (cinematic) dwarfs prove themselves unforgettably charming and loyal companions. The tale animates the age-old clash between fecund youth and menopausal anxiety as Snow White glows with abundant beauty that vexes her aging stepmother's waning sexuality. We are expected to side with youth and health.

Just a glimpse of Rapunzel's face through an upper-floor window renders a passing man besotted. The Miller's Daughter, described but once—and then formulaically and obligatorily, if not grudgingly, as nominally beautiful—seems plain. She captivates no one. Her personality and unremarkable looks are never reported. In the Rumpelstiltskin story, it's not the girl's looks, alluring sexual potential, or charm that attracts the King. Even her doting loopy father driven to distraction by the King's sudden appearance fails to praise her looks with specifics about her eyes, musical laugh, radiant hair, willowy figure, graceful gestures, glowing skin, singing voice, or smile; the King could see these unmentioned details for himself so that praising them in their absence would be futile and obviously counterfactual compared to the father's great lie.

Since she cannot spin straw into gold, by this same order of hyperbole her looks are probably nothing special either. Since her braggart father's claims are patently false, why would anyone hearing the story believe that the miller has "a daughter who is more beautiful than all the girls in this region"? Naturally the horse-mounted King gazing down at the peasant was unimpressed by the evidence of his own eyes. He ignores her until hearing an amazing gilded boast (not even an exaggeration but an impossibility) draws his attention to an extraordinary unproven talent that he demands the girl demonstrate. Before hearing that claim the monarch hardly looked at the Miller's Daughter and was planning no dalliance: she's no fetching peasant girl.

Again, the contrasts are clear.

The beautiful Cinderella crowns her rags-to-riches trajectory with the satisfying bonus of moral vindication. The polite heroine rises from clearing hearth-dust to glitter. She enjoys material elegance, social station, and vast riches while, after scrubbing away the eponymous cinders, her outer beauty appears to mirror her inner virtue. (In some versions Cinderella pardons her stepsisters and welcomes their penitence.) Cinderella's mercy confirmed a cosmic justice that exalted her to the prospect that she would join the ranks of mythical wise queens. Suitably gowned, her soot polished off, the scorned sister Cinderella proves both beautiful and compassionate; ennobling allows her to practice ample forgiveness and make visible an expansive soul that bestows clemency and graciousness. That's one lesson about the workings of Providence, pagan or Christian. Truth will out. Her ascent also counterpoises her nasty stepsisters' chagrin: a second lesson. The higher Cinderella rises, the more miserable they feel, an emotional balance that reflects many real-life family relationships.

Cinderella offers a "role model" for peasant girls dreaming of being plucked from their chores to fame. But are young girls hearing the Tale of Rumpelstiltskin supposed to emulate the Miller's Daughter? As queen she leaves behind all material cares but yet exacts sadistic retribution on her defender. However bloody the Grimms' tales in their day, gloating sadism remains a timelessly unfashionable behavior. It also differs from many best-loved fairytales.

Like Cinderella, Belle (costar of *Beauty and the Beast*), Snow White, the Bible's Queen Esther, and many others, the Miller's Daughter undergoes social elevation and new wealth. But instead of revenge against her tormentors—her father and husband—she destroys poor Rumpelstiltskin who helped her gain the crown. The story presents a confusing message[6]—pretty sordid in all as she treats her benefactor shabbily. The story's attraction must reside elsewhere than in teaching morality. Essentially, this tale lacks any lesson in scruples.

Pleasurably creepy stories often end with a last-minute triumph at the curtain, a jubilant resolution of release from tension. In Rumpelstiltskin's tale, deliverance arrives after doubly accented stress. The familiar pattern supports hundreds of plots, and many jokes rely on the same triple "setup". Three nights of spinning, three pulls to fill a spool, three days of guessing, three names guessed—this near-universal rhythm supplies a cadence essential to many droll stories.[ii] Rumpelstiltskin himself reckons triple time when he sings that "Today I bake" (the first day), then "tomorrow brew" (the second day), and "The next I'll have the young Queen's child" (the third day). A thrice-metrical pattern sustains both high and low art and that array lavishly ornaments Rumpelstiltskin's story. Yet, despite its familiar organization, this story remains uniquely alien. Its seemingly familiar types, a commonplace triple form, and famous themes of magic and human woe—nothing habituates us to it or expunges this tale's remarkable strangeness, which suggests neither its structure nor stock elements distinguish Rumpelstiltskin's story— but something else, unspoken. Beneath its obvious surface an unstated content lingers weirdly in the mind.

The Tale of Rumpelstiltskin occupies a place apart from otherwise-comparable fairy-tales.[7] The story drops into our present as an exceptional legacy because of where it was composed, by whom, how it was transmitted into the present, the disregard and scorn it suffered before gaining serious attention, and how its message (but not its content) adapted to an onrushing future. We might ask: Does the Tale of Rumpelstiltskin mean anything at all? Perhaps that is not even a fair question to pose of a work that was never intended to withstand interrogations routinely directed at high art's literary ambitions. It's certainly not a question we pose to its main audience, children: "OK kids, what was *that* all about? Think about it. Tomorrow morning you'll be tested on this bedtime story. Sleep tight".

Where Rumpelstiltskin Came From

Universally known in the English-speaking world, the tale carries a potent inner meaning. Its significance rests latent far beyond children's fanciful conceptions or even adult's

---

ii. An odd statement or situation repeats to set a pattern of expectations. A third syncopated variant delivers the punchline that breaks toward a surprising direction. (So the last of the three Billy Goats Gruff fares better than his two brothers. The story counsels learning and progress. "The Three Little Pigs" celebrates an evolution to celebrate technological development. "Goldilocks and the Three Bears" always finds a middle ground between extremes.) In really sophisticated jokes the punchline refers to a pattern that already exists outside the joke, meta-humor. Present in the crudest drollery, this three-part order also defines the sonata form beneath the nineteenth century's great symphonies.

deceptive recollections of their own earliest years. Rumpelstiltskin remains a fundamentally baffling story about which we know little conclusively. But even latent meaning can be exposed. And when unmasked this fairytale's inner workings and the storyteller's ambitions reveal redemptive promise and the fairytale's power. To fully grasp how the otherwise incomprehensible tale can be so affecting, we have to learn something about its origins.

★★★

The story surfaced from Europe's subconscious into the world of well-circulated literature in 1808 when Jacob Ludwig Carl Grimm (1785–1863) sent a version of it, called "Rumpenstünzchen", to his teacher Friedrich Karl Von Savigny (1779–1861), a founder of the "historical school" of jurisprudence. The connection between statutes and folklore is not obvious.

Savigny advocated the view, then novel and now prevalent, that existing bodies of law derived from a community's cultural origins and the historical transformations they had undergone as a people. Law embodied no moral absolute, neither divinely revealed nor unalterably inherited from ancients. However unlikely this approach to law, more specifically the study and application of jurisprudence, decisively aided Rumpelstiltskin's voyage into the present.

Savigny was the heir of a long line of landed nobility who had emigrated from Lorraine. He studied at Göttingen and received his degree from the University of Marburg in 1800 where he began teaching, freed from economic concerns by inherited wealth. Undisturbed by political or financial considerations, he committed himself to scholarship. But he was no dilettante.

Savigny's connection to the Grimm family derived from his stature as a preeminent German legal scholar. Jacob Grimm's father, a lawyer, died when Jacob was a child, leaving his mother and her children in a suddenly difficult financial situation. The family suffered instant degradation from self-sufficiency to penurious dependency upon others' good will. As in a fairytale (for example, *Beauty and the Beast*) almost overnight the widow and her family were reduced from running a large and prosperous household with servants to near poverty. Luckily the family's aunt served as a lady-in-waiting to the princess of Hesse-Kassel, and she helped finance the Grimm boys education so that Jacob and his two-years-younger but equally clever brother Wilhelm Carl Grimm (1786–1859) could attend the public high school at Kassel. In 1802 Jacob entered the University of Marburg to study law, emulating his deceased father who had studied there, and, after recovering from a severe illness, Wilhelm joined his brother the next year, also to study law. Compensating for their father's death and their reduced social status as relative paupers at the university, the boys strove to excel and they won the attention of their professor, Savigny. Savigny's classes merged cultural studies, science, and law into an intoxicating blend. Inspired by these lessons, years later, in the "Preface" to Grimm's *Grammar of German*, Jacob credited Savigny with stimulating him to pursue historical investigations. And such studies were hardly inconsequential Ivory Tower pursuits at that moment.

Electrifying ideas swirled through the German-speaking world, a place without an obvious center. No unified Germany then existed; only a cluster of German-speaking principalities descended from medieval fiefdoms. Such an unworkable patchwork beckoned as an opportunity for invasion when the French Revolution overflowed that country's borders. Napoléon rampaged through Europe. In response, a decade after France invaded the German realms, Savigny published an influential pamphlet (with the imposing title: "Of the Vocation of Our Age for Legislation and Jurisprudence", 1814); he argued for resisting the Napoleonic Code's unifying influence. An apparent reactionary Savigny countered the tide of ostensibly modern progressive reform.

French legal theory seemed attractive and was widely proposed as a model to consolidate civil regulation throughout the still-divided German states. But Savigny's opposition arose from his wholly Romantic idea that a legal code, like any other aspect of culture, expressed a community's deepest spiritual identity no less than cooking, music, poetry, and dress. For him statutes supplied part of a peoplehood. Law could not be imposed willy-nilly from above or from outside however noble the academic wrangling that fashioned it. Though lenient or admirable, for Savigny and his followers French law was unsuitable for Germans. Hardly a distant abstraction, its many ordinances and rules govern mundane living, and Savigny wanted the law's intimate relationship to its people to grow from a uniquely and identifiably Teutonic loam. The law touches us all, every day. The ancient roots of folk traditions should nourish what might otherwise be a dry study of legalisms. Law followed lore.

As two embryonic law students, the Grimms were taught to look from present law backward to ancient traditions. Savigny's jurisprudence exposed them to a critical facet of German Romanticism, a movement that aimed to discover or invent cultural expressions consistent with Germany's rudimentary, even tribal, roots. From these roots grew Germanic language, songs, lyrical epics, and folktales. That long-neglected ethos would be refreshed with new forms, cultural and artistic expressions that presented the latest manifestation of purely native characteristics. That was the theory anyway. The *Volksgeist* (the soul or spirit of a people) supposedly represented an unconscious set of urgings unique to Teutonic bloodlines, an urge that supported everything else particular to the German people. Today this once-promising theoretical position has largely become odious by association with its malfeasant offspring.

After its forceful Nazi amplification and willfully vile misprision, the cluster of ideas and corollaries associated with the Volkgeist reeks. Now a repugnant idea, in the early nineteenth century, the ancient foundations of the "spirit of a people" seemed to need discovery, dusting off, and renewal for fresh structures to be erected atop. That's were Rumpelstiltskin comes in. Age-old customs and beliefs would find their complete articulation in the national spirit of a modern state, its laws, and its arts if, according to this theory, modernity arose organically from a trove of half-remembered folkways. In the next century this notion flowered into the nastiest expression of nationalism when zealots assumed that if Germans had once possessed a "pure" culture it must have been corrupted (by somebody) and should be purified by killing almost everybody else in Europe.[8] The process of coarsening Romantic ideas began innocently enough, then stampeded amok.

Among the scholars seeking the roots of Teutonic culture, Johan Gottfried Herder (1744 1803) worked in tandem with the Grimms. Tragically, "students focused on Herder's ideas of nationalism and the German *Volk* and interpreted them in the narrowest possible way".[9] In particular, as Ruth B. Bottigheimer pointed out, an eager student of this theory, Wilhelm Grimm believed "that the tales not only embodied German-ness, but also that they showed Germans how to be German".[10] Misinterpreted or exaggerated, the nationalist idea incubated history's most dire consequences. Herder's concept of nationalism didn't elevate one people above another as he tried to understand the difference between groups. The "volk"—peoplehood expressed as a nation—defined the utmost of human achievement and genius. But those who followed Herder saw no reason for restraint and posited that the German *Volk* possessed qualities superior to other nations. The urge to unify Germanic peoples into a common state and the Grimms' folkloric-linguistic enterprise provided the essential materials, but hardly inevitable direction, for a catastrophe. The rise of a German state did not inescapably lead to the nightmares that followed, but explorers who searched for an early, and subsequently "violated", Teutonic culture provided an indispensable element of what ensued. Accordingly, when "[t]he bicentennial of the Grimms' birth years in 1985–1986 was celebrated by scholarly conferences and exhibits both in the United States" and in Germany, it was understood that "[t]he Brothers Grimm fad [had] ridden the coattails of popular nostalgia, nationalism, and a yearning for a 'positive' celebration after the series of commemorations of Third Reich and Holocaust events".[11] But at its beginning no Nazis loomed as over-eager inheritors of the explorers who searched for prehistoric culture's surviving remnants. The original quest seemed wholly benevolent: excavating ancient mores to yield present law or finding contemporary words that preserved the sounds of distant antiquity.

Rummaging in the past for materials to build a future state, the searchers stumbled upon Rumpelstiltskin. His latent powers revived like a movie's sleeping mummy.

The Search Begins

Spoken dialect—perchance obsolete words or phrases, highly localized language usage, provincial precepts—could reveal a lingering ancient ethos. But you had to know where and how to look and listen. The Grimms became linguistic prospectors mining for nuggets in a hunt that challenged stamina and cunning like other nineteenth-century adventurers who fanned out across the globe to explore the map's "blank" zones. Some adventurers set out to find exotic wildlife and returned with trophies of previously unseen species. Others traveled into the past with a spade—like Heinrich Schliemann (1822–1890) who unearthed Troy and the "Tomb of Agamemnon". A different sort of explorer wandered to the world's far-flung corners to peer at natural splendor previously unseen by Europeans. Along these heroic lines the Brothers Grimm sought an exotic but long-forgotten world. Their treasures were not disinterred from the earth but, overgrown by modern usage, could be transcribed from the parlance of aged speakers. That still-living record yielded the ancient jewels they sought, treasures spoken by elderly rurals who lived in out-of-the-way places undisturbed by the Industrial Age and who conversed in regional dialectics. At least that was the idea—practice was something else.

As Savigny and a few others struggled to unify ancestors with their descendants, Jacob Grimm set off to become a philologist as well as a lawyer and mythologist. And he succeeded, becoming an immortal collector of folklore and fairytales. But first Savigny opened to Jacob Grimm a vista of the past, half-obscured by time's erasures.

At the beginning of 1805 Jacob joined Savigny for a year in Paris to assist the senior scholar with literary investigations. There Jacob wandered delighted through pages of ancient songs and tales. In Parisian libraries he first read the Old German minnesingers—the German troubadours of the twelfth and thirteenth centuries, singers of courtly love who preceded the Renaissance meistersingers. Once he began he toiled ceaselessly to reclaim time-stilled voices; Jacob's scientific outlook harnessed to indefatigable energy kept him cheerfully working until he died. His research yielded abundant scholarly insights published in impressive works like his masterful *Grammar of the German Language*. He also laid the foundation for much modern philology. (Grimm's laws describe the more or less regular changes that speech-sounds undergo through time.) Grimm exhorted his colleagues and scholarly heirs to endorse a scientific outlook. He proposed strict linguistic patterns to organize and correlate kindred sounds within any one language though time or to affiliate word- or sound patterns in related languages. Ideally his surveys for linguistic samples would be gathered in various out-of-the-way places—as a true explorer. To glean such results he could interrogate a cross-section of people of varying castes and professions. But such field investigations were unnecessary. Instead of worldwide travel he often derived examples from old texts that recorded bygone patterns of speech. Less colorfully, he lived amid the best possible representatives to illustrate theories with specimens of Teutonic usage: everyday German speakers.

Optimally, the Grimms culled speech samples—delicacies of oddly antiquated talk or queer bits of commonplace local phrasing native to a district or profession—from interviews with Germans of different regions. In an idealized representation the Grimms tracked half-remembered folktales that elderly provincials recalled from decades-past childhoods, before the Industrial Revolution transformed their agricultural world. At least that was the hope. As conceived the great adventure invited a long and arduous trek throughout Eurasia. In reality Jacob and Wilhelm Grimm gathered most of their material from a closely circumscribed group in their immediate vicinity. While this may seem illegitimate—perhaps deceptive, or at least a curious way to find the long-buried roots of German language and thereby to fashion declarations about an entire culture—it is not. The Grimms did not cheat by staying close to home. Exonerating them requires an explanation.

There are many ways to gather and appraise intangible cultural elements. Museums hold other things, hard artifacts on display in glass cases. We're used to a history of things. Perhaps more important than such admired material objects that can only infer meaning and use, what people carry in their heads identifies them with one group rather than another. Notions about the world (its origins and organization) help us identify us and explain how to relate to those who either share or attack our views. It's an arduous and exacting work trying to harvest and sort such immaterial stuff. Concepts are less easily intercepted in overheard conversations or interviews than catching gossamer. Consequently, harsh disagreement erupts in the various disciplines that make up Human Studies about how to capture, arrange, and construct from such samples a theory of social behavior.

It's generally thought that a theory of community-approved conduct requires wide-ranging surveys. In some fields an accurate or reliable result derives only from abundant data like polls or surveys with results replicated by an open community of scholars.[12] There are exceptions. A language can be sampled from a small population, even if spoken in far-flung—geographically diverse and culturally various—expressions like globe-circling English that is natively spoken from Maine to Texas, Australia, India and, of course, the British Isles. The specimen taken of a language can be small to arrive at a valid representation however large the family of native speakers. For the purposes of a linguistic survey only a tiny sample of native speakers suffices, a point the Grimms well understood. A reliable (indeed unassailable) picture of a language originates from those who speak it. Interestingly, linguists themselves repair to a metaphoric Rumpelstiltskin to describe this situation. The fairytale suggests that the "native speaker is both a blessing and a curse" as the term "remains ambiguous, tantalizingly beyond grasp. If linguists are the weaver-maiden, the native speaker is surely their Rumpelstiltskin, necessary but troublesomely elusive".[13] Invoked by the Miller's Daughter (or linguists), Rumpelstiltskin comes to their aid as a "necessary but troublesomely elusive" helpmate. And the Grimms would concur that as a native speaker of some language, no one has more right, is more entitled, than you to your language. Each speaker, including you, plays a role in building language—a vital function the Grimms appreciated when they stumbled upon Rumpelstiltskin.

Jacob sampled the raw materials of language that he trusted to reflect remnants of, or clues to, old-time speech. He printed some valuable examples in the folktales subsequently celebrated as the Tales of the Brothers Grimm. One of these, among the strangest, became known as Rumpelstiltskin.

Rumpelstiltskin, Any Language's Native Speaker

After Savigny the Grimms next sent the fairytale to Clemens Brentano in 1810.[14] Clemens (or Klemens) Wenzeslaus Brentano (1778–1842) crucially figured in the second phase of German Romanticism. A polymath, he wrote plays, essays, novels, poetry, was a folklorist, editor, and religious writer. In all his work Brentano trusted the folkloric tradition to provide an aesthetic touchstone of literature's value. He received Rumpelstiltskin's tale as a reader ideally suited to sympathize with the story's unrelentingly gloomy tone. Brentano likely rejoiced in its dark twists, though unaware of the tale's origins. Unknown to him and everyone else Brentano had spent his life preparing to receive the story. His exhaustive erudition in Germanic culture predisposed him as Rumpelstiltskin's best and most sympathetic auditor until the tale entered the world of children's literature. Brentano himself had never fully disenthralled from a traumatic childhood. His troubled youth conditioned him to roam in wonder through the shadowy fairytale realm, perhaps to escape into fantasy from an afflicted past.

Conducted to the empire of literature by his mother, Brentano compensated for her death by morbidly immersing himself in the cult of the Virgin Mary.[15] His absorption offered no mere religious solace. Inconsolable, he sorrowfully wandered through an alternately dreary or resplendent natural world. Nature revealed or screened evidence for the hand of a Providence that shaped the landscape and human fate.[16] Driven by an impassioned but unspecified longing and profound regret, he yearned for a lost (personal) paradise. Today we might diagnose him as bipolar without diminishing his creativity in the least. Dismal mania suited Brentano's literary needs as an author, and perfectly conditioned his mentality to accommodate Rumpelstiltskin's unhappy tale. Brentano likely thrilled when he began to read a pre-modern folktale of magic and Hope, an ancient story yanked from the obscurity of a linguistic grave and returned into daylight. And how Rumpelstiltskin was fished from the deeps of a forgotten cultural abyss informs our understanding because when removed from his original context Rumpelstiltskin appears as a strange creature indeed.

If Brentano's Romantic past served him well, his disciples continued to long for that bygone world of heightened emotions and blurry thinking. At the beginning of the nineteenth century, the Grimms excitedly read Brentano's folk-song collection *The Youth's Magic Horn* and began to collect for themselves folktales inspired by Brentano's example. Through the Grimms we remain in Brentano's debt—unlikely feckless dreamer that he was.

While some features of the tale that Jacob Grimm showed to Savigny differed from the main version now in circulation, after it was first dictated and copied down, the tale's essential attributes hardly changed. The type of story was well known, but this variant appeared new. Yet, as has been recognized for some time, many tales called "Rumpelstiltskin" share little in common as during their transmission related but misnamed tales became jumbled. Casual thematic associations or coincidental similarities confused some stories' (perhaps minor) features with others. Conceivably, geographically close dialects from neighboring districts merged separate stories, rendering a muddle. It wasn't easy to disentangle the mess to arrive at a cleanly delineated core story.

Similar tales might appear affiliated because of some shared happenstance feature, a related vocabulary, or ancient or modern misprision that merged unrelated, "[r]adically different stories [which] since they ... concern a girl spinning something to gold ... have been represented [as] variants of the same tale to Wilhelm [Grimm] and to generations of subsequent scholars".[17] This confusion introduces an important point as we will be examining a single artifact: the story (as printed earlier). However appealing secondary versions might be, as everybody is entitled to a favorite, they present confusing distractions— a seemingly harsh judgment until the story's underlying logic exposes its unity.[18] The Rumpelstiltskin story's form of reasoning emerges when we understand the story's narrative that suggests fairytales offer a way to grope toward consequential truths, along with science and myth. That reasoning works only with, and derives from, the story's "classic" version that emerged from the Grimms' editorial process that preceded their last, somewhat twisted, version of Rumpelstiltskin. Before the story switched languages.

The first English translation of Jacob and Wilhelm Grimm's *Nursery and Household Tales* in 1823 met with immediate success, and "German folktales and fairy tales have enjoyed widespread popularity in the Anglo-American world... [ever since, and] American readers are bombarded on an annual basis with dozens of translations, adaptations, and retellings of the stories".[19] Today Rumpelstiltskin's name and story are woven into the English language, his absorption and naturalization complete. Like any immigrant family, after a few generations his accent disappeared in an open and welcoming society. And there is no country as free as literature.

Spoken American or British English flaunts a zesty and almost indiscriminate hoovering of sources: borrowed terms, odd constructions, and a universe of words. Linguistically, we'll give anybody a chance to fail. And in America, as in England before, Rumpelstiltskin proudly shows his papers: a landed immigrant long-ago became a citizen.

A Story Is Reborn

> Tales are born out of necessity and desire.[20]
>
> *Jack Zipes*

In 1811 Wilhelm Grimm recorded the essential version of Rumpelstiltskin from Henriette "Dortchen" Wild (1795–1867) whose family members had also been interviewed to collect stories. Dortchen supplied some of the Grimms' best folktales, and she must have told compelling stories for, just as Scherazade won her king with storytelling, in 1825 Wilhelm Grimm married her.

The daughter of a neighbor, a pharmacist, Dortchen Wild had already known the brothers for twenty years, and Jacob, a lifelong bachelor, moved in with the now-married Wilhelm and Dortchen. An odd trio, they lived snug as any fairytale family. But they never lived in a fairytale's picturesque cottage tucked in the woods. In such an imagined setting, the Grimms might trawl for fairytales from nearby gossipy crones gumming ancient tales of their long-gone girlish days passed in the vicinity. But, rather than foraging in the hinterlands from helpful or cryptic peasants, the brothers largely recorded stories from their sister Charlotte ("Lotte") Amalie Grimm, her friends, and their wider circle of middle-class associates. Lotte's sister-in-law Marie Hassenflug also contributed tales, and her French-speaking family perhaps infiltrated Gallic stories into the mix—diluting the purity of the so-called Germanic culture being resurrected. But Rumpelstiltskin was not an import.[21]

The tale's immediate derivation from Wilhelm Grimm's wife, Dortchen, was no less a legitimate source than the fictitious withered old rural women who more comfortably fit the image of authenticity. Despite the "widespread knowledge of fairy tales . . . observed among his contemporaries . . . we should be wary of indicting Wilhelm and Jacob Grimm of intentionally misleading their readers".[22] There's a caution here. Dressed for the part and ready to spout regionally appropriate blarney, many a roadside huckster waits for the tourist seeking authenticity. The lesson: although the story's unlikely fountainhead appears a middle-class woman (and not a picturesque example of rural Germanic "local color"), we can yet accept the tale as genuine and embrace the legitimacy of this unlikely transmission. Yet Rumpelstiltskin's parentage is disputed.

The fairytale's reemergence, during tumultuous times for Germany and Europe, indicts a custody battle as sharp as any fought in divorce court or across the battle lines of opposing armies, for smaller stakes. Some early collectors of folklore thought this fairytale's pedigree could be, somehow, "pure" and made to reflect national essence, while others believed an illiterate peasantry produced fairytales; more recent scholarship questions that assumption. The roots of this genre may be lost in the tumult of their times:

> The French had been defeated on the battlefields of Leipzig and Jena, but in the fairy tale realm, they prevailed. It was the Napoleonic intrusion that had impelled

FIGURE 1.1   *Clemens Brentano.*

Source: Meyer's Encyclopedia, 1906.

the Grimms to seek an authentic German identity . . . Germany's fairy tales . . . were to a very large extent actually French, not *völkisch* in origin. This conclusion has proven uncomfortable, unpalatable even, and undesirable for many researchers who wish to retain a now outdated oralist history of fairytales.[23]

It's relatively easy to defame fairytale's "outdated oralist history", but there's a problem the newer outlook cannot escape. Wherever and whenever the stories originated their survival depended on a truthful depiction of actualities or their audience would have spurned them. They were told and retold because of their meaningfulness, a profundity that is hard to ascribe to any single author. Especially, this story about Rumpelstiltskin pertains to daily life without depending on the literacy of peasants who might, or might not, have read such a story of recent vintage and put it into circulation as an oral "tradition". Moreover, while the Grimms unwittingly relied on already-published versions of texts that can be traced back to, or resemble, earlier sources in French or Italian literature, there's no telling where those early published versions originated, perhaps from folktales. And such stories existed long before printing or before anybody thought to immortalize with ink such provincial babbling.

Scholars of the Romantic period conceived the body of tales as emanating directly from the folk, an idea that continued into the twentieth century. While recent scholarship can push back the horizon of their birth to a period some centuries before the Grimms yet, to the disgruntlement of scholars invested in the literary origins of fairytales, we cannot peer over the horizon of printing and publication to a time when the stories may have freely circulated as exactly what they seem: folk tales from illiterates. Whatever the earliest printed versions of the texts may suggest about their authorship, in whatever language, the alternative argument may yet prove valuable without in the least diminishing research to affiliate the stories with ever-earlier published versions. The inherent, deeply complex, details of one story in particular argue for its long gestation when it was honed to perfection by repetition to satisfy a particular audience. And that is how this present discussion will proceed. Neither ignoring earlier texts nor concentrating on them, we will instead look closely and almost ahistorically at the marvelously integrated elements of the Tale of Rumpelstiltskin that, surprisingly, paint a complete picture of a society.

★★★

After taking dictation from their friends and relatives, the Brothers Grimm distilled the raw material they transcribed. (Some of the Grimms' contemporaries shunned enhancing their work into literature, instead favoring crude folkish accuracy. Other German folklore collectors reproduced the raw sound of the rural dialects that couched the stories, faithfully rendering both stories and the unrefined speech that ferried tales from the past.[24]) From their interview sessions the Grimms fashioned the folktales passed down into our times as polished and alluring works. Their published stories recall a time when common wisdom was not recorded in linear numerical formulas, data-laden spreadsheet,

FIGURE 1.2   *Friedrich Karl von Savigny.*
Source: © Berlin Public Library.

or charts, but in aphorisms or fables. Formerly the most effective and socially accepted way to convey a truth was in a good tale: Aesop advised on everyday ethics and psychology in fables, while Homer's epics instruct about manly virtues; essential parts of Jewish Scripture narrate stories and Jesus taught in parables. Animals may speak wisdom or self-evident foolishness in folktales where gods and men portray keen insight or blinding pride. In the past, more than today, sages and prophets instructed with moral allegories. To their Germanic inventors and English admirers, the Grimms' stories represented a legitimate way of analyzing and understanding the world, a means of access fully equal to philosophy. As the nineteenth-century folklorist Edward Clodd put it: "[W]hether the stories are 'archaic' or not seems to me to be of quite secondary importance. Whatever be their age they may hold many old philosophies of things, as do much more serious vehicles than fairy tales to this day".[25] These tales were not always accorded this sincere respect. Yet teaching with a story memorably conveys a point and the Tale of Rumpelstiltskin had a message. That bulletin about human relations will presently appear.

This tale, together with the cluster of stories they had gathered, became the basis for 1812 publication of the Grimm brothers' collection *Children's and Household Tales*. (Unlike the previous rendition where the girl's Midas touch unrelentingly turned her threads golden, in this collection Rumpelstiltskin's story exhibits the now-familiar quandary of the heroine's mortal challenge to spin gold from straw.)[26] The first edition included a story called "Rumpelstilzchen" featuring most, but not all, of the tale's familiar attributes. But the 1819 edition of *Children's and Household Tales* formed Rumpelstiltskin into the character we recognize. The Grimms continued to alter the tales until their last lifetime edition of 1857 yet; like only a handful of others, the story of Rumpelstiltskin hardly changed after its first appearance. One scholar proposed that

> Wilhelm Grimm's editorial direction after 1812, the year the first volume of the first edition appeared, was set more by a desire to approach and incorporate the German-speaking "folk" than to embrace bourgeois values, at least as they have been understood in eighteenth- and nineteenth-century Germany.... ["Rumpelstiltskin" in] its earliest extant German version (1810), the heroine's problem centers on the fact that everything she spins turns to gold, which she finds troublesome. Two short years later, the story flows very differently. Now her father boasts (falsely) that his daughter can spin straw into gold; the king hears of this, takes the girl to his palace and says that she must spin roomfuls of straw to gold— or die. A very different tale indeed![27]

Instead of attributing such changes entirely to Wilhelm Grimm's (perhaps heavy-handed) editorial preferences to concoct a document to justify the German-speaking "folk", these variations may indicate a shift toward greater literary integrity. If Wilhelm and Jacob tweaked odd bits here and there, artistic quality guided them to Rumpelstiltskin. But they enjoyed no monopoly on literary skill. Their sources were pretty shrewd too.

The Story's Setting

Rather surprisingly for a psychological drama, Rumpelstiltskin's tale includes a tour that ranges through medieval countryside. Not a travelogue that pins the story to specifically recognizable natural features (and certainly not a mythic adventure voyaging through the imaginary wonders of foreign lands), as backdrop to the main action of personal struggles we travel an excursion that features rapid and dramatic scenic changes. The rural region's dark atmospheric tones evoke pre-modern Germany that would have enraptured Clemens Brentano as he excitedly turned the pages to begin a journey in open farming country surrounding the mill. Presumably in good weather the King and his party recreationally ride up to the mill. Perhaps he's hunting or out to inspect his realm. Thereafter the action moves from clear sunlit space to the castle's dank cell. Although the tale omits at least one intervening year or more as the King and Queen enact the pomp of their ceremonial life and create a child, when Rumpelstiltskin reappears to claim his reward, we enter the Queen's palace apartments. Now she lives in warmer rooms, brightly lit, colorfully decorated with paintings perhaps tapestry or murals, and high in the castle her royal apartment's less damp than the dungeon she first occupied. Next we peer into deep forest where by night and around a fire's long shadows the little man sings his weird and haughty song. Finally, we enter a throne room or large reception chamber (perhaps a room in the suite of her private quarters) that frames the Queen's inquisition of Rumpelstiltskin. (Although he initially poses the riddle, like on the quiz show *Jeopardy*, her answers take the form of questions "Is your name...?") These settings proposed operatic potential that attracted notice from the start, if they did not guide the Grimms' editing. The story conjures both nature and human creations as residing adjacent to a magical world.

The story solicited serious academic attention from its earliest readers—Savigny, Brentano, their students, and folklorists worldwide. That might have sufficed to recommend Rumpelstiltskin universally if non-German youngsters had not quickly and spontaneously adopted the tale with no thought of German peoplehood. Yet, though neither as violent as other fairytales nor engaging in moral uplift, children were unaccustomed to its weirdness, even compared to other tales in the Grimms' collection. Fairytales often warn children to stay on the marked trail—peril lies nearby. That seems good advice. Just off (under) the trail that crossed a bridge, an ogre menaced the Three Billy Goats Gruff. Little Red Ridinghood should have kept her head down and walked straight to Grandma's without engaging a loiterer in conversation. Hansel and Gretel tried, but failed, to find their way back to the proper trail. Rumpelstiltskin's story established a landscape, but the trail through that territory meanders. The landscape doesn't seem to contribute very much, but that appearance can be misleading.

Within the story's terrain each character's residence tells plenty about them. With their home addresses, trades, genders, and family relationships, these essential elements of the story's final published version reveal everything necessary to unmask the main character behind the funny name. But since the Brothers Grimm never set out on this kind of detective work, they cannot be faulted for ignoring the story's symbols.

Unlike a poker game with its hidden cards and bluffing, but more like chess where all is visible if dizzyingly complex this story hides no clues. The clues rest right on the story's surface as they emerged from remarkably cunning arrangements that accent the tale's ribald insinuations. And when those hints finally clarify into a recognizable pattern, they reveal how lucid were the tale's otherwise bizarre narrative lines. Playing before a circumstantial backdrop of an ordinary late-medieval countryside, the creators' assumptions take their place but the story's creators were not the Brothers Grimm.

This tale's mainly unsuspected power accommodates modern intuition. If you first heard Rumpelstiltskin in English you know him; prepare to discover who he was.

The Problem of Meaning

The aspect of Rumpelstiltskin's tale most in need of attention demands that we revive the currently discredited idea that the story might "mean" something. The prejudice against denotation enforced post–World War II academic fashion to flee from assigning the story (or any story) a single, univocal and pervasive, explanation. Ambiguity reigned as an appealing range of possibilities bobbed into view on critics' voyages around the text. That trendy if irresponsible love of vagueness may strike future generations as a surprisingly luxurious indulgence. Avoidance, packaged to resemble humility, faced puzzles that resist analysis but are solvable.

The Tale of Rumpelstiltskin had a purpose. A knowing teller deliberately told the tale to a knowing audience, all of whom "got" some embedded point. The story's early reciters would have found strange a (post) modern idea that one person cannot assuredly convey intention to another, or that the audience principally constructs meaning. On the other hand, it's irresponsible to arbitrarily assign significance where none (or a different meaning) was intended. Yet, as we shall presently see, ample evidence suggests the story's inventors aimed to form an intentionally coherent, wry, and humanely momentous tale to comment on the aspects of a lived adult life. There's nothing arbitrary about Rumpelstiltskin.

Recognizing the difficulty of establishing meaning, some have disregarded the possibility that Rumpelstiltskin obeys a deliberate design and most observers just tiptoe past this enormous potential. If you don't look it isn't there. The first page of an important late twentieth century set of inquiries warned that "folklore studies, it seems, still shy clear of the 'quest of meaning' . . . In the last hundred years rather too much emphasis was given to meaning".[28] How can you overemphasize meaning? The heroic urge to communicate bridges otherwise-lonely human existence by dispatching a message to cross the cosmos that separates people. It's possible, I suppose, to disregard meaning if the results of searching for humanly significant communication prove consistently wrong— as a consequence of applying doctrinaire and academically trendy fashions. I've never heard anybody complain about research that's correct too often or gripe about accurate messages that touch the heart.

Within a famous stone labyrinth a monster guarded the center. In the middle of word-mazes we find ourselves. Rumpelstiltskin names a maze of language erected to hide in its middle a person we recognize; the hidden storyteller speaks about an intimate subject. Roadsigns leading to the maze's heart remain visible, but the route became overgrown, neglected, in time finally forgotten—time to hack away the weeds. In the undergrowth remain long-forgotten guideposts. We have to find the signs and then follow where they point.

Six Roadsigns Through the Maze

Except for professional scholars of folklore who rigorously examine Rumpelstiltskin's sometimes-obscure alternate versions, almost everyone encounters a single rendering of the story; the tale's central features derive from five variants the Grimms combined to make their one. If they merged variants to create something literary, the blending could be tolerated to inform the German audience of its ancestral heritage. Yet a large part of the story's lineage went missing, its origins misplaced before it was conveyed to the

Grimms by Dortchen Wild. In particular, one of the story's lost treasures supplied the source for the peculiar name, variously identified in different languages:

> Rumpelstiltskin goes by many names. Titliture, Doppeltürk, Purzinigele, Batzib-itzili, Panzimanzi, and Whuppity Stoorie are just a few of his sobriquets. Whether he makes an appearance as Ricdin-Ricdon in a French tale or as Tom Tit Tot in an English tale, his essence and function remain much the same.[29]

Within each language's rendering of the story his centrality and narrative purpose may appear more or less similar, but Rumpelstiltskin's "essence" relies on his specific name in our standard version. That's the key, but isolating that quintessence first requires that we locate a purposefully obscured target. Admittedly, it's daunting to treat the cardinal question of his identity and meaning. We're reminded that "[i]mportant and sometimes unanswerable questions have to be addressed before one can approach fairytales knowledgeably".[30] We must ask, Who is Rumpelstiltskin and what does his name mean? This may seem an unpromising inquiry, but it is answerable. In other languages similar characters go by various names:

Danish: Rumleskaft
Dutch: Repelsteeltje
Finnish: Tittelintuure
French: Grigrigredinmenufretin
German: Rumpelstilzchen
Hebrew: עוץ לי גוץ לי (ootz li gootz li)
Italian: Praseidimio
Japanese: ルンペルシュティルツキン
Russian: Румпельштильцхен
Slovak: Martin Klingáiček
Spanish: Rumpelstiltskin and El enano saltarín (the jumping midget)
Swedish: Bulleribasius

This plethora of names might prove confusing. When Edward Clodd wrote about Rumpelstiltskin in 1898, his appendix listed a considerable number of "variants of Tom Tit Tot" with some of the story's sizeable bibliography that had already developed in the nineteenth century. (The character's other names likely mean something distinctive in their language, but—once again, despite temptation to shop around—we are only looking at one story with one English name.)[31] Hastening attention to Rumpelstiltskin's many shifting names and identities bewilders; the situation seems hopeless. Despite variants derived from German that can distract from the real focus, the little man's English name exposes a vista of possibilities.

The name, in the form by which English speakers ubiquitously know it, contributes to the character's personality so that, strictly speaking, "Titliture, Doppeltürk, Purzinigele, Batzibitzili, Panzimanzi, and Whuppity Stoorie" are no more Rumpelstiltskin than chien = dog. These two words (chien, dog) carry different social burdens in their native society. Each word is distinctly tangy in its language, like all words, but refers to a different conception of the same biological reference. Rumpelstiltskin's name—today thoroughly part of everyday English and no longer considered German—came from somewhere: Edgar Taylor's 1823 translation.[32]

Taylor (1793–1839) provided a sensitive transliteration of the German dialect name into English, one of his greatest creations as a translator: *Rumpelstiltskin*. The leading character's name supplies our first clue that points toward the story's significant inner purposefulness and the reason it was composed. Rumpelstiltskin's name directs attention to a room that the story mentions only obliquely, a place not really absent from the story's inventoried countryside but, by analogy, very much part of that landscape. That singularly dedicated room saw the birth of Rumpelstiltskin.

The Map to Meaning

Though *he* is, Rumpelstiltskin's name is not a magic. When he hears it spoken he vanishes of his own volition and not by power of the pronounced name to make him disappear. Its sound does not activate an enchanted spell. Even that clue proves useful: amid the magic that he can perform (entering a locked castle cell, spinning straw to gold, flying on a spoon, etc.). Rumpelstiltskin's name is not a magical formula.

Edgar Taylor's invention of the Rumpelstiltskin name for his 1823 translation of the Grimms' work presented either a cannily intuitive transliteration from the German or possibly the revival of a latent English name for the same figure—or a bit of both. In any case, it was a stroke of genius for when we understand the hidden meanings of Rumpelstiltskin's name as it was originally intended to be understood, many troubling aspects of the story resolve. With the knowledge of his name the story reads like a *roman à clef* with the significance of its six pivotal plot points falling into a happy concordance. Astonishingly, a group of management consultants intuited the story's unity.

Students of administration and office maximization invoked Rumpelstiltskin as a metaphor for an organizational problem: "If we go back to the tale, we can see the importance of paying attention to the relations among all the elements. No part alone makes sense, separate from its link to the whole".[33] And that is true.

To discover Rumpelstiltskin we must consider what he does. As the story unfolds we learn six crucial things about Rumpelstiltskin. These are our roadsigns.

1.   Rumpelstiltskin is a male. Bidden by the Miller's Daughter's despair he attends the girl. He is the only helpful male in the story.
2.   He is noticeably short but not called of the race of trolls, dwarfs, or some other mythical wee-folk.
3.   He accomplishes vital work and performs many magical feats; with magic he easily accomplishes the girl's task.
4.   While Rumpelstiltskin can apparently have anything he wants by sorcery, somehow he still wants a living child—which seems to be beyond his magic. This lack helps identify the kind of power, and powers, Rumpelstiltskin possesses.

5. No one seems to know his name. The girl who becomes queen does not know his name and has never heard the word spoken. (Because so much is at stake, she would not pretend ignorance.) To save her child, over a period of three days she strenuously exhausts all the words she knows or has ever heard—his name is outside her vocabulary and beyond all her helpers.

6. When Rumpelstiltskin does hear his name from the lips of the Queen, he shouts, "The Devil told you! The Devil told you!" Then he vanishes (or self-destructs in various ways depending on the version of the story).[34] Aside from losing his bet, what has changed by this pronouncement to make the climate so inhospitable? Losing a wager feels bad enough, but can he not bear to hear his name spoken?

All six features of the tale can be explained once we understand what the name Rumpelstiltskin means. As a bonus: the name's meaning will, like the signature on a painting, identify the author.

Now that we know the story's history, let's see how its unity was achieved, and why.

Notes

1. This system of classification derives from the work of Antti Aarne and Stith Thompson, *The Types of the Folktale: A Classification and Bibliography* (Helsinki), 1961.

2. Although it differs from the tale of Rumpelstiltskin in all other regards, the Scottish fairy tale of Whuppity Stoorie features a heroine who must guess the name of a helper to save her baby. Accordingly Whuppity Stoorie appears on the same roster as Rumpelstiltskin. What the tale of Rumpelstiltskin decidedly is *not* affiliated with, despite the demand for the girl's firstborn child, is a remnant of the old notion that malicious elves and dwarfs stole unattended babies and replaced them with their own child, a changeling. Heated debates about these rarefied classifications resolve upon subtlest refinements to distinguish various folk-narratives' formal qualities. Some learned folklorists pigeonhole Rumpelstiltskin according to evolving sexual politics.

3. Bottigheimer (2009, pp. 11–12).

4. Zipes (1993, p. 43).

5. McGlathery (1993, p. 77).

6. *Beauty and the Beast* enjoyed wonderfully contrasting movie versions. The French homosexual Cocteau shows Beauty/Belle bending to the ways of the Beast as she learns to accept him. As she comes to trust his grumpy maleness, Cocteau's Belle condones the dismayed Beast's gruffness when he turns with steaming hands to implore Belle to "Forgive me for being a beast/creature". The American Disney version required the Beast to spiff up, civilize by learning deferential manners. Disney's markedly effeminate Beast yearns for Beauty's approval. The version that approves a feminized male Beast resides deep in much American popular culture, and that norm represents the antithesis of Rumpelstiltskin's tale as a smug Queen utterly bests his crippled maleness.

    To woo pert Lois Lane, the almighty Superman approaches her as Clark Kent, nebbish. She rejects Mr. Kent as too mild-mannered, a man apparently conquered by life. Lois imagines romance with a figure of unrestrainable forces, a cluster of masculine powers (like the Beast, also a kind of superman) whose strength her alluring presence can properly curb—like the story of Samson and Delilah. Instances of this type, while not endless, unearth our culture's yet-operating foundational values.

    In the popular movie *Groundhog Day* (1993), written by Danny Rubin and the late Harold Raimis who also directed, the male lead lives a purgatory of infinitely repeating days. During his time under a curse he masters piano, French, and other mellowing skills that smooth his rough cynical edges. (Since he gets only one hour each day to practice with his piano teacher, the writers admitted to a period of 30–40 years of repetitions with an upper limit of 10,000 years—true purgatory on a cosmic scale.) During this period he is daily, like Cocteau's Beast, rejected by the female lead. Finally, when he conforms to her (American) idea of a suitably mild gentleman, she welcomes his remade tempered self. Her approval liberates him from his spell   very much like the Beast. This plotline also guides a witty high-culture classic, as when a gruff and inarticulate male mellows from an apparently inconsiderate iceberg into the gentle, self-effacing, and thoughtful Mr. Darcy of Jane Austen's *Pride and Prejudice*.

7. If Bruno Bettleheim sensed the riches lurking in this story he ignored it; the tale of Rumpelstiltskin does not appear in Bettleheim's well-known study *The Uses of Enchantment*. Neither does Rumpelstiltskin feature in such newer forays as Ellen Handler Spitz's *Image and Insight: Essays in Psychoanalysis and the Arts*, nor her *Art and Psyche: A Study in Psychoanalysis and Aesthetics*, nor her *Museums of the Mind*. Surprisingly, given the purview and tools of that discipline, Rumpelstiltskin too rarely appears in the psychoanalytic literature.

8. The sources for Nazi ideology grew directly, if unfortunately, from the previous century's investigations. For example—though the son of a philo-semitic German Protestant theologian Franz Delitzch (1813–1890), a founder of modern Assyriology—Friedrich Delitzch (1850–1922) became a German nationalist and Jew hater who believed that since the story of Gilgamesh and much Babylonian literature antedated the Bible he proposed replacing Hebrew Scriptures with German folklore.

9. Goldfarb (2009, p. 134).

10. Bottigheimer (2009, p. 38).

11. Blackwell (1990, p. 108).

12. Surveys of probable election outcomes try to canvas as many people and types of people as possible—of different ages, occupations, sexes, races, and regions; people with stated political preferences and those without party affiliation; some who usually vote and others who don't; and people with strong opinions about current options and those undecided. And when completing the surveys according to the best available resources, the polls can often prove wrong: the survey didn't adequately reflect the population as a whole. Similar problems arise when polling for marketing and product placement or to gauge the popularity of a television show or a movie (short of ticket sales, which is a bit like post-election results versus a survey beforehand). Such studies address mass behavior, choices noted in the aggregate.

    Individual cultural choices, preferences that most express our creature selves, prove no easier to ascertain with polls and surveys. Try to develop an "average" recipe for a well-loved dish: many French towns claim to practice the only authentic version of Bouillabaisse or ask an American about the proper form of Bar B-Que and see how many answers you get depending on the respondent's native region, age, and race. Sex isn't even an issue; women don't do Bar-B-Que, mostly.

13. John C. Maher summarized the issue with a series of questions: "What does it mean to be a native speaker? Is it possible to become a native speaker of a language that is not one's mother tongue? Just how special is the native speaker?" (1997, p. 650).

14. In this version of the story, the girl's problems arise from her inability to spin anything but gold. For a full description of this unique version of the story, its sketchy existence as a brief and illogical narrative, see Tatar (1987, p. 125).

15. His was no simple turn to religion for solace. Brentano celebrated his birthday on the day of Mary's birth, September 8 (when he was actually born the next day). He added the name "Maria" to his other Christian names (Clemens Maria Wenzeslaus) and his first published book appeared under the pseudonym Maria. He never abandoned such passionately dreamy gestures, however sexually confused. Lost in a hopeful trudge through Catholic mysticism, Brentano preferred deep emotional verification rather than logical proofs.

    Typical of the second phase of German Romanticism (the so-called Heidelberg school), Brentano mined German folklore and history as the criterion of his own expressive writing. Not surprisingly, Brentano's most effective works are his fairytales. Their richly imagined situations flowed through uncommonly musical writing. But by 1817 his emotional instability, mood swings, and wanderings that epitomized German Romantic ideals took its toll. He succumbed to severe depression and immersed himself in Roman Catholic mysticism to ponder life's questions. Brentano spent six years secluded in a monastery. This melancholic was the Rumpelstiltskin story's second important reader, after Savigny.

16. Discontented with his studies, Brentano traveled throughout Germany, a moody pilgrim seeking an emotional grail that he found in Göttingen in 1801. Still a wanderer, he resettled in Heidelberg in 1804 to work with his brother-in-law, Ludwig Achim von Arnim, as they compiled the text for a folk-song collection *Des Knaben Wunderhorn* (The Youth's Magic Horn), which they conceived as embodying the truest spirit of national German literary traditions. The text was his paradise. In Göttingen with von Arnim, Brentano created a bookish kingdom with vistas opening to an imagined yesterday of glittering chivalry, stately if murky personalities given to quixotic gestures and deeds of epic grandeur—the complete Romantic miasma.

    At the end of the century, Gustav Mahler (1860–1911), a Jewish composer whose works cap the Romantic movement, set the text of Brentano's compilation *Des Knaben Wunderhorn* (The Youth's Magic Horn) as a song cycle. Here irony grows profound and bitter. The growth of German nationalism excluded Jews as an alien nation among the Germanic peoples, while the Jews, no longer defamed merely for being of a foreign religion, now were excoriated for wanting to revivify (Zionism) their own nation (destroyed by Europeans, the Romans). They were accused of "dual loyalty" although disallowed Germanic loyalty. One of the progenitors of pan-Germanism, Brentano was most gloriously honored by a man whose relatives and descendants fled or were murdered by that movement's overripe fruition. Mahler's kin found themselves shunned because they resembled the competent Rumpelstiltskin, a figure sometimes identified with the condition of the Jews.

17. Bottigheimer (1987, p. 17).

18. If you prefer other versions, you are entitled to like one of them better, but the tale's inner logic works with none of the related but fundamentally different stories. Despite what may seem an imposed partiality (mine), this story's inmost meaning explains why this story reliably befriended generations, a strange friend, but a faithful one.

    Indeed, such distractions were noticed as secondary considerations:

    > If ever there was a text that cannot be definitively nailed down, it is the Märchen: an ever-shifting story that renders the biographical method virtually impossible; its Urtext can neither be established nor its oldest version privileged over a later one, because its "contaminations" (to use the loaded term of the folklorists) are as valuable as its "original".
    >
    > *Jeannine Blackwell, 1990, p. 107*

    Even in the unlikely event that the tale should prove a modern fabrication by the Grimms and utterly spurious as a survivor of folk literature, it would have to be seriously studied.

    A monument of our literature, the story's name entered our dictionaries as a word and its hearing became one of the handful of common experiences shared by almost everyone. Rumpelstiltskin is part of the mythology of the modern world, one of the touchstones of near-universal upbringing almost regardless of class, gender, or geography within the English-speaking world. Its Germanic source in academia is finally considering how far it has migrated from scholarly circles, irrelevant to its popular impact while the tale's broad influence justifies and invites inquiries into its origin. The tale of Rumpelstiltskin has deeply penetrated our literary world and has been thoroughly woven into the fabric of our imaginations and memories. The story has become a prominent part of our childhoods. Those childhood experiences, remembered or not, shape the people we have become. If similar assertions once seemed fanciful or merely pedagogic ("Spare the rod and spoil child" and a hundred other bits of crack-brain advice), it becomes plainer by the day that early nutrition, a youngster's patterns of exercise, birth order, familial affection, or abuse—and a host of other kinds of cumulative incidents—shapes individuals so that no two are alike. Exposure to scary stories or tales of beautiful princesses, warriors, or saintly scholars as heroes, all these images and concomitant morals shape the formative climate of the long episode regarded retrospectively as childhood. And we don't need Sigmund Freud or his psychoanalysis (although this invention didn't hurt) to realize how early events and experience prefigure and help determine our later aesthetic tastes, personal joys, and fears.

19. Tatar (1997, p. 8).

The story remains gripping. New editions come forth to greet each generation. The most beautiful—in many ways the most completely authentic to the fable's spirit—appeared in 1986, lovingly illustrated by the masterful Paul O. Zelinsky. Today the critical and speculative literature devoted to Rumpelstiltskin is vast, too broad to even inspect a decently representative sample of the various scholarly and analytic penchants. The present discussion surveys and questions only a narrow portion of that debate. This story's clandestine affective life cannot be guessed from adult literature: a dialogue between participants in a forensic examination who have largely forgotten what they observed as eye witnesses in childhood.

20. Zipes (1993, p. 48).

21. There's some cavilling about how much, if any, influence the Grimms absorbed from Gallic precedent. For example, Zipes (1993) claims that Grimms' 1857 rendering of Rumpelstiltskin treats the story "as a literary fairy tale, which has antecedents in folklore and in the French literary tradition, namely Mile L'Heritier's 'Ricdin-Ricdon'" of 1705 (p. 45.) A few pages later, Zipes more emphatically asserts that

> there are also clear signs that they were aware of the French literary version "Ricdin-Ricdon" by Mile L'Heritier, whose tale also influenced the Grimms' "The Three Spinners". In short, the 1857 "Rumpelstiltskin" is an amalgamation of literary and oral tales that the Grimms carefully reworked to represent the dilemma of a young peasant woman who cannot spin to save herself.
>
> *p. 47*

There seems little point in the present instance to argue against Rumpelstiltskin being an "amalgamation of literary and oral" conventions since I am approaching the story as a fixed entity in English, a work with limited variations whose impact on its audience wholly was independent of its German or French ancestors.

22. Bottigheimer (2009, p. 51).

23. Bottigheimer (2009, p. 51).

24. In the last few years a huge trove of 500 fairytales, some heretofore unknown, were discovered in an archive in Regensburg, Germany, where the documents had lain undisturbed for over 150 years. Only in 2012 a cultural curator in the Oberpfalz region, Erika Eichenseer, published a selection of fairytales from this collection by Franz Xaver von Schönwerth, an anthology he called *Prinz Roßzwifl* (local dialect for "scarab beetle" as the scarab or "dung beetle" buries its eggs in ball of dung that it rolls and buries—an apt symbol for fairytales' caching of ancient learning and wisdom). Nearly contemporary with the Grimms' efforts, these myths, parables, fables, and legends, including many previously unknown fairytales, were gathered in the Bavarian region of Oberpfalz by Von Schönwerth (1810–1886).

Though nearly forgotten today in 1885 Jacob Grimm endorsed Von Schönwerth's efforts: "Nowhere in the whole of Germany is anyone collecting [folklore] so accurately, thoroughly and with such a sensitive ear". In capturing his homeland's tales, Von Schönwerth recorded coarse language that he presented unrefined in its local rhythms and perhaps as a result, unlike the Grimms who won universal acclaim and admiration, Von Schönwerth's research (published in a three-volume book called *Aus der Oberpfalz: Sitten und Sagen*, 1857, 1858, 1859) languished. Also, unlike the Grimms, Von Schönwerth accurately recorded what he heard and did not polish his collection as literature subject to his editing and refinement for bourgeois taste. Eichenseer believed this accuracy made the material more valuable as, "[t]here is no romanticising or attempt by Schönwerth to interpret or develop his own style" (Victoria Sussens-Messerer, 2013). Moreover, curator Eichenseer theorizes the fairytales' "main purpose was to help young adults on their path to adulthood, showing them that dangers and challenges can be overcome through virtue, prudence and courage", a task that would be

congruent with the postulated message secreted in Rumpelstiltskin; in fact, the Von Schönwerth collection does include local Oberpfalz versions of Cinderella and Rumpelstiltskin. As
a result of gaining familiarity with these tales, Maria Tatar exclaimed: "Suddenly I understood
the kaleidoscopic magic of fairy tales: a little twist here and another one there, and you have
a completely different story, yet constructed from the very same bits and pieces" (Tatar, 2012).

25. Clodd (1890, p. 272).
26. Unbeknownst to them, the Grimms' collection contained "German" stories that nevertheless had been imported from France and perhaps elsewhere. Yet Rumpelstiltskin carries no
visible foreign "infection" as the earlier or associated versions bear scant family resemblance
in the crucial details. Actually, the earliest known mention of Rumpelstiltskin appears in a
freely adapted and translated version of Rabelais' *Gargantua* and *Pantagruel*, Johann Fischart's
1577 *Geschichtklitterung*, which mentions a children's entertainment called Rumpele stilt or
the Poppart, a character with a similar name but wholly different lineage.
   Soon after the 1812 edition, Napoléon's forces were ousted from central Europe, which
elated the brothers whose labors, they hoped, contributed to German unification—a vast and
slow political project retarded by the French invasion of Kassel. Along with others of various
political persuasions, the brothers strove to establish legitimized foundations for a culturally
consolidated state to emerge from the shards of despotic principalities that ruled the German-
speaking world. Their contribution resurrected from its collective unconscious a trove of
Germanic fairytales. As a political and linguistic effort, the stories might have been drab agit-
prop had the Grimms been lesser personalities and talents, but, despite the relative paucity of
their sources (mainly neighbors who walked into their house for sessions of dictation), the
stories were, and remain, vital and touching. Their impact has never lessened, though we no
longer hear these stories in the intended political light of their 1812 publication.
27. Bottigheimer (1991, p. 197).
28. Rohrich (1991, p. 1).
29. Tatar (1987, p. 124). In English Rumpelstiltskin is also known as Tom Tit Tot (from *English
Fairy Tales*, collected and edited by Joseph Jacobs, 1884). The equivalent is not exactly the
same, but the present discussion fixes attention on more than these differences. In the story
named for Tom Tit Tot, a mother scolded a girl for eating five pies, but when the King learned
of this feat and inquired about it, the woman lied, saying she had been talking of the five
skeins her daughter had spun at lightning speed.
30. Bottigheimer (1987, p. 17).
31. Clodd (1898) showed that the Irish variant "Trit a Trot" is not Irish; neither is the Welsh
"Trwtyn-Tratyn" Welsh (p. 28). Though Rumpelstiltskin derives from German, as a sister
Germanic language English conveys the name's essence very well.
32. In a published letter of Reinhard Köhler attested to this transformation when he referred to
correspondence of twenty years earlier:

> To the Editor of Folk-Lore.
> Sir,
> With regard to the note of Mr. W. F. Kirby in Folk-Lore (vol. ii, p. 132), I would point
> out the following remark of E. Taylor to his translation of the Grimms' folk-tale, "Rumpel-
> stitzchen" (which word he changed into "Rumpelstiltskin"):
> We remember to have heard a similar story from Ireland, in which the song ran:
> "Little does my Lady wot
> That my name is Trit-a-Trot".
> I drew attention to this remark of Taylor's so long ago as 1870, in my notes to p. 81 of
> Gonzenbach's Sicilianische Marchzen, which Mr. E. Clodd appears to have overlooked.
> Reinhard Köhler
> Weimar, March 14, 1891

33. Smith and Simmons (1983, p. 389).
34. These six characteristics were first identified in Rand, "Who Was Rumpelstiltskin?"
(2000).

2

MEANING IS PURPOSE

Prologue in Prehistory: Guilty Pleasures and the Pleasure of Contrition

> "Rumpelstiltskin" is a disturbing fairy tale, not because we never really know the identity of the tiny mysterious creature who spins so miraculously, even when he is named by the queen, the former miller's daughter. It is disturbing because the focus of folklorists, psychoanalysts, and literary critics has centered on Rumpelstiltskin's name and *his* role in the tale despite the fact that the name is meaningless. Indeed, it reveals nothing about Rumpelstiltskin's essence or identity.[1]
>
> *Jack Zipes, 1993*

But if Rumpelstiltskin's name is not "meaningless", it may supply the key to the whole story. His discovered name may reveal everything about his essence, identity, and the reason he was invented, and by whom. But where to begin looking for the meaning of this unusual name?

Rumpelstiltskin's odd name could signal a rare outcropping of the crushed culture of indigenous peoples. To some folklorists this possibility presents an appealing idea. Wave after wave of prehistoric immigrants moved across western Europe, settling, displacing, intermarrying—and then justifying their occupation. That pattern thrives into the present day. And each displacement and re-settlement fostered its own myth to justify occupying the terrain. The process by which these stories were created and circulated might seem familiar. Like successful movie or TV franchises, the great tribal and national myths spun off junior offspring in fairytales that assumed each race's superiority and vindicated its right to the land. Ancient observers recorded their versions of the succession.

Roman authors were impressed by the height and strength of barbarian Germans they faced when pressing the empire's northern borders. By virtue of cunning and organizational skills Romans deemed themselves more fit to rule than the hulking blonds they conquered. Latin chroniclers weren't just bragging that they had overcome immense physical specimens. Roman authors described the truth. German tribes spawned taller people than the Mediterraneans, and keeping these northern giants at bay taxed the waning imperial armies' strength. Finally Rome diverted such immense resources to contain the robust northerners that the weakened empire could be overrun. Directly and indirectly the Germanic tribes did bring down Rome when in 476 a German chieftain named Odoacer deposed the last emperor. Rumpelstiltskin cannot be counted among the ponderous berserk northern invaders of Italy as he hardly presents good warrior stock. Consequently, as far as the Grimms were concerned, as a distant ancestor of the modern Teutonic people(s) Rumpelstiltskin provided poor materials to found a unified German state. His contribution to the Grimms' project, and hence the reason to include him in their compilation, lay elsewhere. He had mastered special expertise and unexpectedly displayed a too-human hidden imperfection.

Rumpelstiltskin may not illustrate a short instance of a tall German but he could represent a stubby dwarfish example of an ancient race. Before Teutonic tribes occupied most of Europe a shorter and darker Celtic people lived in the forests and along the shores. But even these were not the first settlers. Before the Celts, tribes whose names we do not know inhabited much of Europe. Those pre-Celtic peoples either were preliterate or wrote on perishable materials. We have no trace (except perhaps Basque) of what they spoke or how their words sounded. Shadowy occupants of what became the Germanic lands, the earliest occupants were dark-haired and comparatively squat of stature, and they apparently spoke languages unrelated to German, modern Celtic, Slavic, Lithuanian, Armenian, or Latin.[2] If their prehistoric heritage lingers in modern languages such words or word-fragments survive by lurking invisibly in our midst.[3] Those ancient languages hardly resembled modern European tongues that comprise parts of the Indo-European family of languages. The long-lost alien languages' structures bequeathed scant vocabulary or grammar to their land's invaders. Yet they are not completely gone.

Migrations from the east overwhelmed their languages and culture, but their genes live on in modern Europeans, descendants of subsequent but still prehistoric newcomers who streamed into Europe and whose descendants composed the fairytales. If their stories overlay older local tales or offer a valedictory memory of their European predecessors the tales and Rumpelstiltskin's name might recall the indigenous peoples. Survivors' guilt for displacing the native population fuses contempt with respect; nostalgia for lost crafts mingles with fearful admiration that, when recalled at all, surfaces as magical folkways. If Rumpelstiltskin's shortness memorializes the non-Indo-European speakers encountered by the agricultural settlers who flooded westward in prehistory, then his odd name and his diminutive stature memorializes a suppressed native population.[4]

Evidence of these earliest inhabitants was all around; curious stone tools of the aboriginal Irish and the prehistoric Scots kept percolating out of the ground, to the mystification of the later arrivals. These worked stones posed a special nuisance because Indo-Europeans introduced advanced tillage of the soil, which unearthed long-buried "elfish" flint weapons. These instruments attacked from underground and hinted at imaginary subterranean sprites who aimed to injure cattle. Locals called these pointy rocks from the earth elf-bolts, elf-arrows, or elf-shot. For newcomers to western Europe, such implements confirmed the presence of creatures who dwelled in the earth and could fashion tools to help or harm, depending on how the invisible ones were propitiated. The reality of this unseen world was all around, the question—aside from who these creatures were—focused on the degree of shame Indo-Europeans should feel for driving them out of the sun and into the dank underground.[5]

Rumpelstiltskin's derisive stature, his ill-treatment and humiliating banishment, could commemorate the lingering memory of an otherwise forgotten non-Indo-European race. It wouldn't be the first or the last such arrangement. Germanic and Polish sentimentality dotes on a gone Hebraic culture (if not a genetically identifiable people); their admiration and contrition resembles North Americans' self-indulgent pathos for supplanting the Amerindians (and in Australia the aboriginals). Yet, as they recede, pangs of guilt easily subside into sappy mythology. Once annihilated, now-absent folkways can be venerated even cherished but the land never returns to the surviving remnant of the vanquished and dispossessed. Remorse for genocide sits mute in memory's cupboard, guilt forgotten amid the chattering topics people really discuss: daily chit-chat of living myth, mainly celebrity.

If not utterly ignorable, the scorned, who were defeated and supplanted, could be accommodated in a soothing story of justification, "they had it coming (to them)", which would justify Rumpelstiltskin's rude treatment. Almost a reflex-quick response when needed, such reasoning confers total absolution.[6] Europe's prehistoric conquerors not only superseded the vanquished locals but imagined themselves their heirs, hubris that resembles white people who dress-up to play "cowboys and Indians"; few such historical revelers are Amerindians. Reconstructed frontier towns, really theme parks to a genocidal struggle, come furnished with every motif of a gone western American expansion. Such zany re-enactment proves an unexceptional, indeed perfectly human, coping mechanism for a bad conscience. Another example: after exterminating Europe's last Jews Hitler intended a quarter of the city of Prague for a Museum to an Extinct Race. Anticipating the creation of a macabre post-war theme park the Nazis funneled tens of thousands of artifacts of Judaica from the burning continent to this intended museum where Nazis' twenty-first-century grandchildren could stroll and study the works of a perished people (while undoubtedly eating fast-food modeled on Jewish dishes).[7] Hard to imagine? Today gentile-stocked neo-Klezmer bands flourish in *Judenrein* central Europe. For generations white performers in black-face expressed genuine admiration for entertainers barred from the same American stages by Jim Crow laws. Memory models the past for comfort, and perhaps modeled Rumpelstiltskin.

Conscience-soothing behaviors repeated throughout history. (The Japanese maintain a quaint narrative concerning the indigenous Ainu they displaced.) Fashioning the past to accommodate conscience-challenged scruples, shame and a penchant for self-leniency could explain Rumpelstiltskin's physical appearance. Those same motives could also explain his mysterious name injected into the human world from beyond spoken (known) language.

A lurking sense of Europe's gone indigenous inhabitants might validate the furtive if rarely helpful and occasionally vindictive elfin population, the fairies,

> the little people [who] had inhabited the land first, but had yielded it, however unwillingly, to settle in rocks and caves, woods and streams, as human populations and agricultural activities expanded. Thus deprived of space, the fairy societies came to depend upon human contributions to ensure their perpetuation.[8]

Absent, but vaguely recalled by the Indo-European colonists, Europe's aboriginals might provide a historical source for folklore's short and stealthy race of little people. Rumpelstiltskin would portray the guilty recollection of an exterminated culture, an easily mawkish sort of nostalgia the Nazis prepared in their museum to the eradicated race of Jews, an institution that mocked the culture's creators while accepting their gifts. The Grimms' Germanic readers might find that Rumpelstiltskin represented "the tension between those seeking a national heritage" and a literary item perhaps little more than "harm-less fun for children".[9] In the modern day as in earlier times Rumpelstiltskin's message hinged on whatever politics framed the story. Some residue of that expired culture might yet survive. Considerable evidence connects the pre-Indo-Europeans to the story's nub: the story's implicit admiration for mastery of spinning and weaving—the fiber arts.

Though multi-talented, Rumpelstiltskin quintessentially performs as a fiber-worker and textile expertise supplies the story's essence. Perhaps gently by generations of intermarriage the Indo-Europeans gradually reconciled themselves to these new lands and new technologies—both expropriated. For example, in the Greek language "only the most primitive aspects of weaving show Indo-European names, the rest having been borrowed later . . . the prehistoric Greeks must have learned the craft fairly late, as they were moving into Greece from farther east".[10] Their acquisition of indigenous fiber arts mirrored the situation in western Europe. Was Rumpelstiltskin's odd name evidence of a residual European uneasiness for usurping land whose original owners had taught the Celts and other Indo-European newcomers the advanced fiber technologies? Those very skills Rumpelstiltskin performs dazzlingly. But there's a major problem if assigning Rumpelstiltskin to a long-gone race.

Entrusting Rumpelstiltskin's odd name to a lost world means facing a blank impenetrable wall and trying to guess what is behind it. The obliterated pre-Indo-European culture left only mute artifacts, objects shelved chronologically by archaeologists and labeled by site. Despite the long tenancy by pre- or proto-literate non-Indo-European speakers their language(s) do not survive in any written text or even an inscription. We will never hear the sounds of those lost languages, attend their dances, listen to the music of that gone race, taste their food, observe their clothing or, especially, eavesdrop on their storytelling. All gone. Irretrievable. That immense gap in our knowledge leaves only two possibilities. Ultimately, looking for Rumpelstiltskin's sources in pre-Indo-European culture threatens a blind alley. Yet we had to consider that possibility should real clues turn up. Back-tracking through the tale's German language we can pick up the trail. And thereby figure out his name and his story.

Within the Realm of Memory

It's clear the preliterate non-Indo-European speakers of early Europe left no direct physical traces of their languages; accordingly, when examining the scant fragments that *might* be attributed to prehistory, at the end of the nineteenth century a scholar had to "consider whether the work of collection of materials is . . . sufficiently advanced to justify the subjecting of those materials to scientific treatment".[11] Against early Europe's daunting impenetrability there's finally no reason to credit the preliterate non-Indo-European with originating the figure we presently recognize as Rumpelstiltskin. Or, if he does descend from such distant past, there's no way to know. But for the present discussion more recent sources might suffice. Enough surviving material helps draw a clear picture from pieces that lie scattered about and must be found, recognized as parts of a puzzle, and re-assembled.

More than a century later than the despair of "subjecting of those materials to scientific treatment" the answer echoes: linguistics, genetics, psychology, physical anthropology, geography, and comparative folklore—all resound affirmative. These studies yield positive results that help solve the problem and we can gather a considerable bounty of insight if his name is Indo-European. That is what I propose. Analysis of the "meaningless" name has not been seriously attempted; let us begin.

★★★

Rumpelstiltskin's linguistic roots trace strong affiliations with Indo-European cognates: the languages spoken by Europeans, many other Eurasians, and Latin Americans—including what you are now reading. In different but related Indo-European languages the same syllables mean the same things. The Brothers Grimm knew that words in diverse languages exhibit family resemblances that derive from a common ancestor. Like siblings who bear a striking resemblance to each other because they look like their parents, the descent of words from one progenitor accounts for similarity of sound. When these words are written out a family likeness appears. As genetics can reconstruct a family tree, linguists can unite kindred words of a similar appearance (when shown to belong to the same family) however long they were orphaned. Our story's name preserves one of those orphaned words, a lost relative. And a bitter-sweet word it is, even funny in harsher times.

Rumpel = rumple, to wrinkle by forming into uneven creased folds. This is a commonplace word: rumpled sheets are less inviting than refreshing crisp ones and an automobile accident results in crumpled fenders. The word invites everyday usage; it's not at all obscure. To "rumpel" suggests a compression or collapse. It's different from the even geometry of fresh pleats. The modern term boasts an ancient lineage.

Strictly speaking, the German verb the Grimms chose can be related to *rumpel(n)*, which implies noisiness, uproar, cacophony, tumult, and general mayhem—none of which characterizes our tiny man. But that look-alike association of a German verb rumpel(n) provides less of an explanation of the little guy's name than the present discussion; it's also unconvincing of the story's many narrative variables and character traits, features that Rumpelstiltskin's name should satisfy. Actually, as a verb rumpel(n) relates to a whole different class of supernatural being, as we shall see.

Rumple comes into English from the Dutch *rompelen*. Middle Dutch had an earlier form, *rumpelen*, that restores the spelling of the title character's name. In Frankish—essentially an un-written language reconstructed from etymology, spoken by those tall Germanics who so impressed the late-empire Romans, and the ancestor of modern French, Dutch, and German—this same root spawned the word *rompōn*, "to contract oneself". These olden words offer immensely useful hints when pursuing Rumpelstiltskin's story backward, perhaps to its native situation. From these family likenesses, and using detective's tools invented by Jacob Grimm, we can peer into prehistory. From that preliterate past we retrieve a bit of what people discussed in ancient times or even later when spoken by unlettered medieval peasantry.

The modern words related to Rumpelstiltskin's name derive from the Proto-Indo-European root *Skerbh, which also gives us the Middle Low German *shrempen* ("to shrink, to wrinkle"). That root is akin to the Low German source for the English "shrimp", a pygmy. Not that anybody speaks Frankish anymore, but such related diminutive terms illustrate how (with the "sh" prefix) the Frankish *rompōn* suggested a shrimp or pygmy. And the memory of such words lingers, imprinted in the wider language family.

Calling somebody a shrimp is no compliment. The recipient of such ridicule would be deemed ineffectual and probably small, not necessarily a dwarf. Somebody who is a shrimp can be overlooked as physically unimposing, dismissible. A "shrimp" can be regarded as a mere trifle—a fellow with whom the girl-queen toys once she has gained mastery of him by learning his name. Seemingly only a physical trait, being judged too short carried an insulting moral component. Calling somebody a shrimp suggested a deficiency of honor, a lack of manliness that's still used as taunting schoolyard mockery. The word's unpleasant associations echo through time, from the distant past to the present. More than just a comment about anatomy and height, transcendent cultural baggage associates this word with a presumptive justification for teasing people.

Rumpelstiltskin's main physical attribute seems to be that he appears a runt from his first entrance when he's described as "a tiny man" who entered the girl's cell. Finding a word-root for his name, a word that corresponds to his physique, suggests that Rumpelstiltskin hails from Indo-European stock. But his long name contains syllables that point to other traits, characteristics that render a more nuanced picture of him than as simply a shrimp.

After *rumpel*, comes another syllable we recognize: stilt. A stilt or, in the plural, stilts are tall posts or pillars upon which a building rests. In flood-prone areas stilts can raise small buildings above the waterline. A stilt is also a long-legged wading bird. Stilts add height. Used in pairs under the feet they lengthen the legs. They allow trained wears to take greatly exaggerated movements that extend each stride. Yet, a problem of dissonance arises. His name's two parts quarrel with each other. The added height contributed by a stilt seems at odds with the dwarfish Rumpelstiltskin as his name's first element means to be short or to shrink. Nevertheless—and this is the key to the whole ribald story—the two, apparently clashing, parts do reconcile.

"Stilt" derives from the root *Stel, to put up, to stand, to erect, as in the Greek, *stēlē*. Without modification of sound or meaning this word has come wholesale from Greek into English to mean an upright stone slab. A stele usually commemorates a person or event with a monument having an inscribed or sculpted surface. Those connotations from Greek memorials (standing erect, and put up) carried into Latin *stolidus* to mean stolid, impassive. The word has barely changed in centuries. Related words also emphasize verticality.

From Norwegian comes another stiff upright feature, *stalk*, the main stem of a plant. (The word is unrelated to the verb meaning to pursue by tracking.) From this same word-root arrives the Germanic *stall*, a standing place (akin to *stable*). These terms endure as the name for a compartment to house a single animal: the word stall has hardly changed in meaning or sound during those centuries after English split off from its Germanic forbear. There's also the Frankish *stallion* that carries the sense of "firm and standing". We recognize this word-root and use it without finding anything esoteric or strange about stable or stallion. These commonplace terms in modern English hint at erect stature.

Each of these "stall/stilt" meanings embodies the idea of vertical length, elevation, altitude. Tallness carries exactly the opposite connotations of being a shrimp. (By now the paradox should begin to dawn: a shrimp is antithetical to somebody stalwart. Being a shrimp contradicts possessing a strong, physically stout, or well-built, physique. A shrimp is not a morally steadfast or valiant person.) Somehow the name Rumpelstiltskin merged, or combined both senses. The linked first and the second part of his name embody contradictory qualities of length and shortness which seems impossible as a single idea. The name agglomerates opposites. But there's an ancient logic to how such a mash-up can be visualized. Unraveling the knot requires thinking of words in a way that's highly premodern. We are unaccustomed to our words operating like ideograms—complex signs more usually encountered in Chinese or ancient Egyptian hieroglyphics—yet sometimes even modern words perform that way. Rumpelstiltskin's name presents a cipher composed of (at least two) concrete references to contrary ideas.[12] Placed adjacent to one another these paired linguistic roots—one for shortness and another for length or tallness—provide either an oxymoron (the short-tall, or a crumpled-erect) or a specialized ideogram for a particular situation or circumstance. What word can germinate from two roots meaning both crumpled *and* stilt? Oppositely charged atoms, these antitheses crash together and combine into a new molecule of meaning that remains balanced against disintegration. Rumpelstiltskin's name endures. But how?

The name's singular, apparently irrational, allusion points toward something squat and stubby while also upright, like a stem. Or, if not a thing, a condition that refers to some circumstance that is alternately shrunk or shrinking and tall and slim, a linguistic elevator that apparently goes up and down at the same time. The conflicting and contradictory senses may be coincidental or the clashing meanings can resolve. Somehow "Rumpelstiltskin" refers to some special situation in which both senses remain true, simultaneously; reconciling those two suggests the story's covert sense. Rumpelstiltskin's real character emerges by resolving the quarrelling words that compose his name.

Succinctly, in English, Rumpelstiltskin means a crumpled stalk—and nothing fits that condition better than a flaccid penis. This object, or condition, resolves both word-roots. Rumpled, a detumescent penis deflates the stalk; a rumpel[ed] stiltskin describes a soft penis. And that is precisely how Edward Clodd, the great nineteenth-century commentator, spelled his name preferring an orthography that has since disappeared: Rumpelstilt-Skin.[13]

★★★

The "stilts" part of the name must be accounted equal weight with the first diminutive element. Even though we discover him as a miniature man that first impression should not limit consideration of his complex character. Rumpelstiltskin does more in the story than "be" small. He revealed himself as more than a dismissible shrimp and there's no reason why the opening word-root should take precedence over the second. Both halves balance the equilibrium forming an oxymoron that requires that each section be counterpoised without prejudice.[i] A construction like "icey-hot" only sustains itself as an oxymoron because each half contributes a contradictory component that its fraternal twin cannot cancel.

The "stilts" section of the character's name proves as crucial to understanding his nature as the "rumpled". In fact, the stilts component indicates against what expectation he fails. And failure, to perform, to "measure up", lurks at the heart of a name that carries both humor and pathos—as if the two are ever far apart. (As jokes go, when somebody else falls down it's funny; when I fall down I want sympathy and my pain feels decidedly not funny. It's not that "misery loves company" but that somebody else's misery often proves essential to humor. Since the somebody else, the "other" who composed Rumpelstiltskin's name, suggests his opposite, our first clue about the story suggests that women told it. At the expense of malekind. Specifically, at the expense of malekind's inadequacies. And, like all jokes, by itself the punchline means little unless preceded by contextualizing material. Likewise the following discussion builds a picture of the circumstances that likely created and certainly fostered the Tale of Rumpelstiltskin.) Compounded of disparate and seemingly antagonistic parts this joke called "Rumpel-stiltskin" conceivably enjoyed a long underground life among women who told it to

---

i. The oxymoron conjoins, without any attempt to blend, incongruous or self-contradictory elements. In that sense it operates like an ideogram that holds two things at equal remove to combine each in a new special meaning. Despite its esoteric and almost mystical operations the construction is widely recognized and people ignorant of every other rhetorical device can identify, will cleverly construct and use, oxymorons although this figure-of-speech actually occurs rarely. Somehow it now occupies center stage and everybody knows and uses the term. A Google N-gram reveals that only in the 1980s this centuries-old word's frequency of usage shot up. I know not why this sharp epigrammatic form of expression has become fashionable (possibly because it contains the phrase "moron") nevertheless, in the case of Rumpelstiltskin we espy a true example of the type.

each other, perhaps gleefully. But of course to "get it" we have to understand what the joke was, besides its title.

Only lately written down by the Grimms we lack this taunting story's prehistory. Yet, the merger of two opposites with implied sexual innuendo vaults ages to unite us with the past. The name and the character's actions cache a deep history of affinity between us and them, the original tellers of this story of insinuation. Freud would have endorsed this name's inner conflict and its ultimate reference; he anticipated the present argument that there's an

> abundant use made of symbolism for representing sexual material in dreams" and "many of these symbols . . . occur with a permanently fixed meaning . . . this symbolism is not peculiar to dreams, but is characteristic of unconscious ideation among the people, and it is to be found in folklore, and in popular myths, legends, linguistic idioms, proverbial wisdom and current jokes, to a more complete extent than in dreams.[14]

Freud intuited that, like words themselves, the symbolism by which dreams portray sexuality could develop a durably settled meaning. The symbols' fixed significance could resemble spoken phrases with essentially anchored references. Like words, the images he described are usually exchanged assuming neither ambiguity nor utter haziness. The images of sexual reverie might grow conventional akin to a culture's typically distinctive features, its "folklore, and in popular myths, legends, linguistic idioms". That hardly seems controversial today. But that very symbolic operation rests at the heart of this fairytale.

Rumpelstiltskin may enduringly depict failed or troubled sexuality. The fairytale's sexual configuration survived bowdlerization or suppression precisely because we misplaced its meaning when the institution (but not the problem) that fostered it disappeared. Presently we'll see how the rest of the story confirms the lead character's failures and strengths. Freud's insight advised that folklore's emblems could, and often did, portray every aspect of sex.[15] (And why not? It's one of the few universal experiences, along with hunger, pain, weather, death, joy, and viewing the night sky. To make sense of all these—as constellations order and comprehensibly organize the myriad stars— the human faculty for pattern recognition and formation would, unsurprisingly, invent editorial cartoons for sex. Certain features remain amid shifting emotions and complex relationships. And, regarding constellations, as telescopes peer deeper and earlier into space we could do worse than name a heavenly body for Rumpelstiltskin, as not all the objects of deep space name admirable figures.) Folktales dwelled on the failures of sex, its delights, shortcomings due to physical defects or incompatibilities, sex's mythologized expectations (Prince Charming), and its actual successes. But if we happened upon one of these durable symbols for a less-than-perfect, less-than-romantic situation—the kind of sexual misery typically found in commonplace speech's idiomatic and off-color phrases—would we recognize it? The past was not squeamish.

The stories we've inherited do not turn their eyes away from or ignore all-too-human situations of sexual failure. Fairytales treat human foibles of all sorts and not just the imperfections it's morally polite to mention like greed, foolishness, pride, or gluttony. To address the misery of a flaccid penis, impotence, the Tale of Rumpelstiltskin conveyed a mild, but genuine, dirty joke. That's just the beginning.

Smutty talk nourishes humor, also spices the common sagacity expressed in fairytales. Commonplace speech (what can be plausibly and comfortably said to another native speaker) also configures grand mythologies and literature. Humble fables may illustrate proverbs, adages that subsequently justify the judgments of mundane banter. Thus we give order to the world.[16]

We can discern the wit of Rumpelstiltskin's name generated from cleverly arranged word-roots. Earlier generations would have keenly enjoyed the same perceptions; preliterate societies, especially the Northern European world, lavishly rewarded adroit spoken word-play for entertainment. The performance of verbal wit is no recent invention of stand-up comedy but any prehistoric Oscar Wilde suffered from bad timing— too early an entrance to be recorded before writing.

The next chapters reconcile Rumpelstiltskin's name to what he accomplishes and how he looks. Suffice it for now that his name could summarize his physical condition. When we arrive at the center of this fairytale's linguistic maze we learn how the name Rumpelstiltskin satisfies the story's many other circumstantial demands. Even without discussing the name's etymological basis, a scholar recently deduced that "it is quite clear to some psychoanalysts (following Sigmund Freud) that Rumpelstiltskin has a phallic meaning".[17] Of course "to some psychoanalysts" everything has a phallic meaning in a world uniformly drenched in sexual urges. But in this case the monomaniacs would be correct; Rumpelstiltskin's name carries distinctly phallic implications.

A Third Word-Root

-chen, in German, is always neuter [gender].

W. V. Quine[18]

In the wake of Freudian analysis that challenged even the least introspective to awareness, a 1920 English-language edition of the Grimm brothers' tales lists the story using strange orthography. It's called "Rumpel-stilts-kin". The shattered name deflected phallic allusions, perhaps unconsciously sensed and darkly disquieting: the suffix "skin" visually disappeared from the name. Like the story's Queen, who struggled to speak the unmentionable, editorial revisers could not pronounce the source of their discomfort: the little guy's name. So, before diving into the story's depths let's consider his name's third, if minor, element. Almost coincidentally, the suffix "stiltskin" is composed of stilt + skin, a skin that can stand up, an erect phallus.

That last bit contributes a pure bonus to Taylor's virtuoso translation. If Taylor's highly effective transliteration wasn't a conscious invention then the suffix represents an inadvertent literary discovery. In either case the suffix marvelously amplifies and confirms what preceded it. Approaching the truth those uneasy editors stressed the miniaturizing suffix; the German *chen* offers a diminutive—as *kin* or *ette* does in English. When we want to make something seem smaller or sound harmless or endearing (often "female"), either of these suffixes will do: bomblet, Rockettes, lambkin. (Wilhelm Grimm's wife Dorothy was known by the affectionate diminutive "Dortchen".) Transliteration of *Rumpelstilzchen* rendered the German *chen* into English kin. Once transformed into English the suffix conjures the specialized skin by which we beget kin.[19] Moreover, as none other than W.V. Quine reminds us, the "chen" ending in German is gendered neither male nor female—appropriately for Rumpelstiltskin.

So "kin" represented *chen*. That syllable harmonized with the other two word-roots; together they complete the invitation to a sumptuous feast of sexual insinuation from a woman's viewpoint. Unlike most words of our speech we know exactly who concocted this word, and why. A single translator launched a process that, through myriad repetitions, rendered the word part of the English language. Whatever its former aural or written German heritage the name Rumpelstiltskin now lives as part of English—and there's no returning imported words, they are ours. And so is he.

Droopy but Trustworthy

It would be easy to question the idea that Rumpelstiltskin represents a limp, an impotent, penis; the idea seems outrageously glib at first but every aspect of the story bears out this assignment. (At least one of this story's commentators holds the opposite to be true:

> For some psychoanalysts—from Freud to Graf Wittgenstein—Rumpelstiltskin, the little mannikin, whose name no one knows and whose name changes from version to version, represents nothing less than the penis. Thus, according to the Grimm version, Rumpelstiltskin is a stiff being.[20]

We shall see that nothing could be less stiff than Rumpelstiltskin.) His essential floppiness hides in his name.[21]

The current English word "stilt" was preceded by the Middle English *stilte* which meant crutch, a term of dependency and a way to keep upright. A crutch supports the limp. That implication of helpless dangling, useless, flaccidness intensifies the root-words already encountered. One graphic artist shrewdly grasped this innuendo in Rumpelstiltskin's story—as intuitive artists instinctively leapfrog reason, scholarship, and cogitation. When George Cruikshank (1792–1878) illustrated the story he instinctively grasped the tale's semantics. He sensed the unstated undertone that effected his depiction of the final scene of the name-contest. Cruikshank showed Rumpelstiltskin throwing down a crutch. The fairytale mentions no crutch. Presumably unconscious of the immodest nuances laden in the story's words, Cruikshank nevertheless perceived something about this little character, a lameness that the Grimms cited nowhere but which lurked implicit.[22]

FIGURE 2.1   Cruikshank's Illustration.

Source: Illustration from *Grimm's Fairy Tales*, 1858.

FIGURE 2.2   Dali, *The Sublime Moment*, 1938.

Source: © RMN-Grand Palais/Art Resource, NY ART155516.

The little man's name now animates a single ingredient of English. His name produces a response akin to other charged words first encountered during childhood as we acquire our words flavored by the situation of their first encounter, including this story's title. If it survived only to be examined with scholarly attention vivisection would have killed it but in everyday speech the name prospered amid other English phrases. The word "Rumpelstiltskin" survived and never dropped into obscurity while other borrowed phrases dimly landed in the forgotten bin of obsolescence. Actually, this fortunate word grew more popular.

A Little Guy by Any Other Name . . .

> I am attached to the name Rumpelstiltskin from various popular translations, and vaguely resent the abbreviated "Rumpelstilts" [or] (Rumpelstilzchen). . . .[23]
>
> *Humphrey Milnes*

Analyzing the roots of the English term Rumpelstiltskin compels more than intuition as even the Grimms' German name *Rumpelstilzchen* contains the necessary Indo-European roots to derive the meaning: flaccid penis. But we can disregard the original German when considering English-speaking children who, blissfully ignorant of any word in German, were exclusively affected by the English-language artifact. Anglophone children's appreciation of this story grows without external linguistic knowledge. If Rumpelstiltskin has become a word in English the Tale of Rumpelstiltskin has also achieved total independence from its German source(s). Kids know nothing of Jacob Grimm's career trajectory: his rise from a humbled youth, his reliance on his sister-in-law Dortchen's recollections, their family's cramped co-habitation, early-nineteenth-century cultural history as context, or the tale's Romantic debt to German nationalism. Such grown-up concerns hardly afflict youngsters. But, like its sister fairytales, Rumpelstiltskin originally was performed for a multi-generational audience; the tale was only consigned exclusively to children's literature after the Grimms' publication. In a Devil's bargain, if the story was ghetto-ized and stowed in a sub-genre fit only for juveniles, it thereby gained worldwide fame.

To summarize: the name "Rumpelstiltskin" contains meaningful elements that collectively hint that the word arose from coherent underpinnings. This characterization argues against the claim that began this chapter, that Rumpelstiltskin's "name is meaningless". And that declaration of meaninglessness cannot be easily dismissed coming from Jack Zipes, a scholar hailed as "a leader in this field" (an estimation with which I concur).[24] So, asserting the opposite suggests an original author for the story (not the Grimms, who transcribed and edited Rumpelstiltskin) which entails assigning that unknown author conscious responsibility for meaning. The story's six narrative elements direct us toward the tale's source and its inventors' intentions while, incidentally, confirming that those conjectured authors possessed rare and astute judgment of human nature—related in terms of their expertise in an age-old craft.

Compensation

Let's stipulate that Rumpelstiltskin's name presents a frisky witticism when the story's author(s) designed a coarse name to joke about the character's shortness: limp penis. Crucially, the story expanded from the crude observation that Rumpelstiltskin was stubby; one jibe did not suffice. Rumpelstiltskin's nature disavails him of claiming a long proud phallus but his nighttime song boasts of other proficiencies—one does not brag about having (or being) a short prick. He tries to compensate. Who can blame him?

The story's inventors had plenty of experience with his real-life type. They had seen men strive to offset one deficiency with a surfeit of other performances. For potent men, being a "good provider" or doing the chores impresses some women as superior foreplay. (Bodice-rippers' standard fare: pose the sweating man, shirtless if possible, laboring at some job while secretly inspected by a soon-to-be lover. This delectable tension supplies the sole genuine plotpoint of William Inge's 1953 play and the 1965 movie *Picnic*.) So, while the nubile Miller's Daughter enters the story romantically unattached, when the King threatens her with death her gratitude for Rumpelstiltskin's life-saving spinning might reasonably melt into tenderest affection. No such luck. Competence does not win her.

Rumpelstiltskin's dexterity and generous rescue avail him nothing while the oppo site, charming ineptitude in the lovable schlemiel, provides a literary (and life) staple. (Woody Allen made a career of this.) But Rumpelstiltskin doesn't even get that benefit of the social outsider. Shakespeare understood that ambivalence when he created *Richard III* as physically and morally disagreeable but an unmistakably potent potentate. His tension-filled wooing oscillates between polarities of male competency and aesthetic inadequacy (as a physical specimen); our fairytale separates the two with Rumpelstiltskin to balance the death-threatening King. Richard III supplies both the puissant King and repulsive Rumpelstiltskin. That's not all they share.

What's That Between Your Legs?

Sexually feeble men may "erect" whirling distractions as a compensatory shield of their inadequacies. Either that or slouch into attention-grabbing sulks. The story's inventor correctly understood that psychological dynamic. The fairytale anticipated still-prevalent complex psychological adaptations and inadequacy's resentment that sells pharmaceuticals today. When restorative actions fail enraged flight follows, frustration driven by humiliation. The fairytale considered how men, represented by Rumpelstiltskin, try to offset his handicap.

Some versions (including the first 1808 version called "Rumpenstünzchen") present Rumpelstiltskin riding around his campfire upon a cooking spoon. The spoon's long handle between his legs replaces the erect phallus he neither is nor has. (Other versions switch a ladle for the cooking spoon, functionally interchangeable long-handled objects.) Rumpelstiltskin's tale is not unique in considering anatomical replacements, a prosthetic enhancement. This story just tells it more frankly.

Notwithstanding Harry Potter's Quidditch matches of virtuoso flying, witches apparently ride broomsticks as phallic substitutes. The brooms make them more like men, especially when bright moonlight backlights an airborne silhouette. Craving a temporary phallus between their legs, as outlaws witches achieved a freedom to act more womanly and wanton. Magic emancipated witches, as super-females, to become as powerful as men who enjoy purchase on their lives. When witches reinstated with a wooden replacement a "lacking" part they became women with penises—transgendered. An inadequate male could do the same. The spoon's elongated grip re-sexed Rumpelstiltskin. And that was no coincidence. A cooking implement must possess an extension to shield the cook from the fire's heat and, unlike a table spoon, the longer the better (up to a point). Size counts. The story's choice of implement was not arbitrary. The women who told the story knew about cooking. They knew a short spoon from a long one and a limp dick from a hard one. If the long spoon = phallus, then in its well-known psychoanalytic association, flying = sexual activity. Rumpelstiltskin sports his anatomical enhancement while airborne.

A phallus-spoon and sex-flying mutually reinforce. The noun and verb amalgamate into a compound idea. (Fusing a noun and verb reveals another astute ideogram, like the name. This technique's reappearance as a formal device suggests the original

FIGURE 2.3   Martin Le Franc, *Champion Des Dames Vaudoises* (Waldenssians as Witches), 1451.

Source: W. Schild. "Die Maleficia der Hexenleut", 1997, p. 97.

author's mode-of-composition, a method. The object and action emerge reciprocally dependent.) A poor rumpled dick, Rumpelstiltskin seeks bodily restitution, repaired by his cooking spoon. While his own penis functions improperly he must still acquire substitute fertility if he wants a child. And that is his only expressed desire. He borrows the King's potency to father the child Rumpelstiltskin claims for adoption. Proposing

FIGURE 2.4 *Flying Green Monster Penis,* in *Decretum Gratiani,* 1340–45.

Source: © Bibliothèque municipale de Lyon.

that balance awards more credit to the tale's inventors, not for prescience—they did not "anticipate" psychoanalysis or surrogate birth and are not thereby vindicated by these developments. But they invented a wonderful image for treating a rarely discussed human malady, an almost unmentionable condition until searching for a way to promote Viagra. Then a torrent of coy "Low T" ads recognized the previously secret condition.

Centuries after the ladies who created Rumpelstiltskin Freud arrived with quite explicit observations on this point: "[I]n men flying dreams usually have a grossly sensual meaning; and we shall not be surprised when we hear that some dreamer or other is very proud of his powers of flight". Freud continued by mentioning that a doctor of his acquaintance "put forward the attractive theory that a good number of these flying dreams are dreams of erection".[25] We don't have to agree. But if flying unconsciously expresses erection poor Rumpelstiltskin—whose name suggests sexual deficiency— found a proxy in his spoon-aeronautics long before Dr. Freud elucidated. As with many apparently modern insights, ancient folk wisdom got there first. The prosthetic long-handled spoon redresses Rumpelstiltskin's anatomical lack: this artificial prick, held between the legs and extending straight out as a witch's broom, counterfeits maximum arousal. It offsets and advertises his inability to perform sexually. Rumpelstiltskin presents the namesake for impotency, and acts it, in every way.

The importance of Freud's remarks do not derive from his embryonic "science" which many deride as we move further from the moment in which Freud worked. Behavioral neuroscience may finally overtake and render useless, foolish, or merely preliminary his insights about a mechanistic understanding (that mostly, brain = mind).

But in this instance Freud's associations effectively tie cultural assertions to a time and place. The combined unit (of a flying male who straddles his erect spoon to thereby correlate with Rumpelstiltskin's name) reconciles previously disparate story elements. That underlying unity exposes an outlook that will eventually reveal the identity of the story's creator. The penchant for duplication hints at the literary "style" of an artistic intelligence. But whose?

There's a consistency to the way the story builds units. Each successive element cumulatively tints the other units with wry editorial asides. The flying-verb seems male while cooking, associated with females, ambiguously genders the kitchen implement, yet the spoon's shape appears male. With supreme literary efficiency these elements reciprocate to bolster their complex gender evocations. For a writer that's no easy task. The story's technique for achieving coherence suggests a compositional manner, a style that permeates the whole tale. This method celebrates enjoyably complex polyphony within an aesthetic that arranges the dramatic arc as performance. The Tale of Rumpelstiltskin hints that its creators were present and working in a moment with its own conventions for inventing and reciting stories. The story's gradually appearing deep consistencies strongly suggests an original author (before the Grimms edited alternate versions) or at least a local or period style, a habit of composition, incidentally consistent with how Freud thought.

Rather than presenting a haphazard and "meaningless" accumulation of details, some guiding force oversaw the increasingly intricate story's creation as anything but random nonsense. Now the question is, what did the author(s) want to stress and what point(s) to make with this tale? Knowing these particulars would identify the ideal intended audience and therefore the story's first narrator. Most importantly, the story celebrated a valued skill: spinning. Rumpelstiltskin is a master spinner.

The Distaff Side: Real Men Don't Do Fiber Arts

> What harmony can there be between pupils and nursemaids, desks and cradles, books or tablets and distaffs, pen or stylus and spindles?
>
> *Peter Abelard (1079–1142)*[26]

Otherwise tenderly disposed toward women, or one in particular, the great lover Abelard generally disparaged females whom he identified with spinning fiber (distaffs and spindles). The spindle opposed the pen—learning, philosophy, theology—in an apparent conflict "between pupils and nursemaids". The sour disharmony he shared with many men prompted a fairytale to remedy the situation or at least offer a rebuttal. In case the story's first hearers misinterpreted the gist of the tale or failed to catch how Rumpelstiltskin's name hinted at impotence, they noticed that, overwhelmingly, men did not spin fibers. His dexterous spinning contrasts with normal gender roles. For most of history any male caught spinning suffered a muddled sexual identity. Spinning was women's work, exclusively.

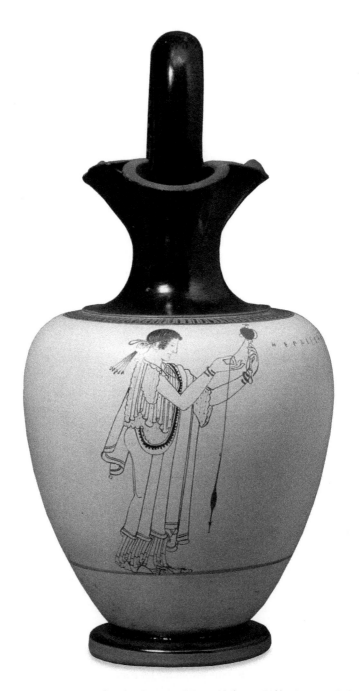

FIGURE 2.5 *Women Spinning* by the Brygos Painter, Athens, Fifth Century BCE. © The Trustees of the British Museum.

Source: By permission of the British Library. White-ground jug, attributed to the Brygos Painter, ID 00034686001.

An essential employment in ancient settlements or nomadic tribes, in towns or in the countryside, at women's rest or during play and even while at other chores, women spun fiber. There were good reasons why females of every age practiced this art, from cradle to grave, in every era.

Spinning yielded an immediately useful product and thus, though it came from unglamorous drudgery, proved of unambiguous worth to the community. Restricted to females, spinning endured the ages barely celebrated. Jesus recognized that spinning epitomized continual travail: "And why take ye thought for raiment? Consider the lilies of the field, how they grow; they toil not, neither do they spin" (Matthew 6:28). His words valenced gender—toiling was male and spinning, female—to illustrate terms for endless work, the arduous drudgery from childhood onward.[27] Jesus referred to women by invoking spinning, an understanding perfectly obvious to everyone until the post-industrial era's urban revolution disengaged women from their age-old occupation.

Subsequent religious figures came to the same conclusion about spinning's gendered associations. Rabbi Papa (c. 300–375 CE) noted that "[Even] a women whose husband combs wool will call him to the doorstep to sit with him".[28] Rabbi Papa meant that a

FIGURE 2.6   *Young Woman Spinning with Servant*, Susa, Iran 8th–6th Centuries BCE.

Source: © Rama, Cc–by–sa–2.0–fr.

FIGURE 2.7 Tomb stele, Hittite, Late 8th–7th Centuries BCE.

woman whose husband practices (the otherwise female) fiber arts—a "repulsive profession" according to Rashi[29]—will not be ashamed to sit with him and be seen together on the stoop of their house. She will show her love and loyalty despite his shameful trade, a disreputable craft for a husband because it implied sexual confusion. In the late classical era wool-working was exclusively women's work. Men toiled, women spun. The reversal of roles threatened loathsome gender-bending such as Rumpelstiltskin practiced centuries later. Despite Jesus' suggestion to desist from such labors no one shirked these jobs because without spinning there was no fiber to make cloth and somebody had to discharge this ceaseless task. The somebody was always women, for good reason.

Spinning had to be learned early to be done well. Youngest girls were taught to spin and perfected the art long before they were marriageable. This essential chore could be performed while nursing or between cooking duties. From childhood onward women performed spinning in every household situation: prehistoric "multi-tasking". And they performed simultaneous tasks without lowering the quality of thread (based on evenness of the thread's thickness and regularity of the turns). During biologically defined and culturally exalted states of a woman's life (menstruation, newly wed, pregnant, post-partum, widow) the rate of fiber production hardly varied. Women could, and did, spin at every hour. As a young child spinning contributed to the family's well-being with one of the few tasks that (along with goat/sheep-herding) required neither an adult's gross muscle power for heavy toil nor advanced mathematical-linguistic skill for bargaining. After childhood, and at every successive age and rite-of-passage, spinning mattered.

When nubile, spinning brought a definite asset to the marriage, so a good spinner appeared more marriageable. The Miller's Daughter knew how to spin, as her loopy Dad boasts that she "can spin excellently, both quickly and fine". Mastering the skill to high perfection hastened wedlock. The community judged a would-be bride desirable if she spun well and only through marriage did a girl leave her father's household and her mother's direct oversight. Competent spinning contributed to sexual liberation and the chance for personal expression when a female became mistress of her own household (under a husband's direction, but at least without Mom). Adroit spinning elevated female prestige among peers and enhanced a girl's desirability to menfolk, which identifies one of the tale's motifs: super-spinning fit for the King.

Although it could be practiced alone the activity also presented certain opportunities for relief from solitude. Whenever women spun together they benefited from congenial company and a chance to share thoughts and compare observations about their world. You can spin and talk.

Before or after marriage, the society of spinning women provided a dignified place to meet and talk about current situations. Spinning with other women continued an age-less circle whose companions shared mischievous tales and memories, cultivated gossip, and passed around sage advice untainted by a nearby male's idea of impropriety. Group spinning offered womenfolk a social activity even while breast-feeding. Practiced in the company of relatives or friends this exclusively womanly art extended the promise of an alluring respite from masculine company and pestering children. In old age, when a widow no longer headed a household herself, in addition to baby-sitting the grandchildren, spinning and cooking could return value for her upkeep in her children's home. Females spun all their lives, as long as their fingers remained nimble. So, Rumpelstiltskin expertly performs useful labor, and not just any activity but work that was highly charged with gender associations. He either usurps a female prerogative to displace women at their quintessential proficiency or (not trying to outdo them) admiringly tries to be more female. The spinners knew which was insinuated.

A Gadget Ordains a Sex

His story would mean less (or something completely different) if Rumpelstiltskin had dug prodigious ditches or picked innumerable apples. In fact, the story would be impossible if Rumpelstiltskin performed any other task than spinning fiber. His tale would never have come into existence, would have no reason to have been told, if he didn't spin since the story's principal points arise from jokes about gender confusion associated with this task. But Rumpelstiltskin does not labor alone in this role reversal. To achieve the same amusing displacement other stories transposed male and female work.

Among "The Twelve Labors of Hercules" one task involved the hero's spinning wool for the Lydian Queen Omphale. The comical notion occasioned ancient drollery: the strongest of men reduced to women's work. The story also inspired some spectacular art. In

FIGURE 2.8   *Hercules and Omphale*, 201–225 CE, Spain.

Source: © Herzog Anton Ulrich-Museum, Braunschweig, Germany.

a Roman mosaic (201–250 CE) in Spain, though heavily built and unmistakably bearded, Hercules wears women's clothing. His left hand holds a distaff loaded with wool. Queen Omphale carries Hercules' olive-wood club and she wears his skin of the Nemean Lion— one of Hercules' important attributes, a cloak that refers back to his killing the beast. (Look who is wearing the pants in this family, to put it in modern colloquial.) The great German Renaissance artist Lucas Cranach, the Elder (1472–1553) painted a biting illustration of the story, *Hercules and Omphale* (1537); as the hero spins the queen's playful handmaids tie a wimple on his head in recognition of his feminization. Only women wore that garment that enhanced their "modesty" by hiding their hair. If you spun you must be dainty if not ladylike.[30] The myth illustrates the quandaries men get into, sometimes for love.[31]

Rumpelstiltskin does not (apparently) love the Miller's Daughter yet he spins for her like a love-muddled suitor. Likewise Hercules evidenced self-effacing affection. Although no Hercules, indeed virility's opposite, Rumpelstiltskin's gender-reversal proves the same point: men do not spin except when enthralled by a woman, and then only in stories, never in reality.

The same witticism motivated a Dutch artist to create the image of a *Cherub Spinning for a Young Woman* as one plate in a compendium of pictures and stories about love, the *Emblemata Amatoria* by Daniël Heinsius (printed sometime before 1618). This image proves exceedingly interesting because it mirror-images many illustrations of Rumpelstiltskin's story. The difference between the Cherub and Rumpelstiltskin derives from the print's caption. An accompanying inscription (in Dutch) points out what happens

FIGURE 2.9 Lucas Cranach the Elder, *Hercules and the Maids of Omphales* (tying a woman's wimple on his head), 1537.

Source: © Herzog Anton Ulrich-Museum, Braunschweig, Germany.

FIGURE 2.10 Daniël Heinsius, *Ambacht van Cupido* (Lovestruck [Male] Cupid), 1613.

Source: In Nederduytsche poemata, Leiden University Library, Self no. 20643 E 32. Web, Emblem Project Utrecht.

when a man falls headlong into infatuation: "That['s what] Happens to me when I woo a woman". The "that" refers to the topsy-turvy condition of self-abasement, reversing gender roles when a man spins. Until recent times the discovery of a man spinning meant sexual confusion. And that's true for Rumpelstiltskin also.

Spinning fiber was not just a predominantly female activity but an act that defined gender—*the distaff side*. (Abelard saw manly learning from "books or tablets" opposed to a woman's "distaffs".) A sex was named for the activity of spinning. Until recently, the word "distaff" indicated what double-X chromosome means today.

Rarely used allusively now, except to be quaint or condescending, the word "distaff" produces a cascade of associated meanings. In the first and unadorned sense, it named an instrument, a tool, a simple staff with a cleft end to hold unspun fiber (flax, wool, jute, etc.). Hand-spinning drew thread from the distaff. The distaff enhanced mechanical efficiency compared to manually handling bunched fibers (tow). The distaff held fibers so they remained untangled until needed thus easing and speeding the process of spinning. And the implement has been around for a long time. And was gender-loaded all the while. An old word, "distaff", first appeared in English around the year 1000 to refer to an already ancient technology. Centuries later Chaucer employed the word distaff unchanged. In "The Nun's Priest's Tale" in the *Canterbury Tales* ("And Malkyn with a dystaf in hir hand"). Three centuries after Chaucer, Robert Burton used the word in *Anatomy of Melancholy*, 1621, to identify properly gendered spheres of activity ("Tradesmen left their shops, women their distaves"). As a household item it supplied a central piece of everyday vocabulary and the distaff featured in all manner of idioms.[32]

The distaff evolved along with the technology of spinning. Still serving the same role of holding bunched fibers, it attached to spinning wheels when that implement was invented, possibly in China during the late middle ages. We'd be mistaken to assume we hear the modern spinning wheel's creaking treadle or in earlier times the sound of hands slapping the tall walking wheel—both likely anachronisms to this fairytale's core ideas. Spinning wheels appeared only c. fourteenth century; before that the act of spinning neither suggested nor was associated with any specific rhythm and hand-spinning required no muscular strength but a repetitive choreography of fine motor skills well-suited to female anatomy. Combining the distaff and spinning wheel vastly increased the amount of thread a spinner could produce in a day. (Unchanged in form from hand-spinning, the distaff typically mounted next to the spinning wheel's bobbin with the fiber-wrapped distaff tied in place by a piece of ribbon or string. On spinning wheels the distaff was placed within easy reach of the spinner who still manually played out the fibers.) The spinning wheel was not widely introduced until the fourteenth century and since the whirring thrice-pulled wheel is essential in the Tale of Rumpelstiltskin, the story could probably not have been invented before then as previous to the wheel spinning was performed quietly by hand with only a distaff and noiseless spindle.[ii] If some form of

---

ii. A prehistoric invention, created at so early a date that no one knows to what era to assign its appearance, the drop spindle makes a twined filament from a mass of semi-coherent fiber. (The process of carding aligns random fibers into a more or less organized mass of parallel fibers which enhances the whole process. Yet, even without carding it is possible to spin directly from animal hairs or fur.) In its simplest

Rumpelstiltskin's tale predates the fourteenth century it must have been a radically different narrative. Based on late-medieval and later technologies Rumpelstiltskin's story or its closest variations preserved a specific outlook on how fiber was spun, by whom, and perhaps most importantly, where.

Since only women spun thread the distaff's connotations enlarged to mean the world of female work and the concerns traditionally considered germane to women. In the *Canterbury Tales* this sense appears in the "Monk's Prologue" ("I will have thy knife And thou shalt have my distaff and go spin") where the phallic knife and cloudy-tipped distaff present plain surrogates for what then seemed unchanging and irreducible sexual characteristics. If you were a man you did not ply the distaff anymore than you had breasts. And a woman abandoning the distaff announced a radical gender-swapping like attaching a penis and shedding breasts—a sex-change operation. This is just how Shakespeare intended his audience to understand things when *King Lear*'s daughter Goneril decides: "I must change names at home, and give the distaff into my husband's hands", meaning that she must unwillingly do man's work as her reluctant husband proved himself unfit for a (male) ruler's difficult and unpleasant responsibilities. Shakespeare flourished the distaff in *Cymbeline* (in metonymy, as Jesus substituted spinning for the idea of womanhood): "Their own nobleness which could have turn'd a distaff to a lance". He contrasted women's work of spinning with men's armed combat just as Chaucer had used a knife to symbolize maleness. With the exception of certain eccentrics, like Joan of Arc, gendered roles endured, sequestered.[33] But when a woman fought she took up the weapons at hand as Hermione relates:

> . . . he shall not stay,
> We'll thwack him hence with distaffs.
> (*Winter's Tale* I:1)

No woman handed her husband the distaff to spin. Period. But Rumpelstiltskin spun and spun marvelously well though he was apparently male . . . how can this be? Clearly distinguished, the workaday worlds of men and women diverged but Rumpelstiltskin mastered a female art that—from the time of Jesus to Shakespeare's day and beyond—separated assigned space(s) and times. Each gendered realm even celebrated its own holidays and festivals.

The day after Twelfth Night was called distaff's day which Robert Herrick (1591–1674), that consecrator of everyday life's vitality and color, celebrated in a poem called "St. Distaff's Day".[iii] On that day women resumed their household chores following the

---

form, raw or treated fibers are attached to a stick that can freely spin. As the stick fills with spun thread or twine—and the newly formed line curls around the spindle—new fiber plays out from the bunched material to be added to the accumulated spooling.

iii. This affinity with the holiday connects lines in Shakespeare's play with its title. The correlation springs from the fact that in life as in fairytales, spinning provided a dowry. A nubile girl's spinning humorously associated specialized female toil with imminent sex. Spinning recommenced immediately after a midwinter's sexual frolic (formerly rowdy Christmastide). Sir Toby Belch advises the wife-seeking Sir Andrew

FIGURE 2.11 Luttrell Psalter, *Woman Beating a Man (Her Husband?) with a Distaff,* 1320–1340.
Source: By permission of the British Library.

Christmas break. Until recently Christmas unfolded a riotous carnival that emphasized feasting, obscenity, openly practiced fornication and playfully inverted social roles that lasted during the revelry. Following mid-winter merriment spinning enjoyed its own holiday to mark its resumption and a return to the "norms" of humdrum life. Though

---

Aguecheek that his lank hair, which does not curl in an attractive way, "hangs like flax on a distaff; and I hope to see a housewife take thee between her legs and spin it off" (*Twelfth Night* I:2). Common speech used spinning as a vulgar synonym for sex and—as usual to please his raunchy audience—Shakespeare extracted every bit of lewd innuendo . . . as does this fairytale.

exclusively female this women's celebration differed from treacly Mother's Day, a recent female-centric holiday; Distaff Day recognized the community's essential reliance on the fruit's of women's spinning. The holiday consequently honored the distaff side. So why was Rumpelstiltskin intimate with spinning and the distaff?

The term distaff referred to women themselves, considered as a group and this sense survived into mid-twentieth century journalism and informal writing. Despite its antiquity—a venerable word from the spinner's obsolescent technology—some women find distaff offensive as a synonym for "female". The word symbolizes a gender limited to the realm of domestic life, "the little woman". The original Glass Ceiling. Spinning's associated tools so severely defined their lives and women's accessible roles that as an adjective in the "distaff side" of a family the implement referred to the mother and her blood relatives. By extension, distaff remains a synonym for "female" in horse racing (especially the American Breeders Cup run by the National Thoroughbred Racing Association as a competition for fillies matched in a separate race). That the word contracted to applications in horse racing suggests that propriety no longer employs it without prejudice concerning women. But that development occurred only decades ago while the Tale of Rumpelstiltskin treasures up a bygone age's lessons.

An Extinct Species and Its Descendants

His familiarity with the now-embattled, sex-determined, term distaff signals how outrageous was Rumpelstiltskin's oddball character. His spinning associated with cross-over gender restrictions related to the female world. As far as the storytellers were concerned Rumpelstiltskin represented no man and certainly no "he-man". But the story intimates that a helpful and infertile (if troublesome) male might not be such a bad thing. Especially if you could make him disappear when his work was done.

The tale ridiculed men more than spinning's obligatory drudgery because lifelong spinning at the homestead offered compensations. If men assembled for outings like hunting forays, women met when they went to the well or stream for water, then visited with nearby friends. The official line claimed the sexes carried distinct burdens executed in different zones of authority and in ways natural to their competencies. The fiber arts colored this worldview. Women spun while walking; in antiquity women carried whorls to spin thread from fiber while standing or strolling, sitting, or talking. In contrast, spinning cannot be done while hunting, fishing, chopping a tree, plowing, or doing anything that requires the characteristic upper-body strength reserved for jobs assigned to male anatomy.

Human males mostly grow larger and more muscular than females—neither trait exhibited by Rumpelstiltskin. These physical differences (express what zoologists call dimorphism in sexual differentiation) helped underscore the story's main point. Small and physically weak for a man, Rumpelstiltskin demonstrates compensating talents that are female. While the women who told this female-celebrating tale might oppose changing places with men to gain purchase on their lives, they definitely did not wish to become Rumpelstiltskin, a shriveled guy who apparently suffered sexual dysfunction. The story revels in a womanhood that mocked various male qualities, the same qualities that furnish material for today's sit-coms.

FIGURE 2.12   Gerard ter Borch, *The Spinner*, c. 1652.

Source: Museum Boijmans van Beuningen, Rotterdam, Netherlands.

Rumpelstiltskin's Shadow Across Literature

In Europe spinning never crossed gender lines, though males could practice fiber preparation or weaving—a gender contrast of which literature took note. (Sometimes literature itself benefited. In the 1780s Robert Burns briefly worked as "a flax-dresser, manually beating fibers in preparation for weaving, before his partner's tipsy wife burned down their shop and propelled Burns towards his poetic calling".[34]) Yet, preponderantly women pursued the fiber crafts with the few exceptions, some notably recognized by mainstream authors.

FIGURE 2.13 Jean François Millet, *The Spinner, Goatherd of the Auvergne*, 1868–1869.
Source: © RMN-Grand Palais/Art Resource, NY.

George Eliot (1819–1880) observed colorful local particulars that her artistic intelligence shaped into a novel, a work that shared the folkloric elements that generated the Rumpelstiltskin fairytale. Eliot set *Silas Marner: The Weaver of Raveloe* (1861) in a crucial moment of the nineteenth century's industrial revolution. She set her story in England's South Midlands where the fictional town of Raveloe supplied the novel's geographic features based on the Warwickshire village of Bulkington. Eliot anchored her tale with minutely accurate details that marked current society's titanic industrial transformation. She founded her story on:

1. the fact that women of all but the highest social classes spun
2. that, as a shared activity, women formed a gender kinship in spinning and related fiber arts
3. certain men also spun and wove although it was understood that a male weaver would need to be supplied by thread furnished by up to twenty women, as spinning was so much slower than weaving
4. for the purposes of her story these male weavers were short—or, more importantly, *perceived to be short* and physically unimposing in stature—unlike the hearty squirearchy or robust agrarian peasants
5. like some half-forgotten memory (of the extinct pre-Indo-Europeans or the "wee folk" who infiltrate the countryside) these outcast men who practiced the fiber arts seemed to live beyond society, not quite pariahs—as their craft's products were valued, used the women's spun thread, and contributed to the rural economy's exchange of goods and services—but neither were they included in mainstream society
6. despite the benefit they provided, these short men (like Rumpelstiltskin) were inexplicably and preternaturally despised, almost the victims of a phobia in the countryfolk, without reason or explanation

The beginning of her book seems a harsh NeoRealist retelling of the fairytale's opening:

Part One

CHAPTER 1

In the days when the spinning-wheels hummed busily in the farmhouses—and even great ladies, clothed in silk and thread-lace, had their toy spinning-wheels of polished oak—there might be seen in districts far away among the lanes, or deep in the bosom of the hills, certain pallid undersized men, who, by the side of the brawny country-folk, looked like the remnants of a disinherited race. The shepherd's dog barked fiercely when one of these alien-looking men appeared on the upland.

Eliot limns Silas Marner so that he, like Rumpelstiltskin, dwells isolated. His only human exchanges are commercial dealings through his work, weaving. He is sexless (like Rumpelstiltskin). Also, he apparently (or so the townspeople suppose) knows magic:

he sought no man or woman, save for the purposes of his calling, or in order to supply himself with necessaries; and it was soon clear to the Raveloe lasses that he would never urge one of them to accept him against her will—quite as if he had heard them declare that they would never marry a dead man come to life again. . . . And where did Master Marner get his knowledge of herbs from—and charms too, if he liked to give them away.

Like Richard Wagner's gnome Alberecht, Silas Marner (an exact contemporary of the "Ring Cycle") found himself spurned by womankind.[iv] Loveless, Marner re-directed his affections from human beings to gold. Like Alberecht's golden hoard, Silas found his hidden cache stolen, which plunged Marner into compensatory toil, comparable to Rumpelstiltskin's.

Silas Marner practiced the sometimes male task of weaving, unlike the exclusively female art of spinning.[35] Male weaving gained a recent fiber-arts companion in male knitting. That technology appeared in Europe no later than medieval times and European knitting possibly dates as recently as the Renaissance. It seems that knitting has been with us forever. But it's a recent invention, and one that occidental men first arrogated. (An ancient form of endless-knot looping called "nail binding" was practiced in ancient Egypt and to the untrained eye the products of nail-binding and knitting appear similar. Don't ask me to describe the difference. They look the same to me and it takes an expert to tell nail-binding from knitting.)[36] As a commercial trade in Elizabethan England, only men pursued knitting through the exclusively male guild of hosiery knitters and, though marooned in office jobs that require no physical brawn, today few men knit. Knitting's exclusivity suggests something of spinning's bygone gender-explicitness.

Confusing the picture, some of the arduous trades related to the fiber crafts evolved into avocations (carding, dying, spinning, knitting, craft-weaving) also almost exclusively practiced by females, regardless of age. Modern fiber arts continue a gendered division of labor that flourish as hobbies transformed from old-time drudgery. To its originators the Rumpelstiltskin story's gender-bending seemed an outlandish re-configuring of sex-roles and much of the story's surprisingly vicious humor depends on understanding who Rumpelstiltskin was and to what class of being he belonged. So we have to distinguish between spinning, weaving, knitting, and the other fiber crafts. Recovering history's endless female toiling to create useful fibers of spun wool or flax reveals the Rumpelstiltskin story's editorial insinuations.[v]

---

iv. Ultimately, the figure who completes this cycle is Samuel Beckett's pathetic loner Krapp (*Krapp's Last Tape*, 1958). The play's cynicism revolves around the question of who is rebuffed in love. Like many predecessors, magical or not, Krapp spurned human affection for his work's allure. At first he found literary toil exhilarating and self-confirming but having given up the love of women—whose rejected beauty and pleasures he bitterly recollects—in old age Krapp discovers himself a literary failure who traded love for work and squandered his life's colossal wager. Like Alberecht and Silas Marner, like Rumpelstiltskin himself, Beckett wrote that "I saw Krapp small and wizened" (Harmon, 1998, pp. 61, 59). Text replaced textile.

v. George Eliot's "great ladies, clothed in silk" obtained their finest cloth from a sad, but oddly male, compound. Beginning in the seventeenth-century English prisons planted mulberry trees in their exercise courtyards. Supplying fresh fruit for the convicts' diet was not their principal justification as the inmates well-being counted for little in that harsh sub-world. As an example of privatization and out-sourcing, prison convicts supplied free labor for the silk industry whose ravenous silkworms fed on mulberry plants. In this context, though only published c. 1840, the ditty (assigned Roud Folksong Index number 7882) makes grim sense of a prison exercise yard:

Lacking a normative male's muscular physique Rumpelstiltskin appears a wimp who performs none of the "heavy lifting" allocated to males. The girl's father works arduously as a miller while her King rides his domain—solid male roles. That distinction, too, quietly contributes to the tale's finely calibrated gender discriminations. By the end of the twentieth century the theme of "the occupational-specific construction of gender in various 'Rumpelstiltskin' narratives", sprawled a battleground in second and third-wave feminist criticism of folklore.[37] Scholars began to examine occupations that traditionally were allotted to one or the other sex—perhaps for good ergonomic or child-rearing reasons. The investigation uncovered assumptions about gender-assignment of household chores that implied how those particular, apportioned-at-birth and unalterable, appointments burdened their practitioners with defined social obligations.[38]

When the King challenges the Miller's Daughter for the third time he offers that "if you succeed, you shall become my wife". She will have become an irresistible model bride—having performed women's work so admirably, indeed magically, to the chore's epitome. Productivity and fecundity: she had it all. If she lacks proper lineage and hereditary status, well, ancestry can be bought. Titles acquired with cash or service in war secured noble rank outright or through arranged marriage. The Miller's Daughter essentially "buys" her title and elevation to the nobility. In this story money drolly trumps vaunted bloodlines. Just as in late-medieval life.

Notes

1. Zipes (1993, p. 43).
2. Before they learned to write the folks who became Europeans spoke an unknown language but once they attained literacy they began to leave us helpful records of their ideas and the sound of their words. Comparing the similarities shared by related words, and other features in many languages, that long-gone speech has been reconstructed and called Proto-Indo-European. It was the ancestor of today's most widespread spoken languages. Proto-Indo-European left no written records of its own but its many offspring, who resemble their parents in a linguistic family album, eventually developed writing systems and used various versions of the alphabet to record their thoughts. The exception is Hittite which recorded its pronouncements in cuneiform.
3. McWhorter (2008) argued exactly this position: that unexpected overlays of new languages are colored by underlying strata. He maintains that an Indo-European language, Gaelic, and specifically Welsh grammar, supplies the foundation beneath English, especially in its weirdly, almost unique, reliance on the pleonastic verb "do". His work dwells an outlier in linguistics' nether reaches: English's (perhaps special) relationship to other Indo-European tongues.
4. See Otto Kahn (1966/7) whose theory is summarized in: McGlathery (1993, p. 78).
5. Oliver Sacks (2012) mentions an alternative origin of all manner of "little people" arising from various kinds of hallucination: "Did Lilliputian hallucinations (which are not

---

Here we go round the mulberry bush,
The mulberry bush,
The mulberry bush.
Here we go round the mulberry bush
On a cold and frosty morning.
[Alternate verse: At 5 o'clock in the morning]

uncommon) give rise to the elves, imps, leprechauns, and fairies in our folklore?" (p. xii) These hallucinations could be drug-induced or the product of mental derangement.

6. Amerindians call the purposeful mis-identification of the conquered with their masters "Apples", red on the outside but white inside. Also "Uncle Toms" (for subservient African-Americans who associate with so-called white values) may, like the apple analogy, be "Oreos", a cookie with a dark outside but a white core. Simone Weil, in one of her best and more cogent essays, "The Great Beast" (1939–1940), urged the occupied French to note how they mistakenly viewed themselves as the heirs of Latinate culture. She reminds her countrymen that Gaul's Roman occupiers had invaded and governed the land as ruthlessly as the Nazis. Hence, France's putative Latinate culture marked subservient collaboration.

7. As that peerless essayist Cynthia Ozick (1977) phrased it:

> How—If there were no Jews—the world would be enraptured! . . . the mother-people of Jesus, the sister-people of Mohammed! A lost civilization: barbarism closed over it . . . Christian ladies [would] study "The Priceless Culture of the Jews" at Chautauqua in the summertime, where there is also a work-shop on talith making *(pp. 107, 207)*.

8. Schneider (1989, p. 198).
9. Blackwell (1990, p. 108).
10. Barber (1994, p. 291).
11. A.W.T. and Edward Clodd (1889, p. 135).
12. Ideograms are often abstracted pictures of objects, superimposed or juxtaposed, that add up to a symbol expressing an idea or a thing. In contrast, pictograms picture a thing whose meaning may be the name of that thing, a related verb, or a concept. The confusion between the two arises as ideograms often employ pictures as well as abstract signs but Rumpelstiltskin's name links together components that are word-roots, not graphic images.
13. See A.W.T. and Edward Clodd (1889).
14. Sigmund Freud, "Representation by Symbols" (1900, p. 351).
15. Freud never discovered the bio-mechanics of mental states. Nor did he claim to, although as a neurologist he knew the telos of his studies in the brain's bio-chemistry. His exploration commenced in earnest two generations later and we do not fault him any more than we fault Copernicus for not getting astrophysics "right". Freud's great breakthrough recognized that dreams are not messages sent from outside the body. Dreams are not communications from gods, ancestors, or a spirit world, not pre-cognition dispatched from another realm as affectionate warning. And if dreams do not arrive from caring spirits there's no reason to propitiate ancestors whose "souls" dwell in another world as they tenderly watch out for our well-being. And *that* realization hugely advanced human understanding. Dreams were "merely" inward messaging that originates in the brain's switchboards. Part of behavior, dreams respond to stimulus.
16. As I understand him, Charles Olson meant something similar when he pointed out that the word and concept of mythology apparently combines *muthos*, mouth + *logos*, words = the words in one's mouth. (See: Charles Olson, 1970, p. 53-*passim*.) The things people really talk about, the words actually in people's mouths. With such talk people impose order to create the world; we bring order from *chaos* as myth-making is anti-entropic, defies increasing randomness. (Olson neither noted, nor apparently knew, that chaos means neither disordered confusion nor commotion but in Greek means yawning—the creation of space within which the universe could occur. Hesiod began his cosmogony by stating that "First came chaos", meaning the story begins by opening a world. As the Greeks could not imagine creating something from nothing, chaos refers to the gaping space into which history flowed, specifically the world.) The here-and-now is an example of mythology: not the eternally distant, but the eternally present. Olson's words-in-mouth suggests the kind of over-the-back-fence chatting that occupies folk dealing with their lives' actualities, the gossip and speculation by which we create some orderly view of the world from necessarily fragmentary insights. In

modernity this chatter of small talk might discuss TV shows, movies, celebrities, but in all ages the central topic, in many guises and levels of confidentiality and disclosure based on trust and self-knowledge, is Sex.

17. Rohrich, "The Quest for Meaning in Folk Narrative Research" (1991, p. 2). Rohrich continued, "Today we might wonder about the audacity of some of the claims [as] we are more aware of the questions of relativity and subjectivity, and the role played by time in such interpretations". In fact, in either German or English the identical interpretation is possible and if the other versions of this story in different languages may contain similar puns, these joking phrases are beyond the bounds of the present discussion. "Rumpenstünzchen" or "Rumpelstilzchen" may represent attempts to transcribe a dialect pronunciation, but the Germanic and Indo-European connotation remains visible.

18. Quine (1987, p. 79).

19. The Grimms' prototypical spelling "Rumpenstünzchen" supplies the same essential linguistic roots as the English name Rumpelstiltskin but the Grimms rescinded this provisional spelling. Perhaps it was mis-heard or the orthography insufficiently captured the sound of the liquid glide that the double Ls introduce in *Rumpelstilzchen*. Aside from the more pleasing sound, in German the L supplies an endearing diminutive: little Hans is Hansl (written Hansel in English) and little Greta is Gretl. Rumpelstiltskin seemed twice as small by doubling the Ls.

20. Rohrich (1991, p. 9).

21. Incapable of virile rigidity, Rumpelstiltskin proves more accommodating than anyone in the story. Nobody could be less "stiff" than Rumpelstiltskin who bends to the girl's will and re-negotiates. On the other hand, the King, who fathers her child, glares inflexible, never relaxing his death threat unsated after two nights of spun gold. The girl's father never recants his lie. Rumpelstiltskin's fault names him a softy and he relents, pliable, except about revealing his name, an act of self-incrimination. The tale forces the contrast. Everyone else is headstrong but Rumpelstiltskin.

22. In Taylor's 1823/1920 translation, George Cruikshank's Rumpelstiltskin illustration faces p. 150.

23. Milnes (1962, p. 144).

24. In her survey of the field, Jeannine Blackwell's full statement (p. 110) comes from her review essay in *The German Quarterly*:

> Jack Zipes has been a leader in this field since his publication of *Breaking the Magic Spell: Radical Theories of Folk and Fairy Tales* (1979), *The Trials and Tribulations of Little Red Riding Hood* (1983), and *Fairy Tales and the Art of Subversion* (1983).

25. Freud (1900/1931, 1965, pp. 429–430).

26. *Letters of [Peter] Abelard and Heloise* (p. 17). Peter Abelard and Heloise (1101–1162) may be celebrated as great impetuous lovers but by standards of sexual equality a millennium later they were deficient, which is understandable.

27. Here Jesus engaged in metonymy whereby one term instantly invokes or substitutes for another term—as opposed to metaphor's gradual exchanges. To say, "He gave up the crown for the pen" (metonymy) would mean to abdicate the throne to become a writer. The substitution is instantaneous. If the poet invites "Shall I compare thee to a summer's day?", the comparison continues as a gradual exposition of analogies (metaphor) to close the gap between the two objects. We began this chapter with Abelard's metonymy used as a rhetorical device where "books or tablets" stand for male scholarship while "distaffs" alludes to the world of women that opposed the schoolroom's "pen or stylus" with the household's "spindles".

28. Rabbi Papa of Nahardea, Talmud [Babylonian] Tractate "Ketubas" 75a.

29. Rashi—an acronym for Rabbi Shlomo Yitzhaqi (1040–1105)—echoed this distinction made by the early rabbis who recorded the Talmud.

30. This point escaped the Flemish painter, Bartholomäus Spranger (1545–1611) whose *Hercules and Omphale* (1585) luxuriates in fleshy nudity. He illustrates the tale's obligatory cross-dressing but misses the story's coarse jest as Spranger's scholastic and courtly wit aimed for a, perhaps overly sophisticated, learned audience.

31. The ancient predicament was never better expressed than by that astonishing poem of love in old age, William Carlos Williams' *Asphodel, That Greeny Flower* (1955):

> I cannot say
> > that I have gone to hell
> > > for your love
> but often
> > found myself there
> > > in your pursuit.

Something very like this must be going through the mind of spinning and drag-accoutered Hercules, or any man who is led by love and finds himself at an oddly unexpected conclusion or midway on an unforeseen path.

32. Among these mainly obsolete expressions "to have tow on one's distaff" meant "to have work in hand or trouble in store". Chaucer's "Miller's Tale" features the line: "He hadde moore tow on his distaf Than Gerueys knew".

33. Obscure male terms symmetrical with distaff (side) include "sword side" and "spear side". These derive from Old English "sperehealfe" and Middle Low German "swerdhalve" or "swerdside"; they ceased to appear in Modern English.

34. Soskice (2010, p. 8).

35. Too often historians overlook the gendered assignment of different fiber arts, with sex-inversions for crafts like hosiery. Many stories present this theme of sex-role reversal as a cornerstone: in the myth of Hercules and Omphale, or Rumpelstiltskin's tale. No less a comprehensive authority than Lex Heerma van Voss of the Royal Netherlandish Academy of Arts and Sciences oversaw the publication of the massive (860 pages) *Ashgate History of Textile Workers* 1650–2000, which despite its comprehensive and utterly admirable coverage of many topics basically ignores the gender apportionment of various tasks associated with, or essential to, fabric production.

36. For example, the Victoria & Albert museum holds a pair of Coptic socks (C. 300–400 CE) that may have been knitted; alternately these socks example nail binding (V&A 2085&A 1900). Because these garments exhibit apparent seams they are less likely to have been knitted. But the differences between how they are made and modern knitting are far from clear.

37. Bacchilega (1993, p. 7).

38. Sometimes the distinctions were definitive and beyond much debate:

> From the early formation of grazing societies up to the nineteenth century, women participated in almost all the work that concerned the spinning. They took care of the animals and helped plant the flax; they cleaned and prepared the wool and roasted, broke, and hatcheled the flax. They did practically all the spinning. That is, spinning became the privilege of women, and it was considered their domain.
>
> *Zipes, 1993, p. 51*

I'm not sure how this claim ("they took care of the animals") jibes with Bronze Age testimony from the *Song of Songs* (1:7) that specifically describes the singer's shepherd boyfriend tending flocks. But each society assigns such tasks as it sees fitting for age and gender.

3
RUMPELSTILTSKIN'S AUTHOR

The Room Where the Story Was Born:
The Poor Girls Salon

> Stranger, I have only a few words to say. Stop and read them. This is the unlovely tomb of a lovely woman. Her parents named her Claudia. She loved her husband with all her heart. She bore him two sons. . . . She was charming in speech, yet pleasant and proper in manner. She managed the household well. She spun wool. I have spoken. Go your way.[1]
> *Roman tombstone, 2nd century BCE*

Lacking alternative employment outside the home women's destiny preordained most girls to a life doubly shrouded in invisibility. First, spinning seemed effortless (and thus incapable of meriting the glory men could win). Secondly, its gendered condition demoted that task's social status to the merely honorable. (If you spun you took your place as a reliable and upstanding woman within your family and community but if you chose not to, well that was unthinkable.) As one scholar put it: "Neglecting one's distaff was tantamount to laziness".[2] Hesitating to spin evidenced a visible character flaw while continuing to spin illustrated womanly integrity, constrained by the norms of severe social pressure. However slender the options, while women spun endlessly at their designated task, pre-modern society offered men only slightly greater vocational choices to "seek their fortunes". Admittedly, versus incessant female compulsion, history offered men only limited liberation, and then at great personal risk. But women who threw off social constraints that pigeonholed them rebelled with (real or symbolic) distaffs as weapons, their defense against men who knew nothing of spinning. But things did change. As one sex gradually deserted or was forced to abandon its age-old work assignment the revolution in family life and community structure produced no rousing anthem of gender insurgency, only stories.

FIGURE 3.1   14th century women spinning together, French.

In the Spinning Chamber

As a communal activity akin to modern quilting bees, spinners gathered to break their boredom and escape family responsibilities. At group spinning a woman could pass time with neighbors, exchange news, weigh life's choices with older or more experienced women, compare bodily sensations, and tell stories. Since the exclusively female meetings were held in a domestic setting—not within official buildings or under state-sanction—records of the spinning bees enter the literature late: "The first written references to spinning bees date to the thirteenth century".[3] They doubtless existed for untold ages before their first recorded account, but, like so much of women's toil, the chronicle of spinning circles' earlier epochs appears blank or only insinuated. Unlike heavy labor associated with men, spinning exacted no outward toll of bodily wear-and-tear, so its burden appeared minimal and un-heroic.[4] If spinning's modest acclaim scarcely featured in the public record or national epics, fairytales glorified and commented upon this women's work. So, we suffer a deficiency of written reports on how the spinning bees operated (who convened them, where they met if they moved from home-to-home) and what occurred in them (in the way of social interactions) but by unpacking certain fairytales we can learn.

Lacking written accounts of spinning circles' agendas they nevertheless seem plausibly congenial sites to hatch, preserve, or perfect stories like the Tale of Rumpelstiltskin, whatever the ultimate source of the kernel of the story. The Rumpelstiltskin story comments ambivalently about the work of spinning:

> Two voices seem to be present . . . one expressing dissatisfaction toward this archetypically female employment, while another voice affirms and extols spinning as a worthwhile enterprise. The latter voice belongs to Wilhelm Grimm, through whom a nineteenth-century value system and its vocabulary entered the tales as we know them today.[5]

FIGURE 3.2 Lhermitte, *"Les Veilles", Evening Work, or The Night Workers,* a spinnstube, 1888.

Source: © 2000–2018 The Athenaeum.

Without understanding where and when Rumpelstiltskin was first told it's misleading to conjure Wilhelm Grimm's Romantic-era mores as this tale's dominant note. After two world wars and too many horrors his ardently hopeful worldview (of a people reborn in their ancestral Teutonic homeland) lost all luster for modern readers. But before he ever heard of Rumpelstiltskin women told that story in a special room.

When women gathered at nighttime to spin they formed a *spinnstube*, German for a spinning chamber. And that institution proves supremely important because, as Ruth Bottigheimer succinctly noted, "[i]t was from female informants privy to, even if they were not an essential part of, this oral tradition [of the spinnstuben] that Wilhelm and Jacob Grimm gathered many of their folk tales".[6] Numerous fairytales portray spinning in a way that suggests the stories' reciters were accomplished spinners; this tale not only included details intrinsic to the craft but also sharp editorial comments about its place in society. Moreover, the Rumpelstiltskin story slyly inserts invidious comments about the extraneous world of men: just the sort of amusing wise-cracks to enliven an evening of group spinning. We gather from these stories that a tone of light-hearted practicality seemed compatible to these regular all-female events. Facts about the spinners' highly gendered precinct and spinning's technology were shared like a sisterhood's password or a knowing wink. From within their community's lively center ladies at an evening's spinning circle assessed their surroundings; they judged the quality of the spinning at hand but also their neighbors' situation and troubles, each woman's status within the circle and locality, the conduct of their menfolk and children, rumors about the greater world beyond the village, and all expressed their observations in appropriate terms. If initial observations were crudely phrased the timeless situation's inherent complexity, repetition, and hours-long duration at each occurrence, cultivated nuanced retellings as surely as any graduate school seminar refined terms under examination. As Maria Tatar noted,

> Spinning occupies a highly ambiguous status—not just in the Grimms' collection but in Western folklore as a whole. Like manual labor in general, it goes hand in hand with industry and achievement, but it is also associated with physical oppression and enslavement.[7]

Resembling other fairytales the Rumpelstiltskin story viewed a basically gentle task, interminable spinning, as drudgery.

The ladies of the spinning bee created their antithesis. Although obviously a master spinner Rumpelstiltskin represents everything opposite to the spinnstube.[8] He dwells isolated in the forest; he spins alone; seemingly he's unaffiliated and belongs to no known community or type; more astonishingly, he is a male who spins. An unsexed male, Rumpelstiltskin aided a woman whom the King installed in a space resembling the story's birthplace—a room for spinning. But, even in this detail, the story resonated with its likely authors: cell or spinnstube, both chambers excluded men. These analogies and numerous parallels suggest that the women who may have invented this tale realistically portrayed pertinent aspects of their lives. That may help explain how, centuries later, the tale still captures imaginations—it's rooted in reality. Unlike the Grimms, the spinnstube's ladies did not compose Rumpelstiltskin's tale as a conscious literary construction for, like all good writing, the women described what they knew best: spinning and men. Some of the men they knew were failures in every way, a topic worth discussing in a safe place, a place away from male encroachment.

Through drear long nights the spinnstube gatherings offered a place where women controlled the agenda as "spinning bees served as meeting places for rural girls and women where they would spin and amuse themselves during the fall and winter evenings".[9] The possibilities associated with such a staid and hypnotically monotonous activity seem bland but busy imaginations excluded from the spinning rooms ran wild as men envisioned all manner of lewdness. "[T]he spinning bees or *spinnstuben*, were controversial, because the assembled company lightened the burden of a tedious and repetitive activity with frivolity and entertainment".[10] Such amusing levity worried the menfolk. Men imagined the spinnstube's sometimes unrestrained vivacity as sexualized merriment but the truth was less intriguing.

Principally, the spinnstube's recreation featured storytelling fueled by everyday incidents. As the spinnstube's inmates attended to their individual and non-delegable work they shared life experiences; they exchanged and sought suggestions to weather vicis-situdes. Better than texting and swifter than electronic communication, proximity conferred intimacy. They would have known each other's lives intimately as "[l]arger villages often sustained several spinning bees, which segregated participants by location, age, social class, or marital status".[11] That specialization by neighborhood, class, or other variants had its effects on the conversation and resulting stories. At the spinnstube a woman gained information about friends' shifting status or threats to domestic situations: knowledge of each other's mental states. This community cultivated both mutual support and cutthroat envy as women's stories of an evening's spinnstube concerned events that wives, friends, widows, and daughters could understand: shared female experiences with fiber-work as the common background. With female liberation beginning only as recently as the late nineteenth century came political enfranchisement but also the end of spinning and some of women's ancient concerns became obsolete; others worries linger everlasting. Times change but human nature has not. Human afflictions like Rumpelstiltskin's impotence persist, along with the emotional hardship it brings to relationships. Exasperation and irritation felt identical then and now. And, then as now, friends talked.

Confidantes at the spinnstube learned when once-bright anticipations had dashed, sometimes repeatedly. The women heard when vaguely formed wishes were checked against realism. Older women advised about which slights had to be grudgingly endured, resisted, or accepted. And they learned where rare happiness likely gleamed through tedium. All this talk helped. The spinnstube provided the arena for group therapy, a venting, a way to speak the otherwise unsaid. While they spun the spinnstube's ladies addressed shared apprehensions: men, preparations for marriage (courting, sizing-up a suitor, or accommodating to an arranged marriage), more or less satisfying begetting of children, preparations for child-bearing, and husbands.[i] Even if their gatherings did not foreshadow the psychoanalytic chamber's explicitness or mimic the priest's confessional in its mannered frankness, the spinnstube's members knew or guessed each other's more delicate secrets, including, specifically, spousal impotence and the generally bewildering problem called men. A uniquely functional world of speech developed within spinnstube that mirrored language at men's workplaces. A place largely prohibited to men, the spinnstube's choicest conversations were not repeated outside for in these spinning chambers women learned from one another to be women.

The Spinning Chamber as Salon

Educationally, the peasants' spinnstube's informal schooling compared to the aristocratic ladies' salons that, in their own version of exclusivity, resembled men's Masonic lodges.

---

i. It is easier to visualize this situation based on an image of a "Spinnstube" painted by Leon Augustin Lhermitte (1844–1926), his *Evening Working*, 1888, (Glasgow Museum, Kelvin Grove Museum, Glasgow, Scotland catalogue #2140, o/c 93.5 x 112 cm). The artist witnessed the last generation of western-European women who practiced this dusk-to-midnight occupation. The spinnstube proceeded as long as it fared unchallenged by popular home entertainments like the phonograph and the even more invasive radio that brought the outside world's norms into isolated villages.

Like the secret society that all women represent(ed) to men, the rites and words spoken by women in these places remained pointedly unknown to males. Unlike the elite and progressive institution of the salon the spinnstube's familiar local cohorts tended to conservative peasant grumbling. They were neither revolutionaries nor intellectuals. Superstition reigned instead of science.

The spinnstube's ladies apparently supported prevailing morals. They hardly questioned inherited values and social structures even if they complained muttering about life's unfairness. The basically conservative institution of the spinning circle neither fomented or condoned bad conduct nor doubted core socio-religious assumptions (whose questioning flirted with heresy or treason). But the spinnstube did, in the anecdotal manner of comparing personal experience, analyze behavior with leisurely meticulous care. After all, there was no rush as the next night the same group would assemble and resume conversation or pick up again the developing story. For generations. Accordingly, the Tale of Rumpelstiltskin neither offers an example of, nor advocates for, change(s) to rectify the rampant unfairness it mocks. The girl overcomes her travail by operating inside the system not overthrowing constraints that defined womanhood or a peasant's life—an endless spinner of fiber with limited other options.

Instead of preaching a remedy Rumpelstiltskin's story ruefully observes human shortcomings. Yet, despite this story being a product of the spinning chamber in some relationship to published material, similarities remain between the intelligentsia's progressive salons and the peasants' conservative spinnstuben. Women established the salons in upper-class homes. In the salon the topic of domestic life was decidedly and pointedly off-limits to the high-minded salonieres—not so at the spinnstuben. Both convened regularly on set days of the week and, while men were welcomed into the female-led salons but rarely if ever into the spinnstube's proceedings, unquestionably women headed both institutions; one examined assumptions (abstracted, ideal, or typical behavior) perhaps to change society's values the other examined actual and local examples of behavior to more or less reinforce extant mores. Thus, though it gathered the politically disadvantaged the spinnstuben were not an instrument of female emancipation but of rather traditional continuance frequented by some sharp-eyed critical observers. And these experienced eyewitnesses espied men who attended the spinnstube's closing each night. Those ladies' comments live on.

Each rural community's verbal signs identified to their spinners which oblivious male targets were ridiculed. Among the male visitors some might glide unawares through the midst of the spinnstube to deliver a spinning wheel, come courting, smoke a pipe indoors, offer to share a drink. But such men were neither enrolled in nor part of the room's real society—they were often its targets. Though a man might be fleetingly present in the room he could not belong to its sisterly community. And such hermetic communities generate their own lore. In each era and for every trade the teller's social prospects and outlook precondition a story's possibilities as the Tale of Rumpelstiltskin describes its own begetting. The heroine was locked in a cell for spinning, an easily imaginable place for the story's reciters. Sitting in a room dedicated to spinning women discussed spinning's actual details as a jumping-off point for fantasy.

In the spinnstube the wry Tale of Rumpelstiltskin likely elicited guffaws of recognition as older women drolly commented on the varieties of worthless men they had known. One authority conceded that

> German folk tales have long been assumed to have originated in or in many cases to have passed through the spinning chamber (*Spinnstube*) where women gathered in the evening and told tales to keep themselves and their company awake as they spun.[12]

And nothing would keep a tired spinner alert like the humor of bashing men's general incompetence and braggadocio, the thrills of a threatened child saved by his Mom in a cliff-hanger, the prospect of supreme social elevation from peasant to Queen, a dash of ironic sexual innuendo and, ultimately, the sweetness of revenge. You couldn't want more from a story invented and told in surroundings congenially sympathetic to women's plight. From such a spinnstube the story leaked out to the Grimms.

A Room of Her Own, and It's Not Virginia Woolf's

> When I was a boy, one day I walked into my grandmother's house from the barn and there were four generations of women in the parlor. They were talking and laughing, but when they saw me they went silent. My grandmother told me there were cookies in the pantry and I should get myself some and wouldn't they taste good. I went for the cookies and while I forget what kind they were, I have always remembered those women talking and laughing and how quiet they went when they saw me standing there and have long since wondered what the talking and laughing could have been about.[13]
>
> *Robert Olmstead, 2013*

Within its confines, beyond male (over)sight and hearing, the spinnstube's women hashed-out fundamental questions of male-female relationships. Like all aggregated folk wisdom, from herbal medicine to cooking, the spinner's examination of sexual relations progressed over many lifetimes. The spinners' stories accumulated sly observations and pared away extraneous embellishment. Repetition sloughed off failed narrative variants. The story traveled and iteration shed purely local observations that translated clumsily to another region (space), dialect, or that passing time rendered obsolete. Through every change of circumstance a fairytale had to prove relevant to survive. "The long winter nights may have lessened the work-load there was little to do in them except tell stories around the fire".[14] In the spinnstube's close setting or with the family gathered before the hearth anything inauthentic in a fairytale violated psychological truth and was discarded. But during all these retellings Rumpelstiltskin's consignment of sharp-eyed observations about human relations floated downstream through history over many generations. By the spinnstube's cozy firelight spinners

FIGURE 3.3   Jean Bourdichon, *The Craftsman or Labor*. From *The Four Conditions of Society: Work*
c. 1505–1510.

Source: © RMN-Grand Palais / Art Resource, NY.

developed their stories for each other's hearing. When retold to children as fairytales,
perhaps with judiciously hidden revisions, those versions concealed from males what
Olmstead wondered "the talking and laughing could have been about". Sisters of the
spinnstube reserved the tale's abounding innuendo for one another.

The world of female companionship and gendered work extended beyond the spinning room, into the kitchen, the nursery, the laundry, etc. From these sex-segregated chambers supposedly came the stuff of the *Kinder-un Hausmärchen*. Strictly speaking these were not at all sex-segregated rooms.

> *Spinnstube* entertainment typically involved courtship play. . . . In the course of a typical evening, young men dropped by to flirt. Although they also devoted much of their leisure to card-playing and smoking tobacco, they ate, drank, and danced with the girls and, carrying their [spinning] wheels, escorted them home. . . . So much did the spinning bees nurture courtship that religious reformers, both Protestant and Catholic, attacked them as dens of vice, seduction and immodesty.[15]

After spinning became industrialized one of the last tasks left to women at home was carding and, although we have no modern reports from spinnstuben, descriptions of carding-circles or carding bees can supply the flavor of the lost institution:

> [Carding] was a tedious process, yet when carried out by eight or ten women gathered in the *but end* of a croft house, the essential chore became a pleasant social occasion. . . [when] the evening's work was finished and the menfolk arrived with their fiddles. . . [work was] put away and the fiddles tuned for a dance.[16]

Which seems pretty much the same routine as followed in spinnstuben: a mix of female-only work, storytelling among the women, and when the men arrived, dancing and whatever followed. As the women spun and talked, imagined sex and courtship cavorted in their minds. They had plenty of time to envision details that ripened in an exclusively female company that contemplated varied relationship situations—until the menfolk arrived.[ii] Toil preceded pleasure. Before co-ed recreation commenced at evening's end, for entertainment spinners advanced the analytic work of spirited female-biased story formation.

Men excluded from the spinnstube's drudgery envisioned these industrious women engaged in a veritable orgy of sex-drenched misbehavior. The workplace spinnstube was bedecked with phantasms of immorality as males projected utter fantasies upon of the spinnstuben: a male phantasmagoria of unleashed eroticism. Excluded from this zone

---

ii. The first graphic record of the spinnstuben sadly derives only from pedestrian copyists' lackluster woodcuts. These are copies of Hans Sebald Beham's print that "is the first surviving example of a spinning bee in visual art" (Alison Stewart, 2003, p. 127). But, notwithstanding its nominal subject, in Beham's riotous print of imagined debauchery only two women spin while the rest cavort or fend off frisky advances. Clearly this illustrates no real spinnstube but a pornographer's idea.

FIGURE 3.4   Hans Sebald Beham, *The Spinnstube*, 1524.

Source: © Ashmolean Museum, University of Oxford.

men remained largely ignorant of what happened in the spinnstube, but that proved no inhibition. In a well-documented case

> most of the evidence and information about spinning bees in Nuremberg comes from the very small group of men comprising Nuremberg's town council. . . . The council included no members who represented craftspeople, the middle or the lower classes . . . or women.[17]

To put it bluntly, and not for the last time in politics, the men who drafted the town's governing ordinances to regulate activities like spinnstuben had no idea what they were talking about. Hence, as caricatured by Rumpelstiltskin, the town's elders proved eminently worthy of mockery about their reproductive organs.

Lacking corroborated evidence of the spinnstube's actual activities the esteemed councilors in their sessions of 1528–1529 referred to "excessive, unchristian actions, and the meetings afterwards outside spinning bees of young, single men who wound and kill each other".[18] But what really riled the town's elders was not drunken males murdering one another but the girls at spinning bees arranging marriages for themselves without their fathers' approval. On the way home from spinnstuben girls discussed the details of love-matches with their potential bridegrooms thereby over-stepping paternal prerogatives endorsed by the church's view of submissive females. The town's elders—like towns' patriarchs everywhere vexed by uppity women taking fateful matters into their own hands—passed edicts (their version of *fatwas*) to restrain them. But women had a way of retaliating: with fairytales' guarded editorials. The Tale of Rumpelstiltskin responds to male fantasies about goings-on in the spinnstuben.

In contrast to the sexual fantasies clouding their description, scant reliable reports of the spinnstuben's moral tone survive. One report hails from 1500 years before the Brothers Grimm began to gather tales. The Talmud described the question that so vexed the medieval town fathers who wanted to control arranged marriages otherwise contracted in the spinnstube. That earlier account explained when to consider a betrothal official:

> A rumor of marriage is recognized not when they heard the sound of an echo [mere gossip] but when they witnessed a room in which there were lamps burning, and couches made up, and women spinning by the light of the lamps were rejoicing for her [the bride] and saying "[So-and-so] is going to be betrothed today!"[19]

You could believe what came from the spinnstube because only what was supposed to leave that chamber trickled out intended for general hearing. The women spinning by night talked candidly (of loyalties to community, family, and sex) and their testimony rings utterly believable as no participant would betray the spinning circle or shame herself. Nobody attending wanted to risk social excommunication: to be ostracized by her spinning-fellows for "premature ejaculation", a theme Rumpelstiltskin also conveyed. As the Talmud slyly observed, statements countenanced by the spinnstube could be received as accurate, unlike mere hearsay, and might carry the legal weight of affidavit. Centuries after the Talmud recorded its description nothing much had changed in Medieval Germany's spinning culture.

Spinning and Destiny

The fairytale's heroine never spins a turn but she depicts female spinners' condition of servitude to the spindle: confined to a room; in mortal peril if she fails to spin successfully; marriage dependent on her efforts. Though fateful and repetitious but not ignoble, spinning earned merit. Despite the chore's ceaseless (in time) ubiquity (in space) throughout their lives, spinners took pride in their labor and distinguished good from shoddy work. Every village, clan, or family sub-unit, informally and maybe even officially recognized a hierarchy of spinners. These women were distinguished by quality of their thread, productivity—that measured their adroit speed and diligence—that yielded a raw quantity of output. The most proficient practitioner gained local fame as a woman that young girls might envy. These masters were pointed out as exemplary by mothers who consulted such sister-spinners about technique. A reputation as the foremost spinner might outlast the lifetime of the woman who achieved such celebrity, might become a myth. But the corpus of mythology scarcely treats tales of famous spinners; women lacked control about what entered the high bardic canon of national myths. Minstrels rarely included spinners as heroines and preferred to sing about famous male skull-bashers, but women framed fairytales. Unlike violent moralizing epics, nothing could be less self-righteous than a tale like Rumpelstiltskin. This story indulges in equal-opportunity mockery of all men.

In a parallel gender universe ignored by national epics, women told their own tales, to each other, then to their children—stories fashioned and perfected in spinning circles closed to outsiders. And those stories conspicuously displayed an outlook far different from the great anthems of tribal epics. Anomalous in mythology, fairytales awarded spinning a crucial role to indicate that a female voice had created or transmitted a story. The uncommon mythic heroine-spinners exhibited cunning and bravery. But insignificant spinners could never eclipse male heroism's deeds of physical boldness that required daring martial craftiness. The mythic spinner performed her deeds more quietly. She's a shrewd observer. She figures things out and solves problems immune to male bluster that she unobtrusively directs through suggestion. It's an old guise but the pretense still works.

We should learn to see the spinner-heroine's unmentioned deeds of everyday dependability in stories that mostly ignored domestic life while, in the foreground, men pursued madcap adventures.[iii] Some myths preserve spinning as the unseen precursor to all that women could, or were allowed to, accomplish. So, while many died, killed by the monster at the heart of the labyrinth, of those sent into the giant puzzle only Theseus survived and emerged victorious because he is aided by Ariadne; she suggested he follow a thread to pilot the maze—a strand of spun fiber, woman's work.

Like the secret at the core of the stone maze's many switches and confusing reversals, a powerful force churns hidden within the Rumpelstiltskin story: women's exclusive powers to make thread and babies. (Concealment proves essential to hide the assumptions behind both stories. Unseen by the male hero Ariadne spun her labyrinth-remedy; in an undistinguished room the magician puts the rabbit into the hat to later reveal it in the spotlight. So, too, stories posit unnoticed elements that dramatically reveal themselves as crucial.) Without Ariadne's thread Theseus is toast, or lunch for the Minotaur. Like his predecessors into the maze, Theseus doesn't spin and never considered this humble tool to navigate the labyrinth. It's beneath his notice. Spinning is female; killing the Minotaur is male.[20] But sometimes spinning did occupy a myth's foreground.

From antiquity though the Middle Ages, and presaging latter-day Christian patron-saints, gods and goddesses presided over specific occupations. Pleasing that divinity

---

iii. Odysseus discovers the shirking Achilles when he emerges from the women's world where he's been hiding in drag; Achilles' interest in handling weaponry rather than adornments or household goods gives him away. The story makes you wonder about the size and girth of the local ladies when the Greeks' most ferocious warrior, Achilles, passed unnoticed just by throwing on the equivalent of a hajib.

FIGURE 3.5   *Theseus and Athena with Minotaur*, 420 BCE, National Archeological Museum of Spain, from the Salamanca Collection.

Source: National Archeological Museum of Spain, from the Salamanca Collection. Photograph Rights © Marie-Lan Nguyen.

helped your enterprise achieve a good outcome. Each God-sponsored chore denominated a gender-related if not gender-explicit task. In this schema goddesses associated with spinning proved essential to how antiquity and pre-Christian Europe envisioned the universe operating.[21] For ancient Greeks and Romans (who inherited Indo-Europeans' parcel of beliefs) archaic myth enshrined elderly spinners as a trio of females who managed fate. There's a logic in this as, "since women were the people who spun, the spinners of one's destiny would have to be women".[22] The Three Fates (the *Moirae*) controlled each person's mortal life.[iv] One Fate spun out a person's life from

---

iv. Spinning carried fateful associations; regardless of social status, Roman laws forbade any public display by a women holding a spindle. Spinning was to be done at home, behind closed doors. Inadvertently beholding

the unformed mass of destiny held on a distaff. Another sustained it and allotted good or bad fortune (the thread's quality). A third cut off the life and ruled death. The Fates had real-life counterparts. This trio of crones portrayed the aged women who ruled an evening's spinning bee. Just so highly did its practitioners regard spinning. (Talking to her younger companions while she worked, a village's oldest and most accomplished spinner imparted lore and personal history that stretched back many generations—and thereby represented the model of potent wisdom and destiny. Life resembled a thread.[23] Specifically, human life advanced as a filament spun by immortals.)[24] The Latin names for these three goddesses curiously reflect their relationship to the spinners' circle.

The spinner of the thread of an individual's fate was called *Nona*, colloquially "grandma". The named perhaps referred to the oldest still-competent woman presiding over the village spinning circle, the woman who won local fame as a spinner. The sustainer of life, who held life's thread in her hands, was named *Decuma*, suggesting expansiveness and sustenance, probably from the root "dec" meaning ten multiples, or increase by an order-of-magnitude. (To decrease by an order-of-magnitude is to decimate.) The last, who cut the thread of life and ended a human's existence was called *Morta*, simply "death".[25] Shakespeare's *Macbeth* preserved the memory of this trio in three witches who either control or foresee destiny. In this drama about man's fate shaped by ambition—allowing, or not, the possibility of free-will—it's uncertain if the witches direct events by their agency, merely prophesy what will happen, or plant insinuations and allow suggestion to take its course. In a lighter mood, Thisbe recites doggerel about the Fates in *Midsummer Night's Dream* (V:1): "O Sisters Three, / Come, come to me, / With hands as pale as milk; / Lay them in gore, / Since you have shore / With shears his thread of silk". The thread of a mortal's life was created at birth.

The idea of a *lifespan* derives from the verb spin, the process by which something is drawn out or stretched. Only subsequently spinning came to refer to "turning or whirling". Rumpelstiltskin extends the girl's life by spinning (quantity of time), then he exalts her worldly condition and her fate (quality of time). Granting him powers handed down from primeval times the spinning bee could not foretell that their ageless craft would almost vanish in the Industrial Revolution. The demise of hand-spinning severed the line leading back to Rumpelstiltskin's meaning. His context in the gendered fiber arts became extinct (cut off by Fate) when the incongruously male master-spinner ceased as a viable myth once a young woman who spins dared to speak his fated name.

---

a woman spinning represented terrible luck generally and, specifically, meant crop failure for the witness. Perhaps oddly, the spinner herself was immune from misfortune for this offense to public decency. The superstition proved long-lived, as Jacob Grimm reported: "if, while riding a horse overland, a man should come upon a woman spinning, then that is a very bad sign; he should turn around and take another way" (*Deutsche Mythologie* 1835, v3.135). Spinning's deeply felt associations cluster life, fecundity, destiny, and death with the mysterious life-giving female power—all linked intuitions that outcrop in ancient lore, including this tale.

Spinning and Fate

Though inconspicuous to non-spinners (most of us) the act of spinning mimics unalterable destiny. (The *idea* of an inexorable fate may have historically preceded spinning technology but fate was eventually identified with its female life-givers. The notion of a fated lifespan and its immutably spun destiny perhaps predates any language now spoken which, if true, locates an even deeper cultural substrate than where the Grimms were tunneling.) Once spun a thread's basic character cannot be amended—like mythic destiny.[26] A spun thread can be doubled or plaited but the constituent thread's basic character, its thickness, coarseness, and length, is determined when first spun. Don Pedro senses, and expresses in terms of fiber-work, that immutable inevitability when (*Much Ado About Nothing*) he understands Claudio's plan and tells him "Was't not to this end / That thou began'st to twist so fine a story?" (1.1)—a line written by a former country boy who made it big in the big city. Apparently nostalgic for the rural life as he composed this play Shakespeare has Leonato moan in desperation "Being that I flow in grief, / The smallest twine may lead me" (4:1), recalling Theseus led by a thread ("twine").

Despite its everyday domesticity once performed humble spinning cannot be changed or rescinded; in simpler times spinning resonated hauntingly to evoke or symbolize irreversible destiny and life's fateful decisions. The breadth of such

FIGURE 3.6   Charles Dollman, *Frigga Spinning the Clouds*, 1909.

Source: Guerber, H. A., *Myths of the Norsemen from the Eddas and Sagas* (London: George G Harrap & Co.), p.43.

associations embraces all human history.[v] Characterizing prehistory's threshold Rumpelstiltskin arrives from a wooded borderland to enter the "civilized" built environment. Though a creature of a much later moment Rumpelstiltskin nevertheless recalls a primeval revelation, an insight bursting like fireworks in the brain of the first people to realize how radical a technology spinning was.[vi]

Spinning resonates magically. It transforms matter like fire metamorphoses solid wood to airy smoke, shiny metal melts from dull mineral ore, or the fire hardens ceramics from mud. But unlike these pyrotechnologies' invisible mechanics spinning arose wholly of human agency, its knowledge perhaps a gift from the gods.[27] The goddess of fiber art, Athena, who spins and weaves, challenged the unfortunate mortal woman Arachne to a spinning-weaving duel. (Arachne was really a weaver but became a spinner in the afterlife.) Defeated by the goddess, Arachne was duly punished—transformed into a spider (an eponymous *arachnid*) in revenge for contesting a divinity. That far-away and ancient myth yet lives in our speech as the creature's name, spider, derives from an old English form of the word "to spin". (It's clearer in German where spider is *spinne*.) And, to the goddess Athena who presides over spinning and weaving, thread-guided Theseus presented and dedicated the slain Minotaur. The story came full-circle: Ariadne's sage counsel born of thread-spinning triumphed in Theseus' homage to the wise goddess who supervises the textile crafts.

Spinning's technological triumph, a progressive step of which humanity should remain unalloyedly proud, suggested a lingering debt owed to the spirit world. Supernatural beings bestowed the world's goodness, however hard-earned by mortals. This obligation was payable to shadowy beings who dwelled in forests, underground, beneath

---

v. The Three Fates were represented in India by an ostensibly male trio of primordial gods: Brahma, Vishnu and Shiva. Unlike the three female Fates' rather blank and unknowable personalities these males possessed suites of richly elaborated attributes. Perhaps such males represented a pre-textile, nomadic, warrior-based, or clerically female-excluding, Indo-European notion. The mythic anomaly of representing a male trio who created, sustained, and ended life may locate the faultline between transitional hunter-gather tribalism and settled society. That ancient India fashioned the fates as male gods suggests their theological construction predates settled pastoralism when nomadic hunter-gathering augmented rudimentary farming and raiding. That prehistoric society which conceived The Fates as male (gods who did not spin) would be amazed at its distantly unimaginable future whose descendants would be represented by Gandhi sitting at a spinning wheel that featured on his nation's flag.

vi. Spinning worked the crucial transformation from a natural to a recognizably (wo)man-made article. The very idea still astonishes me.

In the long retrospect, looking at perfectly serviceable, warm and durable, shearling, I have no idea why anybody thought, or *how* anybody thought, to clip wool from a sheep, hair from goat or dog, and to spin it into threads. Until woven into a cloth treads are useless as clothing or insulation. Then the cloth must be tailored—all to yield a product as warm as the shearling was originally. (Eskimos/Inuit, whose world resembles the early Neolithic condition of our post-glacial ancestors, do not spin or weave but sew skins using sinew drawn by bone needles.) The technology and conceptual transformation of spinning's materials remains simply stunning, unmatched by a very few (some recent) human accomplishments. Spinning is certainly more conceptually complex than striking fire, a process already visible in nature.

FIGURE 3.7 Paul Manship, *Time and the Fates Sundial*, 1938.

Source: Smithsonian American Art Museum, Bequest of Paul Manship, 1966.47.4.

the sea, or in the sky and whose gifts (like fire from Prometheus) accounted for every human blessing.[28] A supernatural male, Rumpelstiltskin surpassed women at "woman's work" but he also practiced the skill of the immortal goddesses who direct human destiny. What could the busy, the crafty, Rumpelstiltskin have in common with these majestic mythical beings, the celestial spinners? A lot, it turns out.

Fairytales vs. Myths of Spinning

Great national legends bind people to their history and land. The legends reflect experiences of war, wandering, travail and triumph, remembered geography, and include or imply a world-explaining theology. In contrast, household tales reflect eternal conditions and not the disruption of regularity by singular situations. Fairytales operate outside history. Myths function within history to metaphorically re-tell the past and to probe causality. This difference between myth and folktales contrasts two views of time as either linear or static.

Women occupied an unchanging timeless world—of endless spinning, the repetitive chores of child-rearing, and cooking. Whatever dynasty ruled or army swept through, women's work remained the same. (Part of a wider movement within disenfranchised peasantry, women's aspirations were those of a female sub-et of misery.) And if history overlooked them fairytales concealed, sometimes not too well, women's desire to gain purchase on the world. Their unchanging background condition and its mostly unrecorded struggles invested storytelling with gendered assumptions. The lone female in the Tale of Rumpelstiltskin stands clearly outlined against this changeless setting. She performs the two laudably mythic tasks assigned woman.

Not a farmer's child, the Miller's Daughter does not shepherd flocks, nor shear sheep for wool, she gathers no flax to rett; according to the only report we have of her in our story she cards no fibers nor, apparently, does she weave. But as a spinner she performs the crucial transformative conversion: a natural material became a utensil when spun. In spinning she performed one of the two primary tasks a pre-modern woman was expected to master. The story includes another wry aside about her nubile status.

Prepared for marriage by attaining proficiency in the skills of spinning she acquires significant money to bring with her as a bride to endow her husband, just as every bride's family was expected to supply a dowry. It's just that she doesn't earn the money herself, although it's gained by spinning. Enslaved to spin for her life, and implicitly for her dowry, she finds herself aided by a figure whom Joseph Campbell classes as a "supernatural helper".[29] To end her fatal spinning, this so-called helper (a businessman with a limp dick) demands her child thereby robbing her both of motherhood and of her identity as a fiber artist: the two essential womanly accomplishments.

While motherhood survives into modernity as femininity's monument, the industrial age jettisoned a skill-set that represented womanhood's former gauge of self-worth. (Bride-wealth, the dowry as an endowment of marriage, is also fading in many parts of the world, although it remains implicit in the Tale of Rumpelstiltskin.) Spinning's usefulness daily augmented gender identity. The pre-modern world enshrined spinning in foundational myths that bestowed merit on its practitioners while, in historical reality, women's spinning antedated the conception of Fate's generative engine spinning away in mythic timeless eternity. Spinning set the model for lived time. And not just in pagan lore. The Bible identified feminine virtue with masterful spinning:

Who can find a virtuous woman? for her price is far above rubies. . . . She will do [her husband] good and not evil all the days of her life. She seeks wool, and flax, and works willingly with her hands. . . . She lays her hands to the spindle, and her hands hold the distaff.

(Proverbs 31:10–13, 19)

The identification of spinning and virtuous womanhood plumbs the deep past while Rumpelstiltskin's story adds an odd gimmick about procreation. For the contemporary two-income family there might be a modern female morality play in this fairytale: the choice of work or children. But, then or now, such choices occur within a context. It's not immediately clear why this is so, that fairytales can still move us, but perhaps the origin of their power arises from the reality that "fairytales originated among the same kinds of urban assumptions and expectations with which city and suburban dwellers continue to live today".[30] Many, so-called modern, dilemmas arrived into the present trailing long precedents of human anguish.

Beneath the head-banging tumult of major myths' heroes, the brutish or wily struggles of gods and goddesses, their toying with a helpless humanity, or the deities' occasionally aiding benighted mortals—spinning continued, quietly in the background, an essential of the myth-makers' worldview, a way to conceptualize time and destiny.[31] As metaphor or a minor allegorical theme it seeped into edges of the mainly male bardic great myths. But in female, and hence unofficial, fairytales spinning could occupy the foreground. The incentives to consider spinning were enormous, as hinted by the furtive lessons of Rumpelstiltskin. He was supernatural, a spinner, and incongruously male.

Notes

1. *Corpus Inscriptionum Latinarum* 1.2.1211; "Inscriptiones Latinae Selectae" 8403, ed. H. Dessau; translation quoted from Jo-Ann Shelton.
2. Stewart (2003, p. 141).
3. Stewart (2003, p. 130).
4. Because it represented the slightest acceptable work, the myth (according to Plutarch) recounts that the male-heavy population of early Rome absconded with the neighboring Sabine women; afterward the Romans sued for their captives hands in marriage. The understandably irate Sabine men inevitably agreed to the marriages providing that the Sabine women performed no work for their new husbands except spinning.
5. Bottigheimer (1987, p. 115).
6. Bottigheimer (1987, p. 115).
7. Tatar (1987, p. 123).
8. As one prominent scholar describes the situation:

    The production of thread, yarn, and cloth for garments was considered so important that, by the seventeenth century, numerous courts had begun a primitive factory system by housing spinners at the court to maintain the production of clothes. Spinning rooms could be found in peasant houses and also middle-class houses, and they were both a work and social place for women, children, and men. This is especially true for the peasantry, which was the largest class to maintain spinning as female productivity up through the nineteenth century. For the most part, peasant women would work in spinning rooms or a room that housed the spindle from morning until evening, and the men and young boys would join them in the evening, WHERE there might be some singing, games, dancing, eating, and storytelling.

    Zipes, 1993, p. 52?

    I'm not so sure that the spinnstuben ("a room that housed the spindle") were occupied day-and-night ("from morning until evening"). Spinning represented a more or less continuance activity introduced into any gap in women's other work. The time dedicated exclusively to spinning, evenings in the communal spinnstuben, would have suited this story's creation in its primitive form before the Grimms roughly drafted their literary opus, perhaps with an unknown assist from previous authors.
9. Stewart (2003, p. 127).
10. Schneider (1989, p. 193). Zipes (1993) summarized the situation when noting that "the spinning rooms were types of cultural centers up to the beginning of the nineteenth century and that tales were exchanged by the women and also men to pass the time of day" (p. 53).

11. Stewart (2003, p. 129).
12. Bottigheimer (1987, p. 115). Bottigheimer goes on to note that "It was from female informants privy to, even if they were not an essential part of, this oral tradition that Wilhelm and
Jacob Grimm gathered many of their folk tales".
13. Olmstead (2013, p. 9).
14. Girouard (1985, p. 73).
15. Schneider (1989, pp. 194–195).
16. As related by James R. Nicholson, referring to his earlier publication, *Traditional Life in Shetland*, and quoted by Nancy Kohlberg and Philip Kopper (2003, p. 80).
17. Stewart (2003, p. 129).
18. Stewart (2003, p. 134).
19. *Talmud (Babylonian)* Tractate "Gittim", 89a.
20. The modern reader or listener to the story inevitably misses such tasks' utterly gender-spe-
cific associations. A man who spins was more than merely anomalous, was almost unthinkable. And for ages this division of labor held true. Rumpelstiltskin presents a sexual middle
ground, a more complicated construction than usually found in the macho world of myths
and, despite his magical powers, it's hard to imagine what he would say in self-defense of his
acquired skills to guys crowding the bar in Valhalla or on Olympus.

   Myths are history's truth (not its authenticity or factuality) which excludes, or does not
deign to note, the quotidian reality of relationships that even the gods botch. Textural difference separate the weight and color of household stories from history and myth. These
differences reveal the traits of authorship. Men wrote history. More specifically, the men who
won wars wrote their history in the language they carried with them (which is not the same
as observing yet again that victors write history). What endures—outlasting wars, changes in
language and religion, all that—resides comfortably in fairytales' description of permanent
household situations. In contrast transient events, like the war at Troy, are at home in myths
where, buffed by retellings, human actions are explained to bespeak universal conditions
of conflict. The two types of story may once have been in a contest but separated so that
eventually one dealt with action and the other with stasis as one type presents the urge, and
sometimes necessity, to change while the other celebrates the tug of tradition and a known
cadence to the year.

   Similarly, Christian Scripture awkwardly combines the wondrous acts of Jesus with his
sayings of wisdom in a hybrid literature. Though embroidered with myth the Gospels narratives arise from the historical moment when the Jew Jesus lived and also impart transcendent
moral assertions that are not stories.
21. Some examples are easy to spot and other instances are more perplexing. A case has been
made that the famous Greek statue of Aphrodite, goddess of love—called by its Roman name,
the *Venus de Milo* (Louvre), because it was found on the isle of Melos—originally showed the
goddess spinning. See Elizabeth Wayland Barber (1994, pp. 236–238).
22. Elizabeth Wayland Barber (1994, p. 235).
23. This trio of women assumed a strange Germanic twist in tale of "The Three Spinning
Women" type 501.
24. Preeminent among Norse goddesses Frig (variously anglicized as Frigga, Fregge, Fregg), the
wife of Odin and queen of Asgard, was a very ancient deity. Her Sanskrit cognate means wife
or "dearly beloved one" (related to the word friend, from the Proto-Indo-European root
pri- meaning "to love", that shares a source with the word sapphire). She supplies the mythic
paradigm of the wife and mother; the constellation Orion's three-star-cluster Belt was known
as "Frigg's Distaff". The Norse, called the bright planet Venus "Frigg's star" *Friggjarstjarna*.

   Some sources associate a far more powerful Celtic goddess, Brigid (or Brighid), with spinning and attributes that the Mediterranean world parceled to other goddesses. These celestial
wives or "dearly beloved one[s]" parallel the Book of Proverbs' human ideal.

   Preliterate Baltic myths lack transcriptions by literate contemporaries from other cultures.
They were recorded only after they became hopelessly muddled; two waves of Mediterranean stories, Greco-Roman and subsequently Christian, overwhelmed Baltic myths. Yet in

their snarled form certain sources distinctly gleam. The Baltic sun goddess spins sunbeams. And the sun, source of life, places her on a par with the Fates.

25. Spinning occupied a central place in early Levantine-Mesopotamian culture and not just the later Greco-Roman world of the Mediterranean. The Bible—using the most ancient, and probably prehistoric, literary tropes—envisions wisdom as a woman, in Greek "Sophia". Mystical Hebrew writers had their own version of this figure in the *Shekhinah*, God's female aspects. This virtue (combining fiber arts and keen discernment, like Athena's) infused action with wisdom or with actions that produced wisdom: "All the women that were wise-hearted did spin with their own hands" (Exodus 35:25). Then again: "All the women whose heart stirred them up in wisdom spun goats' hair" (Exodus 35:26). The quality of wisdom descended from a goddess who spun. Scripture amalgamated this lost goddess with her attribute of spinning. Holding the thread of life's duration in one hand and dispensing life's blessings in the other, she herself embodies life's vitality:

> Happy is the man who finds wisdom, and the man who gets understanding . . . and all the things you can desire are not to be compared to her. Length of days is in her right hand and in her left hand riches and honor.
>
> *(Proverbs 3:13–18)*

Duration measures out the length of life's thread. Its quality is determined as it reaches the spinner's other hand—fate as a spinner.

Fate and fortune melded when the goddess *Fortuna* degenerated into mere affluence.

26. For example, Theseus was "fated" to enter the labyrinth, slay the Minotaur, and escape alive; the thread he followed was his lifeline—in both senses, as his life support and his destiny. Ariadne performed the Three Fates' work as she unrolled the ball of yarn that guided her hero into and from mortal danger. Consistent with the tale of Rumpelstiltskin's jaundiced view of men, Theseus disappoints Ariadne. That ancient motif has been continually up-dated. In the (1956) film of William Inge's (1955) play *Bus Stop*, Marilyn Monroe's character follows her "life-line" across a spatial map, not time. When boy gets girl in *Bus Stop* (as Don Murray takes home Marilyn Monroe) he recapitulates—the rough-hewn but virginal and backwoods sidekick of the city-slicker Gilgamesh—Enkidu who, otherwise ignorant of the world, is humbled and civilized by a courtesan, a worldly woman. Perhaps more than ten thousand years old, the ancient Mesopotamia tale of Gilgamesh re-hashed the story of fate long before movies made clay tablets obsolete.

27. Here I must disagree with Maria Tatar (1987) that "[u]ltimately, spinning has little value. In order to prove effective, it must have a magical quality attached to it" (p. 133). Simple spinning might be devalued by a disgruntled female storyteller who knew it only as drudgery but spinning was vital to the community's life where—after a long process of tilling soil and plowing furrows where scattered seeds preceded plants needing tending and weeding, then gathering a harvest, retting, and other preparations—it represented the penultimate step before producing cloth through weaving.

28. The Miller's Daughter's task of magically spinning appears in lands and languages never visited by the Grimms. A goddess of motherhood and fertility in Inca mythology, Mama Ocllo first taught women the art of spinning thread, weaving cloth, and building homes.

29. Campbell (1994, p. 844).

30. Bottigheimer (2009, p. 13).

31. The unfolding universe's alternative explanatory image involved a great mill: the 26-thousand-year-long precession of the earth's axis through the Zodiac (see Santillana and Dechend, 1969). And "she", un-named, was the daughter of the miller.

4

THE SPINNER'S LIBIDO

If they were spinsters, if they had not had babies, they were forbidden by the mystique to speak as women.[1]

Betty Friedan

Spinning: Erotic Prelude or Alternative to Sex

The spinnstuben's women inserted oblique social comments into their stories. These sly references passed beneath the radar of men who barely listened to the stories even if they arrived early enough to hear them. More typically, as Robert Olmstead reported, women's "talking and laughing" continued until "they saw me [a male, and] they went silent". Male visitors to the spinnstuben were preoccupied with ogling the girls, smoking, flirting, playing music, perhaps ardent courtship, or drinking; they didn't notice a story's change of tone. But the older women observed the scene. Spinning uninterrupted but keen-eyed, they scrutinized the cruising action.

Through the spinners' midst strode examples of manhood on whose fitness the women could comment with the men beyond earshot. This was women's territory. Although men arrived to wrap up the evening's socializing the spinnstube remained a space where female mores held sway just as male behavior dictated norms of tavern life, civic and religious behavior, and set tacit standards for legends of mythic heroism. Men paced the spinning chamber as tolerated trespassers who might helpfully lug the spinning wheels back home. Men were interloping meddlers infringing on, but sometimes augmenting with titillation, women's space that could vary considerably with social class: from well-lit and spacious rooms or a dim smokey hovel. Whatever its character, this compartment tallied among a chain of several gender-assigned rooms in a woman's life, places not merely relegated to women but created by and for them. Significantly, these special rooms had something in common: they were shunned by men.[2]

Each stage of her life appointed a chamber exclusively for female use. Not surprisingly, men festooned these (mostly unseen by them) places and occasions with the most outlandish falsehoods. They couldn't imagine what went on inside sex-segregated rooms when they weren't there.

Along with the spinnstuben, but more securely guarded, the birthing room was foreclosed to men. Court officials witnessed an imperial birth (to insure no substituted heir) but otherwise the pre-modern birthing room resembled a spinnstube. The correspondence of these two spaces arose—not because what happened there coincided with spinning, though a life's fate did begin when babies arrived attached to a chord made by a woman—but because women chose to organize themselves that way when free of male influence:

> The social practices surrounding childbirth emphasized the exclusion of men from women's knowledge. Well before a woman went into labor, she extended invitations to her closest female relatives, friends, and neighbors to support her through the birth. As many as a dozen women stayed with the laboring woman, trying to keep up her spirits by talking, telling jokes, and drinking a special kind of wine thickened with grain. These hours of labor were dangerous and frightening, but the men excluded from the birthing room imagined the women telling jokes about sex, belittling men's performances and reputations. The women invited to the birth were called "gossips",[i] from which our modern use of the word to mean scandalous and intimate personal details is derived.[3]

Such women-only institutions encouraged correlations imperceptible to the grand history largely written by men. Sisterly support groups issued blatant observations about everyday situations observed from a perspective that would have astounded clerics and kings. The comments in women-only zones were attuned to the aesthetics of the Tale of Rumpelstiltskin as a narrative deeply rooted in female experience—regardless of who first wrote it down. And the values that generated the tale run deep throughout the story. Birthing and spinning only seem physically unlike but all the social and emotional support attending them comforted the same people.

At night in the spinning room the story's early tellers confederated sexual intercourse with society's expectations; they merged the body's needs and its disappointments with spinning's insistent but gentle rhythm textured with subtle flax or the wool's smooth lanolin and animal odors. These acutely noted physical associations entwined to represent the world's fate. Like spinning, sex consummated in birth

---

i. The "gossips" also presided at a child's baptism as god-parents or sponsors. That usage goes back to the eleventh century. The word's roots are god + sib (as survives in sibling, one who is akin). Their sisterhood flourished intensely; the same women of the birthing chamber attended the spinnstube. As closest friends they doted at a baptism and celebrated the mother's safe delivery or weeping they dressed the corpse of a friend. Gossips lodged nearby as lifelong intimates.

encircled by the lifelong company of women: the gossip's sisterhood polled the very supportive people as nightly spinning. Of course Fate and Spinning co-mingled when authored by the same sensibility while that interchangeable group membership likely contrived Rumpelstiltskin, a figure less easily integrated into that female world in any *obvious* way. Spinnstube or birthing chamber, selected woman populated rooms to perform their exclusive work as men speculated lasciviously on what was happening out of their sight. Sex, spinning, destiny, birth: these fused in a common female world-view. Womankind's peasant philosophy presumed adroit spinning could win a husband, gain promotion from "spinsterhood"; thereafter sex and motherhood awarded adulthood.

Motherhood Extolled, Begrudging Fatherhood

The miller's daughter gasped. How could she promise such a thing?

"How shall this be, seeing I know not a man?"

Luke (1:34)

Centuries later it's hard to appreciate the life of a generic Miller's Daughter but the story's early reciters knew her well. They knew that spinning entailed endless and "invisible" work (unseen while in plain sight, discounted though essential) but that, as one scholar somewhat delicately described the Miller's Daughter, "[t]he only thing she appears capable of doing is giving birth to a baby".[4] This formulation invites considering how the story rates female usefulness *not* exemplified by spinning.

The ladies who gleefully told it understood that mating is what queens do. Modernity confuses this function with talk of royalty as heads-of-state (ceremonial, as in the United Kingdom, or actual in Saudi Arabia); as bearers of a national tradition (with historical eras named for monarchs in France or Japan); or as chiefs of a racially fictitious national family. Nobody at the court or in the kingdom of Henry VIII forgot that a Queen should not imagine herself as stately, exalted, or honored if she failed to successfully breed. Plentiful benefits followed the discharge of her primary role but job security only accrued when queens produced an heir.[5] Hence the fairytale bargain mimicked actuality; the King understood perfectly what he acquired in this serviceable Queen, and so did the female storytellers cackling to friends while spinning.

Following the King's offer to promote her to royalty in exchange for a final performance of Rumpelstiltskin's life-saving magic, Rumpelstiltskin makes the girl swear that when she is queen "your first child will belong to me". From this bargain a new equation hatches. If consummated, Rumpelstiltskin's contract would grant her motherhood but rob her of parenthood. That's calamity enough but there's more involved; the storytellers, who lived as subjects when all served some monarch, immediately understood the deal's social consequences. Losing her child amounted to more than private woe for this new mother. The Queen would cease to have supplied the kingdom a royal heir. No longer the future Queen Mother her status would plummet. If the Queen grieved

like any childless mother she additionally would endure a demoted and perilous situation. Her tacit omission (taking credit for the golden spinning) concealed the Queen's
source of talent; once enthroned she committed treason by risking the life of the prince.

The Queen's life hinges on the King's never learning who manufactured his gold.
Or that to save her life a commoner wagered the crown prince. (That feature adds a
delectable "I Love Lucy" craftiness: household peace gained by a husband's decep-
tion. And comedy depends on the audience knowing something unknown to the
characters.) Because the King never detects Rumpelstiltskin's role in fabricating his
new-found riches—unlike tales of charming night-visiting shoemaker elves and similar kindly but unseen aids to humankind—this unremittingly cruel story features no
equivalent to a happy iris-out of elves hammering away at shoes through the night. The
Queen would be mad to tell her courtiers or the King what Rumpelstiltskin did or
what she gambled. She remains the only one who knows Rumpelstiltskin's role in her
social elevation and the potentially fearful cost of her promotion from the peasantry.
But the commoners telling the story knew and appreciated household deceit, however
exalted the home.

The story assigns parity to Rumpelstiltskin and the King since if the bargain were
fulfilled both would be father to this baby. One would be the biological father and the
other would, as an adoptive parent, raise the royal child. Like Jesus—himself hidden
royalty—the tale's regal child would have two fathers. The unlikely narrative symmetry
unfolds with more similarities to Scripture. Visible and splendid, an earthly King was the
prince's progenitor while in Gospels a supernatural Father remained invisible and glorious. Substituting for the Gospel's St. John (a carpenter as foster-father) the fairytale's
supernatural Dad would raise the son of the Miller's Daughter. And, accordingly, the foster Dad would not teach him carpentry but wizardry. In Rumpelstiltskin's unimaginable
world the concealed prince trains in, or witnesses, magic. After his apprenticeship to
Rumpelstiltskin how would a mortal regard the lost Prince if he re-entered the human
world to perform miraculously with powers unimaginable to the normal person? Other
narrative features parallel the Gospels.

Unattested by Scripture, Christian legend imagines the dutiful Virgin Mary as a youth
at her fiber-work, placidly embroidering the Temple's curtain and priestly vestments. In
some imaginings while at her needlework she learns she must bear a child who will be
taken from her: the moment of the Annunciation during her needlework. The folkloric
parallel clearly corresponds. While trying to spin the Miller's Daughter hears, and agrees
to, the sacrificial fate of her yet-unborn offspring. Neither of these two fiber-working
mothers-to-be felt relaxed about the forthcoming situation. Uncannily familiar in structural similarities to its prestigious narrative precedent—a story universally known, even
by illiterates—the fairytale's timeless organization delivers Rumpelstiltskin's parenting
arrangement in terms foreshadowed by Christian Scripture. Yet, even from this gigantic
precedent a problem of influence arises. For some scholars,

> far from originating among an illiterate folk. . . [the] stories told to Jacob and
> Wilhelm [Grimm] by their young Cassel friends. . . . had come from books

read by Cassel's girls and young women in the late eighteenth and early nineteenth centuries.[6]

But those books themselves may have had profound folkloric sources as their ultimate derivation. If somebody wrote down a story before the Grimms recorded their version the fairytale could still have long before originated in common folklore. And overarching all such amusements were the great canons, first of pagan then Judeo-Christian lore and text. The entire western world operated in consonance with the Bible and its penumbra of sanctioned and explicative tales. The storytelling spinnstube reasonably derived formal expectations for a story's balance from sacred scripture as scripture's own storytelling arose from an older, and perhaps long-lost, narrative tradition.

Besides confirming ancient narrative standards there's also something forward looking, modern and psychologically genuine, about the child's presumptive destiny. The Queen's offspring would have a magic-working Dad and a ceremonially employed biological father. The Prince would be pretty special if an indeterminate species raised him—a bi-national taught the magical arts by Rumpelstiltskin, a child who spans the worlds of wizardry and humanity. For good reason that rich childhood passes an uncontemplated hypothetical. The first tellers assumed an unmitigated catastrophe if Rumpelstiltskin reared the boy separated from his mother, despite the exciting prospect to children of learning wizardry's secret byways. Eventually Rumpelstiltskin's step- or foster-child would ask about his parentage or try to search out his birth mother and rectify the world's baffling order. At some point the human child would probably note that he has grown much taller and in many ways differs from his "Dad" Rumpelstiltskin. No family resemblance is possible as Rumpelstiltskin seems to have no family and the Princeling is not his kin. That isolation threatened even the young listener who could understand or intuit the tale's unspoken remainder.

Children who considered the story's threatened "abduction" were supposed to automatically concur with their mothers, no matter how wretched their situation. If storytelling mothers feared their child's effective kidnapping, a youngster's fright of separation from the parent implicitly outweighed the otherwise-appealing admission into the magical world (which generated seven Harry Potter books). That tacit understanding, that Mommy loves you, nested so deeply in the matrix from which the story arose that it was not even a "lesson" but a stipulation. This fairytale's assumed female authors sensibly ranked direst possibilities in ways that men might not: impending rape seems more tolerable and less scary than losing the child produced by molestation. Male and female priorities reside differently in this story; the women who told it might have been inured to or accepted rough and joyless sex at their husband's command but the loss of a child could not be condoned. Despite the tale's old-time gender roles the story forcefully comments upon crucial life decisions in terms we easily recognize or can extrapolate to the modern situation.

For the contemporary two-income family Rumpelstiltskin's fairytale presages a female morality play: at the story's heart pulsates the choice of balancing the demands of work or children. The child's viewpoint persists equally timeless. Many children wish that their parents were magical or royalty but few children have one of each.

Replacement Parents

The Queen is threatened with becoming a surrogate mom. She would be reduced to carrying a child to give it up. The story paints so clear a premonition of surrogacy that when the *Harvard Law Review* wanted to survey the legal implications of gestational technology the article was called "Rumpelstiltskin Revisited: The Inalienable Rights of Surrogate Mothers".[7] Today agents match fertile women (gestational surrogates) with barren would-be parents. The spinnstube's ladies could never imagine such bureaus but they understood similar concepts which infuse this story.

She lacks magic to spin straw into gold; impotent, he requires remedy from her, to "borrow" her powers of procreation—formerly a strange idea but commonplace nowadays. Today's fertility clinics gratify wants the storytellers thought impossible except by divine intervention or magic.[8] Yet, the first tellers would never dilute their female identity by permitting even an impotent male to replace their own tender mothering. Again, historical and scriptural precedents guided them. Age-old wet-nursing presented an acceptably partial mothering substitute while the bible allowed child-bearing delegated to a servant.[ii] Artificial insemination and surrogate motherhood secured recent and isometric claims to parenthood. But a mother who relinquished her newly birthed child required no novel technology (the Bible's newborn Moses). That fear lies at the heart of the old tale's tension, an anxiety merely overlain by the suspenseful task of guessing the secret name.

Justifiably disquieted by anxiety the mother dreads her loss but as her child aged into awareness the formerly unsuspecting baby would eventually develop his own perspective on the matter, just as children do in modern cases of surrogacy or adoption. When the boy appraised his options two Dads beckoned. One, a normal and mortal jerk (greedy but conveniently the King who married "down" for money) and the other a . . . what? a species who alchemically spins fiber and flies around on a spoon? But the spinnstube's ladies never allowed that eventuality; the Queen won her naming contest. Later, if she dared tell it, the Tale of Rumpelstiltskin became the royal family's favorite story, the tale with which they bored guests who'd heard it before—a dependably amusing tale repeated for visitors to the castle, a story full of terror with a hilarious resolution. But confused by hearing his possible fate the Queen's child may not think it all that funny. He barely escaped being raised by an unlikely, a singular, personage.

---

ii. Rumpelstiltskin covets her fertility while the Miller's Daughter desires his productivity—actually a commonplace mutuality. How often women hear men wish they could have babies, a biologically imposed chore. (How many women believe it?) Most famously regarding surrogacy:

> Now Sarai, Abram's wife, bore him no children and she had a handmaid, an Egyptian, whose name was Hagar. And Sarai said to Abram, Look now, the Lord has prevented my bearing, I pray that you go in to my maid; maybe I may obtain children by her. And Abram listened to the voice of Sarai.
>
> *(Genesis 16:1–2)*

Her servant's offspring would be counted as the children of Sarai (Sarah), an odd notion in modernity but, like Sarai, Rumpelstiltskin might consider as "his" child a son in which he has no genetic investment.

Notwithstanding a host of other considerations regarding his unknown race/species, the spinnstube prohibited the hyper-competent Rumpelstiltskin from even the chance to successfully raise a child: proficient at everything else, his possible expertise at parenting might diminish the status of mothercraft. He had already surpassed them as spinners. Rumpelstiltskin seems willing to perform child-rearing that, along with spinning, represented the storytellers' reserved domain of female exclusivity. The storytellers had Rumpelstiltskin agree with the spinnstube's mothers that "something alive is dearer to me than all the world's treasures".

The tale's conclusion presents only one possible disposition of the baby's guardianship and parenting. Rumpelstiltskin needs a surrogate gestational mother, a borrowed uterus, and the spinnstube's ladies were disinclined to negotiate; he was given no paperwork to fill out. Accordingly, since his bargain fell through only a special kind of persuasion might work so that "Rumpelstiltskin's approach to the miller's daughter somewhat resembles that of a suitor, albeit one of the childish, regressive type".[9] He materializes in order to help her when she is distressed by two men's foibles, tries to win her favor by gallantly coming to her side with assistance that no one else offers, serves her wishes in exchange only for keepsakes, and finally asks for her child. Unlike a plausibly unattractive suitor but like a "childish, regressive", Rumpelstiltskin never asks to *have* a child by her although she lacks any emotional attachment to the avaricious King.

Rumpelstiltskin doesn't even attempt to gain the boon of her love for, as a repellant little guy willing to foster her child, he feels no human could love him. He apparently recognizes that he represents the ultimate bad blind date. (Some fellow always carries her books home from school, helps with her homework, defends her reputation against scoffers while his infatuation goes unnoticed by his winsome obsession who mates with the dunderhead football team's captain.) Rumpelstiltskin knows the sting of realizing that the Miller's Daughter is more lovable than he. He knows that however useful and loyal he proves himself humans would feel that she more deserves love. Furthermore, he likely knows that such a totally irrational emotional response to her youth and comeliness ignores his past or future accomplishments, proven character, intelligence, worth to the community, and dependability. (Of course, when I say that Rumpelstiltskin "knows" I mean the story's authors knew. The spinnstube's ladies understood the human heart's frailty and some had suffered the consequences of painfully learned lessons.) If lifelong love arose merely from being useful, reliable, and cheerfully devoted, Rumpelstiltskin could win her heart. In an ideal world every well-behaved suitor would conquer. But hearts are not apportioned justly. The pretty face and the vacant personality triumph in a tale constructed by and for women who bitterly knew the handicaps with which they must play. And they were not alone. This corrosive verity's male version festoons Romantic literature ranging from Victor Hugo's 1831 bell-ringer Quasimodo, another repulsive life-saver, to Edmund Rostand's supremely competent, endlessly loyal but ugly, *Cyrano de Bergerac*, 1897. Tenderness traps these two in their era's mannerisms while the fairytale harshly metes out a ruthless and much older worldview. But a worldview newly shaped by the Grimms during the Romantic era when all three fictional outcasts must forego justly earned affection.

Despite the story's lingering medieval fondness for the merciless that now seems scant of mirth, Rumpelstiltskin ameliorates the girl's situation when no mortal man intervenes to soften her fate. We cannot know if remorse, envy, or rage prompted him or if Rumpelstiltskin feels sufficiently guilty that he offers the Queen a way out of her pact. He didn't create her problem (her father and king did) and twice helps her. Compared to unlovable Rumpelstiltskin, fairytale's charming knights and princes coast on their superficial personalities and good looks while performing perfectly ordinary feats of strength and perseverance. Such work comes with the job description of fetchingly handsome knights or gallant princes. (Until William Steig's *Shrek* became a movie in 2001, nobody in mass culture was ever rescued by an ugly knight.)[10] Heroes performed expected deeds that unfailing won hearts and pre-pubescents' sighs. In contrast, this story's authors well knew that parenting tested the long haul when endurance proved love. The last thing mothers or their daughters needed was somebody prone to impulsive brash feats of strength when the women beheld a supply of such promises loitering outside the spinnstube, smoking and boasting. Instead of the absurd puppetry of a handsome prince's rescue the fairytale presents a squinty-eyed assessment of love's typical landscape peopled with fantastic characters who represent recognizable states-of-mind.

Generation after generation, the story appealed to listeners who experienced its anxieties. Its deep emotional truths did not supply the reasons for Rumpelstiltskin's creation as the story's arousal of childhood tensions only sauces the tale's main dish of social commentary. To understand why Rumpelstiltskin was composed we should look at what actually happens in the story.

Enter the Spinsters

> Helena: We cannot fight for love, as men may do;
> We should be woo'd and were not made to woo.
> *A Midsummer Night's Dream (II:1)*

The womanly acumen derived from spinning and its associated socializing inconspicuously outlasted industrialization that destroyed home and manual spinning. As late as in 1887 a book titled *Knitting and Crochet: A Guide to the Use of the Needle and the Hook* still counseled that knowledge of fiber arts (carding, spinning, crochet, sewing and knitting) bestowed skill-sets best acquired in girlhood which served increasingly well throughout life and into "that terrible period to women, when they have lost the charm of youth, without acquiring the veneration of age".[11] That is, knowledge and practice of fiber arts conferred value to women when sexual allure faded. (Spinning related reciprocally to sex. A girl who could spin straw into gold didn't have to look especially attractive, practice winning ways, or appear graceful; exemplary spinning tipped the scales in her favor.) Two essential womanly skill-sets closely allied and while one, procreative sex, carried an expiration date, spinning did not. This dreaded knowledge hung about women's lives into the first decades of the recent era but—as that relationship recedes into the past, bequeathing us only the inadequate term "biological clock"—we can yet glimpse its lingering persistence.

The notion of spinning as an overture to sexuality, especially marriage's religiously sanctioned sex, arrives from the late-medieval but still-common (though diminishingly serviceable) use of the word "spinster". The word meant one who, beyond the usual age for marriage, has not been "abducted" from the spinnstube by a man. Into the mid-twentieth century not much had changed; according to an eye-witness in 1963, Betty Friedan, whoever had not or could not produce "babies, they were forbidden by the mystique to speak as women".[12] She described a spinster—a sexually disenfranchised woman who could yet spin.

Being ignored as nubile reduced a spinster to spin without sexual hiatus. And throughout countless generations when the spinnstube told the Rumpelstiltskin story for amusement, into the early nineteenth century when Wilhelm Grimm's bride, Dortchen first told him the tale, spinsterhood threatened a miserable fate.[13] Rumpelstiltskin's gender-reversed spinning inverted the girl's courtship role in the expected prelude to marriage's sacralized sex. First the spinning, then courtship, then marriage, followed by children. The story's sex-inverted spinner saved the Miller's Daughter from a spinster's sexual death. That camouflaged threat of execution or spinsterhood nested in her endless attempts at spinning. Successful spinning allowed her to live and bear children. So taught the spinnstube.

The story compares spinsterhood's threat of living death with judicial execution or marriage. Rumpelstiltskin, a kind of male spinster, rescued the girl from more than female spinsterhood.

Insurrection of the Spinsters

Not only is spinsterhood viewed as a personal tragedy but offspring are considered essential to the full life and the Vassar student believes that she would willingly adopt children, if it were necessary, to create a family.[14]

"Student Culture at Vassar", 1962

The sadly dated word spinster evokes a female without descendants; her genetic thread cut, she endlessly spins for an extended family but not her own offspring. Even worse, deplorable gender asymmetry colors the word. A similar male lives simply a "bachelor". The male word does not necessarily connote: rejection and isolation within the community and family, ineptitude at properly presenting oneself for the marriage market, or a disfigurement of character or body that forecloses matrimony on all but the worst terms. A chilling final verdict, the word spinster issues an unsatisfactory assessment of personal worth and perhaps even a negative self-appraisal. All derived from skillful spinning or its lack.

Spinsterhood suggests the Miller's Daughter's lot had supernatural spinning not delivered her. Accordingly (although she never spins in the story) her plea for help rescues her before she is redeemed a second time by speaking the arcane word that banishes Rumpelstiltskin. Her gumption illustrates a rarity among heroines A fairytale's typical leading lady may be gentle, morally innocent, self-sacrificing but, frequently, a passive beauty. The Miller's Daughter self-rescues. To further complicate matters about who is the story's potential spinster, the childless Rumpelstiltskin, like a Vassar girl, would "willingly adopt children, if it were necessary, to create a family". Rumpelstiltskin resembles a spinster more than a bachelor.

The story's early reciters and listeners, largely rural traditionalists, engaged in their age-old craft whose expertise they never guessed could become obsolete. The peasantry assumed their course of life endured as normal: you spun alone or spun in marriage but in any case you would spin fiber until the end. The fairytale's tellers addressed that destiny by secreting a frightful message in the Tale of Rumpelstiltskin, a future they saw around them in the unmarried and the widowed. Everyone understood the dire economic warning implied in the word and condition of being a spinster, a state of endless dependency. A spinster's singular and especially demeaning reliance reduced a woman to seeking, and with luck obtaining, sustenance from close relatives if she had been denied the chance to barter sex for necessities. Alternatively, she begged charity from the church or wider community. In village or farmstead requisites included daily nourishment, warm and dry living quarters, companionship, status within traditional society and the hope for an afterlife, protection from depredations, care in old age and sickness; an extended family and children assured these supports. Without that family guesswork tinted every moment with fear. So the spinster spun on. All wore clothing made from the spinner's endless thread and spinning earned life's essentials. Fairytales carefully essayed that complex economic and social tangle tested by helpless female leads.

When Sleeping Beauty revives to the Prince's kiss she rouses from sleep induced by her poisoned spinning wheel. Everyone in the spinnstube understood the difference between the Prince's attentions and spinning's torpor. Though seeming opposite tasks, spinning and sex remained everyday companions to women of the spinnstube. You didn't need a dirty mind for one activity to arouse thoughts of the other. Visual and sensual prompts decorated the surroundings. A student of this technology's representation, Alison Stewart noted:

> Undoubtedly, the sexual behavior characterized at spinning bees has much to do with the phallic shape of the primary spinning implements used at the time—distaff and spindle . . . the word "spindle" stood for the penis in Late Medieval English, French, and German.

And she adds that, "[a]lthough spinning was a female activity, spinning tools assumed unquestionably 'male shapes.'"[15] Following girlhood's initial awkwardness handling these suggestive tools, ladies' practiced ease appeared delightfully risqué. The spinnstube's women who understood such connotations concocted fairytales like Rumpelstiltskin to editorialize about their sometimes eroticized situation. Their story strongly contrasts with others; when Sleeping Beauty first touches a spinning wheel's spindle—against that meeting her protective father had turned the whole kingdom up-side down to rid his daughter of the phallic threat—she "pricks" her finger, a drop of blood flows, and she swoons until woken to love. That's a pretty fair description of a (idealized) wedding night. In this analogy to spinning the spinnstube also merrily described a father's standards for his daughter: nobody (no prick in the kingdom) is good enough. Despite such wry comments, for either a princess or a peasant, marriage offered virtually the only economic path to women's betterment. That may explain why, irrespective of its romantic appeal, so many fairytales hinge on the all-important wedding as the transforming event in a woman's life. And so it remained, endlessly, to escape spinsterhood.

To mirror an optimal reality marriage represented the goal that concluded so many stories. Woman could not own property until recently, not even their own bodies, but in marriage they could, nominally and under the guise of extracting agreement from their husbands, make some decisions about their condition. And tending toward two marriages, but not entering one, the story surreptitiously mimics normal courtship steps as emotional closeness grows. The Miller's Daughter marries the King but Rumpelstiltskin courts her. Not far below its surface Rumpelstiltskin's tale cached a kind of betrothal, an anti-spinsterhood. This story wildly re-contextualized an engagement's typical symbols representing the stages of a flourishing intimacy. A courtship of exchanged gifts and tokens burlesques how real-world partners denote their intensifying mutual bonds to become a couple within their community.

First, a necklace is exchanged. This pretty keepsake rarely binds partners in a marriage but expresses affection—usually from the man to the woman. (But here the woman does the courting and so, like Helena, she might rightly complain that "We [women] should be woo'd and were not made to woo".) In terms of a general symbolism the jewelry does not seriously obligate the giver; unless especially valuable, the necklace might be returned if courting soured. Exchanging the necklace for a night's work indicates that, at first, Rumpelstiltskin envisioned his relationship with the Miller's Daughter as a business deal. He asked for payment and the girl made an offer that he accepted as adequate compensation. A dryly legal formulation of the transaction to her it might resemble courtship to him. Neither friends nor lovers Rumpelstiltskin aids her for increasingly suggestive gifts that insinuate the spinners' wit about sexual relations. After all they had experienced or heard of seduction with a shower of bedazzling gifts and temporarily kind behavior. The storytellers noted an accelerating erotic trend as from the necklace the tale advances toward another plateau of affection.

The story conjures a deepening relationship when the girl offers a ring that recalls, ordinarily "with this ring I thee wed". The ring seals the engagement. (Before the twelfth century marriage was not even a sacrament but a binding contract to unite families. In the pagan ceremony rings "wed" or bound the couple sometimes quite awhile before any marriage rite.) The ring's promise does not secure marriage's ultimate intimacy for Rumpelstiltskin and the girl but heightens the story's role-reversal as ordinarily males furnish engagement rings. Finally, the girl's coerced promise of a child impersonates the commitment by which partners publicly enter matrimony (regardless of any private understanding to have children or not). The very word derived from the understanding that motherhood, *mater*, rests at the institution's heart. Children secure the matrimonial deal. Though not his biologic child, the promise of parenting unites Rumpelstiltskin and the future Queen in an ersatz courtship. They pass through the stages of mock courtship, a counterfeit wedding arrangement based on the bond of children, and a future of surrogate parenting.

In these similarities Rumpelstiltskin and the Miller's Daughter achieve something like the structure, if not the intimate tone, of a marriage. She promises to give him a child and then as Queen she learns to say his true name and thereby gains absolute control over Rumpelstiltskin. With his secret name she can summon him (from sports on TV, from among his friends, or in whatever worlds he travels) or humiliate him. The women who created this story parodied the outlines of a marital relationship, however repellant or impossible to consummate, between a fully human woman and impotent Rumpelstiltskin. Thus three kinds of marriages appear in the story:

1a.   The "real" marriage of a Miller's Daughter to a king as an atypical social pairing;
1b.   Her father's inferred though absent marriage partner, the miller's wife.
2.   Rumpelstiltskin's courtship of the Miller's Daughter with its three stages of increasing familiarity from a trinket to "wedding" ring to the promise of a child: fulfilled with the marriage-like knowledge of his secret name that represents his genuine nature unknown to others.
3.   The matrimonial background in storytellers' lives: their backdrop of wryly rational heterosexuality colored the editorial comments delivered to unmarried auditors.

While cataloguing men's failures the spinnstube discussed the worlds of marriage closed to spinsters and perhaps yearned for.

Art Not for Sale

Social cohesion accounted for the spinnstuben's popularity as an all-female society. The spinnstube promised a night out: away from the house and marriage's obligations or daughterly confinement. Men had their taverns as refuge. The spinnstube delivered its "members" from male supervision, escape from children, a break from endless cooking and cleaning, flight from the tedious care of dependent old folks, relief from annoying siblings—all problems incumbent on womanhood. In addition to mental relief, as escape, mechanical efficiency recommended the institution as

> [s]pinning technology, whether with distaff and spindle or with pedal-operated wheel, was portable. Thus, when the work was a by-occupation of the long winter evening, it made sense for neighbors to assemble in one place, save on light and fuel, and spin together.[16]

Practicality may have birthed the institution but the results of gathering a community's women in one place produced cultural artifacts of surprising quality and resilience: the fairytales.

The spinnstube's ladies supplied their own entertainment with a special flavor. Unsupervised by men as at a few other times, female conversation prompted a climate conducive to ideas and metaphors unlike what generally circulated through mixed-gender society's patriarchal mores. Almost invisible to the gaze of (predominantly male) literature's high art, women achieved something aesthetically unsuspected. When crucial bits of conversations were repeated and purged of superfluous components an artform was born, verbal at first but eventually transcribed into books. Though women practiced the folktale's art the stories were first studied by men. The tales were collected by Basile (1575–1632) in Italy,[17] Charles Perrault (1628–1703) in France and, during the next century, by the Grimms in Germany. But the zone of folklore had become so feminized that collections like the "Thousand and One Arabian Nights", issued from a women's mouth, Scherazade.[18] (Scherazade presents an alluring women, like the Bible's Esther who also wins a king of limited attention-span.) Mother Goose knows no male equivalent. After all, what's spookier, an old woman telling a story or an old man? What's more intriguing, a young woman telling a story or a young man? That storytelling was professionalized by male bards or griots reflected men's freedom to move unfettered between villages, throughout society, while women were sequestered—ostensibly to "protect" their modesty, honor, virtue, etc.

The professional storyteller, likely imagined as an old man, chanted above the smoke in a Persian tea-room, near the central fire of a Greek megaron, or to thoughtfully mead-sipping northerners in their timber hall. Unlike stories purveyed by men to men, when examined carefully for their differences from national myths fairytales frequently exhibit distinctly female eroticism. The contrast stands clear. In the spinnstube's temporary and much-appreciated cocoon women sheltered from otherwise behaving subserviently to the patriarchy (religious, political/feudal, family). Gathered in spinnstuben women protected each other's secrecy and told stories developed for their own pleasure (like belly-dancing that was never intended for male eyes). With years of re-telling the tales progressed—from frivolous or guarded recitations of local conditions, personally idiosyncratic complaints, or editorial insights about neighbors' disputes and miseries—to a deeper analysis of universal human circumstances. Though vernacular the tales were not witless time-wasters, empty mental calories.

Popular mass entertainment did not become stupid until it could be profitable on a large scale. Unlike the rural, agrarian, or peasant ladies of the spinnstube who entertained themselves industrial-age workers could be taught to find amusement as consumers. Finally, with mechanically advanced devices a miracle of merchandizing appeared: purchasers were convinced that buying wares was itself a creative act that bestowed distinction. Owning a Smartwatch made the buyer a patron of taste, an act of discernment like commissioning the Sistine Ceiling. The gradually evolving but decisive changes for art's commercialization proved dramatic. In advanced societies—possessed of and by electronic communication—it becomes silly or mercenary to talk of contemporary folk art. Formerly, as Tolstoy proposed in his 1898 essay "What Is Art", the common people supplied high art's basic materials. And the fairytale represents the most evolved folk art (since, unlike an "autographic" object attributable to a single individual who carved, painted, wove, or composed it, although some think fairytales may derive from masterful authors).

The fairytale's communal authorship mimics, or presages, the generations-long and cumulative contemplation of high art's formal properties. Compressed within a single fairytale rests the same experimental formalism as drives in a series of high art's works that critique their predecessors. Instead of a string of evolutionary works the successful folktale abridges development to present a unique exemplar, notwithstanding that many tales exist as variants of common themes all in search of their perfection. In this way, though decidedly not high art, fairytales nevertheless work like formalized artistic exploration.

A prime example of this type of development, Rumpelstiltskin's story passed through uncelebrated spinning rooms and generations of nameless women's gleeful recitations; purified of extraneous matters it became a deeply resonant tale of revenge, almost a comedy of revenge.

In some ways it fits the pattern: the powerful are cruelly brought low. The King was fooled about his bride's talents and thus who she "is", which might be funny if you're telling the story to other women in the spinnstube. Also, the apparently all-powerful Rumpelstiltskin finishes the tale humbled. He exits bitterly as Malvolio in *The Twelfth Night*, a pleasingly sadistic ending for pre-modern audiences.[19] Or the Tale of Rumpelstiltskin might be a tragedy of revenge (*Hamlet*). Basically humorless on its surface, Rumpelstiltskin's story recounts enchained calamities sinking downward: tripped by a fool's boast a lust for gold drags the realm's heartless commander into marrying a witless peasant; she threatens the kingdom's heir while jeopardizing a Queen's standing and sanity. All the personages descend until everyone, and especially Rumpelstiltskin, faces ruin.[20] Comedies and tragedies of revenge flourished as Renaissance forms employed by Shakespeare and his contemporaries. Though high art grazes on folk art we cannot know if Rumpelstiltskin's tale (and its sister folktales) supplied materials for Renaissance literary ideals. Perhaps it survived by evolving toward such models if it had not anticipated them. Conceivably, the Grimms formed Rumpelstiltskin to resemble a conventional and venerable literary pattern.

The tale's initial audience included neither Renaissance playwrights nor their paying public (of law clerks, prostitutes, and gentlemen) but the spinnstuben's women and subsequently modern children. However darkly mysterious a story, it's young auditors found "Rumpelstiltskin" neither a tragedy nor a comedy but a tale different from others and even to children's minds not quite classifiable. Perhaps to remedy sugary marital fables, the canny and skeptical spinners offered no consolation in a palliative ending and they added no note of false promise. Rumpelstiltskin's story ends with him more miserably an outcast than when the story began: still impotent and now humiliated. Formerly, before he met the Miller's Daughter, he lived as a proud polymath rejoicing in his bachelor's competencies. But helping her and undergoing a mock courtship cast him into losing a custody battle that degraded him into spinsterhood.

Hardened by life's realities the spinnstube's senior women proposed as grim a spectacle as found in Greek drama or modern "realism" for Rumpelstiltskin's story ends with the Queen immured in her castle with a loveless match. The storyteller's ingenuity had ripened into something truly masterful. But real appreciation of their profound invention awaited modern inquiries.

The Imagination as Female

The famous Viennese doctor would have disagreed about some things discussed by the household's fiber-spinning ladies who sat and chatted through the evening. Yet, perhaps Freud arrived at no greater truth than the wisdom encoded in this fairytale. In a really interesting insight—because it's inadvertent, an unintentional "Freudian slip" by the doctor himself—Freud fosters the masculine point-of-view that "the remarkable phenomenon of erection, around which the human imagination has constantly played, cannot fail to be impressive, involving as it does an apparent suspension of the laws of gravity".[21] He thought his statement advanced his case for dreams of flight which conceal musings on the great priapic penis. Coincidentally he revealed another proposition. A statement that powerfully implied how this story came to be.

Like the rest of us, Freud was wont to and well-aware that he committed unintentional self-revelations. What layman call a "Freudian slip" psychoanalysts, following Freud's 1901 conclusions, refer to as a *parapraxis*: a statement that resembles an inadvertent mistake that may reveal the speaker or writer's unconscious attitudes, desires, or motives.[22] What we think of as unintentional acts or statements may arise from intentions we did not know we harbored. All sorts of things jumbled in the unconscious can prompt the slips of parapraxis. Some hidden prompts to parapraxis were planted in early life—including hearing fairytales, some of them recounting shocking or worrying experiences that may later awaken in the unconscious.

As a kind of revealing parapraxis, only one thing fits Freud's description of what surrounds "the remarkable phenomenon of erection, around which the human imagination has constantly played": the encompassing vagina. What else constantly plays *around* the erection? The vagina plays, inventively frolicking for its own amusement, "around" as it grasps and circumscribes the erection.[23] The vagina embraces the erect penis (indeed it cannot clasp a limp penis like Rumpelstiltskin). That identification makes female anatomy home to the instinct of "the human imagination" the faculty that invents and tells the tale (while Rumpelstiltskin plays the toiling fall guy). Freud's triumvirate—Play, Erection, and (surrounding/grasping/clasping) Around—unites three concepts that unlock the inventiveness behind the Tale of Rumpelstiltskin. But he was not the first to discover this un-named configuration. Probing at human nature with intuition's tools, literature got there first. Freud clustered the same items as Shakespeare (or his coauthor Fletcher) in *Henry VIII (All Is True)*.

Contemplating having to "leave / so sweet a bedfellow" in his divorce from Catherine of Aragon, King Henry laments:

> But conscience, conscience—
> O, 'tis a tender place, and I must leave her.
> *(2.2.141–2)*

The King invests "conscience", the *moral imagination*, in his wife's vagina. If this lament seems ambiguous the playwright hastens to explain himself. Immediately Shakespeare, the Stratford glover's son, invokes cheveral (a flexible, indeed stretchy, leather used in making gloves) to clarify his interesting conjunction. The next scene spells out what Shakespeare has in mind when he blends the vagina and (the moral) imagination. When Henry takes a new lover to replace the Queen (and to produce a male heir), the Old Lady who chaperons Anne Bullen (Anne Boleyn, his second queen) advises her that despite the young woman's protestations at assuming royalty's sometimes onerous burdens:

> Beshrew me, I would,
> And venture maidenhead for't; and so would you,
> . . .
> You, that have the fair parts of a woman on you
> . . .
> Of your soft cheveral conscience would receive,
> If you please to stretch it.
> *(2.3.24–34)*

With the consistency by which the writer's unconscious inseparably welds such associations, in *Hamlet* the prince attributes this same womanly trait to de-naturing masculine heroism when he laments (3:1): "Thus conscience does make cowards of us all".

Four hundred years after Shakespeare, Freud connected these same elements. But less formal authors, who may have predated Shakespeare or were his contemporaries, arrived at this same invention except that the Tale of Rumpelstiltskin evidences the viewpoint of women talking candidly to other women about sexual disappointments.

According to Freud's self-revelatory conjunction, if the penis designates action then the female matrix associates with the imagination. Being proceeds doing. But it's not that simple. Women's presence and child-rearing presides over the imagination (work's productive yield)—spun thread, children, fairytales.[24] Women telling Rumpelstiltskin's tale would agree: men may do proud deeds and boast of them but with our imaginations (as defined by Freud and explained by Shakespeare) we re-configure the world and people it.[25] Ingenuity unites "doing" with "imagining" or "conceiving" in both the mental and biological senses. Some who engage the Tale of Rumpelstiltskin believe that it recounts "persecuted woman and female creativity symbolized by spinning".[26] Thereby bridging both qualities.

Rumpelstiltskin's first act of sorcery so casually insinuates into the story that may pass unnoticed.

> It was in vain that the poor maiden declared that she could do no such thing [as spin straw into gold], the chamber door was locked and she remained alone. She sat down in the corner of the room and began to lament over her hard fate, when on a sudden the door opened,

and in walked Rumpelstiltskin.[27] How did he get into the castle and then into the cell? Just his entrance into the scene violates a secured, and probably guarded, precinct the King set up. Rumpelstiltskin can apparently invade any location he wants without flying, an activity which, in the best Freudian sense, he might reserve for recreation or pleasure.[iii] That distinction reveals something curious.

Let That Be a Warning to You

Young listeners received the tale's droll, if half-understood, observations dispensed by a cadre of masterful reciters—seasoned veterans of domestic politics. Perhaps grandmotherly figures offered the tale as a generational exchange to daughters and granddaughters. The recipients were rapt: youngsters who hungered for every scrap of intelligence learning to master their bodies and manipulate their surroundings. But children are shooed from the room when grown-ups talk in seeming riddles purposefully concealed children. Juveniles overhear adults whispering about the body—about death, sickness, health, and sex. As children slowly acquire worldly skills they are trusted to share adult confidences about money, politics, private religious beliefs, and the secrets of man-woman relationships. The children learn to accept harsh verities. Some secrets pertain to body parts rarely mentioned, and then circumspectly with euphemisms. Mostly adults

FIGURE 4.1   Illustrated by Margaret Evans Price, 1921.

Source: in *Once Upon a Time*, ed. Katherine Lee Bates (Chicago: Rand McNally).

iii. Since he appears into the locked cell that confines the Miller's Daughter and disappears from the girl's castle cell unaided by his aeronautic phallic spoon, he clearly doesn't need it to travel (by telekinesis?) only to fly. Optional as transportation, the spoon is his evening "amusement" while he uses magic to get around, to appear in, and disappear from places. Magic's for teleportation, the spoon's for fun. Even that canny distinction the story's authors included in their composition to re-double the spoon's contextual meaning.

obliquely communicated what seemed cultic truths.[28] The Tale of Rumpelstiltskin could hint at one of those truths—that marriage and (consequent or preceding) sexual relations rarely delivered a "fairytale" happy ending. In this folktale sex takes a beating. The consummation of the Miller's Daughter's marriage goes unmentioned. Most fairytales avoid the bedroom but not many encompass before-and-after childbirth as does Rumpelstiltskin's tour of virginity to motherhood. Yet, an uncharacteristic detail suggests the first storytellers editorialized about the royal marriage's sexual health. The tale is not crowned with the formulaic "They lived happily ever after" a phrase that implies intimacy; the equivalent standard closing in French fairytales is "They lived long lives and had many children". (French fairytales taught kids that you can't be happy without sex and family and maybe the German spinnstuben agreed—before the tale migrated to England.) Instead of such fecundity the Tale of Rumpelstiltskin ends with this curtain-lowering: "And he never was heard from again". That's it. That's the finale. Nobody gains "happiness" although the Queen smugly escapes her bargain, relieved at retaining child custody. Once Rumpelstiltskin exits offstage many invented futures can be imagined but the spinning circle's ladies, who were all too-familiar with high rates of infant mortality, vaguely suggest only loveless royal sex to produce a replacement heir(s) as insurance.

This bitter story departs from syrupy stereotypes. In this tale's universe the King and his Queen markedly did *not* "live happily ever after" and poor Rumpelstiltskin's self-banishment sealed a loveless tale. Maybe in some forgotten past the Miller loved his absent wife but the King married for greed. The unloved Queen lives a fraud, likely condescended by her blue-blood court. She mortgaged her son. Whatever her respectable reputation she knows it a sham. Helpful Rumpelstiltskin wanders somewhere (expelled from the world of humans) dazed with rage and shame. The story's creators, who had tolerated many hurts that modernity has softened for women, afflicted Rumpelstiltskin with sadistic public humiliation; the spinnstube thereby planted in their listeners both a taste for revenge and hope of liberation. The story's retaliation exquisitely framed their ire.

These women had legitimate complaints against husbands and the patriarchy ruled by a regal crown or Bishop's miter—both throne and pulpit fountains of derision at female "weakness" (for, among other things, causing mankind's Fall by tempting Adam). But if the Tale of Rumpelstiltskin subversively mocks male-dom this perplexing story's reprisals represent different ways to get even.

The spinnstube could prepare a young woman to accept harsh realities about actual, not idealized, men. A girl's later wonderment or disappointment could be lessened if, perhaps intuited or forewarned, she understood that most aspects of male-female relations were fraught and not the stuff of "fairytales". There are a few Prince Charmings around. She could hear these lessons before she sadly related her own less-than-exemplary incidents; and her disappointment would be reported to the spinnstube, the already-knowing community of older women predisposed to sympathize. The story cached small but quite astute and grow-up hints about anatomical reality. It furtively offered sharp confidences about the threat of spinsterhood, spinning as a passport from girlhood, courtship, loveless marriage, and onward to motherhood.

Notes

1. Friedan (2013, p. 181).
2. Women were barred from serving in the church and climbing its career ladder. They were prevented from joining almost any gild. They were subject to agnatic [salic] law which decreed male inheritance of estates that passed titles and land over the heads of would-be female heirs. They could rarely claim even the property brought into marriage except when otherwise negotiated by contract (today called a pre-nup). They lacked political voice much less a vote. Perhaps a not wholly accurate but nevertheless a fair description pre-modern society suggests two teams, women versus everyone else.
3. Fissell (2004, p. 70).
4. Zipes (1993, p. 49).
5. In twentieth-century England this point was apparently lost on noddy Princess Diana. Her principal job was breeding heirs and everything else—her personal bonds of affection to courtiers, dispensing highly visible and photogenic comfort to people worldwide, cultivating self-serving publicity, the quality and fidelity of her relations with her husband or her in-laws or possible lovers—was secondary. She thought her job concerned glamour, service, and mutual sexual devotion; in other words, she bought the "fairytale" version of royalty. That illusion would have amused the peasant ladies who spun and invented a wryly entertaining tale exactly to mock such pretense.
6. Ruth B. Bottigheimer (2009, p. 50).
7. *Harvard Law Review* (June 1986), pp. 1936–1955.
8. Providing a negative proof and re-directing attention from the oedipal model, Bruno Bettelheim noted:

   > In fairy stories which help the oedipal girl to understand her feelings and find vicarious satisfaction, it is the (step)mother's or enchantress' intense jealousy which keeps the lover from finding the princess. The jealousy proves that the older woman knows that the young girl is preferable, more lovable, and more deserving of being loved.
   >
   > *(1976, p. 113)*

   Never post-menopausal though impotent (a virtually congruent condition) Rumpelstiltskin is unthreatened by the youthful Miller's Daughter but envies her fecundity as much as an aging stepmother.
9. McGlathery (1991, p. 177).
10. Although the list may seem lengthy, compared to other fairytales derived from works by the Brothers Grimm, Rumpelstiltskin's treatment on film is scanty.

Movies:

Rumpelstiltskin, 1915 (execrably including a character called "Jim Crow")
Rumpelstiltskin, 1955
Foul Play, 1978, where Rumpelstiltskin's name supplies a running joke triggered by a character's dwarfism (played by Billy Barty) and another character is named "Stiltskin".
Rumpelstiltskin, 1985 (TV Movie) a twenty-four-minute animated feature (Family Home Entertainment) narrated by Christopher Plummer with Al(ec?) Baldwin voicing the King.
Rumpelstiltskin, 1987
Rumpelstiltskin, 1995
Rumpelstilzchen, aka "Rumpelstiltskin", 2007
Rumpelstiltskin, 2012 (Short)

Video:

Goldilocks and the Three Bears/Rumpelstiltskin/Little Red Riding Hood/Sleeping Beauty, 1984
We All Have Tales: Rumpelstiltskin, 1992

TV Series:

Shirley Temple Theatre, 1958
Jackanory, 1965
Rainbow, 1972
Faerie Tale Theatre, 1982
Reading Rainbow, 1983
Grimm Masterpiece Theatre, 1987
Grim Tales, 1989
Happily Ever After: Fairy Tales for Every Child, 1995
Fairy Tale Police Department, 2002

TV Episodes:

Rumpelstiltskin, 1966
Rumpelstiltskin, 1987
Rumpelstiltskin, 1989
Rumpelstiltskin, 1982
Rumpelstiltskin, 2008
Super Why!, 2007
Rumpelstiltskin, 1958
Rumpelstiltskin, 1987
Rumpelstiltskin, 1989
Rumpelstiltskin, 1995
Rumpelstiltskin's Last Straw, 2002
"The Tower" episode written by Robert Hull for the TV series *Once Upon a Time*, first broadcast on Disney's ABC television March 23, 2014.

11. Quoted from *The Needle Arts: A Social History of American Needlework* (1990, p. 52).

12. Friedan (2013, p. 181).

13. Zipes (1993) mentioned this element to make a slightly different point:
    The Oxford Universal Dictionary states that spinster was "appended to names of women, orig. to denote their occupation, but subsequently as the proper legal designation of one unmarried" (1944:1971) in Middle English. By 1719, a spinster was synonymous with old maid. In French the term for spinster is vieillefille. There is a connection to filer or filare: to spin. In German, eine alte Spinne is an ugly old woman. To spin is spinnen, and spinnen can also mean to babble in a crazy way.(p. 55)But the word-root's connection is not principally derived from "to spin" but to a strand of thread, fil (affiliate), as in filial, pertaining to a son or daughter—through the male line. Thus: Latinate fil or fils, relates to Germano-Celtic fitz as prefix in Fitzgerald or suffix in Meyerwitz, or vitz. In Slavic the forms are written witz, wicz, or vich. A highly contracted form retains only the F sound as in Ivonovich shortened to Ivanof, the equivalent of Ivanhoe, etc. At least one of the two prominent linguistic theories (fostered by the Grimms) sees this lineage deriving from the Indo-European root *bheu, to be, to exist, to grow. An example is the Latin fierī, to become, as in fiat, but also related to filius, son. So, the gendered word spinster returns us to the three fates who bring into existence (to be), then sustain (to exist), and chose the mortal's fate (to grow, or not).

14. John Bushnel (1962, pp. 509 ff). Quoted from Betty Friedan (2013, p. 173).

15. Stewart (2003, p. 130).

16. Schneider (1989, p. 193).

17. Writing a series of frame stories told in his native Neapolitan dialect, Giambattista Basile (1575–1632) authored what seems the earliest collection of fairytales published in 1634 as

The Tale of Tales, or Entertainment of Little Ones. The Grimms admired the work for its nationalist outlook.

18. A frame story (or frame narrative) the collection uses a technique that probably originated in ancient India around the first millennium BCE (and used for the Sanskrit epics, the Mahabharata and Ramayana) whereby a central story contains successive stories-within-a-story.

    Over centuries, frame stories moved westward and the first known reference to the Thousand-And-One-Nights appears in a ninth-century fragment of an eighth-century collection where the title indicates a very large number of stories, not really a thousand. The definitive version with almost 500 stories, covers material datable to the sixteenth century. The Thousand-And-One-Nights' stories accumulated as the frame story moved west; some are Arabic in origin (brought to the Middle East by Mongols), others from India, Iran, Iraq, Egypt, Turkey or Greece. Set in Persia, India or sometimes China, the Thousand-And-One-Nights tells of a king whose wife betrayed him and in revenge against womankind he daily married a virgin and killed her the next day at dawn however Scherazade contrived a scheme to save herself and thus end the sexual battle.

    On her wedding night Scherazade began a story, leaving it unfinished at a cliff-hanger moment just as dawn broke but promising to conclude it the next night. The childish king reluctantly granted her wish the first night but the stories—some of which are themselves frame narratives, and include Aladdin, Ali Baba, and Sinbad the Sailor—so enthralled that years passed, the king grew to love her and in some versions they had sons, and the royal degree was eventually revoked as the king repented of his inhuman scheme.

    Whatever their origin, either as folktales or as the work of professional storytellers, to gain plausibility, this universe of stories were put into the mouth of a woman, albeit a beautiful one whose allures only complimented her recitation. But, then again, if female invention made Rumpelstiltskin repulsive, a heroine can be devised as the perfect entertainer.

19. Rumpelstiltskin doesn't threaten well-deserved reprisals that are certainly within his power, unlike the equally abased Malvolio who snarls, "I'll be revenged on the whole pack of you" [*Twelfth Night* V:1] grimly coloring that nominal comedy's last moments with a chilling warning.

20. Rumpelstiltskin's descent raises the others' fortunes, as when *King Richard II*, abdicating his throne and crown, taunts Bolingbroke just as the new-minted Queen taunts Rumpelstiltskin, her benefactor.

> On this side my hand, and on that side yours.
> Now is this golden crown like a deep well
> That owes two buckets, filling one another,
> The emptier ever dancing in the air,
> The other down, unseen and full of water:
> That bucket down and full of tears am I,
> Drinking my griefs, whilst you mount up on high.
> King Richard II *to Bolingbroke (4:1)*

21. Freud (1900/1931, 1965, pp. 429–430).

22. These "slips" occur when interference from the unconscious rises into the everyday world and mars the conscious execution of speaking or gesture to produce an apparently faulty action. The product of conflicted thoughts may reveal the existence of unacknowledged and subconscious mental processes.

23. Here Freud recalled his favorite writer, Goethe whose concept of the allegorical Eternal Feminine represents creative inspiration. The very last line of Goethe's *Faust* Part II (1832) declares: "The Eternal Feminine draws us on", a line that supplies the equivalent and predecessor of Freud's "the human imagination . . . constantly [at] play".

24. Storytelling ladies contested Robert Graves' formulation in his 1964 book's title poem, "Man Does, Woman Is".

25. At his early (nutty, Romantic, bombastic, wonderfully sonorous) best Ezra Pound played these two against each other in his 1912 poem, *An Immortality*:

> And I would rather have my sweet,
> Though rose-leaves die of grieving,
> Than do high deeds in Hungary
> To pass all men's believing.

26. Zipes (1993, p. 44).
27. Taylor (1823/1920, p. 148).
28. Society's beliefs could be formulated and communicated in stories, scripture, or edicts: stories for the young, commandments and laws for adults. The difference in modes of transmission marked each society's rites-of-passage. Societies transitioned from truths couched in myths to ultimate expression as laws. See Rand (2012).

5

FAIRYTALE CONTRACTS AND COMMERCE

Magical Helper or Legal Villain

> I made her an offer she couldn't refuse.[1]

Perhaps an outcast, a lone forest-dweller alien to the female spinning chamber's spirit of community, Rumpelstiltskin deviates from Campbell's idea of a "supernatural helper". He more fully resembles a supernatural she-male who plies his androgynous mastery of gender-defining work. But why? Who is he? When he gallantly allows the contract to be renegotiated, Rumpelstiltskin tests an idea of pre-modern jurisprudence and personal responsibility: the rigorously fulfilled mythic/fairytale bargain. Within fairytales' weird context these imaginary contracts seemed neither contrived nor impossible fictions as imagined by non-lawyers whose limited understanding of legal codes arose from being the law's usual victims. It also helped if you believed in magic and the supernatural, neither of which were irrational worldviews before modern science explained how things work. (Legal scholars, the Grimms and Savigny, enjoyed a long historical view of jurisprudence and perhaps saw folklore's many contracts as incomparable precedents.) The situation prevailing between Rumpelstiltskin and the Miller's Daughter recognizes the "if" and "then" nature of their relationship: if I do this, then you are obligated to do that. Sometimes the unforeseen consequences of such fairytale or mythic deals blow up in results that become splendidly tragic, trivial, or (if a joke) amusing.

Endlessly ironic as their implicit details surface, fairytale's agreements resembled lawfully structured arrangements, perhaps enforceable by a human court; their "fine print" appealed to an illiterate and largely lawyerless rural society with a keen appreciation of sharp dealing.[2] The appeal of spooky contracts never waned. Washington Irving's story "The Devil and Tom Walker" updated the sticky Faustian supernatural contract in 1824.

FIGURE 5.1   Illustrated by Charles Robinson, 1911.

Source: in *The Big Book of Fairy Tales*, Walter Jerrold (ed.) (London: Blackie & Son).

Stephen Vincent Benét revived the binding contract in 1936 for "The Devil and Daniel Webster" that, significantly, changed the venue from a human court to avert a mythic bargain's dire consequences. A human jury understood the mythical contract's obligations and mortals bound by folk wisdom must adhere to binding bargains. In a human court with a mortal jury, Rumpelstiltskin's agreement, though reached under duress, might withstand a challenge by the Miller's Daughter. But that challenge would affirm that their give-and-take assumed the form of a negotiation, albeit with feeble haggling. The heroine (if she is one) enjoys no time to ponder Rumpelstiltskin's offer, and she makes her compact with him under drastic duress.

Their transaction hardly exemplifies a free market when a willing and unconstrained seller dickers with a un-coerced purchaser. It's a deal she must take or die, which makes it no deal at all under extreme compulsion. There's an implicit distinction here. When kings (emperors or military officers) command, the executor (a subject of the realm or soldier) has scant choice but to perform the action. Kings command but Rumpelstiltskin offers. He never orders the Miller's Daughter to do anything. The story clearly distinguishes the two kinds of wishes. Specifically the King barks that "[i]f by the next morning you have not spun this straw into gold you will have to die". On the other hand, Rumpelstiltskin negotiates; when the girl tells him that "I have nothing left that I could give to you", he suggests a counter-offer: "Then promise that when you become queen, your first child will belong to me". An easily overlooked word and concept, his "then" means "in that case" or "if that is (truly) so" or "if you wish me to stipulate that such is the case or state-of-affairs". The word introduces a vista of human responses. The point being that this noddy country girl overlooked a card she could still play. Her predicament may not be as bereft as she fears.

With no alternative apparent to her, the Miller's Daughter concedes the deal. Her renegotiation to recover her son in the ensuing vocabulary contest only underlines the fact that she had previously engaged in a binding compact—otherwise there'd be nothing to renegotiate.[i] (When she learns the secret name to gain the upper hand, she herself dismisses any possible renegotiation: she reveals herself a hardened adult peasant. Her cleverness seemed humorous, then.) The Miller's Daughter can, and does, escape the fairytale/mythic bargain. Since Rumpelstiltskin ultimately lost the child that represented his payment, we have no idea what the bargain cost him. He drew down magic from the reservoir of his powers to save her, and that magical storehouse might not be inexhaustible. (He was, after all, the original "small" businessman.) In his supernatural world he may have squandered reputation when bested by a mortal, and that too represents a sacrifice. She offers nothing to repay him nor any consideration of how the

---

i. It may seem odd to talk about re-gaining her son since the Queen never losses him. Yet, here too, peasant storytellers understood a fine distinction. They dealt with millers like the girl's father so rurals knew that grain left for milling would be returned minus a commission taken in milled flour; a miller takes possession of the farmer's property and gains ownership of some agreed-upon part of it. Likewise, if someone buys something from you and you agree that the purchase will be paid immediately but on a certain date the goods will become the purchaser's, it doesn't matter if the seller still possess the goods—ownership has transferred on the agreed date. Likewise, since Rumpelstiltskin's contract remained in force the child became his whether the Queen surrenders the Prince or not. Hence, for the child to remain with its mother requires re-negotiation. Or a broken contract. The former seemed possible to the storytellers, the latter, an unthinkable abrogation of a verbal contract, would shatter their society.

broken contract diminished him. Our sympathies might be divided if we consider the loss on both sides. There was, after all, a contract. She had something to offer.

★★★

Into a female world arrived a "safe" man, harmless because (we are beginning to believe) impotent, but helpful. He can neither rape nor inseminate; he attempts neither. One observer speculated:

> Were he a lecher, or the type of the oversexed dwarf, he might indeed have asked for her body. The point, however, appears to be that, on the contrary, his desire is to become a father, without having to be a lover, much as a little boy might dream of becoming a parent, yet abhor the thought of doing what is required to achieve that end as nature dictates.[3]

(Of course, if Rumpelstiltskin is supposed to be a homosexual, he wouldn't be interested in coition but might yearn for fatherhood.) Yet Rumpelstiltskin probably did not "abhor the thought of doing what is required"; he just could not perform. If he could there'd be a whole different story.

While a "little boy" might abhor descent into the alien and repulsive female body, if women first told the story, they would find nothing loathsome in their own contribution to baby-making. This important difference translates us through the looking-glass of normative male to a normative female viewpoint: Rumpelstiltskin does not decline to impregnate the Miller's Daughter. He can't get her with child, and he's never offered the opportunity as he never asks. And she certainly doesn't volunteer as long as he's willing to take trinkets in exchange for his work. If Rumpelstiltskin could have sexually consummated his bargain, he would have fathered the child himself. But in a story composed by women overt prostitution cannot win the day, only the usual sort of sexual bargain: marriage.

The Miller's Daughter typifies the dull good girl; not for her recreational premarital sex or conceding its attractive possibility or admitting she knows anybody who enjoys it and how to perform "it". She certainly would not use sex as a bargaining chip. Yet the Grimms faithfully, if unknowingly, reproduced the inherent isometry in the Tale of Rumpelstiltskin for "[w]hile spinning could indicate the sex act, it simultaneously and more importantly epitomized the virtuous woman, incongruous as these opposi-tions may seem . . . virtue, more than sex, was the historically dominant association of spinning".[4] The storytellers featured the key to their beliefs within the story: "I have nothing left that I could give to you", states the Miller's Daughter, which would be true if we consider only goods, not services. There's the usual comforting assistance she can render a healthy male—even a kiss of feigned gratitude from a sexual dullard. As they stood outside the story modeling this tragi-funny tale, storytellers created the Miller's Daughter an ideally innocent figure who has no idea that Rumpelstiltskin is incapable of sex. In desperate straits other good girls resourcefully swapped sex for their lives, but in so doing, remarkably and perversely, they ceased being good girls and become clever, sullied, or heroic. That's not what the tale's creators proposed for the Miller's Daughter.

The spinnstube's storytellers improved on trading middle-class sex for subsistence in marriage (the accepted term for this arrangement is "homemaker") when the Miller's Daughter is forced to marry the King. She had no choice but to become Queen. When she soothes her womanly contrition talking with the court ladies, she can truthfully claim that she did not marry for money. But, first, coerced by the King she had to negotiate with Rumpelstiltskin without offering him sex for his spinning. She never even considered it.

Once sexually experienced and a young mother, the new-minted peasant-queen could counsel her ladies-in-waiting exactly as Shakespeare's chaperon advised: "I would . . . venture maidenhead for't; and so would you . . . that have the fair parts of a woman on you . . . your soft cheveral conscience would receive, If you please to stretch it". The working-class women who invented this tale imagined the life of a Queen amid gorgeously gowned courtiers swanning around the palace. But instead of guessing about court life, the ladies of the spinnstube knew, and did not have to invent, the life of a miller whose unsophisticated Daughter remained innocent of the possibility of trading Rumpelstiltskin sex for her life, or prostituting herself even for prestige and wealth. That abstinence shows no lack of initiative but her ignorance. The tale's composers weren't about to endorse whoredom, a rival institution to their well-being. Harlots paraded as their adversaries. (Fairytales assigned alienated affections to stepmothers who threatened children. But adults knew stepmothers as replacement wives—they arrived after the catastrophe of a mother's death.) Too many husbands and boyfriends had frittered away their time, affections, health, and wealth on drink and floozies. Regardless of how this fairytale originated, the spinning circle's ladies valued stability in their lives along with continuity (tradition), their society's seasonal regularity, and lifelong predictability. Loose women were unwelcome in their midst and certainly not as heroines. Accordingly strumpets were barred from fairytales. Ladies of that essentially conservative institution, the spinning chamber, would scorn learning that the Miller's Daughter proved quick-witted or worldly enough to trade sex for her life and ennoblement. She even lacked the vocabulary to name the terms to negotiate such a deal.

Business Is Business

> The King thought "Even though she is only a miller's daughter, I could not find a richer wife in all the world".[ii]

It's deplorable that casual or nonchalant usage made Rumpelstiltskin a stand-in for evil. More a martyr, Rumpelstiltskin names an esoteric female entertainment as "[f]ew tales in the Grimms' collection are so crass as 'Rumpelstiltskin' in depicting purely economic

---

ii. Which recalls the song (written by Terry Britten and Graham Lyle and released in 1984 sung by Tina Turner) "What's Love Got to Do With It?" Nothing.

FIGURE 5.2   Illustrated by John B. Gruelle, 1914.

Source: in *Grimm's Fairy Tales*, Margaret Hunt trans. (New York: Cupples & Leon).

motives for marriage".[5] The King himself recognizes how incongruous the situation would appear: to pluck a peasant girl from obscurity and place her on the throne. It's unlikely that he's unconcerned about how he's perceived because he threatened the girl's life if she appeared insubordinate and failed to fulfill his command. More consistently with the rest of the story, this King can tolerate fellow monarchs regarding him as a money-grubber. He has no other reason to marry but unadulterated greed. Certainly the Miller's Daughter herself advertises no distinguishing charms. No third-party observer mentions the Miller's Daughter's beauty as her "saving grace". She exhibits only one talent: spinning—just not as well as the King thought.

While the Miller may love his daughter and she him, and while the King might eventually love his wife and she him, and while the Queen may love her son, this story omits any explicit "positive" emotions. Instead we encounter avarice, gloating, shame, pride, sadism, and horror. Romance or love is just not on the menu. The story retained a certain reality for, as the spinnstube well knew, an arranged marriage awaited most of the story's original tellers and its first hearers. Yet an arranged marriage hardly threatened the worst fate compared to spinsterhood. The real problem of an arranged marriage was not a lack of initial love but finding yourself wedded to disappointing blunderer. The Tale of Rumpelstiltskin hints at that possibility, albeit tactfully. There's a hidden comment about the hard facts of failed mercantile endeavors: a stinging but piquant satire (at male expense).

★★★

Taylor's 1823 translation begins with the formulaic "In a certain kingdom once lived a poor miller", without further mention of his trade or financial condition.[6] Perhaps (because he was "poor" and lacked worldly goods) the miller had "in this world only a beautiful daughter" and no substantial assets. Two centuries later an observer surmised, he was a "poor peasant—father of a daughter whom he despairs of marrying off, because he can afford no dowry. This is a hard-working, simple man, who struggles to provide a living under harsh circumstances".[7] Often enough spinners who relished this story owned even less than the miller. But they enjoyed the enterprise of a girl who supplies her own when her father "can afford no dowry". That gloating detail of female ingenuity leads to other insights to cumulatively paint a keen editorial picture of events.

Calling the girl's father a "poor" miller declares him an incompetent since in an agrarian community the capitalist miller might top the social pyramid as the wealthiest person in the neighborhood, excepting the lord of the manor. It took considerable capital and highly specialized technological know-how to erect a mill, to obtain an ideally suitable location near flowing water where a mill race could be constructed. (Often nobility owned watermills and rented them out to millers. A royal lease might have occasioned the king's inspection tour of his prized property.) Other capital-intensive infrastructure that reached into the countryside supported a widespread system with a mill's thrashing gears at its heart. The mill's site should be reachable with decent roads to bring in crops and haul out the pulverized meal to market. The whole operation had to be nearby to farmland, not just any site would do. So including a "mill" in the story insinuated prime real estate owned or rented at the nucleus of a supportive network of skilled labor and expensive engineering. In a farming society whose members wielded only simple hand tools, the miller represented the cutting edge of capitalist technology; he operated a large and highly complex machine, really a stand-alone factory. (His father's prosperity as a miller allowed the young Rembrandt to chance the iffy career as a painter.) Turned by water- or (later) wind-power the mill's whirling shafts and gears drove finely calibrated mechanical parts through their dynamic but precise motions. Learning to operate a mill meant an apprenticeship's training and subsequent experience of how to make those, sometimes subtle but crucial, manual adjustments that governed the entire gyrating and extremely powerful operation. For his services the miller claimed a percentage of all the grain milled, regardless of whether it cost the farmer dearly to raise that season's crop. In good years or in bad, through drought or locusts, the miller took a fixed percentage. The miller prospered relatively insulated from ruinous crop failure that raised the price of his share; he welcomed deflation or war that increased the value of his tithe. A "poor miller" is a nebbish. And this one delusionally boasts as well, which might explain why he was poor.

The story's creators editorialized by reporting his occupation as they piled defects upon the man: a liar, a coward, a business failure (because poor)—a true warning to nubile girls and a joke to older woman.

Crimes Against the Crown

"I have nothing left that I could give to you" the girl replied.
"Then promise that when you become queen, your first child will belong to me".

Everybody in the tale emerges more or less grubby.

As a cautionary tale Rumpelstiltskin falls apart. The storyteller can't forewarn anybody, even the child-listener, against the evils and consequences of bragging because the boastful miller remains unpunished while his daughter, a bystander, is imprisoned for his lies. Ultimately the miller gained exalted rank and presumably lived richly as the royal father-in-law. Father and husband can safely be called psychopaths. The King casually issues death threats but emerges unscathed for his greedy hauteur. That seems one of the story's few universals in whatever variant: "Whether we look at German, Scottish, or French versions of the tale, the King whom the heroine marries makes it clear just why he finds this humble girl so irresistible".[8] Yet, of course, he is right; he could not find "a richer wife in all the world" as his new-found wealth comes, not of this world, but from a supernatural source. He's happy, in his way. Then there's the story's namesake. Shabbily abused, in some versions of the tale Rumpelstiltskin undergoes his final humiliation not in the Queen's private chambers, where no one can witness his shame, but amid assembled courtiers. But there's a problem with envisioning that resolution of the story, however richly satisfying for the Queen. The sadistic detail of public embarrassment would cost her dearly as the Queen would have to divulge to the onlookers her madcap treasonous bargain: she put at risk the royal heir, though yet unborn.

Pre-modern storytellers understood what that meant: the risk of sedition argues against the emotional luxury of a public outing with its shaming and instead strongly proposes setting the final scene as a private meeting in her royal chambers. (A tale of appalling ingratitude, in Taylor's version once Rumpelstiltskin was openly trounced in the naming contest, "he made the best of his way off, while everybody laughed at him for having had all his troubles for nothing".[9] The "everybody" imagines attending courtiers who snickered at Rumpelstiltskin's now-public flaw. But that's an implausible motif.) Despite the tempting pleasure of humiliating him in public, the Queen likely chose a quiet guarded room that, like her former cell, only Rumpelstiltskin can enter unobserved. The Queen would sensibly confront Rumpelstiltskin away from the assembled court. If she insists on his public degradation the Queen proves herself perfidious should anybody ask "Who was that little guy, anyway?" More costly than trading trinkets for magical spinning, gaining a merciless laugh at Rumpelstiltskin's expense would reveal to the kingdom's convened aristocracy that she had bet the true heir of the blood-royal for a peasant's life—her own.

It wouldn't take the King long to figure out that having gained three rooms packed with gold, having fulfilled his promise to wed her, and having produced an heir—he had no further need of this self-confessed peasant traitor, whose child would be renounced once he procured a new heir. The King gained considerably by repudiating her but realized little from her continuance on the throne once he learned she could never again spin gold. He could dispose of the "disloyal" Miller's Daughter for a more politically advantageous aristocratic heiress. So many benefits accrued to ousting the peasant-queen. Nuptials with a new Queen from the nobility could convey significant alliances and perhaps title to serious real estate, not just a rural mill. A new bride would deliver sexual variety to the marriage bed. A new bride would produce a successor of untainted pedigree. And the King keeps three brimming rooms of gold.

As imagined by the spinnstube's canny ladies, given all the situation's liabilities the Queen probably waived the otherwise satisfying chance for Rumpelstiltskin's public humiliation. Both as coherent literature and as psychological insight the Tale of Rumpelstiltskin can teach us a lot, just not about everyday morality. Again, as in so many of the story's details, there's a reason for that fine distinction. The story begins outside our moral universe and never touches modern values.

Lessons to Be Learned

Nobody ever concluded a recitation of Rumpelstiltskin by saying "Let that be a lesson to you", as there's no obvious moral lesson to learn. Yet the story imparts guidance, just nothing intended for our world. As they respected verbal business contracts, even promises, and appreciated implicit fine print, the spinnstube's ladies would have understood the distinction between morals and ethics. Rumpelstiltskin's tale deals in the latter.

The tale's deficiency of an obvious moral sermon initially proved no handicap. Its lack of preaching only appeared an imperfection when modernity enlisted fairytales for child-rearing, which disadvantaged the story compared to other, sweetly redemptive, tales. Now Rumpelstiltskin's story competes against more accessible and straightforwardly chaste fare: cleaned-up versions of fairytales mass-marketed to urge prescriptive behavior.[10] In contrast, this story's conspicuous shortage of any meritorious concluding precepts helps account for the absence of a successful movie version. Instead of morals Rumpelstiltskin's tale advocates a distinctly primeval, though not outdated, ethical stance: verbal contract lore. Again, the Grimms and Savigny thought they hit legal pay-dirt. Not only does the story's central agreement specify what goods (a child) will be accepted for (Rumpelstiltskin's magical) services but the King's short-term, thrice-renewed, contract had to be fulfilled in a timely manner, by dawn. No cunning lawyer could have drawn a tighter contract than the spinnstube's ladies. Wary victims of sharp dealings, they shared many evenings when they refined the tale and closed loopholes. Experience showed them how the world worked, even without attending lawschool. To the storytellers' sense of propriety, self-obligated conduct seemed respectable, even exemplary. The alternative, breaking your word, exposed unthinkable rascality. Their story taught that verbal contracts are binding; the Queen's word seals her bond and Rumpelstiltskin adheres to his terms, even though each suffers for keeping their word.

Scrupulously following his agreement, disgraced Rumpelstiltskin still honors the bargain despite his great loss by it as he abandons the child, his payment. Unlike the Miller's Daughter, whose tears moved Rumpelstiltskin to leniency when her weeping summoned him to work for her, defeated he exits without protesting the revised contract. After all, he could have departed screaming "It's Not Fair!" In Rumpelstiltskin's story of anomalous helpfulness children glean the lesson of abused trust which, at least partly, explains the story's peculiar effect on its youngest hearers who are otherwise denied fairytales' usual heroic rewards. The story's threat of maternal abandonment felt real enough; its comments about greedy nobility editorialized along lines children already heard at home, remarks that informed them they were the aristocracy's ready victims; its evident guidance about the principled value of verbal bonds, their word engaged weighty responsibilities not easily discharged—all this seems trite now but informed a wildly Romantic view of the peasantry as a source of wisdom.

Despite the child's lack of analytic powers there is no "need to label one's first reactions as 'sentimental nonsense,' when, in fact, such reactions represent an authentic *moment*—often, even, a *charged* moment—in the history of one's own aesthetic response" [stress in the original].[11] Kids get it. This tale flaunts no dapper renegade (the demobbed soldier of the Grimms' *Twelve Dancing Princesses* who follows young ladies as they repeatedly lie to their Dad) or Hans Christian Andersen's dissemblers in *The Tinderbox*, a tale contemporary with the Grimms' work.[12] In Rumpelstiltskin's world those who enter into pledges remain inexcusably bound by them. In the village and the castle, in the Tale of Rumpelstiltskin, your word counts and cannot be rescinded.

The Queen never doubts that she must give up her child, having so pledged. An idealized Queen does not shirk her responsibility however barbaric the deal; playing within the rules she seeks another bargain to replace, not abrogate, the first. The Queen cannot imagine being free of her bargain but she wants to supplant the onerous debt with a lighter tariff and to her amazement she gets off the hook entirely. It doesn't matter if we find the baby-for-gold trade repugnant; the story never debates the transaction's appropriateness. The Tale of Rumpelstiltskin details how pledges remorselessly bind and, therefore, the need to live with the unpleasant consequences of vows. Procedural and ethical restrictions secured an illiterate community that lived on reputation and handshake deals, even after writing became accessible in nearby towns. The story implicitly details what circumstances may invalidate a spoken contract: nothing. Forgiveness is simply not on its moral menu.

The tale occurs, not just before but, outside Christendom. Its rural commoners self-govern with ironclad peasant law. Arriving from that fierce world it's a useless errand for moralizers and modern commentators to assign the Tale of Rumpelstiltskin a mawkish up-lifting value. The story treats only people who are morally flawed.[13] It cannot mean whatever we want it to. Or indicate whatever we want it to. On the other hand, it can mean nothing at all. And some do think that speaking Rumpelstiltskin's name signifies nothing. But then, if his name means nothing, we have to explain the rest of the story's homogeneity and why uttering this word changes everything. Once Rumpelstiltskin's name is spoken, like a candle blown out, the light vanishes from a delicious dark fantasy of revenge.

Justice, Then and Now

Rumpelstiltskin may have been swindled. That raises two points: Who exactly is the story's hero? Who entraps who? Can fleecing Rumpelstiltskin of his rightful gain constitute heroism? The Queen cheats her rescuer yet derives every benefit from his labors for which she paid nearly nothing. (Services or goods obtained for free are either gifts or stolen. Rumpelstiltskin ended up with a necklace and ring he did not need.) A sad form of heroism indeed. But for the story's creators a brutally witty, if apparently acceptable, kind of female valor.

When helpless, the girl accepts his aid but when potent she effectively defrauds her benefactor. Not a merciful Queen—and what use is power if not clemency? She never offers to recompense Rumpelstiltskin for his lost wager. Cruelty distinguishes her from her fairytale peers. Cinderella also rises from obscurity to emerge Princess (future Queen) but Cinderella forgives her tormentors, her heartless stepsisters. The Miller's Daughter shows no compassion once delivered from her distress. So, aside from defending motherhood's sanctity, what cause or justification can the Queen champion? Is she the hero or villain? It depends on who you ask and what you ask. A judge might inquire if she has acted in self-defense and a lawyer (Rumpelstiltskin's for example) might cross-examine about her due-diligence, what actions or inquiries did she undertake to correct her problems and anticipate their consequences. Similar admonitions about commitments may have laced an evening of communal spinning.

Much nearer the bottom than the top of society's ladder the spinnstube's women could be cheated of their labors and endlessly submitted: to husbands, fathers, nobility, clergy, millers, or Rumpelstiltskins. Despite any smoldering anger spinners felt for real and notorious men Rumpelstiltskin might deserve better if he were not explicitly the butt of the joke. But any justice he deserves exists outside the story's framework, a situation the storytellers chose simply to ignore. Does the story dispense justice? Even in a morally ambiguous world apt to be unkind and unforgiving can the conclusion be called Just? Hardly. The end reeks of revenge without fairness.

There's less real justice in the Tale of Rumpelstiltskin than in *The Merchant of Venice*, another story in which the female protagonist (Portia, a countrygirl like the Miller's Daughter) outsmarts a canny outsider.[14] An outsider living as a stranger, alien in appearance and manners even in Venice's cosmopolitan majority community, Shylock presented high art's version of scorned Rumpelstiltskin. And Rumpelstiltskin represents the ultimate outsider. From a host of folklore's assorted supernatural creatures it's impossible to assign Rumpelstiltskin to any tribe. Though he tries to ingratiate himself, he belongs nowhere. But lives by the old-time rules.

A Negotiated Child Unobtainable by Magic

> In a salon, people do not write, but talk. Talk presupposes the presence of others; writing, their absence.[15]
>
> *Barbara Hahn*

In the spinning chamber women exercised their craft amid small talk and swapped rumors. They traded health tips, child-rearing advice and apparently amused themselves at the expense of (mostly absent) men. In Rumpelstiltskin's story their entertainment conformed to a pre-modern taste for cruelty as women stacked the odds for their amusement. Three adult males, each flawed in various ways, paraded on stage with blemishes as their principal qualities. The baby, a fourth male, lives wholly dependent on a woman, his mother. Even allowing for human imperfection, we only know the story's men by their moral deformities; none appear reliable or honorable. Within this scornful framework the fairytale's foremost conundrum can be put to rest: "It remains unclear, though, just why the dwarf wants the child".[16] By now the answer should be obvious. Although Rumpelstiltskin can work magic to obtain whatever he wants he cannot procreate. Only a phallus can create a living child while getting a child evidently exceeds his magic powers.

Apparently a human child seems otherwise unobtainable in his world, except by theft—and Rumpelstiltskin is not a night-thieving imp. That he craves a *human* child suggests some possibilities. A human baby might represent an especially desirable breed, a temptation known to people who smugly walk a rare dog breed as living jewelry—an immodesty visible in any large city. If not prideful, why bother obtaining a human? The story sidesteps an unspoken cannibalism—the witch's preferred cuisine in *Hansel and Gretel* or the Giant in *Jack and the Beanstalk* who gloats that he'll "grind your bones to make my bread"—but something else drives him to seek a distinctive luxury item. The story hints at another likelihood: Rumpelstiltskin is a unique being. There are no females of his kind with whom to mate.

It's hard to think of which is sadder, that he is personally incapable of procreation or that Rumpelstiltskin represents the last of a soon-to-be-extinct race. Either case flattered the storytellers. Fairyfolk especially esteemed the children that women abundantly produced and accordingly children were preemptively guarded against curses, spells, or abduction by fairyfolk who prized them. (They could also be seized by Jews and Gypsies, those other mysterious races.) Human infants crawling around their mother's feet tantalized non-humans as an extravagant commodity more precious than gold to beings who could conjure unlimited wealth. The story assumes and reinforces that message. Because creating a baby exceeds his magic, to Rumpelstiltskin the gold he gives the girl means nothing; in effect, the story that apparently marvels at gold and magic really extols motherhood. The spinnstube's women created a story in self-praise. Absent from the tale themselves—except as a hapless surrogate spinner—the spinnstube framed their spinning sisters as the real heroes. They endure men. They make children. They spin. To aid their mutual survival they regale comrades with stories of potency, and its opposite, that rewards motherhood.

A father engendered the girl, and the miller's powers of procreation rest implicit— he a virile male. The King impregnates his Queen, demonstrating his potency when his royal child issues from her womb. Three generations of potent males line one side of the ledger: the Miller; his son-in-law, the King; his grandson, the infant Prince, whose potency remains to be proved but is presumed healthy. Counterpoised to this trio, a male without a positive relationship to fecundity, Rumpelstiltskin, lacks any sexual connection to the Miller's Daughter. That's neither a small nor universally accepted notion. Recently authors argued that "in contrast to earlier versions, the Grimms' 1857 narrative moves away from [emphasizing] women's productivity to their reproduction, thus naturalizing the protagonist's persecution to the point that scholars have seen the villain in this tale as her 'helper.'"[17] If the story's only female apparently monopolizes fecundity then moral weight shifts from Rumpelstiltskin as helper to outright villain. Things are not that simple. Male reproductive competence conceals women's real concern.

The King virtually rapes the girl—for what is sex under threat of execution but rape? She could not recoil from her sovereign even if she shuns the job of Queen. Her father indentures her. Rumpelstiltskin saves her. True, his fee was high but the spinnstube's ladies knew that as fiber workers essential to their community they were valued only slightly while as mothers of male heirs their worth was payable in gold, up to the price of a kingdom—ask Anne Boleyn whose offspring, short a Y chromosome, became Elizabeth I but cost mommy her head.

A mother's pricelessly fruitful womb might yield a realm's or common family's male heir. But "even" a female child exceeded Rumpelstiltskin's powers in a story that invidiously demonstrates that, like every male, Rumpelstiltskin depended on a woman's fertility. The fairytale nicely balanced many considerations with keen-eyed reporting on the unvarnished state of affairs as Rumpelstiltskin's payment, the royal baby, completes the male spectrum: father, husband, son. Only relationship to a female defines these conditions. (Other functional male roles—brother, uncle, or cousin—reside outside the tale, as affiliation creates them, not direct lineal sexual descent.) Exclusively with a woman's aid a father gains a new title when previously he was called but a man; husband does not exist without wife; son is impossible without mother. In contrast to the story's three-part division of male roles, all female avatars combine in the idealized Miller's Daughter. She progresses from a maiden-daughter, becomes a women-wife, a mother (and also a Queen, the grandest administrative expression of a people's household).

In the story's aftermath, which commences as the tale ends in a raucous scene, the three males fade into insignificance. The Miller's Daughter stands alone, triumphant, hearing or not her court's approval, if they are present. Yet her fertility's victory over impotence depends on another's mercy. Unlike the rapacious King, Rumpelstiltskin does not seduce the girl. Neither does he enslave her for a fixed period. He does not enchant her to do his bidding. These "usual" options would be useless to him. He needs neither a slave (as he can accomplish whatever he wants) nor a sex-slave/concubine. Nothing to him would be more useless than a mistress. Since he cannot employ her sexually he neither requests, nor does the miller's girl volunteer, sexual favors. Generally speaking, he is competent at trades the world will pay for as Rumpelstiltskin first barters a few trinkets for his labor to accustom the girl to doing business. Neither her guardian angel nor fairy godmother, his services are not free. Here's the tale's keen-eyed observation about the sex-trade: it's highly asymmetric.

Even among healthy and handsome specimens, males are not well, or often, paid for heterosexual prowess—by a long margin compared to females. (That bitter joke lurks at the heart of the 1969 movie *Midnight Cowboy* made from Leo Herlihy's novel.) Rumpelstiltskin's charms consist solely of a provider's. Seducing the girl in the only way he can, he entices her into the world of commerce. Finally, the Miller's Daughter catches on and under maximum duress agrees to offer the sole item he cares about. On the third night of magical spinning, divested of anything of value she had brought into the castle, she moans that "I have nothing left that I could give to you", and Rumpelstiltskin presents his first and only proposition, "Then promise that when you become queen, your first child will belong to me". Magic can apparently compel some but not all things, the story teaches.

With word-magic or the proper rituals mortals can summon the gods but nothing will hoist a droopy dick. That cruel joke went around the spinnstube. The story mocked flawed males' antics. Yet, unlike the Miller or the King Rumpelstiltskin is not morally defective but physically. If the phallus is often an aggressor the limp penis is despicable, even dismissible—a disdain that paints Rumpelstiltskin's otherwise seemingly generous character. This story portrays women's revenge. This tale relates how the competent and proudly self-sufficient are brought low to obtain a child, women's purview.

How Rumpelstiltskin Gained a Bad Reputation

Because he wishes the contract honored and delivery of the child he was promised, Rumpelstiltskin appears vengeful or malevolent, which seems unfair. Viewing him as hateful grew into a widespread misapprehension. Recognizing him as an English word the *OED* defines Rumpelstiltskin as "The name of a vindictive dwarf in [a] German folk-tale". Why vindictive? What retaliation does Rumpelstiltskin take? On the contrary, he proposes a second chance, an exit clause.

Rumpelstiltskin generously offers to disobligate the Queen from any payment from a contract that spared her life and bought her new-minted nobility. If he were really a scoundrel Rumpelstiltskin would never accede to this re-negotiation. When things go bad he just leaves, exacting no penalty or reprisal. Despite his leniency, many judge him harshly.[iii] The unjust view of his malevolence prevailed and by the twentieth century's first decade an otherwise sympathetic book illustrator—unsurpassed for exposing the tale's dark magic—could be faulted for concentrating on "the elvish character of many" of the Grimms' "stories [that] precisely fits Mr. [Arthur] Rackham's talent",

> and the illustrator . . . is naturally at home with Rumpelstiltskin, the evil fairies and the witches who figure so largely in German folk tales . . . Mr. Rackham . . . has made himself an adept in creating oddity and ugliness, but he seems to have lost at the same time something of his power over human beauty. . . . He can invent inimitable dwarfs and gnomes and evil spirits, but he is rarely happy with his heroes and heroines[18]

With Arthur Rackham as their guide the general imagination crafted poor Rumpel-stiltskin as the opposite of a hero, though he saves the day from human's cupidity. He averted a catastrophe made and abetted by (male) mortals. Pigeonholed among the "evil fairies" he became an oddly Germanic diabolic figure, his strangeness, purely ugly—not a tolerable "difference".

Recognizing how Rumpelstiltskin entered English the OED further notes that the name is "used allusively" in what can only be called a completely modern perversion. Apparently George Orwell first used the name that way in 1949 when emigrant Rumpelstiltskin found unsteady employment in another language after the Grimms unintentionally created a word in English. Rumpelstiltskin now lives among us a vital expression, a universally known story. He paid dearly for his resurrection.

A prominent scholar was mystified by any "concern for a villain whose name is just as meaningless as the scholarship that has been absorbed in naming him".[19] That seems an uncharitable judgment. He can be invoked properly, with precise reference to his story and his role in it, or Rumpelstiltskin can be conjured inappropriately with ill-fitting acquired connotations. Used accurately, like a chemical whose properties cannot be exchanged with any other, requires knowing the word's proper implementation and contrary to common usage Rumpelstiltskin was neither a rascal nor brute. Degraded without warrant, he betrayed no one. He only tried to correct a defect over which he had no control. This requires understanding him as neither a "villain" nor as somebody whose "name is . . . meaningless". So, then, what is he?

---

iii. Perhaps his lenient gesture, like those of other semi-articulate literary monsters—Quasimodo's awkward fondness for Esmeralda or the Beast's tortured love of Beauty—demonstrates Rumpelstiltskin's fundamental affection for the girl. His relenting suggests a natural tenderness, even sympathy, for her situation. We'll never know. When he arrives to claim the baby that represents his agreed-upon fee the Queen checkmates him only because he yields to her request to re-negotiate.

Notes

1. Speaking lines written by Mario Puzo, Michael Corleone recalls that his father, Don Corleone, "made him an offer he couldn't refuse"; subsequently Don Corleone repeats his proposal, "I'm gonna make him an offer he won't refuse". Michael then, when forcing a LasVegas hotel buy out, repeats the line which reappears in several variations throughout *The Godfather* epic. Long before Mario Puzo wrote about, or Marlon Brando portrayed, the Godfather Rumpelstiltskin offered a contract the girl couldn't refuse. The bargain carried fine print and consequences beyond her reckoning, the kind of deal that Faust entered.
2. In a grand contract Agamemnon knowingly traded a daughter at Aulis for a wind to drive his ships. He believed he made a bitter but necessary deal with fate. Unbeknownst to mortals Agamemnon set into motion his own death delayed by a decade, then his wife's murder as retaliation and her lover's revenge murder, slain by the king's son and daughter. Such mythic irony served as intentionally pedagogic, as the lesson taught by Midas or Jephthah (1 Judges 11:30–31). Rash promises and vows frame time-bound mortals who cannot guess what details and unforeseeable consequences they have omitted from the bargain. The limits of human understanding inform the "three wishes" situation, often a joke, when the second and third are squandered to cancel the imprudent first wish granted. So essayed was the essence of the concept of Justice.
3. McGlathery (1991, p. 177).
4. Stewart (2003, p. 138).
5. Tatar (1987, p. 124). The Miller's Daughter remains a blank although some supposed her a richer construction. While Rumpelstiltskin's figure depicts established characteristics, "Not so with the heroine. Although she is almost always a young girl of humble origins, her other attributes and abilities change dramatically from one tale to the next" (Tatar Ibid.). When the girl changes radically we are dealing with a different story.
6. Taylor (1920, p. 148). In Taylor's day mills were still mainly water-driven. Some (more in Europe than America) were wind-powered, while newly instituted steam-driven mills were a rarity.
7. Smith and Simmons (1983, p. 382). The authors continue in the managerial vein: "The poor father may be taken as a metaphor for the mid-level administrators in a cumbersome public service bureaucracy who were responsible for creating a new service organization in an ronment increasing demand for service and limited resources".
8. Tatar (1987, p. 123).
9. Taylor (1823/1920, p. 150).
10. In Disney's *Sorcerer's Apprentice*—one section within the 1940 compilation *Fantasia*, an octet of animated novellas—the glowering wizard, a father-figure, at first trusts his assistant. Betrayed, the wizard first remedies the physical catastrophe then corrects his pupil, his chastening viewed as just and paternal.
11. Spitz (1991, p. 69).

    As in many of childhood's first experiences with art, the encounter can be terrifically moving even if the reasons for its effectiveness feel vague. Such potent feelings are scary and exhilarating if the artistic means rest utterly beyond what a child can analyze. Some prior world of experience antecedent to the artwork (fairytale) lend great depth of feeling to early introductions to genuine art. The qualities marbling Rumpelstiltskin are carried thereafter in the hearts of the attentive listener and disentangling those clotted meanings that reflect on impending adulthood is no light matter.
12. A bit to the north of where the Grimms were working, the Dane (poet, playwright, author of travelogues and novels but especially fairytales) Hans Christian Andersen (1805–1875) earned immortality for stories whose characters and structures derive from traditional tales as told in the spinnstuben. His indoctrination into this world was twofold.

    First, although Andersen's father (Hans Christian, Sr.) had received only the most elementary education he read to his son—especially stories from the *Arabian Nights*. He thereby introduced his son to the world of literature, a craft that offered the boy a path out of wretched obscurity and his detested lower-class existence. With a personality as Romantic as Brentano's, after his father died in 1816 the dreamy youth's further descent paradoxically opened to him an unusual course illuminated by his talent.

Andersen's now-widowed mother (Anne Marie Andersdatter) was uneducated and worked as a washerwoman. His autobiography (translated by Mary Howitt, 1799–1888, as *The True Story of My Life: A Sketch*) relates how,

> After my father's death I was entirely left to myself. My mother went out washing. I sat alone at home. . . . There dwelt in our neighborhood the widow of a clergyman [and] This lady opened to me her door, and hers was the first house belonging to the educated class into which I was kindly received. The deceased clergyman had written poems, and had gained a reputation in Danish literature. His spinning songs were at that time in the mouths of the people.

So embraced by an educated widow Andersen heard a literary version of spinning songs after industrialization had begun to wipe clean of folktales the urban collective memory of such common rural pastimes. This model of a literary version of folkloric forms, Andersen rode to immortality.

Actually, Andersen heard the ancient stories told by old rural women who had been gathered in the spinning room of the asylum where his grandmother worked. As he related it: "Close beside the place where the leaves were burned, the poor old women had their spinning-room. I often went in there, and was very soon a favorite". He frequented the place and listened to stories that few men had heard in their original context, an experience that imbued his own later work with a zesty authenticity. Compared to the Grimms, who gathered their stories from a handful of sources, Andersen was inspired by a deep personal knowledge of the spinnstube's many wiles. The countless hours and evenings spent in just such a spinnstube at the asylum contrasts to Dortchen Wild's experience; she was very likely the brother's main channel of transmission for this fairytale. So, we are left with a paradox: Andersen composed new stories as autographic literature although he represented that rare male regularly admitted to the female intimacy of the spinnstube while Ms. Wild—who, when a girl, may have entered a circle of women spinners but had subsequently moved into the middle-class living room—became the actual source for her memories of a former life.

13. I know of only one other significant artwork that regards people who are, to a person, morally repugnant. In Sam Peckinpah's *The Wild Bunch* (1969) for over two hours not a single respectable human being appears on the screen, adult or child. The film shows no black-and-white contrasts of good-and-evil but only beautifully nuanced shades of nasty. Likewise for the tale of Rumpelstiltskin. Great art rarely presents obvious contrasts, a trait that keeps Rumpelstiltskin ever-fresh.

14. And more than the Jew/Gentile contest on which the modern and especially post-Holocaust intelligence fixes, the play seems principally a competition of Urban/Male vs. Rural/Female with the latter, Portia, winning Shakespeare's heart. Whatever we think or suppose we know of him, Shakespeare expressed his preference by quitting London and retiring to the countryside.

Shakespeare would probably be surprised at the enormous recent attention directed at Shylock's Jewishness (that echoed Marlowe's *Jew of Malta* with Shakespeare's slightly kinder, but still cruelly comical, version). To the play's author Shylock seemed merely a plot device. The former lad of Stratford had been drilled in elementary Latin and who subsequently excelled with adroit language play. As an adult playwright recalled he Cicero's praise for the "little book of the Twelve Tables [that epitomized] the fountains and sources of the laws [that may] assuredly . . . surpass the libraries of all the philosophers" (*De Oratore* 1.44). When it came time to account for Shylock's atavistically heathen rage, the Stratford lad remembered The Twelve Tables edicts about debtors:

> One who has confessed a debt . . . shall have thirty days to pay it in. After that forcible seizure of his body is allowed. . . . On the third market day let [his creditors] divide his body among them. If they cut more or less than each one's share it shall be no crime.

(Table III: 1–2)

15. Hahn (2005, p. 149).
16. McGlathery (1991, p. 177).
17. Bacchilega (1993, pp. 6–7). Bacchilega continues, noting that, "[b]y refocusing our critical attention on the value of spinning and the changing conditions for women spinners during the industrial revolution, this essay identifies a relevant socio-economic context shaping the protagonist's persecution".
18. *The Burlington Magazine* (December 1909, p. 172).
19. Zipes (1993, pp. 43–44). Zipes' ire was raised at the categorization of the Rumpelstiltskin story as tale type 500, "The Name of the Helper", a classification that accentuates his assistance when Zipes would prefer to seem him as victimizing the girl.

6

SUPERNATURAL ZOOLOGY

He's Not a Troll or a Dwarf

> A tiny man walked into the room.

Aristocrats favored gaudy self-aggrandizing-epics. Peasants' stories rewarded figures who resembled the tellers. Regardless of when they were first transcribed, and by whom, the Grimms' stories, "had their origin in peasant culture that arose in conscious opposition to the feudal state's ruling class".[1] As a delicious escape from tedious chores and a occasionally violent world spinnstuben dispensed mockery. Their ridicule could assuage long-simmering anger at causes amply deserving retribution: aristocracy, clergy, husbands, men. Necessarily, that anger could only simmer: retribution languished, centuries deferred for self-preservation. With drab reality relieved by the Church's promise of a glorious afterlife the women themselves conjured a parallel world of fun and justice. Their imagined world empowered peasants and sometimes showered them with riches and ennoblement: the quiz show for guessing Rumpelstiltskin's hidden name.

If too rarely in reality, in these stories the peasantry's rulers, ponderous figures in armor mounted on immense horses, could be bested with wit. This lesson supplies the most robust strand in Aesop's fables whenever a clever but puny animal-surrogate defeated the baffled mighty. The pattern seems universal.[2] But Rumpelstiltskin conforms to none of the customary types of weefolk. Those exotic creatures—who, rarely observed by humans, scurry about while peeping from underbrush—may help or hinder mortals. Taken together the tales preserved a menagerie of lively creatures who flitted through shadows and could navigate the underworld. Some were large (the diverse races of giants, ogres, and dragons) but other creatures passed unnoticed in the landscape until their affairs intersected with human beings. Though apparently plentiful such rarely seen beings enjoyed starring roles alongside slim princesses and handsome leading men. Some who shared Rumpelstiltskin's diminutive size occasionally displayed their varied talents and keen wit when trying to wheedle benefits from humans or ogres they could not hope to overcome by strength alone. Yet Rumpelstiltskin resembles no racially identified group among the fairyland's folk. Some miniature supernaturals exhibited one or more of Rumpelstiltskin's characteristics but none bore all his traits. In many ways, he's in a category by himself and apparently belongs to no dwarfish nation. If Rumpelstiltskin had real ancestors, rooting through his family tree should uncover them, based on family resemblances.

While Rumpelstiltskin might conform to the general class of "fairies" his character never softened over time and he escaped being embroiled in twee Victorian *fairyland*. On either side of the English Channel versions of that aesthetic prevailed until high modernity swept away the mainstream taste for spiritualist pseudo-science. Superstitious peasant kitsch, part-and-parcel of the Romantic-age, inspired the Grimms, Richard Wagner, and a host of others.[3] The nineteenth century portrayed fairies in children's stories that ignored their formerly sinister reputation as often dreaded and powerfully cruel sprites. In olden times fairies might, at their whim, befriend or prove dangerous to humans. Middle English "fairie" derived from Old French faerie, from feie, fee, which descended from the Latin word *Fata* (from "fatum" meaning fate) the goddess of fate.[4] Distantly related to the Fates who spun life's thread such formerly non-trivial beings were taken seriously.

Beginning in the middle ages fairies assumed sometimes-diminutive human form. They dwelled on earth, like mortals, and they possessed magic powers often used compassionately toward humans with whom they lived in close relationship. Though Rumpelstiltskin lives apart from people and he can act compassionately, yet fairies are different beings from him. Fairies could be of human size or less than 3 inches (7.5 cm). Distinct from gnomes, these sprites often lived underground or within stone heaps where they guarded cached treasure—the medieval recollection of randomly discovered Roman or Viking hoards. Rumpelstiltskin lives in a house in the forest, a dwelling that distinguished him from a typical fairy. (While several herbs were potent against fairies they so cherished other plants that mistreating these herbs could bring down the fairies' revenge. Yet no residual Druidic or arboreal themes color the Tale of Rumpelstiltskin: another vindication of his being a different race. He emerges not *of* nature or as its caretaker but an industrious and talented being who acts upon nature.) Not every little creature was a fairy. More than one tribe inhabited fairyland in both its Victorian and old-time versions. That imaginary place functioned less a unified nation than an empire.

Fairyland included varying types with diverging and often conflicting interests. They could be offended by humans' tomfoolery regarding inter-species relations. Some were imps, unsavory and evil creatures, but Rumpelstiltskin's mercy indicates he was not one.[5] Some were elves, lively and small, mischievous or malicious spirits in the form of tiny humans.[6] (Probably the only figure of this sort who remains robustly present: an adult conspiracy conveys an elf, Santa Claus, who transits childhood by an Underground Railroad of time, not space. Modern Santa arose in Victorian times; his cult sustains that febrile era's overwrought Romantic hopes against modernity's onslaught.[7] The craze for fairyland ranks among Victorianism's weirder aspects and to moderns may be the period's least accessible feature though not the most repugnant. If the once-vigorous races of fairyfolk saw what the Victorians did to them they'd be mortified, which may explain their scarceness these days.) Originally, a spirit of any kind, in later Germanic folklore elves became Lilliputian creatures classified as either fair-skinned "light" or "dark" elves who were black. But Rumpelstiltskin is presumably "flesh-colored". His story makes no mention of his skin tone.

Notably naughty and impulsive, though occasionally merciful or at least cooperative, elves could cause illness in humans and cattle. Like a burdensome night-visiting incubus, elves sometimes sat upon a sleeper's breast inciting bad dreams (the German word for nightmare, Alpdrücken, "elf-pressure", suggests a heart attack which victims describe as the feeling of an elephant sitting on your chest). But Rumpelstiltskin seems a homebody at night except when summoned by a distress call from the miller's daughter. By night elves stole human children to substitute changelings (an elf or fairy child); like Rumpelstiltskin, they tried to obtain human babies.[i] Why the fairyworld valued human babies at such a premium holds a flattering mirror to humanity, especially motherhood. This theme panders with self-congratulations on our species' desirability. That motif continued after rural fairytales gave way to industrialized entertainment; B-grade science-fiction movies depicted repulsive (never alluring) creatures flying across the universe (that is, entering our world from fairyland) trying to abscond with humans (usually white females for breeding—pure Rumpelstiltskin).[8] Neither willfully roguish nor capricious, Rumpelstiltskin hardly belongs to any elfin species.

Contrasting with agile elves and often beautiful fairies, gnomes (from the Greek Gnōmē, intelligence, from *gignōskein* "to know") appear in medieval mythologies as dwarfish and often physically deformed (usually hunchbacked) subterranean goblins. Gnomes guard mines of precious treasures deep in the earth.[9] Some gnomes lived in the ground but Rumpelstiltskin was not a gnome. He harbors no treasure but gives it away. Neither his actions nor appearance demonstrate that Rumpelstiltskin is a fairy, gnome, troll, elf, or any usual type. Perhaps related (on his mother's or father's side?) Rumpelstiltskin's unlikely to be a leprechaun or a pixie; he was thoroughly German before immigrating to the English-speaking world and neither Ireland nor Cornwall may claim his direct ancestors. And yet.

On first glance, Rumpelstiltskin might resemble a "kobold", ungovernable spirits who haunted dwellings in German folklore.[10] Like Rumpelstiltskin, temperamental kobolds can become outraged, but kobolds become most irate when not properly fed. I do not know how you feed a kobold, but probably like Santa Claus you leave out an offering.

---

i. The updated threat of unknown changelings (familiar faces substituted for unearthly ersatz versions) inserted into our surroundings provided splendidly spooky pleasure for multiple remakes of *Invasion of the Body Snatchers* (1956, 1978, 1993).

FIGURE 6.1 Olaus Magnus, *Gnome*, 1555.

It was easy to feed a Brownie—one of the small industrious fairies or hobgoblins that inhabited houses and barns in England and Scotland.[11] Their noisiness at night related them to a cluster of other supernatural miniature people, especially goblins who dedicated themselves to pestering a household by snatching nightclothes from sleeping people, moving furniture at night, banging on pots and pans, and then escaping without detection after noisily rapping on walls and doors.[12] This latter trait, a penchant for cacophony, deserves consideration.

Some supernatural beings, especially one class of raucous ghosts, haunted a locale or a particular family member. Known by their sounds, these were the *poltergeists* (from the German, Polter, noise or racket, or poltern, to knock, and Geist, spirit). Small but irritating occurrences, noises with invisible sources, had to be explained and disturbing sounds like an old house's creaking boards were attributed to poltergeists.[13] These boisterous spirits acted unpredictably and their cacophonous movements frequently sounded maddeningly repetitive.[14] They rarely meant to physically harm their targets but only to harass humans with unexplained creaking, exasperating rasping, indefinite rappings, nighttime scraping just loud enough to wake you, and grating—noises you could hear but whose source remained undetermined.

While they guaranteed a nuisance, poltergeists are not interesting because they annoyed people (Rumpelstiltskin exhibited no irritating sonic habits) or because their name migrated into English but because they supply a crucial link to their Germanic cousins, the ancestors to our story's lead character. So, what was Rumpelstiltskin supposed to be?

Gnomes and Others

Despite his size, his story does not describe Rumpelstiltskin as a dwarf. He presents no misshapen version of an outwardly handicapped or disfigured man. His impairment is real enough but invisible. Although the story never mentions Rumpelstiltskin exhibiting any deformity besides his paltry size, nevertheless Edgar Taylor's 1823 translation used the word "hobble" to describe Rumpelstiltskin's walk. If his gait falters, if he carries a hunchback, is crippled, or is a midget—such handicaps suggest impairments of strength and size, defects from robust manhood that qualified him for women's work. Accordingly, however rare a creature, Rumpelstiltskin cannot be characterized by dwarfism's abnormalities. The tiny man may belong to a type unknown, perhaps occurring nowhere else in fairytales.

Except for being height-challenged Rumpelstiltskin's normalcy befuddled academics who couldn't pigeonhole him; one scholar recognized Rumpelstiltskin's unique status but tried to resolve the problem by classifying him with a known, if inappropriate, ilk: "By far the most puzzling of the gnomes in the Grimms' collection is the dwarf in 'Rumpelstiltskin.'"[15] Rumpelstiltskin may be gnomic in his aphoristic way of speaking—terse, verging on riddles,[16] no-nonsense negotiations—but he is not of the cavern-dwelling race of short men called Gnomes. Rumpelstiltskin lives in the forest when not "on the job" solving people's problems or creating new ones. But gnomes typically guard treasure. Their shriveled appearance and great age (as portrayed by Richard Wagner's fog-dwelling Nebellungen) suggests that the formerly amorous gnomes traded worldly love for immortality.[17] For want of love they gain arcane wisdom to control glittering ancient hoards that drive mankind mad with longing. (The unearthed gold perhaps referred to the wealth of early medieval Burgundians or Norse hoardings.) Tolkien improved this riff by picturing that quintessence of yearning, Gollum, decaying with a drug-addict's rationalizations. According to this view a Gnome, or gnomehood, depicts a stage of devolution, a degenerative condition of physical and moral decay caused by bitterly rejecting love when first rebuffed. Rumpelstiltskin is not one of these creatures.

Rumpelstiltskin stands sentinel over no treasure but barters his skill for woman's fecundity. Disdainful of its value he gives away the spun gold he creates.[18] He does not hoard but proves generous.

Worldwide, numerous mythic traditions feature gnomish races who spurn love for wealth, traits that reverse Rumpelstiltskin's situation as an impotent workaholic who traded wealth for love (or at least love's product and principal insignia). He anticipated sad modern versions of a small toiling man without a lover but eager to gain the services of a Trophy Wife or, more precisely, her child. He labors but cannot procreate or, alternately, because he labors his heart has room for neither lust's energy nor love.

Spawned in an agricultural age when much of the population lived closely dependent on personally fostering growth and fecundity this fairytale addressed a difficult human truth, discussed in whispers, in the company of women, and then heavily coded. Before the late industrial era—that diverted emotion from attentive craft as piecemeal factory labor alienated pride in workmanship—women already knew the age-old afflic-tion. A hollow homelife foreshadowed interminable and thankless chores (including spinning) from which they were supposed to derive dignity and identity. Neglectful spouses, stingy of emotion or charm, were married to gain social promotion followed by a swarm of, perhaps unwanted, children who could, at least, award the pride of mother-hood as warrant against the curse of barrenness and the plight of spinsterhood. Long before the Romantic Novel's bitter lessons of loveless relationships, in simpler times amid cloud-dappled fields of wheat and flax, with sheep grazing in the background, women already knew their disquieting conundrum. Into such a world appeared this story's male helper. He establishes neither an emotional exchange nor sexual bargain. Certainly not a Gnome or any other obvious elfin type, in the richness of his psycho-logical situation, Rumpelstiltskin exceeds most folktales or even the thinly sketched personalities of pre-Renaissance literature.

What to Call a Unique Being?

The Grimms initially named their starring player Rumpelstilzchen, which translates from the German as "little stilt rattle". This seems nonsensical until, recalling the actions of a poltergeist, this word's implications spin as thread from the inchoate vocabulary mass on a linguistic distaff.

The brothers capriciously applied a word referring to a vertical post, specifically a stilt-pole that provides a building's structural support. A rumpelstilt or *rumpelstilz*, a stilt rattle(er) named a kind of noisy goblin called many things throughout Europe. This sprite made noises by rattling posts and rapping on planks, similar to a rumpelgeist (rat-tle ghost) or poltergeist (noisy ghost). In modern English this concept's only survivor is the talk-like-a-Pirate exclamation "(Well) shiver me timbers!" That phrase connotes something like "Well, I'll be!" because the news—like hearing a cannon-shot aimed at you or discovering that your ship's run aground—shook the whole vessel and disturbed the hearer's tranquility. A clue survives in the word, "rumpus", a riotously noisy distur-bance. Perhaps a fanciful construction, rumpus sounds like what a rumpelgeist would do.[19] Few similarities connect this ancestry with the Rumpelstiltskin we know and the discrepancies open a schism between his German and English versions.

Perhaps the Grimms interpolated the name Rumpelstilzchen to conform their dis-covery to a known Germanic pattern. But his English name resembles nothing else—a problem not of translation but of categorization. Many weefolk resembled Rumpel-stiltskin in some ways, but not others, or in every aspect. If some supernaturals exhibit a family resemblance none provides an exact fit. Rumpelstiltskin's supposed Germanic forebears possessed different temperaments, practiced dissimilar skills from his, and their stories assigned then folkloric commissions unlike the rescue job of the puny creature we know. The Grimms perhaps realized that they had appropriated an ancient name that contradicted this fairytale's character because, if they recognized the dissimilarity with their source, the brothers changed his name in successive editions of their stories.

With his translated name, English-speaking peoples adopted the Brothers Grimms' resurrected Rumpelstiltskin. That success in the Anglophone world might have surprised the Grimms but not disappointed them. They thereby achieved of one their goals: reversing literary and cultural entropy. If not a distantly remembered author's invention that diffused through a semi-literate population, the Brothers Grimm gathered a disordered and almost wispy allusion, personified as a figure who could sharply re-focus the fairytale's hidden references. The Grimms probably never understood the story's suggestive ramifications. That may not have been true of the group of women from whom they gathered the tale. Ultimately, the spinnstube's ladies proposed him as an example of someone to be used, mocked, and then dismissed—and for some women that represented an ideal of sexual power.

The Price of True Love

Absent from Rumpelstiltskin's story is True Love, that mainstay of fairytales.

The king does not love a miller's daughter; he performs no quest for her. Quite the contrary, she labors for him under duress. About as loveless a situation as imaginable, the tale involves various business transactions: trading labor (spinning gold for child-bearing after suspending a death sentence) with fringe benefits (elevation to highest nobility) and bartering (privileged information, Rumpelstiltskin's name) for a child. It's all so tawdry. If Sleeping Beauty's first night with her—probably exhausted—Prince passed as an actual snore—after he performed the requisite grueling quest for her—then the Miller's Daughter's first night with her king constituted violent ravishing. The choice of death or sex is usually considered rape and there is no reason to call it anything else in this story. Or in life.

The Queen does not love the King (which was never a queen's job regarding her spouse). She solely cherishes her child. Once crowned she may become the legally and church-sanctioned victim of sexual molestation of which Rumpelstiltskin is innocent. Castles and spinners' huts knew rapes and ravishments. Marriage for love was the exception.

Unlike warmly appealing fairytales the spinnstube's women did not devise the Tale of Rumpelstiltskin to essay the merits of true love, that tenderly imagined surcease from a sexual desert. At least some of them recognized life's everlasting anti-sensual attendants. They knew lack of desire when you'd prefer not to fake it. They suffered over-work that colored any welcome respite with lingering fatigue. And the spinnstube's women, like working women everywhere, endured drunken or brutish husbands seeking their own sexual release with scant thought of illness, birth, motherhood, child-rearing, and women's underrated economic contribution. The story entombs their dreariness. (Not that life was great for a male serf or peasant either, just vexed with different sorrows. The story treads a fine line between anti-male observations and its sly pro-woman feminism.) Romantic yearning, sexual delight, or marital companionship—all are absent for a good reason. Quality sex thrives on leisure but Rumpelstiltskin represents an inveterate worker.[20] When not reduced by religion or necessity to grinding child-begetting, sex is play(ful), ideally "recreational" and famously enjoyable. But impotent Rumpelstiltskin cannot engage in procreative sex, so he works. Maybe it's the other way round. those who work unceasingly cannot consider sex or are too weary to perform.

Symptomatic of work-induced fatigue that could cause impotence, Rumpelstiltskin labors to "self-actualize", as his therapist might have told him. He boasts of being a competent brewer—no mean skill-set in a society that hardly drank water, a questionably hygienic liquid—when, at meals of the highborn or low, beer offered a sanitary quaff, especially in Germany as the medieval English favored ale. That he will "*tomorrow* brew" suggests that after his work on behalf of the Miller's Daughter he plans to service another client requiring beverage. Rumpelstiltskin's efforts feed and clothe himself and sometimes his customers. But Rumpelstiltskin chooses his 'clients' and their tasks, they don't hire him.

It's uncertain for what he ultimately works and how he decides which cases to take on, at what price, which to defer, and which fretful mortals he will ignore. Rumpelstiltskin lives as a free-agent.[ii] (Since Rumpelstiltskin aligns with no group—troll, gnome, elf, imp, dwarf, or leprechaun—he makes his own rules unrepresented by a trade-union's hierarchy. In contrast, most supernatural beings operate by rules so regulated that merely naming a type sets limits on their powers and assumes their fatal weaknesses—few mistake werewolves for vampires, and so forth. The moon governs werewolves; giants and ogres are usually stupid; vampires avoid daylight; zombies crave certain culinary preferments, etc). Rumpelstiltskin roams unconstrained by other creature's shop stewards or guild traditions.

We are not told how Rumpelstiltskin, a singular creature, learns of the plight of the miller's daughter, or anybody else he may choose to assist or comfort. Does he have phenomenal natural hearing? Does he, like God, answer prayer? But he attends to her, compensated with various payments of increasing value, unlike a slave who works without pay or a genie who toils under a spell's compulsion. His brewing, spinning, baking, levitation, self-sufficiency, and supernatural hearing and competencies he has mastered of many trades—none of this, unfortunately for him, spares him final, inescapable, humiliation. Within blossoming fecund nature he wanders barren. Meanwhile, if the Miller's Daughter ever heard of True Love nobody mentions it, which leaves Rumpelstiltskin's story bereft of one of fairytales' principal engines. But a different force moves the plot.

Rumpelstiltskin's need for a surrogate procreator means that without mentioning longing or pleasure the king performed sexual congress for him. Rumpelstiltskin was delegated to do a woman's spinning while the King was delegated a man's role in screwing.

---

ii. Before any tight-lipped trench-coated private eye with a sketchy background took on a murky case that began with a desperate dame, a class of private elves heard anguished women's hard-boiled stories. Some bedded their clients, some didn't. That's the way it is when you reach out for extra-legal aid. If he had a business card it would read "Rumpelstiltskin Private Eye—Have Spoon, Will Travel". A sucker for a sob story, he's a tough guy. He's a freelancer without a girl Friday. He relies on women for nothing but trouble and to incubate children.

Notes

1. Tatar (1997, p. 9).

   For untold centuries, Rumpelstiltskin's Germanic ancestors lurked in folklore's background. Feared or cherished, these creatures occupied a special place in the story-tellers' affections. Beloved bit players in regional genres, the tales' little people represented the triumph of intelligence over brawn whenever supernatural wee-folk displaced hulking champions for top billing. Frequently their adept wordplay and dexterous manual skills prevailed over brute force, a trait that evidenced the story-teller's sympathies for feudal society's largely defenseless under-class.

2. Darling of Southwestern Amerindian tales, the trickster Coyote lives by his wits, a figure beloved for his shrewdness. Such agile trickster characters rarely survived urbanism and industrialization. As smokestacks sprouted from the landscape Rumpelstiltskin's story spread in fame, then flourished when read in bedrooms far from shadowy forests through which princes might ride or goblins dwell. Rumpelstiltskin's new urban acquaintances likely never saw a spinning chamber but—though deprived of the rural background and the originating language's flavor—industrial-era childhoods welcomed the story.

3. Not only did High Art's practitioners (Wagner) become enmeshed in the Victorian fairy aesthetic of Romanticism but the aesthetic happily accommodated outright mental cases. The lunatic artist Richard Dadd (1817–86) painted in an effort compatible with his contemporaries the Grimms. After he had illustrated (1842) *The Book of British Ballads*, but while confined in a psychiatric hospital, he mainly pictured minute details of the Victorian fairy world.

4. Fairies appeared either beneficently, as beautifully dainty and ageless winged women clothed in gleaming white gossamer clothing, or mischievously as the tiny creatures protective of the household hearth (formerly the purview of the Roman goddess *Vesta* or the Vedic *Agni*). Because fairies could manifest themselves as comely or handsome beings (soulless like animals) who lived much longer than humans, such loveliness disqualifies Rumpelstiltskin from conforming to them. Nobody ever called Rumpelstiltskin attractive.

   Though fairies are reputed to snatch children and leave changeling substitutes, Rumpelstiltskin used no stealth trying to obtain a child. He had no intention of planting a counterfeit. (Fairies also abduct adults, taking them to fairyland, a kind of pre-Christian abode of the dead from which humans could not return if they ate or drank there—as in the myth of Persephone.) A Celtic variant of a creature found throughout Eurasia, fairies and their lore abound in Ireland, Cornwall, Wales, and Scotland. Part of Ireland's national tradition celebrated fairies as leprechauns who appear as a dwarf humans characteristically sporting green clothes and hair.

5. A class of minor demon, the Imp, was thought to be the Devil's offspring. Now an imp exclusively refers to a small and low-ranking demon, perhaps less abstractly and more malevolently a fiend, or a mischievous child more commonly and colloquially an urchin. The ancient but obscure word for this class of creature—that derives from Germanic etymology hailing from Latin and Greek—meaning "to graft" was, in obsolete usage, a young plant or tree's shoot. Hence in an equally long-outmoded usage "to imp" served a transitive verb that meant to splice or graft. The term might therefore refer to a sapling (from Middle English impe, from Old English impa, from the extinct verb impian to imp), or a sucker, slip, scion. Eventually this juvenile status referred to a child, specifically of the devil, or of hell. While the mischievous imp compares to a fairy or fiend, imps were specifically smaller demons of lesser potency and rather than unfailingly evil or destructive imps could play harmless tricks and deceptions on humans. Though always small and unattractive they were sometimes even helpful to people yet imps specialized in disturbing pranks like misleading travelers in unfamiliar territory or switching babies. Nevertheless, since they are primarily both small and immature Rumpelstiltskin could not be an imp as he is no child; though diminutive he is a fully adult male. This class of creature refers to a minor irritant having very little diabolical power to do wholesale evil; so, once again it seems, Rumpelstiltskin belongs to none of fairytales' common

species. A close relation to the Prince of Darkness, the Devil might be expected to know an imp's name, if Rumpelstiltskin is one.

6. The name Elf comes from Middle and Old English ælf, ãklu to Old Norse alfr, perhaps from Latin albus, white (as in "Albus Dumbeldore"). Though elves eventually lost their status as a distinct race and blurred into the general category of fairies, Johann Wolfgang von Goethe's poem "Der Erlkönig" ("The Elf King") and J.R.R. Tolkien's *Lord of the Rings* (1954–55) considered elves as a separate identity and so ought we to figure out if Rumpelstiltskin was one.

7. Riding the wave of this sentiment, Tinker Bell earned a starring role in J. M. Barrie's epic of *Peter Pan* (1902–04) the tale of a pre-pubescent youth subject to two females' otherwise quite grown-up jealous territorialism. In his dreamworld of Neverland all manner of magical creatures surround Peter who, unlike Rumpelstiltskin, does not need a child, being one. Victorians heard Peter diagnose the mortally stricken Tinker Bell, "she says she thinks she could get well again if children believed in fairies! Do you believe in fairies? Say quick that you believe! If you believe clap your hands!" (lines 276–280). That line would fall flat if written today yet the plea echoes from venerable theater. Amazed at the lifelike statue of his sixteen-years lost wife, Queen Hermione of *The Winter's Tale*, the Sicilian noblewoman Paulina implores King Leontes (5:3) and the gathered courtiers, surrogates for the audience out front, that ("she could get well again") to animate the sculpture:

> It is required
> You do awake your faith. Then all stand still;
> On: those that think it is unlawful business
> I am about, let them depart.

Unlike Santa Claus, in whom adults don't "really" believe but must pretend to act on belief, if Barrie's audience actually thought their kids were being exposed to Black Magic: children in tow they'd race for the exits. In Shakespeare's day magic threatened a more serious matter.

8. Baby-barter endures into the modern world—in many forms. Science-fiction creatures from another world enter our space from impossibly far away and typically come from a "dying planet" a situation like Rumpelstiltskin's sterility (he may be the last of his race) and his abrupt entry from an unimaginable world. Countless "B" movies feature an extraterrestrial character in a rubber suit (or a "monster" like King Kong, 1933) carrying a limp or unconscious—screaming and struggling or wide-eyed with terror—(white) woman showing considerable leg. And, after a generation of Cold War inspired fear-mongering, this situation was semi-parodied in Nicholas Roeg's *The Man Who Fell to Earth* (1976), with its beguiling and blankly attractive visitor. He too arrives from a dying world, an arid place of obstructed fertility. Like Rumpelstiltskin, Roeg's visitor performs industrial wonders and for his efforts is rejected by the human female who witnesses his true nature and is relegated to a kind of exile (which provides the skeleton of Rumpelstiltskin's story). The rebuttal in the movie *Starman*, 1984, posits no monster for inter-species fecundity. This Rumpelstiltskin-story's construction sells popcorn, unconsciously suggests a date's exciting desirability, and glorifies the movie-goers' species, just as the spinnstube's ladies planted women's self-worth in their tale.

9. The Swiss alchemist "Paracelsus" (1493–1541) (whose real name was the improbably wonderful Theophrastus Bombastus von Hohenheim) coined the word in French from the new Latin *gnomus* to describe creatures resembling dry, gnarled old man who could move through solid earth as fish move through water—clearly not Rumpelstiltskin's mode of travel nor was his neighborhood underground.

10. Like Rumpelstiltskin kobolds helped with household chores and sometimes sang to children. Well, Rumpelstiltskin is helpful, and he sings too. Rumpelstiltskin, like a kobold, grants a home's occupants beneficial services like Rumpelstiltskin's spinning. But kobolds also disobediently hide household and farm tools. Kobolds are likely to kick over stooping persons. Some kobolds dwell in caves and mines. Others frighten unfaithful wives. And some witness the clergy's secret sins. (Their equivalents, Cornish knockers, were benevolent mine spirits who guided Cornish tin-miners to the ore they supplied for Greek and Roman bronzes.)

11. Disliking other gifts, Brownies relished the cream, bread, or milk left for them, but Rumpelstiltskin mentions none of these human delicacies as favorites. We have no idea what snacks he preferred. Rarely seen, brownies were heard at night when they helpfully cleaned and did other housework, sometimes waggishly leaving a room disheveled.

12. Casually speaking, Rumpelstiltskin might have been a goblin (from Middle English *gobelin* via Middle French from Medieval Latin *gobelinus*) a name derived from Greek *kobalos*, rogue. In European folklore, goblins were ugly or grotesque sprites. Their homeliness recalls how the miller's ungrateful daughter tacitly rejects Rumpelstiltskin even before he offers his companionship—it's just out of the question for him to propose friendship. (A sub-species, the *hobgoblin* was a particularly mischievous goblin.) Unlike Rumpelstiltskin, goblins are naughty, malicious, and sometimes are actually evil, which Rumpelstiltskin is not. But goblins are wandering sprites and Rumpelstiltskin, if he has a home base (his hut in the forest) wanders afar when summoned. He rides into town, as unexpected and useful as the Lone Ranger, and leaves again having solved one problem but creating others.
    Goblins lived in grottoes, in which Rumpelstiltskin did not.

13. Indistinguishable from German poltergeists, other belligerent or naughty brownies like mummarts carried local English names: in Yorkshire, boggarts, and in Scotland, bogles; hence a bogey, a variation on bogle, a frightening bogeyman, or a bugaboo. These relate, perhaps as first-cousins, to the Germanic pophart or poppart called rapper or thumper.

14. In olden times, this useful family of sprites served as a pre-modern way to understand the world. Unlike the Dodo but imaginary, poltergeists did not go extinct but survived into the twentieth century. In a description of the waning relationship between Sigmund Freud and his then-disciple Karl Jung we learn that in March 1909, "Jung visited Freud in Vienna, and in Freud's office the two had engaged in a heated debate about the veracity of occult phenomena. While Jung, an advocate of the paranormal, was driving home his point, the men heard a loud noise behind a bookcase, which Jung described as a poltergeist. Freud denied the supernatural origin of the noise, but Jung correctly predicted the mysterious sound's recurrence. Freud was reluctantly convinced". But only temporarily. (Matthew von Unwerth [2005] pp. 41–42.) When it comes to poltergeists, by their sound ye shall know them.

15. James M. McGlathery [1991], p. 177.

16. Short aphoristic verses asserting traditional moral wisdom characterized Gnomic Poetry. The biblical book of Proverbs represents a collection of gnomes. The Greek word gnome means "moral aphorism" or "proverb" either to goad laudable action (what one ought to do) or to indicate a truth. From the early Greek writings of Hesiod to Homer, the sixth-century-BCE poets Solon and Simonides, and the elegiac couplets of Theognis and Phocylides—all display a propensity for gnomic verse. Aphorisms collected into anthologies, called gnomologia, became instruction manuals for the young. Compiled in the 5th century C.E., the gnomologia by Stobaeus was widely circulated throughout the Middle Ages. That book may account for, and provide the model of, the frequent gnomes in Old English epics and lyric poetry, while Old English gnomes were themselves collected in the *Exeter Book* and the 11th-century Cotton Psalter.

17. German Romanticism's principal musical exponent, Richard Wagner (1813–1883) immersed himself in Scandinavian, Icelandic and German sagas. From these materials he drew plots for his gigantic Ring cycle of operas while developing some of his loonier ideas that dilated on nationality and race. The crucial scene is described when: "[At] the sight of the gold and the talk of the [Rhein] maidens ... a change [overcomes the horny and uncouth gnome] Alberecht. Since his love is scorned, and with the gold he can win the mastery of the world, he will foreswear love and win power" (Ernest Newman [1928/30] p. 164).
    Guided by the lure of riches and work, gnomes are the opposite of Buddhism's "enlightened-beings", the Bodhisatvas, whose spiritual knowledge translates into exemplary glowing health (buff bodies), temporal powers, and a take-it-or-leave-it attitude toward wealth (desire). Rumpelstiltskin represents neither a gnome who suffers from spiritual deformity's outward symptoms nor is he a misshapen dwarf. If he were easily categorized, Rumpelstiltskin would not be "By far the most puzzling" little man of the Brothers Grimm.

18. To those who spawned this tale the idea of "creating" wealth did not mean what the phrase now indicates. A gold-based society can only increase its wealth by finding more of the precious metal—as Rumpelstiltskin does to the delight of the king. This quest kept alchemists in business for centuries as they promised to create gold without having to mine it. Alternately, you could trade for it with other nation-states to augment your hoard, as medieval German linen exports to Spain returned a balance-of-trade surplus in gold. Or you could steal it with statecraft's age-old strategy of warfare (organized theft). But to moderns there's another idea for wealth-creation. Instead of viewing wealth as a static quantity (gold, for example) and squabbling over slices of a society's unchanging pie—make the pie bigger. Rumpelstiltskin creates wealth. In economic terms he hoards no capital but introduces new gold (an extractive industry) into the system while brewing or baking (skill-based manufacturing) to generate pristine value-added riches that dilate the available asset pool. Rumpelstiltskin is a Keynesian!

    In a modern, dynamic, worldwide invention creates more wealth, as do introduced efficiencies, or innovation. This distinction separates the present of human possibility from an otherwise psychologically accurate, and surprisingly modern, symbolization of human relations in Rumpelstiltskin's story, a characterization that, for all its psychological truth, remains firmly rooted in a stagnant medieval worldview.

19. An unruly spirit even in a noisy family, as he moves household objects the rumpelstilzchen causes creaking or clattering. That ruckus/rumpus remains familiar as evidence of haunting. Typically such creatures cause unseen objects in the next room to crash to the floor—a seemingly minor but unnerving occurrence. Such trivial events can be as spooky as observed objects that gyrate or scrape about by themselves, as if animated or touched by unseen agents: definitely goosebump-inducing. These unexplainable details ornament campfire stories. The peculiarity of such noisy creatures might furnish us with a meaningful clue except that Rumpelstiltskin does none of these things (being neither noisy, nor invisible, nor prone to misplacing human belongings). Accordingly his demeanor and appearance as related to other creatures, his genealogy, and the mythic zone from which he hails—all remains murky.

20. Outstanding sex in the peasantry found its moment in the mid-winter recess from work, the Saturnalia a.k.a. "Christmas". Then well-fueled with alcohol and a suspension of (almost all) social mores sensuality reigned. Puritan clergy loathed the holiday, hence its complete reconstruction in modern times along wholesome lines.

7

THE TALKING CURE

The Courage to Speak Truth

Rumpelstiltskin's story survived and grew in appeal not because spinners invented a satisfying tale of men's buffoonery, another among countless examples from Comedia del Arte to TV sitcoms, but because subsequent generations sensed its deeper organization. Rumpelstiltskin rescued stable and loving family life by insisting on a "talking cure". That would make Rumpelstiltskin the father or patron saint of psychoanalysis. (Psychology strongly, perhaps inordinately, shaped the present discussion of the plausible figurehead for such studies and resulting therapies.) Rumpelstiltskin insists that for her freedom the Queen must say the unmentionable, the shameful thing that must not be uttered. At the final moment her amazing life's vicissitudes prepared her to utter the disgraceful word and she acts accordingly, desperate to save her child and herself. Unlike other fairytales' wan heroines, the speaker self-emancipates. In that act of liberation she unveils the story's heart. Here some comparisons illuminate the differences.

Few fairytales introduce an active female protagonist. Most advertise the worth of a passive, and therefore implicitly "virtuous", heroine saved by males. In contrast the Miller's Daughter eventually takes charge of her situation. By comparison, Sleeping Beauty appears an acquiescent dupe possessed only of beauty and a gift for flight, not confrontation. Indeed, she's known for "sleeping". Born into a pitched contest between her parents, Sleeping Beauty loiters morally inert in her own story until she is rendered physically incapacitated. Within a tale about exterior appearances, she is trapped unchanging in ageless comeliness; she's unable to advance her cause, bodily rigid. Sleeping Beauty performs as both the tale's victim and also the sexual recipient who "should be woo'd" without having to pursue her lover. Perforce silent, and therefore witless, she gets along on her beauty.

Male action contrasts to female submission as the valiant Prince fights to reach Sleeping Beauty. He penetrates a (Freudian) thicket to awaken her with a kiss. Her fairytale reflects physical maturation and mother-daughter conflicts though by modern standards Sleeping Beauty hardly presents an ideal heroine. She exhibits neither intelligence nor guile and because she demonstrates no acquired skill, like spinning, her fame derives from a congenital talent, her gorgeous face and body. She was (and is) a type the spinnstube's women easily recognized and with whom they had to deal: the stunning female, perpetually "helpless", forever rescued because of her beauty. (Perpetuated by Marilyn Monroe, this prototype grew unfashionable and reciprocally fades as feminists win equality for womanhood.) Real-life ladies envied and hated her. They also invented or repeated the tale of the Miller's Daughter, who took matters into her own hands to get even by speaking the truth about a man's inadequacies. Akin to the finale of The Emperor's New Clothes, speaking the truth ends the story with a male's retreat in humiliation, this fairytale glorifies what real life may not always celebrate: whistle-blowers or truth-tellers. She is rewarded for speaking unpleasant Truth. Other stories contrast with the Miller's Daughter.

Mostly passive and only intermittently the moral hero of her own tale, when her stepmother seeks her destruction Snow White does not confront her but flees. Attended by wee-folk she is roused by another (Prince). After her escape, which shows highly motivated awareness of her perilous situation, everybody works for Snow White whose self-preservation consists of light house-keeping for her hosts. The Miller's Daughter takes action. She swindles poor Rumpelstiltskin, which the tale presents as cleverness and daring born of desperation. But only inadvertently she summoned Rumpelstiltskin to solve her immediate problem; though despairing she never knew she was calling on his services. She pronounces his shame-loaded name to nullify the disaster wrought by her father and husband. Unlike helpless females in so many fairytales the miller's daughter practices initiative—her last act being the most important.

The ladies of the spinnstube anticipated Freud's praxis when they foresaw the two central tools of psychoanalysis. One was architectural, the other verbal. Specifically, the spinnstuben ladies forecast the analyst's sealed room as they aired grievances, probing toward the un-said. In that room confidences were blurted, perhaps surprising the speaker as much as the listeners. Or carefully framed, tentative, or metaphoric statements were pronounced with growing recognition. For the many things that pre-modern women needed to talk about the spinnstube foreshadowed group therapy. In the Tale of Rumpelstiltskin laboring women illustrated a way to heal that recognized the power of the hidden-until-enunciated, as a predecessor to psychoanalysis. A miller's daughter became a mother, an adult, a threatened queen who utters the thing she thought she could never say . . . and her problem goes away.

One of the great submerged themes of Rumpelstiltskin, calling the unmentionable by its proper label, asserts the importance of naming. Speaking explicitly and thereby bringing to consciousness, reigns a therapeutic standard in many forms of treatment, beginning with psychoanalysis but also taught in at least one fairytale. The Tale of Rumpelstiltskin hinges on a women shamelessly uttering, perhaps in public, what had been overheard in private, a word plausibly reconstructed to refer to something never openly discussed. A psychoanalyst succinctly said that, "The purpose of analytic work . . . is to discover Rumpelstiltskin's name".[1] Women knew this long ago. Their disappointment: speaking the forbidden name did not always solve their problem(s) but did bring the difficulty to the surface where, exteriorized and illuminated in the spinnstube's conversation, the problem could be shared with friends and thereby diluted. By itself the relief of speaking and being understood provided no cure to the women of the spinnstuben or psychoanalyst's couch. But it could begin the process. Not every hurt gets better or goes away or when you can name it, as happens in a fairytale.

Medical theory (before behaviorists' infatuation with neuroscience and bio-chemical neurotransmitters) supported the gist of Rumpelstiltskin's story. Rumpelstiltskin's hidden name, that sly pun, suggests the story's underlying "rationale" of ridicule. A flaccid prick contradicts the great generative symbol of the phallus: the magnificent Sanskrit *linga*, the Priapic urge. The laughable detumescent thing lurks contemptible, a mere "prick", not a proud "cock". Accordingly, polite society does not discuss it and certainly young maidens do not speak it, or "mouth" it. Even if girlfriends of the miller's daughter speculated giggling about sex, they probably never theorized about erectile dysfunction . . . no drug commercials informed them. For young girls, sex might be anatomically odd and difficult to imagine, perhaps disgusting, romantic if vaguely fulfilling, even brutal to contemplate, but not a mechanical breakdown.[2] Because no one speaks his name the girl never heard it and as Queen she does not know the word. She did not learn the word as a girl and no one spoke it to the new queen. Court etiquette precluded crude talk near her person. Having lived a sheltered life she neither heard this word for a limp dick, nor heard of it.

Earthy acquaintance with the 'facts of life' would be different if she were a *farmer's* daughter and pointedly she is not—a deliberate detail. The spinners of flax or wool lived closer to the earth than a mercantile miller. The story implies that rural spinners were more knowing and worldwise than the petite-bourgeoisie who invested in mills and left the peasant class. The little man's obscene name, even if she knew it, would be a vulgar word for this girl to utter but less so if she had brought animals to stud or watched the results of mating. But a miller's daughter knows little of such couplings or their failures. When Rumpelstiltskin hears his name he assumes the Queen would never speak so foul a word, a term impossibly far from her daily life and a word which she could not have encountered in her upbringing. Where could she have heard such filth? He shouts out the probable source: "The Devil told you! The Devil told you!"[3] Yet, this is no morality story that opposes the forces of good and evil; the Devil has had no part in it. Rumpelstiltskin "is never once described as evil . . . but he suffers the sort of dreadful fate normally reserved for witch figures".[4] Why? He's the only one who helps the girl.

Two mortal paragons parade their (male) flaws to illustrate pervasive human traits but they are not thought evil or associates of the devil. What fault or wickedness resides in Rumpelstiltskin's actions? Again his contemptible name unlocks the answer. To free herself she must say the thing prohibited by her instincts, upbringing, and self-imaging as a good girl. But once said she is liberated.

Balancing Work and Play

Story-tellers perhaps savored the name's ironic implications without which the tale's rich orchestration proves otherwise unexplainable in either German or English. Indeed, the central figure's characteristics—irreconcilable with other fairytale personnel—supply the one fixed point in this story's variations: he must be short, talented at women's work, perhaps a workaholic who dwells alone, and be known (or unknown) by an unspeakable name. Once the tale's punning name plugs into the Rumpelstiltskin story a whole society's cautionary outlook travels in time toward the present. Rumpelstiltskin resembles somebody who regrets spending too much time at the office, a lesson he learned only after the doctor gave him bad news. Proud of his honest labors, unsurpassed skill, and fine products, he nevertheless wants a family when he finds that work alone cannot emotionally fulfill him.

The spinnstube's astute women prescribed lightly, knowing every life and every marriage represents a bargain, a personal gamble. Some make Rumpelstiltskin's discovery on their own, others need help (now, often professional) to externalize intimate exchanges. Even when not shared but only silently recognized from over-hearing others' talk, self-revelation could flourish in the confidential climate of the spinners' nighttime community. But eventually truth would out. The mutual compassion of small communities tempered a stern view of enforced agreements, like marriage vows; the women who composed this tale anticipated the therapeutic psychoanalytic situation, including group therapy, AA meetings, and so forth. The spinnstube foreshadowed the sealed analytic chamber, a place where "anything" can be said.

As in the bygone spinnstuben, in the psychiatrist's office distressed speakers trusted the listeners' confidentiality. The speaker's sincerity, her agitation or calm, were presumed to honestly, if not accurately, represent unreconciled relationships. As private as the analytic chamber that excludes all intruders, the spinnstube's inviolability remained sacrosanct. (If men were present certain statements remained unsaid. Or these comments were presented in crafty disguise to cloak sharp observations or the true butt of jokes.) The spinnstube's ladies had assembled future psychiatry's elements for the talking cure without guessing that medicine would someday replicate their all-female institution.

No statement left the room in a form recognizable to outsiders. Like Las Vegas, what happened in the spinnstube stayed in the spinnstube. And, like the psychoanalytic chamber's patient confidentiality, the speaker's identity remained unknown to outsiders if the group chose to keep their female speakers' secrets.[5] The ethos of self-preservation ruled in womanly company for one confidence betrayed meant all were in jeopardy. Their bond foreshadowed the woes of a psychiatrist who breached patient confidentiality: disaster for both parties if a patient's name or identifiable troubles escaped the analytic chamber. But sometimes sound therapeutic reasons urged highly personal matters to be discussed by near-strangers—matters of sexual performance, as the story intimates.

Rumpelstiltskin's Humiliation on Display

A pre-modern woman hearing the Tale of Rumpelstiltskin might note how this story proposed a pleasant reversal. Though we're used to women who are eroticized, in this

story female anatomy trailed normative maleness.[6] The Church endorsed and promulgated this relative ranking based on Scripture, a theological grading that began with
Adam's priority. Rumpelstiltskin's story considers (and, of course, quietly rejects) that
reverential hierarchy so invidious to women. The fairytale mercilessly satirizes male
'shortcomings' and men's moral and physical imperfections. In most realms of public
life males enjoyed decided advantages over women but all their pretenses crumbled
if an adult male was found sexually deficient. Cruel inadequacy furnished the humor
that played at the expense of Rumpelstiltskin's impotence but fairytales were dependably sadistic. Rumpelstiltskin's tale proved consistent with the genre. Some accepted
fairytales' situations which, if taken literally, were revolting; others believed the stories'
time-bound offenses resided in the past but were nonetheless dangerous.

In his "Introduction" to these stories John Ruskin noted the overt brutality of the
Grimms' collection: "Children should laugh, but not mock; and when they laugh, it
should not be at the weaknesses or faults of others".[7] This story mocked another's weaknesses and therefore raised two challenges: first, to convince the listener that Rumpelstiltskin "had it coming" for some fault and, secondly, that it might be usual or acceptable
to discuss impotence in public, however guarded the terms. (Basically incomprehensible
to children, the tale craftily cloaked its actual references and taunted a weakness beyond
the ken of youngsters. The story alludes to irreducible facts of failed adult relationships
and merciless vengeance wreaked as in divorce court. Though aestheticized, these tales
descended from barbaric entertainments that impressed Arnold Schwarzenegger, who
recalled that in his Austrian childhood he read "these terribly violent stories by the
Grimm Brothers. I mean, the cleaned-up versions are nowhere near the horror stories
we used to read".[8] Ruskin noted this tale's coarse ungratefulness but the source of the
ingratitude remained invisible or unspecified. Later therapies would name the condition and its cascade of marital consequences although the fairytale already, if guardedly,
alluded to a medical evaluation already well-known to the spinnstube. However genuinely heartless to moderns who might prefer a bit of sensitivity in treating his condition
(if you believe him afflicted) or his helpful person, the story cruelly outed Rumpelstiltskin's impairment.

Different fairytales promoted different values, but none delicately. In a rough age
that enjoyed bear-baiting, public executions of astonishingly imaginative cruelty, the
taunting of village-idiots as good-natured fun, and ritualized public brutality whose
sport we would find revolting, impotence could be hilarious, except to the man and
his spouse. To ward off ridicule the condition remained a private matter or was secretly
examined in ecclesiastical courts that determined if the marriage sacrament had been
consummated. Talk about humiliation. While examined by priests who, though sworn
to celibacy, were presumably anatomically normal males, the defendant would have to
demonstrate an erection, sometimes coaxed by one or more prostitutes hired by the
court. Improbable as this sounds, here is the contemporary record of precisely such an
ordeal of 1441:

> This witness and the rest of the other women warmed [and] touched the said
> [John's] yard [virga] with their hands, embracing him around the neck and kissing

him. . . . . [His member] was not able to rise nor stand but because of feebleness [was] at all times as if white, dead, empty skin down to its end [document damaged] having scarcely the length and breadth of the fingers of this witness.[9]

These bizarre ecclesiastical courts' insistence on demonstrated performance nevertheless convened for a legitimate legal purpose. However odd as evidence submitted in a judicial proceeding public exhibition of sexual competence represented a reality as Rumpelstiltskin's story evolved. Men required to perform sexually (or be found incompliant of a sacrament) could not have been more poignantly embarrassing for all parties. The tribunals of sexual competency heartlessly mirrored Rumpelstiltskin's enraged frustration as observed by the fairytale's single witness (or royal courtiers standing in for the assembled clerics). Who could have invented such a metaphor for trial by erection? Just as men were barred from the birthing chamber, virtuous women were banned from the ecclesiastical chamber's sexual test. But the spinnstuben's ladies could muse about such proceedings—and who wouldn't—just as men conjured events in the birthing room and the spinnstuben. (Reality surpassed most luxuriant imaginations. In

FIGURE 7.1 Ecclesiastical Court Examining a Husband for Impotence from Gratian's *Decretum*.
Source: Walters Collection Ms. W.133 Fol. 277.

one proceeding a woman testified that she warmed her naked breasts by the room's fire and then held and rubbed the trial husband's penis and testicles . . . to no avail.[10] Maybe each woman of the spinnstube secretly thought that *her* charms could raise an insensate member but as the Rumpelstiltskin story intimates, some cases are hopeless and not the fault of womanhood.) In this way the Tale of Rumpelstiltskin mirrored females who contemplated proceedings as closed to them as the rooms that excluded males. And uninformed by facts, women's imaginations yielded results as outrageous, with the genders reversed. Just as men fantasized about the male-free birthing chamber's Gossip or the spinnstube's male-free animated enthusiasms, hearsay and supposition surrounded a sexual spectacle few beheld.

Across the unbridgeable gap of gender difference the spinnstube's ladies might pretend to understand such trials. Female contemplation of these tests and their underlying condition might survive if crafted into a fairytale about sexual failure. In such a fairytale a woman crudely names the malaise rather than a court of clerics. Naming is crucial. But the name must first be known to be spoken.

Secrets of the Spinning Room

The spinnstube's women knew that men suspected of impotence were publicly (in front of strangers) humiliated. Modern readers must confront the question of those women's competency to understand such proceedings. Could they address this personal disaster in the artform available to illiterates or do the fairytales they recited or composed mean nothing urgent or important? Despite its many congruencies with reality which hint the Rumpelstiltskin tale addresses male impotence and its consequences, were the story-tellers actually constructing such a connection? The stories' psychological truth(s)—the reason we keep returning to them—suggests that this tale like other such stories builds from a core nugget of human reality. It truly reports on psychology in the way that art can be true.

To continue an evening's conversational flow (to say nothing of human decency) the story-tellers wouldn't tease an already vulnerable spinning sister who confessed that she might not be getting enough physical attention. Sympathy offered a more appropriate response than derision. Nor would much be accomplished by conspicuously jeering at a reported sufferer's impotence (an actual male of their community). The spinnstube's ladies might allow generalities to seep out of their conclave but divulging particulars would turn self-destructive. The spinning room's inmates' mutual deference verged on professional courtesy arising from sisterly support. Only a fool would mock another's misfortune that might soon become the taunter's own misery. That lesson the fairytale taught to bolster a code of secrecy by demonstrating the consequences of violating sisterly silence. For, in Rowley's words, "Rumpelstiltskin is someone who cannot keep a secret. In other words he cannot tolerate intense excitement to the full, but rather, just as the babe is about to become his and he is almost achieving his end, he reveals his secret, his name. He too, then, as it were ejaculates prematurely".[11] Accordingly, the story implies a profound consonance of sexual inadequacy and incautious speech.

These two inferences re-double the meaning of each 'shortcoming'. The equation of hasty speech and premature ejaculation matches both failures, as the spinnstube's ladies apparently intuited a correspondence only re-discovered by medicalized psychology. Secrets should be kept, cautioned the spinnstube, and no place is safe to utter them for even in deepest forest lurk unseen (and malicious) ears. The only secure place to divulge personal secrets or problems remains the spinnstube. Today perhaps the only secure place to divulge personal secrets or embarrassing problems is the psychoanalytic chamber.[i]

Believing he is alone when he sings to himself, Rumpelstiltskin does not really blurt out the secret that will undo him. To his knowledge he's not "telling" anyone, not even a trusted friend; prideful of his work, he declares his identity without indiscreetly sharing. Yet he stands convicted. For the story's tellers—subject to a severely unforgiving behavioral code now virtually eliminated from the developed world—being alone in deep forest at night and remote from a town or anyone, provided no excuse. Location and select company meant everything about divulging secrets: a lesson to young auditors. Ladies of the spinnstube heeded the old motto that even "The Walls Have Ears". If you wanted feedback and advice, the spinnstube offered a place to share secrets and then only guardedly—perhaps in a fable or, circumspectly and shrouded, as a story's metaphor to consider "what if" propositions.

Rumpelstiltskin appears twice contemptible. A blabbermouth, he desecrates the spinnstube's inviolate secrecy while the premature-ejaculation hypothesis argues that Rumpelstiltskin's inventors believed he deserved dismissal for sexual misdeeds. Despite working as a spinner, his other unspoken but implied performance failed womanhood aesthetically as an anti-sensual lapse. Failing to erect at all he further compounded his bio-mechanical malfunction. As a premature ejaculator, Rumpelstiltskin represented a worthless performer even when/if aroused.[12] Such fine distinctions, recognized by late Medieval women and modern pharmaceutical companies, propelled the creation of a classic.

The Tale of Rumpelstiltskin may diagnose a problem long before pharmacology beckoned a temporary cure. But the tale offers no immediate solution except properly naming things, a braver course (and more modern) than tritely concluding that a charming prince's arrival unties life's knots. The ending of Rumpelstiltskin's story cannot be told without its lingering brutality, frankly dark and medieval in its delectation of cruelty. To achieve an almost musical resolution the tale must include its full quotient of mercilessness. Final degradation. In public. A painful theater of confession.

---

i. This complicated trope can escape into endless permutations, speculation that I bequeath to psychologists. They may spin as long a thread as they like from this Freudian tangle. There's an interesting parallel here as the mass(es) of unspun fibers from which thread emerges are called roving(s) and spinning organizes the incoherent mass into consistent simplicity—with a beginning and end, like a narrative. Similarly, without a map psychoanalysis initially meanders through the unformed matter of dreams, half-remembered recollection, and painfully misunderstood incidents. The investigation charts what first seems a pathless wander until analysis extracts, or spins, a coherent narrative, a clear map backward through the roving, the thread through the labyrinth.

Talk as Therapy

Rumpelstiltskin's story caches hints about how an awakening consciousness yearns to name. Fairytales could probe the edges of knowledge and these human quirks, once observed and critiqued in their personifications, amusingly highlighted life's actualities. Each story editorialized about some relationship or idiosyncrasy. This tale suggests reconciliation through conversation. But utterances of a special sort.

The spinnstube's women favored story-telling as their mode of exploration, unlike the later upper class and more celebrated female-led Salons that would have been left wondering if a guest wandered off into an extended metaphoric story. Unlike the salons, spinnstuben enjoyed neither access to, or interest in, dialectical-scientific inquiry or knowing references to high culture. On the other hand, the scientifically inclined, who are supposed to compose non-metaphoric observations about the world, often ducked their task. The two institutions shared surprising similarities besides their foreseeable differences.

Women led both. One convened the foremost available minds to address topics chosen for the informed assembly. One gathered locals. But even neighborhood women could prove the best prepared to address topics brought, however circumspectly, before the evening's assembly of spinners. One moved forward with a conscious agenda that in reality functioned while partially blind to its own implications and results while the other made no pretense of an intellectual program yet produced metaphors and (fictional) personages as vivid, as frequently invoked today, and influential as any in our culture—possibly excepting sacred scripture. We occasionally glimpse the story's pervasive infiltration of the English-speaking world when a psychiatrist remarks that "Several of my women patients have brought it [the Rumpelstiltskin story] up at various times for different reasons".[13] The reference proves both poetic and startling: Rumpelstiltskin returning to his job of rectifying women's lives.

One psychoanalyst reported, "Patients have experienced me as the miller, a braggart who makes them take all the risks and do all the work, or as Rumpelstiltskin who can do magic but who will ultimately take away their most treasured possession".[14] Once hesitant but finally trusting, the story's female speaker risks 'transference' when she expresses to another person statements un-said to any other. The female patient, unlike in the Tale of Rumpelstiltskin, forms a bond of trust with her therapist-conversant. The Queen, far from gaining Rumpelstiltskin's confidence, drives him away, to her delight. But in the modern setting, after risking vulnerability by speaking the unspoken and, however hesitantly, discovering vast relief in a new trusting relationship, the patient's ensuing adulatory identification with the analyst may, potentially, meld the dual attraction and repulsion that Rumpelstiltskin holds. Only he, the diminutive man, can help her in the shared and secure room (the castle's spinning cell, the spinnstube, or the protected analytic chamber). Neither the story nor the modern therapeutic situation is simple.

As in the fairytale the female patient's collaboration with the analyst may cost her sex's relationship to reproductive triumph. If the analyst becomes identified with Rumpelstiltskin the patient may identify the analyst-Rumpelstiltskin with the penis—sometimes just a prick, a nudnick. (The correlation presents a clear example of phallocentricism, which the story's tellers meant to deflate as "the droll-looking little man in the fairy story is the penis—the wonderful magician who can accomplish everything".[15] Yes, Rumpelstiltskin can "accomplish everything" except the principal job of a penis. His inability to perform that assignment leaves him free to master all the others. The story implied that everyday penis-wielding men may get the—psychoanalytic or more muscular household—job done but mess up everything else.) That seems the drift of some clinical literature. Like the penis, the psychoanalyst toys with precious delicacies.

The story's first tellers professed no high regard for the male organ or its reputed merits, especially when it repeatedly failed to inflate. Why, getting an impotent male to enlarge was like trying to spin straw into gold: utter frustration all around. The story's phallic undertones and implicit carnal themes express no pleasure. And more than pleasure is missing. The tale resembles life's workaday plainness through which trudge highly flawed humans. Excepting the main character's supernatural talents the story barely resembles many fairytales' escape into florid emotional fantasy. At the finale the Queen stands alone with her child, and that's it for happiness. The phrase 'cold comfort' fits her discovery in a loveless marriage holding the child of that union, wedlock secured by a lie that she maintained by humiliating her benefactor.

The curtain comes down on a bitter opera. A story actually well suited to the scale and intensity of opera: reneging on her deal offers the Queen her only avenue for pleasure but at the cost of a betrayal of trust that she must rationalize for the rest of her life, beginning when the curtain falls. The King regards his money and his heir. The addled father marvels that his boast came true. The Prince awaits his kingdom. The Queen enjoys her high station. The courtiers snicker at the peasant girl masquerading as a queen. And Rumpelstiltskin escapes truly miserable. The lot need therapy as Rumpelstiltskin, psychiatrist or spinner, magically relieved the girl of a drear life before a word of healing coaxed from her threatened healer.

Healing Takes Time

Relationships unfold as a process accomplished *in time*, a performance that in retrospect becomes a narrative.[16] We tell ourselves our own narratives quietly, as self-justification or to feel guilt, or aloud in stressful situations, or in talk-therapy. In either case, time supplies the crucial ingredient, as in this fairytale. On either end of the story time symmetrically measured the Queen's three nights of spinning and her three days and nights of guessing. (Her irresponsible father's daughter, she solves none of her problems but off-loads them to somebody else and finally, discovering the source of her irritation she speaks the offensive name to commence understanding through revenge. That's the narrative flow of events.) Her recognition could blossom instantaneously or in "three days"—an interval that might symbolize years of searching, perhaps in private introspection or on the analyst's couch. The Tale of Rumpelstiltskin would hardly be the first such compression. The Queen's anguished days of questioning and probing may represent as symbolic a period as many scholars suggest were the six "days" of Biblical creation—eons in fact.

The "three days" of spinning may represent the years of her youth passed toiling and the "three days of guessing" her complete maturation, her reconciliation to reality.

After mellowing to her life and adjusting to a radically altered reality she can utter the thing she could not but some interval, actual or suggested, had to pass. Knowledge of her body—gained in marital sex, the birth of her son, and lactation—frees her to shed affectations of propriety. And that maturation took more time than the year-or-so encompassed by the story. She finally knows she is flesh, subject to age and its limits. Concomitantly, her ability to speak the unspeakable arrives only with difficulty as it would to any sentient adult which, finally, she represents. The Miller's Daughter has become one of the spinnstube's senior members, experienced and knowledgeable, worth listening to because she can call things by their real name.

Sheltered from indecency in girlhood, as an adult she is again shielded. A Queen encounters few contradictory viewpoints. Few speak coarse opinions in her presence or utter uncouth words, a segregation from reality that forestalls her illumination. All this assumes that the story intentionally accommodated truths of human nature. The story's successful representation of life's conditions vouches for its ability to touch us as successive generations valued Rumpelstiltskin even if its auditors could not say how. Remarkably, not moderns or even Renaissance authors but perhaps rural illiterates, the spinnstube created or promulgated a fairytale that ends with the heroine verbalizing the previously un-sayable utterance. The story-tellers believed in the efficacy of speech. Why not? They were engaged in a verbal universe as they spun.

★★★

So we come to the nub of the question. Women who frequented the spinnstuben had experienced a husband's impotence, had heard of a neighbor's sexual calamity discussed at an evening's spinning circle, or knew about courts that tried male impotence. Women knew. Their awareness laced evenings' conversations however circumspectly they broached this delicate problem. Like all life's conundrums this subject prowled their stories' background if not featuring as a central topic. It doesn't even matter who first told the story or in what form, eventually Rumpelstiltskin came to resemble an all-too-frequent infirmity that had to be discussed. The alternative—that women lived in close quarters unaware of an eternally human problem or that their conversation and story-telling evaded reality and spun purely fantastic tales that, even unconsciously, disregarded their world—would suggest the women remained willfully ignorant and only discussed irrelevancies. I hold neither to be true. This story encoded complex female relationships with male-kind as expressed in terms of the agricultural world they knew. This notion's best proof is the story itself and how the parts reinforce the entirety.

Notes

1. Rowley (1951, p. 144).
2. Over the centuries the condition has elicited as much humor as sympathy and considerable legal interest when marriages could not be consummated. See: McLaren, *Impotence: A Cultural History*.

3. Another variant will do almost as well, though not as colorfully: "Some witch told you that! Some witch told you that!" cried the little man. (Edgar Taylor [1823/1920], p. 150.)
4. Bottigheimer (1987, p. 182).
5. Cuddihy (1974/6) likened the analytic chamber to the *shtetl*, the Jewish village where anything could be said. Freud only recapitulated that setting and did not invent it. The patient might associate the analyst, "who can do magic", with Rumpelstiltskin. But Rumpelstiltskin was impotent and nobody wants an impotent analyst, figuratively or actually. (Hasn't the patient got enough problems without listening to the shrink's kvetching.)
6. Femininity seemed derivative according to the prevailing Biblical account of a male "birthing" womanhood. As the King James version tells it, "And the rib, which the Lord God had taken from man, made he a woman, and brought her unto the man. And Adam said, This is now bone of my bones, and flesh of my flesh: she shall be called Woman, because she was taken out of Man" (Genesis 2:22–23).
7. Ruskin (1920, p. vi).
8. Schwarzenegger (2012, p. 9).
9. Kane (2008, p. 5).
10. See: McLaren (2007).
11. Rowley (1951, p. 144, n.4).
     The story's edifying tropes may include splitting and redoubling of certain characteristics. In the Rumpelstiltskin story the protagonists, or components of them, may be represented by other whole entireties or by parts (synecdoche). Like many another story, a palace of mirrors can be erected of the materials within Rumpelstiltskin. Indeed, the body-as-phallus may be represented by the manikin Rumpelstiltskin, which would be a wandering phallus, perhaps the king's, in search of a name. These roving references, seeking valence throughout the story—and the endlessly reflecting quality of the mirrored characters—suggests the depths that so appealed to the story's hearers.
12. The women knew that erection is not necessary for orgasm and that despite his magical talents Rumpelstiltskin is unable to hold out for the duration.
13. Martin Miller (1985, p. 73). Without beginning to excavate Freud's discussion of the antithetical meaning of primal words the Rumpelstiltskin story appears a primary example of folktales' advocacy of the "talking cure".
14. Martin Miller (1985, p. 74).
15. Rowley (1951, p. 144).
16. These relationships include a marriage, friendship, siblings, an adult's affiliation with childhood, and so forth. Fairytales relate to their readers as the parties to psychoanalysis are liable to William Carlos William taunt (Patterson book 1), "Divorce! Divorce! the sign of knowledge". Ellen Handler Spitz (1994) pointed out that psychoanalysis, "by extending the individual's range of consciousness, does not interpret *away* discordance but rather, by converting unconscious conflict into conscious contradiction, actually *expands* the individual's capacity for experiencing and tolerating the absurd", (emphasis in the original) p. 67.

8
THE DEVIL VERSUS MOTHERHOOD

Something Else Not Mentioned

Not everyone cavalierly dismissed Rumpelstiltskin. Before asking for her child some reciters mention Rumpelstiltskin in kindly terms: "So her little friend took the ring, and began to work at the wheel".[1] His character appears uniformly compliant throughout the story and, if not actually agreeable or charming, he seems consistently submissive to the girl's wishes; his obedience represents one of his hallmarks. First he's helpful as "her little friend" who shows up to solve a problem and then he's cooperative and re-negotiates his contract. Why has Rumpelstiltskin been called devilish? While the listener's sympathies shift through the telling, "When we speak of Rumpelstiltskin, we do not worry ourselves much about his curious desire for a child, but rejoice instead that the heroine manages to cheat him at his devilish game".[2] Rumpelstiltskin suggested the contest that she won, which hardly makes the guessing game devilish. But the finale's accusation ("The Devil told you that! The Devil told you that!") raises a classic case of guilt by association. Why would Rumpelstiltskin think the Devil knew his name and reported that secret to the Miller's Daughter? A stickler for legality, punctilious as Shylock, Rumpelstiltskin appears neither cruel nor rancorous; those are not his faults.

Either the story pointlessly invoked the arch-fiend (merely interchangeable with an expletive) or Rumpelstiltskin's outcry reveals something else about our story's inventors.[3] Why invoke the Devil's despicable name when the Tale of Rumpelstiltskin otherwise ignores the struggle of the universe's titanic moral forces? The Devil's plans for humanity (and his minions, Demons) do not drive this fairytale's hidden narrative engine about personal failings and personal growth. Nothing suggests that Rumpelstiltskin confederates with the Devil or that he belongs to Satan's crew. So, how did Rumpelstiltskin play a "devilish game" and forfeit a friendly reputation for the Devil's companionship?

Speaking His Name Makes Him Vanish

"The Devil told you that! The Devil told you that!" shrieked Rumpelstiltskin.
And in a fury he [jumped on his cooking spoon, flew out the window, and] disappeared.

To the evening-gathered women who told this story, the Devil authored their world's great woes. Everyday miseries could be attributed to meddling wee-folk or men but the big troubles came from a higher power. So it might prove highly significant that Rumpelstiltskin's cry of misery ends the story by invoking the Devil, the implacable force that opposes Christianity's God. But perhaps Rumpelstiltskin screams his name as amorphous evil—the sum of all bad luck but not an anti-theology. Rumpelstiltskin names a Devil who roams the world but Christianity's notorious Devil did not, in fact, inform the Queen of her foe's name. Rumpelstiltskin assumes that, as propriety otherwise forbids naming his condition, she could only speak such a foul word after contacting wickedness and sullying herself with carnal matters. For the Devil to visit this story other apparatus must be functioning: theological and mythological accessories that allow the arch-fiend's attendance.

The tireless opponent of goodness, sometimes called Satan: the Bible envisions this entity as an advocate who argues for mankind's penalty in the celestial court.[4] Others conceive him as Lucifer the fallen angel.[5] A Manichean version of universal good and evil in conflict imagines God's lesser twin; as cosmic decency cannot suppress evil the two forces struggle in equilibrium. Grafted onto our story's final moment, the Devil's presence contributes something inextricable to the whole.

The other characters lack names—but are identified by epithets, titles, or relationships—except for two: in the forest Rumpelstiltskin names himself and at court he indicts the Devil. Thus he supplies the story's only names, if they are names. As did pre-lapsarian Adam in his garden (Genesis 2:18–19) Rumpelstiltskin performs as the namer. One of the story's more acclaimed modern readers observed, "Though the name Rumpelstiltskin may have no revelatory meaning, the act of naming itself is significant".[6] In everyday life we overlook how profound that deed once was. Naming was not a casual act taken for granted. Naming denotes a thing or person we can point to distinct from the rest of the universe; sometimes, as at birth, we are privileged to assign a name. Mostly we use a name to summon a single individual from the jumble of myriad objects littering the world. Formerly naming was serious business; people routinely assumed different names for distinct social or professional functions or stages of life—and in some cultures or situations continue to. In the past naming was much more important when spoken words and especially written words and names possessed coercive magic.

Names could summon. Names revealed innermost truths. Rumpelstiltskin's name likely *means* something that elicits his response when he hears it declaimed. And what it means is unsuitable to be spoken by young women. Here the story gestures away from contractual relationships or human failings and points toward evil. The Miller's Daughter can finally free herself by saying the offensive word not usually articulated by a woman of any social standing while in answer Rumpelstiltskin shouts the diabolic term: a name, a title, a force. An odd exchange, of names, amid anonymity.

There's Evil in the Story but Is Rumpelstiltskin Diabolic?

> Fortunately for the credit of a study which is by many regarded as frivolous, our research brings us more often than not, and sometimes when least suspected, near some deposit of early thought, some strivings after a philosophy which embraces all life in one common origin and destiny; and in sympathy with instinctive feelings of the barbaric nature which are ultimately verified by reason and experience.[7]
>
> *A.W.T. and Edward Clodd*

The fairytale world rested on the bedrock of paganism.

After their Christianization, Northern Europe peasants still distrusted newfangled imported ideas about fate and salvation. Furthermore, there was no reason to replace what had worked, to discard a body of beliefs that had performed so successfully for so long. The residue of that suspicion survives in a wealth of pre-Christian holidays (like Christmas) and customs (like Santa Claus) that yet thrive, unconquered, and exported around the world embedded within Christianity. Especially Northern Europeans globally dispersed colonial cultural spores that included Old World ideas which could function without aristocratic or churchly patronage, viewpoints that simply disregarded Christian theology. And the neither ruling aristocracy nor the Church created or sanctioned fairytales, a body of stories that passed unobserved through high society or if noticed could be dismissed as the moronic playthings of the peasantry and women.

The spinnstube's stories ignored the new faith's worldview, even if that Christian faith was nominally observed in church as insurance against horrors to be visited upon non-believers while it also provided colorful new patron Saints to continue the old festivals. Yet Christianity lacked the vigor to displace old ways that guaranteed crops and could explain the unexplainable ways of fairies. It took some delicacy to espouse one faith and attend church, practice its rites and sacraments, while yet holding steadfast to a worldview that (more surely) animated nature. The tales' authors neither contested (a punishable heresy) nor claimed to have foreshadowed Christendom although, inevitably, the influence of scripture's oft-repeated narratives peeps from behind the tales' motifs and structures. Heathendom remained unchallenged in fairytales, neither an inferior outlook (requiring excuses or apologies) nor an 'outsider' perspective on life. Folktale's outlook continued to operate long after the demise of actual paganism. Yet, eager to avoid confrontations that were inevitably lost when dashed against overwhelming forces, folklore never attempted to define itself as a more advanced and morally superior position from within Christendom. But nor did the Church embrace fairytales and Christianize wholesale. Whatever the Church's misgivings, which were substantial and eventually largely victorious, the two worldviews nicely coexisted except on most Sundays. So, mildly tolerated though tainted with pagan origins and outlook, high culture occasionally compared the two worldviews.

In contrast to the harshness of folktales, *King Lear*'s pagan cruelty invites baptism and the introduction of Christian mercy as Lear—who swears "By Apollo!" (I:1)—lives in a forerunner British world. His wretched suffering advertises the need for a thorough civilizing/Christianizing. But no such invitation to moral evolution emerges from the Tale of Rumpelstiltskin. Rumpelstiltskin's universe neither precedes nor anticipates Christian conversion as none of the story's humans feel motivated to do the "right thing". Each of the tale's mortals strives only for desire (gold, a crown, his daughter well-married and himself exonerated, her life spared, her child returned) while supernatural, and presumably pagan, Rumpelstiltskin inexplicably relents and renegotiates his deal. Yet to the story-tellers he can hardly represent a moral summit. His tale smugly ignores any chance to improve a society where all play by the same rules and none protest the "unfairness" of gender-weighted situations. This fairytale without a concluding adage does not implore for progress, moral, theological, social or sexual.

Rumpelstiltskin's story ignores compassion, aside from that practiced by the title character; if the Devil rules without mercy and God reigns compassionate, where does Rumpelstiltskin stand in this moral spectrum? Closer to the divine than devilish. Yet if goodness alone satisfied him, Rumpelstiltskin wouldn't trade for increasingly dear and more intimate payments: his wages as a mercenary, not a do-gooder. Although we're not told how Rumpelstiltskin chooses his clients if he acted from compassion the story's ending would not occasion a bitter laugh but a catastrophe as through their own devices in banishing him mortals lost one of their few supernatural allies against life's misfortunes: a Christ type. Rumpelstiltskin aided (a portion of) innocent humanity against its own evil instincts (pride, greed, and murder) only to be driven away. So, where does Rumpelstiltskin fit into the spinnstube's moral perspective?

Invoking the otherwise truant Devil, this tale disregards the grinding gears of a moral cosmos where God presides. The Christian God reigns implacably opposed by the Devil who seeks to control the universe in an endless tug of war. Such moral struggles grapple in another dimension, irrelevant for Rumpelstiltskin. Yet he operates as consistently as by moral stricture, just not the Christian variety.

Rumpelstiltskin cancels no portion of the debt owed him, never absolves the Queen of relinquishing her child but, remarkably, he allows her to hazard a gamble in which she risks nothing and he all. She fails to graciously reciprocate. In her triumph the Queen neither forgives him nor treats him kindly once having secured her son. By modern standards this imbalance reflects a uniformly harsh environment where ruthless judgement prevails. For its peasant reciters this story's non-Christian world illustrated the need for—as they'd been told, and perhaps some believed—a means to personal absolution as redemption followed detours of ill-judgement called "sins". But this story espoused vengeance and its route to personal redemption passed through sorcery. In a fairytale that tacitly celebrated cruel reprisal, nobody emerges innocent. But such was magic's allure in the spinners' nominally, or ostensibly, Christian community whose recently acquired Christianity applied only a veneer.

James Carroll (ordained as a Catholic priest) put it bluntly: "Because evangelization of most of Europe was by the sword, imposed by victorious rulers on vanquished subjects, in contrast to the grassroots spread of the faith before Constantine, the Christian religion was never fully authentic in much of northern Europe—nor was it purged of superstitious magic".[8] The Miller's Daughter prays to neither God nor the saints for rescue from her cell. It would never occur to her. Nor does she invoke religion against Rumpelstiltskin; she laments a plight that saints cannot comfort nor angels aid because they, feckless in that realm, are barred from the world of fairytales which they eventually displaced. The spinnstube's outlook, beyond history and barely acknowledging changing epochs, conjured Rumpelstiltskin dwelling in that sometimes-vicious pre-Christian "once upon a time". For some story-tellers that—only recently lapsed moral climate, if not actually memorable to the spinnstube's older ladies who recalled living the old ways—worldview remained still resonant in their lives. Only lately passed in peasantry's imperceptibly slow transformations, the age before Christian mercy underpins the tale. The story operates by sorcery, itself both a premonition of technology while a religious implement. And at one point the story rests tangent to religion. Clearly overkill, there's no apparent reason for Rumpelstiltskin to name the arch-fiend, yet reason there is.

★★★

> Pope Francis does not just criticize the excesses of global capitalism, He compares them to the "dung of the devil".[9]

Rumpelstiltskin occupies the structural place a villain would be found in other stories. Therefore, substituting (and consequently mistaken) for evil, he's afflicted with a villain's customary fate. In formal contrast, the Queen lodges at the story's heart (appearing before Rumpelstiltskin and remaining on stage after his departure). She occupies the position that the 'good' victim typically inhabits the heroine's place of innocence as if it's "her" story. But if this is "her" story the Miller's Daughter corresponds to Belle, Sleeping Beauty, Cinderella, and so forth although the Miller's Daughter hardly exemplifies a moral champion. She just wins, smugly.

Though victimized by all she takes no conscientious ethical stand that contrasts with the other characters. Moreover, without interrogating its source she readily accepts supernaturally tainted aid. If it helps her, she's willing to deal in black magic and with a miniature magus. In the real world of the spinnstube this would have made her a witch and other people so accused were burned at the stake. The ladies of the spinnstube knew of that fate perfectly well as most of the Inquisition's victims, dragged before formal ecclesiastical courts or informal mob proceedings, could have been their friends, women helpless to defend themselves against charges of witchcraft. The Miller's Daughter gets off scot-free. And even seems to earn our sympathy. How can she be "good" and employ, or benefit from, anti- or pre-Christian sorcery? Even if through an intermediate, a magical sub-contractor.

Rumpelstiltskin's appearance, his similarity to others who offer "Devils Bargains" and his finally screamed 'ejaculation' yields the misprision that Rumpelstiltskin is a demon.[10] Even a "negative proof" suggests that Rumpelstiltskin is no demon, supplied by none other than Freud, who noted that, "In ancient civilizations, in myths, fairytales and superstitions, in unconscious thinking, in dreams and in neuroses—money is brought into the most intimate relationship with dirt. We know that the gold which the devil gives his paramours turns into excrement after his departure".[11] Pope Francis seems to agree. Gold abounds in the story of Rumpelstiltskin and it remains precious. Not only does it not become "excrement after his departure" but everyone lived, perhaps not happily but certainly well, on that gold. A cheated outsider, Rumpelstiltskin cannot belong to that order of beings who turn gold to merde. Absent from the ranks who serve the Devil, he is not a demon at all and this is not a moral tale. Okay, then, what is it?

A Detour: A Note About Spinning Gold

Spinning straw into gold sounds impossible. But the women who authored and refined this story knew something that moderns don't.

In other stories, magical beings convert roomfuls of flax or straw into finely spun gold but Rumpelstiltskin spins something else and the story's determining attribute arises from the technology of cultivating, harvesting, and spinning flax—facts that the spinnstube's women would have known intimately as it justified their nighttime gatherings.

To transform raw flax to a spinnable filament the plant undergoes the process of retting (controlled rotting) by which bacteria and moisture dissolve or rot away cellular tissues, pectins, and other gummy substances that bind vegetative fiber bundles. Once loosened from the stem the resulting threads can be separated for textiles. In olden times bundles of harvested stalks were weighted with stones and submerged for one or two weeks in stagnant or slow-moving waters, such as ponds, bogs, sluggish streams, or rivers. The large amounts of water required for flax preparation limited where this procedure could be done without fouling a potable watersource. (Because retting demanded copious clean water today concerns for water purity require the downstream flow from retting to be purified of the gunk created by this Neolithic process.) Retting's dregs worked unfortunate changes on water and land but the plant thereby yielded to a marvelous transformation.

Once water penetrates and swells the inner cells the plant's outer layer bursts open. This release hastens further absorption of both water and decay-producing bacteria but the process can run amok and—as in baking or fermentation of wine or beer that requires practiced mastery—an experienced eye must skillfully appraise retting time. Under-retting makes fiber separation difficult; over-retting weakens the fiber. Where water is limited or too precious for such use, slower dew retting proves effective only if the climate yields heavy nighttime dews followed by warm daytime temperatures. Practiced from deep prehistory the process continued unaltered as each generation acquired the expertise to judge controlled decomposition by eye and feel the fibers' progressive loosening. Such specialized knowledge connects this fairytale's essential elements. The ancient craft's details inform Rumpelstiltskin's tale in ways imperceptible to the modern reader but that contributed highly visible elements for the spinnstube's ladies . . . who knew the difference between water- and dew-retting.

FIGURE 8.1   Illustrated by Dik Browne, 1946.

Source: "Rumpelstiltskin", *Classics Illustrated Junior*, 11 March 1946.

In dew retting, harvested plant stalks are spread evenly in grassy fields or sometimes on platforms; the combined action of bacteria, sun, air, and dew encourages fermentation to dissolve much of the stem material surrounding the fiber bundles. (Dew-retted fiber is generally darker in color and of poorer quality than water-retted fiber.) As it happens, we possess a terrific copper-age document describing this part of the procedure:

> And the king of Jericho was told that during the night Israelites came into the city to spy out the country. Thereupon the king of Jericho sent to Rahab, saying, "Bring forth the men that came to you who entered your house, because they came to reconnoiter the whole country". But the woman took the two men and hid them, saying, "Men did come to me but I didn't know where they were from. And at evening as darkness was falling at the time the city gate was about to close, the men left, but I don't know where they went. Pursue them quickly for you will overtake them". But she had brought them up to the roof of the house, and hid them under stalks of flax which she had laid out on the rooftop.
>
> *Joshua 2:2–6*

As archaeology has confirmed, Jericho's walls were famously stout, tall, and broad. Rahab hauled flax stalks up two or three stories to the roof of her home inside the city's casement walls to get them off the ground where field insects could eat them before the morning dew and strong Mediterranean sun worked to ret the flax.

If the self-employed, and apparently successful harlot, Rahab used the roof of her digs to ret flax, so could anybody in Jericho with a penthouse. She either leased her rooftop for extra income and let renters lay out their harvest, retted her own fiber for spinning (in her spare time) or, as part of her one-woman-brothel within the city's walls, she prepared flax for others.[12] (As a sole practitioner perhaps municipal authorities required her to operate her rooftop for the common good.) Whatever immediate demands convinced Rahab to use her upper floor for retting, if the spinnstube's ladies ever thought about it (they surely noticed this detail when preachers extolled the Lord's might and the faith of the Children of Israel at Jericho), they might cluck their tongues at the hospitable strumpet's sexual mores but the story came alive to those who knew the feel and aroma of dew-retted flax. The laborious work of laying out flax stalks had to be carefully timed to the seasons. Depending on the weather, after a couple of weeks the fiber could be separated, which demanded a workforce intimately familiar with the decaying stalks' texture. These arcane procedures of an antique industry wouldn't matter much were the results not recorded in the Tale of Rumpelstiltskin. The Germanic story-tellers knew of what they spoke, as did their English-speaking inheritors in an age when country folk still routinely practiced these rural arts as, in and out of the spinnstuben, peasants were as familiar with the botanical particulars as the spinnstube's story-tellers.

While the essential bacterial actions and cellulose decay operated mysteriously—the mechanisms of bio-mechanics unknown to its ancient practitioners—flax retting crowned other crucial prehistoric bio-chemical industries, some still practiced today. Wine's fermentation is controlled rot (curtailed by exhaustion of sugar in the grape juice or when rising alcohol levels kill the microorganisms). Brewers arrest beer's malting

FIGURE 8.2 Illustrated by George R. Halkett, 1882.

Source: Grimm, Jacob and Wilhelm, *Rumpelstiltskin*, George R. Halkett. (illustrated and translated) (London: Thos de la Rue & Co.) 1882.

once the seeds (barely, rice, or wheat) sprout to convert the desired amount of starches to sugars. Yeast's effect on bread dough harnesses mold's actions until halted by baking that kills the yeast. Used for thousands of years these bio-technologies relate to retting and spinning. And Rumpelstiltskin brewed, baked, and spun. Hardly a haphazard cluster of talents when seen in the light of their underlying similarity. They were all quintessentially identified with women. Until women were pushed out of these trades or, like spinning, they were mechanized.

Rumpelstiltskin the Brewer

[The] decline of brewsters is a specific instance of an important general trend: the association of new technologies with men. . . . Since in so many cases the development of new technologies resulted in increased male involvement, it seems that we might be right to conclude that technology has a 'masculine face.'[13]

All of Rumpelstiltskin's competencies were practiced, more or less exclusively by Medieval women. He spun, he baked, he brewed. But in the late Middle Ages women were deposed as professional brewers. Specifically in England, noted Judith M. Bennett, the story of beer's late-Medieval acceptance by "brewers and drinkers is a story of urbanization, immigration, capitalization, and professionalization. It is also a story of masculinization".[14] Women's brewing, and Rumpelstiltskin's usurpation of that trade, like his expert spinning, contrasts with the Miller's capital-intensive and very male-dominated technological infrastructure. (Rumpelstiltskin never trifles with the story's other exclusively male vocation, kingship, a sexually unambiguous trade. He and the king never confront.) When this fairytale appeared in its current form milling grain was masculine and 'technological' while brewing was a trade in transition, threatened by the men represented by Rumpelstiltskin: "In 1300, brewing was a ubiquitous trade that required little specialized skill or equipment, conferred minimal trade identity, and offered only small profits. As such it was accessible to women, it was a good trade for them".[15] In a trend that moved at different rates in different continental countries, the skills that women had perfected Rumpelstiltskin performs.[16] And, at one time, everything of which Rumpelstiltskin boasts were female arts.

We now see that nothing could have been less happenstance than his seemingly silly midnight forest chant. Every one of his competencies was highly gendered, which further suggests that, as part of his swaggering song, his name was not meaningless either. Other consequences arise from this observation, corollaries that tint the rest of the fairytale. Such meticulously detailed attention to the household and money-making activities of a pre-modern woman strongly reinforces two ideas: that the fairytale was composed by and for women and that, regardless of whenever it was first written down, its exquisitely particular choice of imagery were unlikely to have originated in a male's literary exercise but emerged from a popular and long-gestating process. Its intricately gendered structure saturates every element with women's sexual identity that argues for some recollection of an oral tradition rather than a professional author's voice.

★★★

No misunderstanding teller (including the latest generation before the Grimms recorded Rumpelstiltskin) revised parts to violate its agricultural-technological assumptions. The story secreted an image that flax workers would appreciate, as no clumsy alterations by an urbanite garbled the tale or introduced internal incoherence within its deeply buried structure. A modern cloth and fiber specialist, recognized that "the source for the image is not far to seek. Flax that has been retted in standing or running water turns golden; flax retted in the nightly dew is pale silver".[17] When properly processed the plant spontaneously yields golden thread. It's like magic. But it's not devilish. The spinnstube's ladies knew gleaming gilt appeared automatically in the course of preparing water-retted flax, and they could be proud of that mastery. An unexplainable alchemical transformation occurred as they watched and coaxed it into existence. And that metamorphosis referred to another part of the story, a detail that preceded Rumpelstiltskin's magical spinning.

The raw fiber's baffling golden transmutation trumpeted the storytellers' intrinsic pride in living near abundant water required for water-retting's gold. That lavish use of water accounted for a deliberate detail: the Queen's Dad ran a mill. Flax retting and water-milling arise from the same resources. The spinners were also pleased about not having to stoop to dew retting: these particularities suggest Rumpelstiltskin's storytellers spun water-retted flax. And they made up stories using their everyday knowledge.

But instead of flax the story-tellers had the sadistically greedy King supply only straw, upping the ante. In reality the miller's daughter likely spun flax but nothing in the story demands that she spin flax. Spinning contributes the story's crucial element, not the choice of fiber which adds some subtle technicalities.[i] Beginning with the spinnstube's ladies' deference to their own high-quality agricultural product and their spinning skills, the story-tellers extrapolated an even better spinner than any of them. They invented a super-spinner, a compromised man who could adroitly perform an otherwise highly gendered skill.

Domestic Dangers

> She tried spinning the straw but it just got tangled in the wheel. The straw certainly did not turn into gold.

The change from yellow straw to gold represents an anchoring detail the spinnstube's ladies borrowed from reality to hint at Rumpelstiltskin's identity. Women noticed many things change color. Pale dough precedes golden bread (and Rumpelstiltskin is a baker). White cream yields golden butter. As a brewer, Rumpelstiltskin watched greyish wort become golden beer. The story-tellers' unglamorous humdrum jobs regularly saw their non-magical labors turn stuff golden. But sometimes mundane chores inexplicably go awry and fairies are blamed. Somebody had to be at fault when a woman did everything right but the product failed. Rumpelstiltskin's distant cousin committed exactly those domestic crimes.

i. Today threads or yarns of wool do not recall the color gold while in olden times colored fleece—usually brown, tan, orange or black—was more sought-after than pure white. After more than a century of breeding bright white fleece for uniformity a recent renaissance of natural fibers promoted a resurgence in colored wools. The story assumes many details about an agricultural (not a pastoral) society used to spinning flax, which summons distant parallels. Jason's search—northward, from the Mediterranean, into the Black Sea— for the Golden Fleece recalls a Neolithic way of mining gold flecks. Prehistorically, a fleece with corners weighted with rocks was submerged at the bottom of a shallow quickly running mountain stream. The heaviest particles, tumbling specks of gold rushing down from the mountains of Asia Minor, dropped from solution and tangled into the curly wool. Coated with gold dust when retrieved the fleece became legendary to Mediterraneans who laboriously mined in the earth. As in the northern European tale of Rumpelstiltskin's gilded spinning the Mediterranean myth of Jason's quest united gold and with a fiber, wool.

FIGURE 8.3   Illustrated by Henry Justice Ford, 1889.

Source: in Andrew Lang (ed), *Blue Fairy Book* (New York, 1965, originally published in 1889).

Rumpelstiltskin behaves a bit like Puck, who travels under different names as he magically helps and hinders household chores.[ii] Shakespeare has an expert, another fairy, describe Puck's work in baking and brewing:

ii. By trade and mischief they both seem related to the Irish pooka, or púca. To this clan belongs Harvey, the giant white rabbit, hero of Mary Chase's 1944 play and made into the successful movie of 1950. Also the Welsh household spirits *pwcca* descended from Pouk, a name for the devil. Once potent, Puck's authority shrank until he became only a misleader of night travelers who favored other minor-league pranks like spoiling milk, frightening young girls, and tripping old ladies.

Either I mistake your shape and making quite,
Or else you are that shrewd and knavish sprite
Call'd Robin Goodfellow:[18] are not you he
That frights the maidens of the villagery;
Skim milk, and sometimes labour in the quern
And bootless make the breathless housewife churn;
And sometime make the drink to bear no barm;[19]
(A Midsummer Night's Dream *II. 1*)

Rumpelstiltskin too is cast as a "shrewd and knavish sprite". Like Puck, distressed women (the miller's daughter) call upon his aid or blame him for magical transformations that, they know not how, arise from their labor or fail to materialize in spite of all their work (like raising an impotent penis). On the farm, throughout the village, in the spinnstube, giggling or malign spirits account for nature's concealed forces that produce unexplainable but visible changes for better or worse. Or no change at all. Rumpelstiltskin serenades himself by proudly recounting his mastery of the biochemical arts of brewing and baking, to which we can add golden retting. Accordingly, women who knowingly told this tale included details to tacitly confirm significant craft-specific words. They knew what they were talking about. Spinning. Men. Retting.

Spinning While Stoned

> Lilliputian vision (little beings—elves, dwarfs, fairies, imps—are curiously common in these hallucinations).
>
> *Oliver Sacks*

Mostly the spinnstube's ladies spun wool or flax while the incarcerated miller's girl tried to spin straw. There's an alternative to consider. Another fibrous plant yields spinnable filaments—hemp. This plant also undergoes retting. The hemp plant's slender woody stalks are hollow except at the tip and base while the stalk's inner bark furnishes hemp fibers. Hemp processing compares to handling flax while woven hemp fiber resembles linen; both linen and canvas (from *cannabis*) have been produced for untold ages. From long and intimate association the ladies who spun hemp knew a thing or two about this plant. What they knew could supply the sub-text for a joke, just another giggle barely audible in this story's straight-laced telling.[20]

If she had been trying to spin hemp fibers long into the night and absent-mindedly chewing its leaves—the plant's celebrated by-products derive from the intoxicating leaves processed into hashish or *bhang*—the girl's brain might have accumulated enough of its psycho-active resinous ingredients to show her a tiny man. Stoned on hemp she could converse with him and imagine he could do wonders. The Miller's Daughter perhaps inadvertently saw visions coaxed by marijuana resins that altered a state of awareness. In all times and places drug-induced visions transported the recipient to tangency with the divine; those experiences have seemed "true", though often terrifying.

Regarding that sacred raised consciousness, Oliver Sacks asked "Why has every culture known to us sought and found hallucinogenic drugs and used them, first and foremost, for sacramental purposes?" And then, with special relevance to the current question, Sacks goes on to note

> The effects of cannabis, mescaline, LSD, and other hallucinogenic drugs have an immense range and variety. Yet certain categories of perceptual distortion and hallucinatory experience may, to some extent, be regarded as typical of the brain's response to such drugs. . . . There may be micropsia or Lilliputian vision (little beings—elves, dwarfs, fairies, imps—are curiously common in these hallucinations).[21]

Does she really encounter him? Except for the handmaid's witness (who appears in some variants of the story, or sometimes a huntsman in the woods who overhears the song) only the Miller's Daughter sees Rumpelstiltskin.[22] Without witnesses to his reality, Rumpelstiltskin could be a hash-induced hallucination. Much depends on what fiber she spun.

A Central Question: Where Has Mother Gone?

> The movie [*Interstellar*] starts on a farm, and you see a grandfather's love for his grand kids and the children's love for their father. (Mom had died sometime earlier).[23]
> *David Brooks*

Despite its bizarre idiosyncrasies Rumpelstiltskin's tale displays structural constants found throughout fairytales. Those same rudimentary story principles survived into the present day. Popular narrative forms, like movies and TV, subsequently inherited fairytales' penchants for specific organizing principles. One of the strongest of these formulas required absence, a character to be missing from the action.

In the fairytale, we meet cruel and frightening people, the least deranged of whom appears a scary gremlin-like miniature man. But there is one person we do not meet. Discounting some variants' superfluous maidservant, neither a mother nor an older female appears in the Tale of Rumpelstiltskin—an interesting but not unique detail, by itself.[24] Beset by flawed men, the girl becomes a queen with no mother to protect her.[25]

The nameless girl's absent mother refers to a hidden name even more obscure than her's or her father's who is identified by his trade. In succeeding centuries he will carry the trade-derived name Mr. Miller bestowed on his wife. (Anonymous even at its ending, the Queen draws to a close somebody else's story in which she is never named. Called many things—a child/daughter, prisoner, worker, wife, queen, mother, victor— her name, wrapped deep inside the story, remains as secret as was Rumpelstiltskin's, but for different reasons.) Yet, in a way familiar to high art but less obvious in folklore, the absent mother prowls the story just as Richard Strauss bid dead Agamemnon haunt Elektra from first to last note, influencing all but nowhere present as a character appearing in the opera. When she finds herself alone in her stone cell that first night the Miller's Daughter likely cried for the one who taught her spinning, her missing mother—she'd never heard of Rumpelstiltskin.

Males also managed households: Belle's father without a wife or Hansel and Gretel's Dad with his venomous second wife. But a competent single male parent threatened motherhood's status. Single fathers in fairytales are widowers (where is the miller's wife? or Belle's mother?) or male parents who take in foundlings or step-children. Here reality entered, another authentic touch. Fairytales acknowledged the often too-real situation of abandoned or orphaned children while asserting mothers' rights. Mothers endured inalienable life-long responsibilities with direst consequences if delegated. The spinnstube's ladies, mothers who bore every hardship to retain and raise their children, thought alternative prospects too distasteful to countenance.

Lacking a mother character Rumpelstiltskin's story might confirm Bruno Bettelheim's notion of how girls learn to disengage from mother to gain independence.[26] That process differs from what adolescent boys endure. The difference of gender outlook between boys and girls may account for qualities of a story crafted without Mom, a story that therefore avoids female generational friction. Without the conflict of a mother the nominal heroine, the Miller's Daughter, cannot be "kept captive by the selfish, evil female figure and hence unavailable to her lover", as Bettelheim styled quintessentially oedipal female stories like Rapunzel, Cinderella, or Snow White.[27] Yet the Tale of Rumpelstiltskin could scarcely help girls navigate childhood's treacherous passage into womanhood if its cached references were meant as a strictly adult amusement.

Apparently neither a bedtime story nor a moral lesson, the Tale of Rumpelstiltskin was composed for a grown-up audience not at all innocent. But if intended as a usefully instructional guide to negotiate adolescence the fairytale might conceal a hidden lesson, a warning from older females to the nubile.

Initially by adults for adults, Rumpelstiltskin's story roamed from teller to teller with its targets sufficiently disguised so that anyone could safely hear it, children even, or the butt of its derision: men. Rumpelstiltskin could be belittled, even dismissed, for challenging motherhood by suggesting he become a single father. That rejection seemed warranted despite the countervailing considerations: his supreme proficiency at the quintessential female task.

If his adoption of the Queen's child was not scotched, the story's latent prospects might appeal to peasant children; those kiddies might consider the temptation to learn magic and enjoy a full belly (because Rumpelstiltskin bakes and brews). The spinnstube's ladies, who ignored sexual barter as a narrative possibility, honored motherhood above maidenhood. The latter was a commodity invented by men—the artificial so-called "purity" of virginity that could guarantee paternity after it was purchased in marriage. Virginal status can thrive along a continuum ending with "family honor" and all that corollary nastiness. But the Miller's Daughter does not avoid pre-marital sex with Rumpelstiltskin; she's clueless that it exists as a bargaining chip, and he can't perform so never tries to barter for it.

This message was not for children. The story's lesson encouraged other women to reconcile to reality. The Miller's Daughter who lacks a Mom will protect her own child because she was left defenseless by her father.

Updating the Motif of the Lost Mother

The Rumpelstiltskin tale may conceal the unspoken reason why mother, the Miller's Wife, has gone away: some tragedy kept her from attending to her child or correcting her wayward husband. This absence commonly threads childhood entertainments, right into the present day. Though in plain sight, that loss disappears, almost invisible and unquestioned. Modern entertainments concoct the same crises, as when Donald Duck finds himself saddled with the care of his three motherless nephews—Huey (initially spelled Hughy), Dewey, and Louie.[28] In the years of Donald's media stardom nothing explained what misfortune robbed these boys of parents. We never learn how or why they were entrusted to their uncle whose sailor suit suggests that previously he lived a peregrinating and audacious life. Donald's adventures ended when fate dumped surrogate fatherhood on him. What circumstances grounded Donald, self-obligated by conscience to foster three boys (well, ducklings) who are not his own? No wonder he's so grumpy.

Formerly a mariner Donald finds himself beached, an uncle-father. He endures a humdrum landlubber's existence and not surprisingly under the circumstances, like the Miller, he's prone to emotional excess. He suffers as a tortured hero surrounded by successful and carefree relatives who goad him while he struggles for subsistence, henpecked by a demanding, vain, and sexless, girlfriend who never delivered hinted erotic charms.[29] And then there's Donald's moronic but unaccountably flourishing friend Mickey, whose unbearable success testifies that witless charm and luck trumps gritty enterprise. Of course Mickey's upbeat: a fairytale prince, he graciously cruises through the world spared real defeat that withers the soul. Life never beats Mickey down. He's the Prince who has only to stoop and pick up a glass slipper that pilots him to perfect love. (For a hefty fee Mickey probably does the motivational speaker's circuit while Donald stands up at AA meetings.) Folklore long foreshadowed these models. Like Rumpelstiltskin, Donald Duck was fated to entertain children who enjoy tragedies visited upon a once-noble figure crushed by fate. (Lear with training wheels? Where's Cordelia's Mom?) From the days of the Grimms until those of Disney, little changed.[iii] Mother-loss sentimentalizes all it touches.

---

iii. Perhaps an intolerable model today, early TV had its *Bachelor Father*. That kinky trope played dull parental proficiency against the goofy but poisoned humor of *The Life of Riley*, *Father Knows Best*, or Rumpelstiltskin's story. Latter-day versions reaped guffaws at the expense of questioning the capabilities of an otherwise fully competent male. (As a group, *straight men* can still be broadly mocked in ways the majority culture prohibits when addressing racial stereotypes or women.) The men in such comedies functioned as a sole parent with a potentially provocative but appropriately sexless bond with their daughters or

Merely creepy entertainments to a youngster prove devastating when contemplated by an adult who—having passed through genuine travails and witnessed others' misery—understands how really calamitous are fairytale's misfortunes. Of all possible perspectives on a fairytale nothing so distinguishes its meaning as the observer's position on the parent-child spectrum. Hair-raising tales target childhood's fears fretted with undertones of physical deprivation, hunger, dismemberment, and abandonment. But unspoken among these, separation from the mother usually requires the father's help. Or the child may blame the hapless father anyway. Though a fellow-victim of the mother's abandonment or death the Miller, the girl's own father, betrays the child; he could not protect her from whatever took off the mother.

The story entangles two motifs. In this tale the "bachelor father", which Rumpelstiltskin wants to become (or a cannibal), meets the "absent mother", the latter a prerequisite for the former.

★★★

Adults created Rumpelstiltskin's story to address troubling problems unguessed by juveniles, aspects of a woman's world which some fairytales gloss-over by ending with a hopeful maxim or moral catchphrase. These up-lifting endings lend optimism to a lingering or oncoming crisis. Yet for young auditors Rumpelstiltskin's tale threatens something they, not adults, fear: the Queen might imminently abandon her baby. That anxiety of being forsaken or rejected by a parent proposes a catastrophe that youngsters can really feel. Other than that dread, why should a child care for a boasting oafish father, an avaricious king, or a nondescript girl? All seem worthy of derision. Maybe the real-life child who hears the story suffers such a braggart father. But aside from that empathetic minority all child-auditors understand fear of abandonment.

Rumpelstiltskin's tale assumes death or desertion ruptured a natural family structure. The shattered pattern of an ideal family leaves this story without a familiar narrative type to play the "baddy". No step-mother, evil or not, enters the picture. The Queen abjures a blended family when an otherworldly helpmate offers (or demands) to "adopt" her offspring. Rumpelstiltskin's tale contemplates him as a future step-parent of an unknown race, a situation that, although deflected at the last moment, casts the traditional step-parent's shadow into the story. By circumventing any female-to-female conflict Rumpelstiltskin's story seems engineered to anticipate and confute

---

nieces. Somehow this supposedly subversive "joke" continues to be foisted on a public that claims to seek gender equality but nevertheless laughs at movies whose only humor portrays male's horrified ineptitude at changing diapers. Rumpelstiltskin would have had no trouble changing the baby, teaching it to fly, to bake, spin fiber, and brew, and so forth while also getting in a little softball practice. He was the prototype bachelor father. Or he wanted to be. Everything depends on who tells and who hears the story. The adult's perspective differs from the child's. Or women's.

psychoanalytic expectations. Well, that's not surprising, considering that early psychoanalysis, indeed early psychiatry and other fields of medicine, viewed human behavior (and anatomy) as normatively male. To understand Rumpelstiltskin's tale literature's default axis must shift from the Y chromosome. And without re-polarizing our viewpoint or shifting gender perspectives the tale means little. But once oriented to a female's expectations the Tale of Rumpelstiltskin unfolds an opulent bounty of human observations.

A Surrogate Mother's Care

> She sent her most faithful handmaid throughout the countryside to discover the little man's name.

Reciting Rumpelstiltskin's tale as blunt grotesquerie produces lopsided sexual asymmetry. That unevenness smears much of the story's nuance into unintelligibility. In contrast, the fairytale's structure stands sharply defined by two tests/ordeals:

1. Introduction of the players in the countryside
2. Ordeal of spinning
3. Marriage and baby
4. Re-negotiation
5. Rumpelstiltskin self-names in the forest
6. Ordeal of naming
7. Triumph and Rumpelstiltskin's exit

Compared to that narrative's clear-cut peasant organization an unbalanced sexuality apparently arose from the bourgeois redactor's own psycho-literary proclivities. As in many fairytales he co-edited, Wilhelm Grimm preferred to isolate helpless females to fret alone. But in the story's 1810 version the heroine was "accompanied by a faithful maidservant who she sends into the woods and who learns the dwarf's name and reports this information to her mistress".[30] By enlisting an older female the young heroine alleviates her mother-less situation.[iv] Injecting the maidservant recreates a mother figure, a caring older woman who alleviates problems rather than reinforcing the story's basic

---

iv. In some versions the maid espies Rumpelstiltskin at his homestead. In other variations a woodsman makes the report. Sometimes the distressed girl-queen wanders distraught through her kingdom herself and discovers the name in a peregrination that symmetrical corresponds to the King's tour of his realm at the story's opening. Without the eavesdropping handmaid the Miller's Daughter seems bereft of female companionship and surrogate mothers. The story's stripped-down version, with the fewest characters, presents an uncluttered plot: no woodsman, no handmaid, no anonymous peasant reporting to the castle. Aides minimize the Queen's desperation-driven gumption; consequently, her autonomy differs from other fairytale queens when she, acting consistently alone, earns the right to her freedom by enunciating the therapeutic word.

lesson: when it comes to the men in your life you're on your own as a woman who, at best, finds solace and advice in the spinnstube.

The superfluous matronly figure quickly disappeared and "by 1812 the hapless queen suffers alone, companionless, and learns the dwarf's name only fortuitously through her husband".[31] This latter arrangement makes even less sense as it skews the plot away from otherwise caustic relations to men. Conspicuously, this clumsy device robs the Queen of the secret that must forever be kept from the King; reliance on him warps the wonderful underlying gender-based structure. Happily that version largely vanished.

In another variant a woodsman or hunter overhears the fireside song, which is at least logical: a woodsman would roam . . . the woods. But such a figure unnecessarily and confusingly counterpoises the harmful men in her life with a useful figure who adds nothing to the tale's basic outlook and smug conclusion. The story's only useful male must be Rumpelstiltskin.

As a narrative device, male-female opposition implied a naturally balanced order. That symmetry perhaps operated with more pronounced differences in languages other than English, languages that assign gender to words. Writing for the 1912 edition of the Grimms' tales, a century after the story appeared, the philologist Friedrich von den Leyen (1873–1966) categorized the Rumpelstiltskin story as evidencing indefinite "Primitive Belief". It's true an ancient worldview operates at the heart of the story, a perspective likely to paint everything with gendered language, but the story also features keen-eyed observations about human reactions and relations. And those insights prove anything but crude or unsophisticated. Little changed when addressing highly inflected and gendered language: "Most of the critical attention devoted to Rumpelstiltskin . . . has remained concerned, as Clodd [1889] was, with survivals of primitive belief evident in the story".[32] The vehicle for "primitive belief" evaporates in English that easily sheds extraneous details to expose the elegant story's crux. The fairytale's cunning observations about human relations could not be less innocent or undeveloped, if by "primitive" we mean, without invidious prejudice, philosophy that can become outdated and rendered obsolete by modern science. Discounting only the element of magic required to explain so many of the baffling physical transformations required for pre-modern technology (brewing, baking, retting's color-changes, etc.) the Tale of Rumpelstiltskin appears less superstitious and more up-to-date than many surviving commonplace beliefs.

Finally we see that in her search for her mother the miller's daughter at last found her, in herself. She has become the mother and she learns what that means. As the spinnstuben well knew, when you become a mother all relationships to the world change. Rumpelstiltskin was nothing but a useful helper to a sexually ignorant girl. But to the mother of the prince Rumpelstiltskin threatens to become a monster against whom the story's only mother rages implacable and remorseless. Absent at the beginning, motherhood's arrival looms over the story's finale.

The story's subtle observations about human relations reflect actual behavior, accurately told in the weirdest metaphors. Paternity cases, surrogate motherhood, mixed derision and sympathy for male impotence—these remain current as advice columns' reports of woe, or the banter of TV talk shows. And another seemingly current theme: an

FIGURE 8.4   Herbert Cole in Ernest Rhys, *The Huntsman Spies Rumpelstiltskin*, 1906.

Source: London: J. M. Dent & Sons.

absent mother, deserted, fled from her lying husband, or dead, but whose lack allows the story to dodge the problem of her daughter's female supervision and guidance. Everywhere in Rumpelstiltskin's story female sensibility drenches circumstances with an outlook that recognizes its helplessness to alter the girl's estate roiled by her father's lie and her monarch's blind greed. Rather than a Prince Charming the story-teller wants a man who can get you out of a jam, work tirelessly, and not expect to be thanked with a fuck. And one appears.

What Follows Nobody's Idea of a Happy Ending

In verbal form the stories were malleable, each teller adding flourishes or introducing different characters but a fairytale's printed record forever fixed its form. On the page the story entered a different world as surely and decisively as Rumpelstiltskin appeared among humankind, perhaps not fully prepared for him. Though the story's original tellers worked manually, and were probably rurals, not every woman who subsequently related the story was poor or agricultural. Illiterate house-servants and peasant laborers supplied the penultimate link in a chain that ended in literacy as the bourgeoisie learned of Rumpelstiltskin. "Most of the Grimms' contributors were of the middle class, and 80 to 90 percent of the tales are from young girls or women".[33] Thus, knowingly or not, the Grimms portrayed a female perspective on the world-at-large as filtered through middle-class concerns. Despite the story's social promotion, from lower to middle class, it conveyed women's apprehensions. And carefully studied the tale reveals those womanly cares.

As the Grimms sorted different versions they often purged women's prejudices, legitimate gender valences, and wry insights about agricultural, sexual, and home toil. Once published, the page omitted brittle laughter's vocal punctuation to indicate sarcasm in an otherwise undistinguished description. The all-knowing crones' sideways glances warned listening girls about the hyped-up pleasures of sex and its never discussed failures. A good story-teller's significant pauses editorialized about how men had stacked the social deck against women. Those meaningful silences never made it onto the page. Accordingly, we should re-consider Rumpelstiltskin as literature that lacks the spinnstube's spicy recitation: verbal nuances and eye-rolling to express how these personified allegories reflected a woman's world, all missing from printed versions. As an artifact on a page, the product of a recent era's collecting and publishing, the story lightly comments on the then-prevailing social climate.

These stories exist in time in addition to the fixed forms of gender relations from long-ago and virtually static ages that saw scant social progress or mobility. Fairytales portray gender conflicts without recourse to a panoramic backdrop of widespread social revolution. And why would they? The spinnstuben were neither seminars nor salons. The ladies of the spinning circle were not historians. They never compared texts but shared bitter or happy experience, memory, hearsay, and legend. Those circumstances, largely eradicated from official records, slowly altered with time.

Despite the Grimms' collecting at the dawn of a revolutionary era and this tale's evidently droll view of men and the aristocracy, fairytales barely hint at widespread unrest given long-overdue expression in (North America) 1776 (and in Europe) 1789 and 1848.[34] During that era more than governments changed. So did art.

Authors from the realm of the emerging middle-brow literary novel colonized the psychological zone between the individual and sociology, an area largely ignored by fairytales. The Tale of Rumpelstiltskin hints at deep discontent with a haughty King, any king who may dispose of his subjects at whim, while the story also ignores suggestions of how to dilute or overthrow the rule of patriarchy—that the girl should be held responsible for her psychopathic father who "owns" her. Such investigations awaited another, more literate and expansive, form. The novel's bookish empire sprawls from high myth to fairytales and within it stitches a domain where Jane Austen's people mingle with Dostoyevsky's and Philip Roth's, a population that fully understand one another despite centuries and putatively dissimilar experiences. Yet book-length, self-conscious, literary ambition and commercial success in translation—none of this compares to a fairytale's flawless manner of expression that captivates masses. And captures their allegiance when young. More people know Rumpelstiltskin than Silas Marner, though Eliot paints a fuller picture of that textile-worker's world and, despite critical enthusiasms for "canonical" figures, all manner of 'famous' literary inventions remain but cult figures while the spinnstube's less aspirational ladies crafted an individual universally recognized. No literary character outside the Bible lives as enduringly in imagination or as well-known as Rumpelstiltskin and his colleagues. But fairytales lacked self-recognition of their social commentary. Though active beneath their narrative surface, the stories' frequently implicit discussion of society muted when fairytales were snatched from the stories' generative spoken-word environment and printed while the novel has no existence except as published. In short, Rumpelstiltskin compresses its psychologically insightful material with admirable poetic concision but lacks the dimension of social awareness that distinguishes the novel.

If we seek women's rare pre-modern cultural achievements one need look no further than these fairytales. The Tale of Rumpelstiltskin gains elegance the deeper we examine its structure.

Notes

1. Taylor (1823/1920, p. 149).
2. McGlathery (1991, p. 188).
3. The story apparently disregards even a glance at Christian ethos, which it might have included as a bit of insurance against Church censure if the story had been composed by a single author. The tale of Rumpelstiltskin never installed the usually ponderous, and presumably required, moral contraptions of parental bedtime stories of moral fables. There is no moral struggle as all. Each character operates from a uniformity of belief and they understand one another within this compact. Their fairytale world exists complete, self-sufficient, and seemingly lacks nothing; it harbors no notion of Progress and points to no evolutionary step leading toward some higher and more perfect existence. Shared assumptions keep the story's limits tidy, the contents morally homogenized.
4. "Now one day the sons of God came to present themselves before the Lord and Satan [Hebrew: the prosecutor] also came among them. And the Lord said to Satan, Where have you come from? Then Satan answered the Lord and said, From going to and fro in the earth, and from walking up and down in it" (Job 1:6–7). English preserves his juridical function in the deep etymology of the word "devil" that derives from the Greek for accuser, who impeaches our faults, or the slanderer.
5. "How you have fallen from heaven, O Lucifer, shining day star, son of dawn! You have been cast down to the ground, who once devastated nations!" (Isaiah 14:12). A German invention associated with the Faust legend, Mephistopheles, the soul-bargainer or soul-collector is not in the same league as the Devil.
6. Zipes (1993, p. 45).
7. A.W.T. and Edward Clodd (1889, p. 136).
8. Carroll (2011, p. 340, n. 38).

9. Yardley and Appelbaum (2015, p. 12).
10. For Gonther-Louis Fink (1991) the story of Rumpelstiltskin, "revolves around the hero-ine's attempt to ransom herself or to circumvent the stipulation of the contract, so that in the end the little demon is chased off as a cheated devil" (p. 151). Others repeat Fink's claim of demonhood for Rumpelstiltskin. Jane Schneider (1989) later referred to, "misfits like Rumpelstiltskin, who were nasty and yet helpful at the same time" (pp. 178, 208). Com-mentators who introduce the notion of evil into a reading of Rumpelstiltskin's character do so reflexively, imposing a mental habit to discover or create oppositions absent from the tale where evidence of genuine evil proves scarce though human lapses are rampant.

    Apparently getting his just desserts, Rumpelstiltskin vanishes as if being punished rather than fleeing in humiliated frustration. He disappears of his own volition—no small point; he is neither banished by the Queen's order, nor magically compelled to depart when his name is sounded. He retreats from shame. To miss the source of his disgrace clouds the essence of his indignant departure and therefore his nature, his identity.
11. Freud (1900/1960, p. 174). Writing only a few years before Freud, in 1889 Clodd defended his folkloric "study which is by many regarded as frivolous" but that, nevertheless, "sometimes when least suspected" uncovers "some deposit of early thought . . . ultimately verified by reason and experience".
12. While waiting for clients, her off-hours spinning may have supplied a crucial element in the Biblical story: the red thread that saved her life, as a thread had saved Theseus:

    "Look, when we invade the country, you will tie this line of red twisted cord to the win-dow from which you let us down. Bring your father and your mother, your brothers and all your relatives of your father's household to your house". (Joshua 2:18) . . . so she sent them on their way and they left; she then tied the crimson cord to her window. . . [during the siege] Joshua said to the two spies, "Go to the harlot's house and bring the woman out here as well as all that she has, as you swore to her". And the young men that were spies went in, and brought out Rahab and her father and mother, her brothers and all of your father's household and left them outside the Israelite's encampment. And Joshua saved Rahab the harlot alive, and her father's household, and all that she had; and she dwelled in Israel even to this day; because she hid the messengers, which Joshua sent to spy out Jericho. (Joshua 6:21–25) The sexworkers trade and spinning repeatedly implicate one another as they remain intimately related to female self-identification.
13. Bennett (1996, p. 78). While Bennett describes the situation in England the pan-European trend to gender-displacement seems usefully recalled. She continues, noting that "In England, beer was an alien drink, produced by aliens [from the continent, mainly Germany, Denmark, and the Netherlands] and drunk by aliens" (p. 79).
14. Bennett (1996, p. 78).
15. Bennett (1996, p. 145).
16. As Bennett further notes, "If women had once independently brewed hopped beer for profit in towns such as Ghent or Cologne, by 1400 that day was long past" (1996, p. 83).
17. Barber (1994, p. 246).
18. "The best known and most often referred to of all the Hobgoblins of England in the 16th and 17th centuries" (Briggs [1976], p. 341).
19. As far back as ancient Egypt the frothy liquid that appears atop alcoholic dairy fermenta-tion, barm, was used as a bread starter in home baking (see Rand, 2011). In different ren-derings of Rumpelstiltskin's campfire song, the tasks of brewing and baking change place. In reality, when these industries are practiced to mutual support only unleavened bread could be baked before brewing was completed. To raise a fluffy leavened loaf required barm, another detail recorded in Moses' story in Exodus. It's easy to bake leavened bread with yeast, even if you're on the move crossing the Sinai peninsula. When leavened bread was co-produced with brewing, as in ancient Egypt, the out-going from the land of Phar-aoh meant eating unleavened bread.

20. To insure an adequate supply of rope the U.S. Navy planted most of the Midwest's now-wild hemp. Nautical minded France remains the world's second-largest producer, only some of which ends up in the heels of espadrilles, which are now often soled with jute or other grasses. The fiber connections—affiliations of filaments—grow more engaging: sailors tugged at hempen ropes beneath hempen canvas sails and told their "yarns" while artists painted on stretched canvases, often smoking cannabis.

21. Sacks (2012, pp. xii, 102).

22. If the Queen publicly stages her final audience with Rumpelstiltskin (not alone in her chambers) to feed her appreciative courtiers' delight in cruelty, witnesses would see him or something worse—the Queen shouting an obscenity into empty air. Did she actually behold Rumpelstiltskin or only imagine him during a drug-addled fright? Perhaps the stress of recent events completely deranged her. If Rumpelstiltskin was real the danger of public disclosure is obvious. If Rumpelstiltskin was not real she risked publicly disclosing her dementia.

23. Brooks (2014, p. A 27).

24. In some versions the girl is succored by the handmaid, who is "motherly" in saving her life and fortune, just as Moses' mother attends to him in disguise.

    "And Amram took him Jochebed his father's sister to wife; and she bore him Aaron and Moses. ." (Exodus 6:20). . . . "And the name of Amram's wife was Jochebed, the daughter of Levi, whom her mother bore to Levi in Egypt: and she bore to Amram Aaron and Moses and Miriam their sister" (Numbers 26:59). . . . "And the daughter of Pharaoh came down to wash herself at the river; and her maidens walked along by the river's side; and when she saw the ark among the flags, she sent her maid to fetch it. And when she had opened it, she saw the child: and, behold, the babe wept. And she had compassion on him, and said, 'This is one of the Hebrews' children.' Then said his sister to Pharaoh's daughter, 'Shall I go and fetch a nurse for you of the Hebrew women, that she may nurse the child for you?' And Pharaoh's daughter said to her, 'Go.' And the maid went and called the child's mother." (Exodus 2:5–8) The story hides other missing names. Like many women the Miller's Daughter does not get top billing in a story whose action she often commands. There's a good reason why the Bible and subsequent literature revere the hidden name. In the articulation of the private or hidden name the spiritual and material worlds converge; uttering the name acts tangentially as a language action akin to performative speech or magic. Enunciating the private name could be either, depending on the situation.

25. The Miller's Daughter functions as motherless as Belle, whose Beast is partially replaced in Rumpelstiltskin's story by the greedy King as her tormentor. Ellen Handler Spitz notes how often in fairytales women-on-women confrontations represent the central clash of personalities and willpower; accordingly, "psychoanalysis has tended, in its discussions of its entanglements between women, to weight negative aspects—recalcitrant guilt, envy, and rage" (1991, p. 157).

26. This absence may suggest something of the hardship of separating from the mother. When discussing the organization of children's stories Bruno Bettelheim (1903–1990) noted that, "The oedipal patterns of a girl are different from those of a boy, and so the fairy stories which help her cope with her oedipal situation are of a different character" (1976, p. 112). Bettelheim suggested that, "What blocks the oedipal girl's uninterrupted blissful existence with Father is an older, ill-intentioned female (i.e. Mother)". Whatever one makes of this (perhaps dubious) theory any such tension is obviated in the Tale of Rumpelstiltskin: no mother.

27. Certain fairytale motifs emerge neither conspicuous nor evidently useful, at first.

    Shut up as in a cocoon, like the Miller's Daughter in her castle, Rapunzel is a prisoner until some one, a Prince-lover, breaks into her cell. Alone in her room, Rapunzel intimately regards fibers—her own long hair which she combs and brushes but does not spin (being, already, a coherent thread). She then constructs an artifact of these natural strands plying them together into a rope. Subjecting fibers to industry she wins a promised freedom's tenderness. The Miller's Daughter earns her freedom by engaging a surrogate master of fiber-craft. Rapunzel sings alone in her tower which alerts the Prince to her presence and supplies her identity; solo singing in the nighttime forest revealed Rumpelstiltskin's identity while, perhaps if we assign agency to his hearing, a wailing Miller's Daughter's cries alerted Rumpelstiltskin to her presence. Noting such subtle symmetries the Jungian interpreter, Donald Kalsched (1996) observed a confrontation with "The Prince, representing the outer world in its 'otherness'" (p. 148). Likewise, Rumpelstiltskin does not merely intrude upon the confined girl but also breaks into her circumscribed rural life with news of a world of craft, of real and apparent magic, and opens to her the vista of the aristocracy which, with his help, she may enter. He resembles the visitor from the Big City with word of another way of doing things, perhaps attractive but certainly different and challenging assumptions.

28. At the heart of many fairytales dwell sexually charged males or sexually compromised males. Often these are disguised. In the orbit of a cruel stepmother, Hansel and Gretel's henpecked father's unstated sexual contract is evidenced by his overbearing wife. She—lacking children of her own, which suggests lowered erotic and maternal interests—tacitly limits or abjures messy coitus. She finds children an annoying intrusion in her life with her new husband. There's also Jack's youthful bravado to show himself as the household's manly "good provider" by climbing the Beanstalk and thereby overcoming his previous, childish, silliness when squandering precious resources. Belle's widowed father evidenced his potency in siring three daughters, one of whom (like King Lear's offspring) loves him best and modestly, and so forth.

29. Like the urban legend's victim, she's the neighborhood girl who, broadcasting a sexy aura, does "it" for everyone else, but has never delivered/performed for anybody you know. As far as he's concerned Donald's provocative girlfriend dallies sexless.

30. Bottigheimer (1987, p. 108) who also notes that "the heroine's problem in the earliest extant Grimm version revolves around her inability to spin anything but gold from her flax", regarding other differences besides the presence or loss of female companions.

31. Bottigheimer (1987, p. 108). This spousal aid also characterizes the Celtic version of a name-guessing tale, "Tom Tit Tot" (see Briggs, 1976).

32. McGlathery (1993, p. 78). Though composed of harsh and abrupt incidents psychological truth is never marred by groundless beliefs unthinkingly parroted (unlike Medieval scholasticism that preserved worthless Greek "science" instead of examining reality, which the spinnstube's ladies evidently had).

33. Gonther-Louis Fink (1991, p. 146).

34. The original storytellers' pre-Enlightenment society discouraged or forbade plastic remakings of personality. People did not develop to fulfill yearnings but only discharged the role that social order imposed at birth. Girls became wives and mothers, jobs that—whatever other daily burdens social class imposed—dictated duties preeminently in fiber-crafts. Personal self-improvement and social betterment awaited successful European revolutions. Rumpelstiltskin simmered, semi-consciousness in the imagination as a cry for reform during an ages-long season of unarticulated discontentment. A generation after the revolutions of 1848 art tested these roles' rigidity with Ibsen's *Peer Gynt*, 1867.

9
THE UNKNOWN NAME

"I will give you three days time" he said. "If by the end of that time you know my name, you may keep your child".

Community and Strangers

"Suddenly the door opened and a tiny man walked into the room".

Rumpelstiltskin invades humanity from the outside. Into the cold cell holding the miller's daughter he projects (what we might call) a glimpse of an alternate universe. To story-tellers who believed in the efficacy of magic, in the existence of all manner of fairies, that other world rested just adjacent to their own, a place but slightly less exotic than tales of fairway Cathay.

From some dimly viewed and hardly imaginable borderland with its own zoology and rules, Rumpelstiltskin enters humankind's reality. Before he appears we known nothing of him. He arrives like a Western hero or a roaming knight whose stories typically disclose only vague biographies.[1] (In this genre's conventions, the gunslinger arrives and then leaves settled society without giving his name. One of the best such "Western" movies is really an "eastern", Akira Kurosawa's [Tsubaki] Sanjuro, 1962, in which the hero saunters in from dim unknown whereabouts; he offers no name to identify himself but a number.) We've learned little about Rumpelstiltskin even when the story ends.

Like many cowboy heroes—independent and solitary figures circling at the outskirts of civilization—once Rumpelstiltskin proves his worth and solves the story's major problem, he finds himself unwelcome in society. The hero of the Western re-discovers that his ways are not the ways of society, that community chafes him while his presence threatens society. But, even while positing a similar lone hero there's a fundamental difference between what this fairytale supposes and what became a mainstay of popular culture. Unlike the taciturn Western Hero uncomfortable in his surroundings (encroaching civilization) Rumpelstiltskin doesn't move on voluntarily but is ejected for discomforting the one he helped. He shares some but not every trait of cowboy champions of the oppressed. Or Rumpelstiltskin anticipated these types.

While he works Rumpelstiltskin makes no small talk, the spinnstube's sustaining elixir. "The little man took her necklace and sat down at the spinning wheel. He pulled three times—whir! whir! whir!—and the spool was wound full of gold thread. She was amazed. He fitted another spool on, and—whir! whir! whir!—three pulls and that one too was full. And so it went until morning, when all the straw was spun and all the spools were full of gold". Rumpelstiltskin exhibits a principal mannerism of the cowboy loner. He's the strong silent type . . . only not tall or handsome.

The legendary rogue male living outside society—the solitary actor, the spiritual or anti-social hermit, gunslinger, Japanese ronin, questing knight errant—rarely converts his energetic non-sexual behaviors to sexual. At least so goes the myth. That particular fantasy created, not so much a type of gallantry or courtly love but an expression of awkwardness around people. The loner's discomfort in society generally causes him to live outside civilization while personal commitments have caused him pain. But, nevertheless, they enter into human society, be it beleaguered settlers, a village under attack, or a girl forced to spin for her life. These heroes infiltrate society to temporarily remedy what nefarious humans set awry, not to get laid. Fitting that corps, Rumpelstiltskin fully complies with the up-dated myth that extends to figures like Batman (unless Bruce Wayne's relationship with his "ward" hides intensity not sexual ambiguity). These solitary figures represent true celibates by choice. They serve humanity from beyond society's bounds, entering unexpectedly from afar: moral comets that depart, perhaps never to return.

Talented and quick-thinking, the mythic cadre of roaming strangers restrain or repress otherwise normal desires. (Primarily males, who knows Wonder Woman's erotic life?) Such figures tacitly acknowledge that they possess such cravings when noting a pretty girl's attractiveness without proceeding to everyday sexual attentions. Muscular or fast-draw heroes (pistol, sword, fists-and-feet) appreciate and can distinguish beautiful from homely women but act like eunuchs; these males do not tarry for intimate relationships. (Shane! Shane! but nobody called Rumpelstiltskin back.) Such loners tempt the local girls precisely because, though potentially violent and physically powerful, they remain sexually harmless to any woman around. They evidence a "bad boy" who, otherwise alluring, proves benevolent and works for justice. A woman could muse on so sexually delectable a hippogriff.

Storied tough guys charm women while remaining ambiguously neutered. However incongruous his physique, Rumpelstiltskin fits this manly group of unsummoned solitary hero do-gooders. He is helpful, arrives from beyond society, and he neither rapes the Miller's Daughter nor suggests sex as payment. But unlike this class of presumably virile but abstaining wanderers Rumpelstiltskin never chooses to refrain from offered sex, as might Batman or Ivanhoe; he has no choice physiologically. His lack of options contrasts with the good-guy Western gunslinger, masterless samurai, or the roving knight. Otherwise self-sufficient Rumpelstiltskin wants only to trade for what he himself cannot propagate and when Rumpelstiltskin comes in from the forest—where he dwells tangential to the human world—the community's rules suddenly apply.

He sees nothing amiss when bartering for a human life. The story implicitly scorns that deal although different societies would not disparage Rumpelstiltskin's transaction. (Men customarily barter their labor for the chance to couple, perhaps to raise a family.) Other communities purchase slaves, discount women or children, celebrate polygamy, and trade in or decimate humanity wholesale—activities with long traditions. Swapping goods or money for a living person can represent enslavement, serfdom, extreme sexism, hostage-taking in warfare, religious denigration that authorizes sacrifice, or wholesale colonialism. Each are widely sanctioned in various places and eras and even the most heinous constitute somebody's precious "heritage". But Rumpelstiltskin must barter for a child he cannot engender because the women who created the story knew malekind, especially its deficiencies. (Rumpelstiltskin's creators noticed compensatory male swagger which they slyly immortalized in the tale's braggart father and the predatory king. Among eminent recent tales the background infirmity that haunts Rumpelstiltskin's story finally appeared in *The Sun Also Rises*—written by so physically active a man as to suggest an over-compensating author, not a genuinely sympathetic view of impotence.[2]) The spinnstube's ladies were not alone in drafting such a literary device. Educated composers wandered into that psycho-narrative territory.

Richard Wagner dubbed his dwarfish mist-dwelling race "Nebellungen"; they faultlessly portray the deflection of sexual energy that psychologists call "Sublimation".[3] (Psychoanalysts regard sublimation as "the transformation of love withdrawn from others into ambition in the world—an impulse that, at the same time it produced effects in the world, enlarged one's sense of self".[4]) It's everywhere in fairytales, and always signals an outsider like Rumpelstiltskin. Sometimes a solitary such figure may live in fraternal fellowship or sistership beyond society. But, though loveless, Rumpelstiltskin remains so proud of his competencies that he sings of them, exhibiting an "enlarged . . . sense of self". He's hardly alone in demonstrating this syndrome in fairytales.

Snow White's rescuers, conceivably Nebellungen, mine in the earth for treasures unseen by mankind (Disney got this part right).[i] Like the Nebellungen or Rumpelstiltskin, Snow White's dwarfs remain de-sexed even when erotic provocation sashays

---

i. Opening at the end of 1937, and generally released in 1938, the movie's hit song "Someday My Prince Will Come" epitomizes the powerless girl's wishing for a male's rescue from what Betty Friedan would subsequently diagnose as socially and psychologically malignant. Because neither the Brothers Grimm nor other sources specify their identities, Disney invented names and individual personalities for the princess's hosts. Disney bequeathed us a suggestive pantheon of traits but rejected many provisional names for these dwarfs who labor in a diamond mine. Thanks to the diamond cartel's tireless advertising diamonds merged with formal proposals of marriage. Hence, celibate dwarfs labor to supply goods for mortals to validate (impending sexual) fulfillment.

right in their midst. Not merely polite to their guest they curb obvious emotions to remain steadfastly dependable, un-aroused, though sensible to her allure. (A menopausal queen's envious wrath had already certified the girl's beauty. The miller's daughter lacks such third-party confirmation of any loveliness. No one testifies to her beauty or wants to punish her for it, least of all the story's nighttime reciters.) Disney's dwarfs are not unfeeling, their names suggest a full range of passions, but live as sublimating drones. Their names recognize a spectrum of feelings labeled Happy or Bashful (who recognizes the girl's fresh allure) while another stutters in sexual excitement and another performs the elaborately gracious refinements of courtly love. ("Doc" an avuncular type seems wholly aware of the girl's luminescence in their dark forest.) Grumpy who— perhaps burned too many times by failed relationships—has turned his back on personal bonds, a true Nebellungen. (So, while Snow White moves around their digs gleaming with youth's radiance where is the, comically restrained by his colleagues, dwarf named Horny? He would have disrupted his colleagues' sublimating labor and broken the mold of this psychological type that was intuited long before modern psychiatry.) The dwarfs achieved a competent and a complete social unit before Snow White arrived and after she leaves they'll re-establish their scheduled proficiency. Not of these diligent miners' home-body ilk Rumpelstiltskin reverses the dwarfs domestic situation. While Snow White invades the dwarfs' world to receive their help and temporarily shatter their un-sexed fraternal routine, Rumpelstiltskin injected himself into human affairs to deliver a costly remedy from beyond, with profound sexual consequences.

Rumpelstiltskin's world adjoins humanity's at a single point. There his need for sur-rogate or delegated fulfillment must balance his otherwise, apparently unlimited female adroitness. He roams self-sufficient as a cowboy untethered to the life of townsfolk except that the Miller's Daughter can fulfill Rumpelstiltskin's hope to become a sur-rogate or adoptive father—and that possibility summons him from another world. Rumpelstiltskin never requests recreational companionship (like the Frog Prince) or physical satisfaction when bargaining with the Miller's Daughter. Or even companion-ship, like Belle's Beast. Instead, like any true cowboy, errant Rumpelstiltskin assumes new responsibilities and solves somebody else's problem to thereby gain fatherhood and become a stay-at-home.

Nameless Lone Wanderers

Rumpelstiltskin's diminished condition offered the story-tellers something positive. The sublimated sexual urge performs vital work. Drudgery and sex rarely mix in legends of courtly love. Toiling postpones sex. Consequently, aside from "dirty jokes", most stories praise great deeds of delayed gratification: sex deferred until after dragon-slaying, which suggested Andromeda as a terrifically salacious painter's subject. Was Sleeping Beauty's courageous Prince up for a night's gambol after travails to reach her side, or did he col-lapse and sleep for awhile? Sleeping Beauty's first night with her Prince was probably a subject she gingerly brought up with her girlfriends or therapist. Rumpelstiltskin's story warily side-stepped the whole question of romantic or perverse affections by ignoring a common fairytale motif, true love.

True love propels the quest and resolution of Snow White, Sleeping Beauty, Cinderella, Rapunzel, and multitudinous famous tales. To adults it may appear fairyland's least satisfying element as the spinnstube's experienced women knew that love contributed an essential but not sufficient ingredient to enduring marital satisfaction. One-sided infatuation left you open to exploitation and too often even True Love preceded woe (Rapunzel). Nobody in the Tale of Rumpelstiltskin seems remotely aware of "true love" except the King's love of money. (And the King threatens the Miller's Daughter with execution, hardly the basis for a grand relationship or the harbinger of a terrific marriage. In his dotage the King's fondly warped recollections will paint him a purely innocent actor laboring in his realm's best interests as the Queen seethes with a sharply different remembrance. "Remember how we met?" The story acknowledged realistic marital failure as candidly and caustically as Edward Albee; this tale doesn't expect them to thrive as a married couple anymore than any other royal couple's happiness depended on compatibility.) If he felt love's massive emotional jolt, the perennial outsider Rumpelstiltskin might abandon his calling and settle down. Unlike the love-tamed cowboy Rumpelstiltskin will not domesticate for a wife but might for a child.

Rumpelstiltskin travels invulnerable to romantic attachment, yet the roaming outsider, nameless but helpful, is nevertheless done in by a woman. When he hears his name pronounced the narrative motif of the "nameless stranger" collapses. That's consistent with a story pattern that still survives, indeed flourishes.[5] Certain Western tales would vaporize if we learned the Cisco Kid's birth name was Aaron Feldman. A character's murky past can be flooded with our assumptions, right or wrong and unchallenged. A nameless but helpful stranger must remain nameless because if his back-story ripped into the foreground motivation would replace altruism. Verne got this right by naming his submarine captain/inventor Nemo, no man. He represents a man outside morality, Nietzsche's hero. For the audience's view of Nemo or powerful loners the incentive to act on past hurts cannot equal a coolly developed moral philosophy; we hope that goodness arises from the urge toward decency not retribution, a problem that dogs The Lone Ranger. Likewise, no one knows what motivates Rumpelstiltskin to aid mortals. And yet, in this too, the spinnstube pioneered narrative invention or mimicked high art that grew from the folkloric culture the ladies practiced all unknowingly.

Like the questing heroes of grand epics, Rumpelstiltskin travels alone (perhaps shedding romantic bonds but in any case unencumbered when we meet him), a wandering stranger, mysteriously nameless, beneficial if not sympathetic to the sufferer. He's everything revered epics require of a hero but in a compact fairytale, without Romantic illusions that clot some legends. Nothing about this tale sentimentalizes, panders, or exploits the audience. We're not either manipulated with a happy ending or given sympathetic insights into any of the characters' provocations to action. Brutally outing Rumpelstiltskin reveals more than he cares to share.[6]

How to Rescue a Tarnished Name

There's still one name left over
And that is the name that you never will guess,
The name that no human research can discover—[the]
. . . .
Deep and inscrutable singular Name.[7]

T.S. Eliot

Evidently the "secret name" or the "private name" gives purchase on the earthly body. Accordingly, "Superheroes" (Batman, Superman, Wonder Woman) invent secret identities. They protect identities unconnected with their famous personalities that function like "stage names". The superhero's constructed and highly visible existence will be jeopardized if his/her/it's public identity can be united with a concealed private life. The flip-side of how mythology works, unlike true fame, modern celebrity allows an otherwise unacquainted somebody to casually mouth a person's name making it a cipher. (It's not only the Lord whose name can be taken in vain.[8] It's just a lesser sin when invoking a personage of whom the speaker lacks real access or knowledge, a vice called "name-dropping".) Real-life celebrities' confidentialities became involuntarily exoteric when publicly aired.[ii] But without mass-media this situation could not have blossomed into sore and bitterly ironic vexation; it remained a private and isolated matter for fairytales, legends, and a very few of history's truly famous. Alfred Lord Tennyson conjured an exasperated hero Ulysses (written 1833, published 1842) who spits out his irritation: "I am become a name". He has become a celebrity. A man named by anybody. Tennyson's poetic line—a composition contemporary with the Grimms' promulgation of Rumpelstiltskin's tale—addresses the effrontery of distant and unwashed people mouthing a name as fame's cheap coinage to adorn dubious stories: Fleet Street as imagined in ancient Greece. (Updated, this could furnish an imagined television "Access Fairyland". This hypothetical show's audience would be the TV-viewing spinnstube while knitting, carding, or spinning, watching instead of talking.) Names and fame react intricately. And recognizing that potential abuse the authors of the Tale of Rumpelstiltskin included a motif that often approvingly features in dark national epics to signal interesting complexity while that same attribute might be easily disregarded in fairytales.

---

ii. Like Rumpelstiltskin's "outing", certain newspapers circulated these identities that were supposed to remain hidden. Paparazzi using long camera lens annul private space snatched into the public. Tabloids illustrate what was never meant to be public after motorcycles/scooters or lurking photographers cut through traffic or time. Such industrial-age intrusions and resulting revelations feed impertinent readers/viewers engaged in the pornography of knowing intimacies concerning persons they have never met—celebrities. Or in Rumpelstiltskin's case, obtaining confidential information never intended to be shared. Rumpelstiltskin suffers the tabloid-like exposure of somebody happened upon in a private moment.

What's in a Name?

> The name of any being, whether human or superhuman, is an integral part of that being; and that, to know it, puts its owner, whether he be deity, ghost, or man, in the power of another, often involving destruction to the named.[9]
>
> *A. W. T. and Edward Clodd*

Rumpelstiltskin allows the Queen to haggle about a price to which she had already consented. She might show a bit of gratitude and try to stick to her deal; instead she pouts and offers nothing while he graciously defers payment. Rumpelstiltskin makes her a counter-offer: instead of paying her debt all she has to do is win a guessing game. Not only will she be released from her vow, she will keep her life, new riches, her nobility, the safe-guarded secret of her success, retain her child, and she will secure something else as well. By saying his name the queen acquires dominion over him as throughout the range of ancient belief systems to learn a private name gains controlling puissance over the body of the named. In 1889 Edward Clodd noted this feature of the story: "It is a part of that general confusion between names and things which is a universal feature of barbaric modes of thought, an ever-present note of uncultured intelligence".[10] A name designates the living body, a person's mortal part, anchored by the name to an identity. The name supplies more than an arbitrary label.

Personality disconnected from body can be called the soul but to actually call it, to summon the soul, requires a name. Not every belief system holds this to be true but the tellers of Rumpelstiltskin's tale believed it, as do most occidentals.[11] Even death does not expunge the name. Though perhaps immortal as an enduring spirit existing before birth and continuing after death, a soul carries a name that labels the deceased person who in life possessed that transcendent soul. And in death names a ghost. If we didn't generally believe this—for pharaohs and Liverpool longshoremen—we wouldn't put names on graves, an otherwise useless locator of people who no longer need an address and have ceased receiving mail or returning calls.[12] There are other kinds of exclusive names we do not know.

A hidden name misdirects attention from persons present who harbor a secret identity. That's why the Lone Ranger wears a mask, to be two people at once.

Those with a secret identity possess another self eclipsed by the person standing before you.[13] Batman ('really' Bruce Wayne) or King Richard the Lionheart traveling incognito—both are dually, but not entirely, present "elsewhere" from where we seem to encounter them. While in Sherwood Forest carousing with Robin's Merry Men as he returns from the Crusades and prison, King Richard the Lionheart's absence from court exerts a force as a chess piece applies local and distant pressure wherever placed on the board. (Players of both chess or the Great Game maximize force by positioning.) A figure in Gotham's high-tone social, philanthropic, cultural, and dating scene, Batman maximizes his moral power by exerting his 'other' presence in the city's nefarious districts. Rumpelstiltskin operates a bit the same way, never letting civilians learn his identity. And his presence among humans means his absence elsewhere. But we know not where that is.

Those with dual identities oscillate between parallel spheres of activity, other universes of moral potential. While this may sound metaphysical, headlines commonly announce, "Executive Found in Lovenest with Long-time Associate", "Trusted Investment Guru Runs Giant Ponzi Scheme", or "Strait-laced Preacher taken in Dragnet of Red-Light District"—secret identities, secret behaviors with undreamt powers, secret names galore. While a commonplace in fiction and the news, "The belief in the interdependence of names and persons is evidenced in the mystical ideas of ancient peoples concerning the names of their deities".[14] And a miniature supernatural being, Rumpelstiltskin dwells on the lower rungs of the ladder whose summit reaches the higher theology of the great gods and, eventually, monotheism.

Rumpelstiltskin's hidden name parallels Moses' story in the Bible.[15] Borrowing narrative devices from the Bible—itself adapted from unrecorded myths, clan legends, Babylonian stories, and now-lost prehistoric narratives—conferred a credibility unconsciously imparted to Rumpelstiltskin's tale. One of the Bible's most poignant moments describes a mortal's thwarted attempt to learn the name of . . . what? an angel, a supernatural being? an aspect of God?

> Jacob was left alone; and there wrestled with a man until the break of day. When he saw that he could not overcome Jacob as he wrestled with him he touched the hollow of his thigh and Jacob's thigh was dislocated. He said, Let me go, for day breaks. Jacob said, I will not let you go, except you bless me. He said to him, What is your name? He replied, Jacob. He said, Your name shall no longer be Jacob, but Israel ["Strives with God"] for as a prince you have power with God and with men and have prevailed. Jacob asked him, Tell me, I pray you, your name. He said, Wherefore is it that you ask after my name? And he blessed him there.
>
> *(Genesis 32:24–29)*

Three sorts of names mark this brief account.

The supernatural being asks Jacob his name, which the mortal gives. The man no sooner reveals his birth-name than it is changed, introducing the second kind of name, an assumed identity (unlike Batman or John Le Carré) comparable to a married name or a Papal name that indicates a new rank and situation. When Israel attempts to learn the third, unknown, name he is instantly rebuffed for cosmic insolence: "Wherefore is it that you ask after my name?" The *wherefore* does not only mean, Why do you want to know? (Of what use will it be to you and what use will you make of the name? Because the name is apparently of some use to those who know how to employ it.) The snub also implies, Who are you mere mortal to be granted such familiarity? The name confers intimacy.[16] Likewise, Who is a miller's daughter to be admitted to the ranks of supernatural beings who may call Rumpelstiltskin by name?

From his behavior we know Rumpelstiltskin's answer: nobody. She is not entitled to such knowledge and should not possess or speak his secret name. Holding his name she would control him. That represents the biblical mode of thinking, or at least a way of thinking consonant with Scripture. And the spinnstube's ladies heard the Bible's inviolable narratives every Sunday vehemently bellowed from the pulpit, preached again on Feast Days and on Holidays, carved on church façades or worked into stained glass, and told by itinerant preachers. Those ancient stories imbued hoary archetypes; sacred texts supplied approved templates for any stories they might spin. Especially, the Bible conferred a distinct manner of considering names, a manner of thinking about names that must have been consistent with the story-tellers' own worldview.[17] Or became so.

Supernatural beings have names that humans are not meant to know—unless the beings announce themselves. Scripture and folktales suggest it's dangerous to learn these names. Biologists might describe Biblical and folkloric narrative similarities as "convergent evolution"; they present two cultural entities that, though radically different in constitution, come to resemble each other as they perform similar essential functions. As certain creatures of different animal kingdoms might exhibit striking similarities resemblances appear in all manner of artifacts that attempt to render analogous services—and a story remains an artifact.[18] Such similarities develop for good reason. To the story's reciters in the spinnstube any likeness to scripture bestowed gratuitous rewards: the twin advantages of heightened believability and a sense of literary merit. In a pre-scientific framework (which is not necessarily chronologically determined but an educational and cultural condition, as plenty of people alive today eschew a progressivist scientific outlook), definitions of truth relied not on empirical evidence, repeatability of test results, or a resemblance to observed nature. What counted as a test of veracity was congruence to the corpus of legends and especially Biblical tales that conferred plausibility; the basis for belief evaporated if you doubted the Gospels, clan or national legends. Whatever resembled these texts was prone to believability, and Rumpelstiltskin's story rested on a narrative foundation akin to certain Bible stories.

And Finally

Hidden names act powerfully. Only some people are entitled to learn them, to intone them, perhaps magically, and thereby call out the name's owner which compels attendance—a subpoena. (Witnesses summoned to legal or royal court are commanded to appear when their names are publicly recited.) As a form of witchcraft, fairytale genies or demons were summoned by announcing their names, which forced them to appear. Unless such knowledge was deceptively obtained the secret name remained the prerogative of the named, a gift to bestow. But if, like any leaked and unauthorized information, the name was not freely given then possessing the name breached the bond between the summoner and the named. And more even than his surprise at hearing his tormentor's improbable discovery, Rumpelstiltskin's decorum was violated. Rumpelstiltskin hoards his precious name and he's compelled to flee in disgust at its unwarranted and revelatory use.

In addition to losing his bet and the proceeds of the transaction, Rumpelstiltskin loathes that the Queen gained this summoning power over him, to enslave him by tugging the chain of his name. He came to her of his own choice and he wants to keep things that way, himself a free agent to come and go—anonymously.

★★★

The etiquette of names sounds archaic and complicated. But hardly obsolete such proprieties continue a standard yet upheld, think: "identity theft". In this modern form of personal invasion the victim often remains ignorant of how the private information was obtained. (The Queen obtains Rumpelstiltskin's name by the equivalent of "dumpster diving" when she acquires discarded data. He should have used password protection as indicated in other stories that foreshadow information-theft, like Ali Baba's discovered cave with its password, "Open Sesame!" using both upper and lower case, a space, and a graphic symbol.) This crime has a history, including impersonation, fraud, and magically wielding the name to coerce, an outrage this miller's daughter committed upon Rumpelstiltskin. Even today those of otherwise serene dispositions, apt to forgive-and-forget minor crimes against property, become enraged and miserable when victimized by identity-theft or other unauthorized access to their secret information.

Today the name and the person may not be "one" (in a primitive notion that recognizes no difference between identity's two magically bound elements) but they come darn close to equaling the same thing when somebody else has power over your name. In a former age Rumpelstiltskin's embarrassing name controlled and described his person as Amerindians' names address personal traits. He chose not to share that name with mortals, especially those in arrears for life-saving favors. A human who learned Rumpelstiltskin's secret would gain the ancient and terrible power of reciting his hidden name to designate the soul, the core of being. If he has any friends, they know his name but no one else need recognize or understand it.

Body and soul join in the name. The connection attracted Edward Clodd and his monograph about Rumpelstiltskin's tale regarded it as among a "world-wide group of stories in which lies the savage idea that a man's name is a part of his very self, and that whoever can find out that name has the man in his power".[19] By "savage" he did not mean Rumpelstiltskin's tale featured uncommonly violent incidents as, though it threatens death, the story lacks the physical brutality of many of the Grimms' stories.[20] Despite the stories' anarchic sadism, by "savage" Clodd meant primitive, as coming from feral prehistory, the substrate of human behavior. The ancient notion of unifying the name and the named persists in our legal and religious world in an atrophied state (as you can legally change your name, and many do at marriage, or assume a nom-de-plume, a stage-name, or a nom-de-guerre). If formerly the link between name and identity furnished a core belief for early civilization from that primal condition of society fragments of the notion survive as biblical plot-points and enduring modern superstition. The idea proves crucial to understanding Rumpelstiltskin's tale which, though a far simpler achievement than the Bible is, nevertheless, not mono-dimensional.

Notes

1. Many heroes emerge from biographies as vague as the background of Shane, who like young Lochinvar came out of the west. Some heroes burst into a narrative with a completely intact back-story that they insist on reciting to explain motivation. (Richard Wagner tended to prefer the latter form of introduction, endlessly.) Other champions lived mysterious histories unknown to the audience. The enigmatic hero emerges from a veiled history while a hero's accessible past can explain present action and outlook; the two types create very different kinds of plots. It helps to understand the slights, ambitions, and private hurts that motivate characters. Some stories develop from the personal impetus to right a festering private wrong rather than the convergence of great historical forces. Homer, who after two-and-a-half millennia remains surprising in his insights, combined micro and macro scales. Though cast as the clash of civilizations, the *Iliad* unfolds as the cascading calamity of various personal offenses and egos. Subsequently these insults were excessively remedied, even disastrously (the alienation of a wife's affections, the sulking pride of the warrior Achilles, the high king's haughtiness) but there are alternatives.

   The hero of *Beowulf* kills monsters to (over)compensate for affronts endured in his scrawny youth. Perhaps surprisingly subtle for an early Medieval work that seems all bloody thunder and chest-thumping, his psychological back-story, his motivation, was carefully inserted. Beowulf's elders discounted the boy's unpromising chances. (The epic's sulking wimp presaged his likely descendant, another indignant royal Dane, *Hamlet*.) Thus, as Seamus Heaney translated the seeming under-achiever:

   > He [Beowulf] had been poorly regarded
   > for a long time, was taken by the Geats
   > for less than he was worth; and their lord too
   > had never much esteemed him in the mead-hall.
   > They firmly believed he lacked force,
   > and the prince was a weakling; but presently
   > every affront to his deserving was reversed.
   > *(Seamus Heaney, lines 2183–2189, p. 149)*

   The youthful Beowulf endured insults he redressed thereafter, "back story" or "motivation" in modern parlance. Heroes who suffered traumatic childhoods compensate with reckless disregard for their own lives (like that modern Beowulf, Batman tries to single-handedly amend a society that allowed his parents' murder). The Japanese ronin (as epitomized by Toshiro Mifune's performances in Sanjuro and Yojimbo) moves a solitary figure of supreme competencies without a personal history.

   Because Rumpelstiltskin featured in no other story—no prequel to "his" Tale that might supply any idea of why he acts as he does—we know nothing about Rumpelstiltskin's motivations.

2. As Bettelheim (1964) points out, referring back to Freud's original work, psychoanalysis cannot tell us why a work of art is great (p. 47). Yet, the *tale of Rumpelstiltskin* lacks no artistic intelligence in its formal complexity; its reach into candor remained uncharted until 1926 when Hemingway featured impotence in a male-authored story. Unless one counts T.S. Eliot's agony of romantic inaction, endless hesitance and possible impotence, "The Love Song of J. Alfred Prufrock".

3. A theoretical "Rumpelstiltskin Syndrome" would describe the inability to talk about premonitions of sexual dysfunction; the syndrome would address love's alienation when transposed into work. This hypothetical syndrome marks the sexually inexpressive spouse or lover whose energies pour into the workplace's humanly meaningless (if profitable) drudgery. He's recognizable as the one who finds identity, not in leisure-time play, sex, creativity, community service, or even pride in workmanship but in mere toil or profit (how much you own when you die, as if life is a game with a finish line). Yet he wants a family, perhaps a "trophy family" as proof of his completeness. It's a question of priorities. Rumpelstiltskin wants a child without

compromising the solitary life he appreciates as a shining example of diligent resourcefulness. I am certain that poor Rumpelstiltskin was many times cited as "Employee of the Month". Such people pridefully point out their "productivity" while doling miserly parcels of their Quality Time—as if a genuinely loving person ever denominates love's obligations. Such a person never says why s/he lacks a child, but neither do many busy people who want to be "completed" by a child, whatever that means. Despite the ease of recognizing this type, there is no such psychological syndrome named for this little guy.

4. Unwerth (2005, p. 124).

5. In September 1944, DC Comics tapped Rumpelstiltskin in a transformed version as Mister Mxyzptlk for *Superman #30*. An unusual comic book supervillain of diminutive statue lacked excessive muscularity or superpowers equivalent to magic. Like Rumpelstiltskin this rascal arrived from (the 5th Dimension) outside humanly experienced nature to harass Superman with pranks he relished, more a jester than inherently evil. Significantly, as another parallel with Rumpelstiltskin, this impish figure's frolicking chaos could be halted by tricking him into saying or spelling his name backwards which, like Rumpelstiltskin's spoken name, made him disappear back to his extra-dimensional home(land).

6. Outing the secret name concludes Puccini's *Turandot* but—as the hero's name is revealed—a cold maiden's heart melts in blossoming love's vulnerability while, in contrast, without his secret name Rumpelstiltskin stands defenseless and mortified.

7. T.S. Eliot, "The Naming of Cats", in *Old Possum's Book of Practical Cats*, 1939.

8. One of the Big Ten Rules pretty clearly states this relationship: "You shall not take the name of the Lord your God in vain; for the Lord will not hold him guiltless that takes his name in vain" (Exodus 20:7).

9. A.W.T. and Edward Clodd (1889, p. 154).

10. A.W.T. and Edward Clodd (1889, p. 154). Clodd continues in this vein that such naming raises "a confusion which attributes the qualities of living things to things not living, and which lies at the root of all fetishism, and idolatry; of all witchcraft, shamanism, and other instruments, which were as keys to the invisible kingdom of the feared and dreaded".

Subsequently Clodd somewhat refined his phrasing poignantly adding: "however grotesque the term given to the story, there abides the fact of discomfiture and defeat through discovery of name; and this fact seems to me linked to that worldwide crude philosophy which confuses names and persons, things living and things not living, making them alike instruments of good or of evil, as the case may be" (Edward Clodd [1890], p. 272).

11. In mystical practice the soul merges into the universe (samsara, nirvana). The observer becomes the observed. Non-mystical systems envision the soul (redeemed or not, in heaven or hell) as eternally witnessing, discretely and individually; accordingly, the Ghent Altarpiece's central panel depicts worthy individuals assembled in the afterlife to everlastingly behold God. The personality of the named associates with a history of actions (taken and declined) and a family (the one into which you are born) formed around the name, a social class, and a place.

12. No one has said this better than Basil Bunting at the opening of *Briggflatts* (1966):

> A mason times his mallet
> to a lark's twitter,
> listening while the marble rests,
> lays his rule
> at the letter's edge,
> fingertips checking,
> till the stone spells a name
> naming none,
> a man abolished.

13. Apparently, half the population of McLean, Virginia, and Chevy Chase, Maryland, work as CIA/NSA 'spooks' with sham day jobs of dullest employment. The 1994 movie *True Lies* drolly shot the lead couple's home in Chevy Chase precisely to emphasize the joke. Eerily

(Jamie Lee Curtis) the female lead's father (Tony Curtis) played the reverse role of pretend spy with a dull cover in 1960 for *Who Was that Lady?* set in Manhattan; both movies end in the ruination of a high-rise building. Stories follow forms, some ancient, all coherent, with surprising echoes.

14. A.W.T. and Edward Clodd (1889, p. 155).

15. In Hebrew Scripture, Moses was privy to God's private name inextricably tied to monotheism:

> And God spoke to Moses, and said to him, I am the Lord: And I appeared to Abraham, to Isaac, and to Jacob, by the name of God Almighty, but by my name Jehovah was I not known to them (Exodus 6:2–3). . . . And the Lord said to Moses, I will do [what you request] for you have found grace in my sight, and I know you by name. And Moses said, I implore you, show me your glory (Exodus 33:17–18). . . . And the Lord descended in the cloud, and stood with him there, and proclaimed the name of the Lord.
>
> *(Exodus 34:5)*

The gods of polytheism flourish, becoming many avatars, each with a different name. That variety of names signals their vitality, whimsicality, deviousness, and their complex evolved origins. The gods may disguise themselves and wander the earth unobserved, with an assumed name—sometimes taking mortal lovers, people who guess (or not) their beloved's identity, with various consequences. (Different myths from many traditions blend divinity and mortality. An avatar of Vishnu, Krishna appears on earth and sports with a bevy of cowgirls; Jesus, consubstantial with his Father, is born of a woman and relates to others as a man while performing miracles, acts that violate natural laws. That is, Jesus only gradually gains awareness of a secret identity, a god.) Knowing what to call such beings confers knowledge of their essential natures, whether supernatural figures in the Bible or magical little men who can spin gold from straw.

16. In a parallel passage that repeats the same vocabulary—on learning that he will father a Nazirite (Samson), "Manoah said to the Lord's angel, What is your name that when your tidings come to pass we may do you honor? And the angel of the Lord said to him, Why do you ask after my name which is unknowable?" (1 Judges 13:17–18).

    There's also a feature of scale, of the puny human looking up at the immensity of divinity and seeking proportion, a quality captured by Rainer Maria Rilke's first *Duino Elegy* (1912–22); "Wer, wenn ich schriee, hörte mich denn aus der Angel/Ordnungen?" (Who would hear me if I screamed amid the ranked tiers of angels?)

17. The tale of Rumpelstiltskin arises from the same substrate of human nature as guided the Bible's oral composition in the generations before it was transcribed. The cunning artfulness of a folkloric hero survives in the Gospels' record of Jesus's life; he is portrayed as something of a wily cynic (more properly a philosophical Cynic) who often answers questions with questions, loathe to reveal his name or identity: "And Pilate asked him, Are you the King of the Jews? And he answered him saying, You said it" (Mark 15:2). He's not about to easily give up his identity or to allow others to define him: part snide rebel in the mold of James Cagney or James Dean, part super-hero with a secret identity. Christian Scripture retains some of oral folklore's typical characters, protagonists known for tricky stratagems—Til Eulenspiegel, Loki, or Coyote.

18. Elsewhere I have discussed this fundamental limit on cultural operations, see: Rand (1980).

19. Clodd (1902, p. 112).

20. Clodd saw this as the story's very essence and certainly its most gripping motif:

> We may leave such references, for whatever they may be worth, as clues to the origin of Rumpelstiltskin; and, reluctantly avoiding digressions on topics suggested by subordinate incidents of the story, as, e.g., the origin of spinning, often ascribed to denizens of the forest and the under-world, deal with its philosophy as indicated by *the central idea of all its variants, the nucleus round which the incidents have gathered. This, put into fewest words, is the notion that the name of any being, whether human or superhuman, is an integral part of that being; and that, to know it, puts its owner, whether he be deity, ghost, or man, in the power of another, often involving destruction to the named.* (A.W.T. and Edward Clodd [1889], p. 154)
>
> *(emphasis added)*

10

A BAD REPUTATION, UNEARNED

Anachronism is a real problem, trying to make sure that ideas and attitudes that we hold as obvious components of our world are not inserted into a reconstruction of the past where they were foreign. It's sometimes called "presentism", projecting commonplace notions from the here-and-now back into the distant or recent then. In Rumpelstilt-skin's tale, easily overlooked assumptions supply the story's essentials; these elements describe human reactions that seem modern, which makes them suspect. Such details should not be discarded for fear of Presentism or anachronism as the story really stipu-lates these ideas and without them we'd have a different story.

Beauty and Its Lack

> Say the secret word and win a prize.[1]
>
> *Groucho Marx*

Sometimes what we don't say rings more eloquently than the formulaically muttered. Despite a "happy" ending for the Queen, Rumpelstiltskin's tale unreels no love story. It's pretty bleak. No one describes the King as 'handsome' in the offhand manner of fairytales. The story-tellers understood how aristocracy's easy life and luxuries spared the nobles' looks while the spinnstube's besmudged audience withered in the struggle for daily subsistence. The faces that told this story grew creased with time, leathery from the sun, reconciled to hopes expressed in stories when reality sapped any realistic expectation of improving their condition. The spinnstube could distinguish the cod-dled from the calloused. Speaking by smoky rush-light as spindles twirled, in a reveal-ingly tender observation the narrator described the prince as "a handsome baby boy". We can imagine that grandmotherly connoisseur of babies spinning in the night while addressing younger women. More surprisingly, the miller's daughter is only grudgingly and tritely described as 'beautiful,' a backhand compliment from her sisterly competition as, "The miller's daughter in 'Rumpelstiltskin' is poor and beautiful, but otherwise wholly undistinguished".[2] Her putative "beauty" was only gratuitously invoked as she won Queenhood exclusively through Rumpelstiltskin's efforts. Her other talents glimmer meagerly. She's an unpromising spinner, a hapless and untalented country girl.

The story narrates that the miller "had in this world only a beautiful daughter"; her prettiness appears solely in his highly prejudiced eyes unless confirmed by somebody else in the story . . . and nobody else mentions the girl's looks. When the miller realizes that his initial boasting fails to impress the King, he inflates his claim: "I have a daughter who is more beautiful than all the girls in this region and can spin excellently, both quickly and fine". This bold promotion does not cause the King to doubt the evidence of his own eyes: the miller's daughter is not "more beautiful than all the girls in this region" unless that district is pitifully bereft of pulchritudinous damsels. The King ignores the miller until he adds the show-stopper about gold.

On first sight the Miller's Daughter holds no appeal for the story's only available virile male, the King. He barely glances in her direction only beckoning to his bodyguards to deliver her to the castle. The silence of other witnesses testifies to her ordinariness. Even though "the king and his court came riding by and stopped before the home of the miller" no courtier mentions the girl's appearance as her (relative) beauty never figures in the story, even after her elevation to the Queen. If she possessed it, her beauty would have changed the story's essential dynamic, as beauty is a talent, possessed by many in varying degrees, cultivated or not. When modern literature painted a similar scene the results rang realistically.

Jean Anouilh had England's first Plantagenet ruler Henry II (1133–1189) opine to his counselor Thomas à Becket (1118–1170) when they—in similar circumstances, also riding through the countryside—come upon a peasant girl:

King What do you say to that, if it's cleaned up a bit?
Becket (Coldly) She's pretty.
King She stinks a bit, but we could wash her. . . . If we made her a whore and kept her at the palace would she stay pretty?
Becket Perhaps.
King Then we'd be doing her a service, don't you think?[3]

Were the Miller's Daughter really attractive we'd have a different story (more like Anouilh's sharp detail about royal/peasant relations) as beauty would have turned the King's gaze. Instead, only the miraculously gilded claim sparked his interest.

Visually unimpressed by the girl the King never mentions how lucky he is to marry such a gorgeous woman. (Purportedly she's more beautiful than all the girls in the district, but that's what her babbling deranged Dad thinks the King needs to hear as the awed peasant scrambles to make conversation.) The story's lack of further comment dismisses the Miller's perfunctory claim, which shows how shrewd the storytellers were. The spinnstube's reciters temperamentally differed from authors of modern kitsch "children's literature" because they were not talking to children. No smarm here. This miller's daughter possesses insufficient charm (and, apparently after her marriage, she's sexually untalented) as she's too plain to restrain the King from killing her without lots of money heavily augmenting her attractiveness. The spinnstube's women knew what they were doing in this detail, too.

A miller's daughter represents any woman of the spinning circle: normal people, only commonly pretty, or worse. She could be one of them. Her only credible attribute was her ability to spin and all the spinnstube's women possessed that virtue.[4] But that prerequisite sufficed to qualify her to be Queen. The spinnstube wryly observed how an otherwise disreputable and imperfect couple were glorified with titles.

What a pair: an unhandsome perverted king and a fairytale queen whose beauty (unlike Helen's) would not launch a single ship. Yet, she prospers despite her plain looks. An ugly Rapunzel would have died lonely in her tower. A plain Sleeping Beauty might have caused her rescuer to reconsider and let her sleep. Only a weirdo necrophile would kiss the 'corpse' of an unattractive Snow White. And an unsightly Cinderella? *fuggedabotit*. Beauty is a beast. The story's female listeners could imagine that they too were fully competent for queenship as—with droll feminism or proto-democracy—the tale implies that a miller's daughter only lacks money (gold) and a title to become suitably royal. It follows that cultivated speech and polished manners layer mere affectations upon the ruling class, veneers easily applied to a miller's daughter, a peasant like them. She came from their ranks and was in no way special. This wry assumption of underlying social and sexual equality generated another feature of this story; admittedly these minor assumptions—frankly only faintly visible with the narrative matrix—introduce accessory themes that together, coming from the perspective of the spinnstube's ladies, aggregate to constrain the story into forming the shape that we know, and no other.

After Beauty Comes Manners and Experience

> All the odd names that she had ever heard.

Rumpelstiltskin enchanted an everyday spinning wheel that he found in the cell. The spinnstube's women practiced on just such un-enchanted wheels; their story surmised that with supernatural help their own wheels could elevate them and remove the peasant's stinging abasement. They knew too well the anonymity sneeringly accorded them by the nobility. To aristocrats these nameless generators of wealth, growers of food, weavers of cloth, and breeders of common soldiers, were but subjects. Part of the scenery, drab women were rarely addressed by name. And names or their lack play varied roles in this story.

Does the Miller's Daughter introduce herself or ask to become acquainted with her savior? No. Thoughtless and ungrateful—she should have. Some courtesy would have obviated the tribulation of discovering the missing name.

For three days she spews out every word she knows, to no avail because, frightened or ill-mannered, she never bothered with minimal politeness. She never asked the ugly guy to introduce himself. For this slight, the girl will undergo the quiz of her life certain that she has never heard the word Rumpelstiltskin with her child at stake. "All through the night the queen sat thinking, and through the next day she paced and thought, recalling all the names she had ever heard". She exhausts every phrase and name she knows as she frays her brain.[5] Grasping for salvation she heeds every outlandish word anyone will tell her. No one thinks to mention to a Queen the dross of language. Even if they had the wit to think of it no one would mention a mild curse word, the name of a limp penis.

Whatever its subsequent literary history as it descended to modern times, if composed by peasant women forced to defer to their 'betters' this motif suggests the spinnstube's amusement as the story carried a wry message about social refinements. Under threat of painful penalties spinners had to pretend that blue-bloods were their betters. In the presence of aristocrats, peasants spoke a eccentrically contorted vocabulary of titles, honors, and pleasantries. Accordingly, as the peasants conceived high society simple barnyard facts about the birds and bees could not be called by their real names by 'persons of quality' who therefore never received a full picture of the world and lived isolated from reality.[6] They didn't know the dirty words or what they stand for.

Nestled deep in the Tale of Rumpelstiltskin, this joke assumes the nobility's ignorance of country matters. That presumed obliviousness extended to other essential facts. The former provincial turned city playwright had Hamlet taunt Ophelia on just this point. The prince tests her fastidious reaction when she protests to maintain her honor or her genuine ignorance; hence she protests "too much" knowing the facts full well but, according to Hamlet, pretending otherwise. Likewise, if the Miller's daughter knew "the secret word" she'd preserve her modesty by simulating ignorance until the ultimate moment. For at that last possible instant before her baby is snatched away she would say anything to retain her child, and break the fussy model that Ophelia wants to preserve through feigned innocence. Accordingly, with the stakes so high, the Queen could not utter a word unknown to her.

Until her luck runs out, is she lucky to be ignorant? Did she, hoping to be mistaken for natural-born aristocracy, pretend to a delicacy of manners when elevated to the nobility? Is she unconsciously fussy, a prig, or does she self-consciously maintain her public guise of pretending innocence of any "dirty" words. If it means anything at all this word suggests a vulgarity far below a peasant's conception of her regal bearing. Did she forget the word or did she never hear it while growing up?

The Power of His Name

> Late that evening the little man arrived. "Now, Mistress Queen" he said, "what is my name?"
> So the queen asked him, "Is your name Konrad?"
> "No".
> "Is your name Paul?"
> "No".
> "Then, perhaps your name is Rumpelstiltskin?"

Unlike mystic words, or sequences of otherwise incomprehensible nonsense that a sorcerer might knowledgeably intone, it's uncertain if saying Rumpelstiltskin's name invokes or initiates magic.[7] He's magic but his name is not. That is, Does saying his name compel him to flee or, having heard himself "outed" as a sexual dud, does he prefer to limit his humiliation?

Perhaps sounding his name summons supernatural forces to repel him or puts him under a spell that binds him to do the Queen's will, and she wants him gone. (She somehow attracted his attention without saying his name so the name cannot compel him to appear—as does the name of a genie. Should you ever need to summon a genie.) Saying Rumpelstiltskin's name requires no special experience, or accompanying bizarre ritual, no amulet need be held; nor does it arise from arcane mystical knowledge that the Queen gained after ceremonial initiation to mysteries discovered in a dusty tome of wizardry. It's apparently not a magical word, like "Open Sesame!" or whatever the Sorcerer's Apprentice said to vitalize his uncontrollable broom, which means that saying "Rumpelstiltskin" can't backfire on the speaker. The person vocalizing the word/name "Rumpelstiltskin" entails no repercussions for pronouncing it or even mis-pronouncing it. Aside from Rumpelstiltskin's discomfort when hearing his name, uttering it apparently carries no consequences but proves the speaker's worldly knowledge or ill-manners. In her case, when the Queen says "Rumpelstiltskin" she frees herself of a terrible obligation and announces her adjunct membership in the legion of disappointed women.

While a potent male initiated her pregnancy, she presumably now knows of impotence cases, rumors heard in the spinnstube. Or she experienced some disappointing bedtimes with her king. Neither coitus and childbirth nor lactation introduced her to this word about the failure of corporeal reality.

When the Queen learns it she articulates the contemptible word with delight, to save her child. The utterance indicates part of maturation's inevitable program for women. Sex's ideal and threatening aspects are learned first, its failures and quirks later. In this story's final linguistic 'adventure'—as real a test as any knight's before a giant or dragon—we discover the "process [by which] the adolescent loses a previous innocence suggested by their having been 'simpletons,' considered . . . merely somebody's child".[8] No longer a virgin she perceives the alternative facts of life. No longer inexperienced she perceives sexual failure and not just the "fairytale" version of love-making. And she demonstrates that she is nobody's sexual simpleton but pleasures herself to the extreme. Postponing consummation of the trial the Queen enjoyably savors withholding the name until it pleases her. Then the little prick withdraws.

In a delighted fantasy of mental foreplay she anticipates her action's effect, a point the story explicitly stresses. The former miller's daughter contemplates her ensuing power over the "tiny man" as she toys with false alternatives. (Unstated: Rumpelstiltskin could have lied when he heard his name. "Nope, guess again. Rumpelstiltskin is not my name; what a disgusting word. Keep trying". But he honestly remains bound by the terms. What would she do if he lied? like her father, a master prevaricator.) She finally rolls the word on her tongue: a sonic implement to end her ordeal. Reciprocally, while it frees her, the spoken name instantly becomes an instrument of torture that metes psychic abuse upon her only benefactor.

Eleventh-hour sadism defines a girl about whom we otherwise know little. But cruelty expresses the endpoint of her developing emotional range, bringing her even with

her psychopathic father and heartless husband. The Miller's Daughter's behavior caricatured or epitomizes different female models; as she undergoes various stressful situations
her reactions illustrate the spinnstube's expectations. A victim of men (apparently all
her life), she's helplessly involved in her father's and the King's stupid machinations. She
fears for her life, a captive in the castle's makeshift spinning chamber, really a prison cell.
She experiences dread at the prospect of losing her child but we learn nothing about
her as a wife or mother. Elevated to the nobility she quickly learned to be haughty to
her benefactor and, quite reasonably given the threat, delights in gaining the hidden
name. Finally she exalts to inflict pain when released from her bond. Given the chance
to express her gratitude, she rejects her savior and dismisses Rumpelstiltskin without
thanks but despicably persecutes him with his name (that describes a lamentable condition). With the Grimms' characteristic brutality, "Once she has ascertained Rumpelstiltskin's name she finds it hard to resist the temptation to engage in the cruel game
of playing dumb as she rehearses various names".[9] So recently innocent when plucked
from the countryside the woman now possesses the knowledge to humble the only
figure who ameliorated her condition and to the story-tellers her conduct appeared
acceptable because he's just a droopy prick. The spinnstube awarded her permission to
act this way. Or they would have changed the story.

The story-tellers lived in a world vastly crueler than what governs their descendants in the developed world; the story reflects a harshness unknown to their daughters.
Or forgotten. Laughing at handicaps (or less-permanent suffering) supplied sumptuous
entertainment when public executions occasioned moral amusements and crowds paid
to watch animals tortured to death. But, despite the unkind culture that imagined him,
perhaps Rumpelstiltskin gave offense to justify his humiliating treatment.

The Well-Guarded Chamber

A tiny man walked into the room.

The Queen's abrupt emotional relief is understandable. She experienced rapturous
whiplash when escaping terror as she instantaneously alleviated the threat to her child.
Overheard in the nighttime forest that strange word solved the riddle and allowed the
Queen to vehemently expel Rumpelstiltskin from her world. All should have been
well but was not. Either her flawed character or some other inherent cause stirs her
retaliation, revenge that might seem excessive. She could have self-liberated by speaking
his name, and then thanked him. But she is far from gracious because Rumpelstiltskin
transgressed, not against her child or the kingdom, but against her directly.

The miller's daughter recollects that Rumpelstiltskin rudely entered into her spinning chamber, like a violation, yet not. Although despair summoned him, despite his
service he encroached on her "private" place, a chamber forbidden to all others' access
(until morning). Rumpelstiltskin performs symbolic intromission when he bursts uninvited into the cell of the miller's daughter. He's not unwelcome but is uninvited because

in all the world, at that moment, only her cell's space came under the girl's jurisdiction. She supposedly controls that chamber to produce something precious. The story's motif of enveloping female anatomy re-doubled and occurred more than once. He enters the cell uninvited. Feminine enclosure echoes in the "gifts" (really payments) given to the night visitor: a necklace loosely encircles without piercing; a ring more tightly encompasses the body. The "gifts" harmonize with the close receptacle of the condemned girl's room and her own female role as repository. Rumpelstiltskin penetrates architectural space but, impotent, cannot bodily enter another. And for that actual violation he must pay when he cannot perform the intimated trespass.

This obscured theme of invasion colors other stories, but less subtly. Notwithstanding all its creepier elements, the Tale of Rumpelstiltskin contains no obvious threat of violation as does, for example, Little Red Riding Hood's leering hungry and lecherous wolf or Rapunzel's punningly sacrosanct chamber. Quite the opposite. Gratitude should have showered unlimited appreciation on her savior according to courtship's doctrine that, "Power is the Ultimate Aphrodisiac".[10] She wouldn't have been the first or last woman to attach herself to a drab short older man [Aristotle Onassis] whose worldly power and wealth promised to lavish comfort and security. When Rumpelstiltskin finds the Miller's Daughter she lives in poverty, lacks luxuries or social standing, has not achieved womanly "completion" through marriage or motherhood . . . and he affords her all that. At the beginning of the tale she's a nobody. She represents exactly the opposite of what she becomes with Rumpelstiltskin's assistance, aid that should afford him unlimited forgiveness as she leaves behind an impoverished life, miserable, virginal, forsaken, and servile—before she controls his fate. Helpless in her debasement the Miller's Daughter wails in frustration until Rumpelstiltskin invades the only place she can call her own, a dungeon cell that no one else is supposed to enter, until dawn when she will be executed. If he cannot ask for sexual payment and she's witless to offer, the symbolic invasion still grates on the story-tellers. Their gathering-place saw the story's birth as the convivial spinnstube substituted for the tale's alternative cold lonely spinning chamber, and neither place countenanced male aggression.

A Rape by Any Other Name

A year passed.
The queen brought a handsome baby boy into the world. She hardly ever thought of the little man. But one day he appeared suddenly in her room.
"Now give me what you promised me", he demanded.
The queen was horrified.

A year earlier, faced with an impossible task the girl's frenzied mind desired some un-nameable assistance, a thing beyond virginal imagining. Yet when Rumpelstiltskin answered her unspoken plea, he entered without permission. Aid arrived brusquely into her chamber, a helpful friend turned abuser. However gentle, the incursion in his role as the prick Rumpelstiltskin intruded into a locked cell and here the story-tellers noted how violation does not depend on the rapist's satisfying adroitness but on consent: date rape. She never gave him permission to enter.

Not an assault, nevertheless Rumpelstiltskin's entry infringed on a locked space and this aspect perhaps flattered the story-tellers' verbal craft for forming analogies that elevated their moral self-appraisal. The castle's chilly locked room replaced the cordial spinnstube while both zones of womanly creativity refer to the exclusively female chambers where children are made.[11] Despite its raucous reputation the spinnstube's ladies would never let anybody in uninvited.

Just another male in the wrong place, somehow Rumpelstiltskin bursts into the sealed room. He comes through or ignores a locked door the King had (foreshadowing a husbandly prerogative) bolted shut. Beckoned by the girl's pure hope, Rumpelstiltskin's arrival was not greeted with joy but with suspicion; in fact, "the miller's daughter was dumbfounded". The story proceeds utterly without metaphor: like an adulterer Rumpelstiltskin enters into a place prohibited to all but the King, the chamber to which the monarch/spouse alone has the key and right of entry. The comparison hardly exaggerates. The story-tellers precluded any confusion of their heroine's pleas with a possible seduction.[12] Without threat of impregnation Rumpelstiltskin enters to afford himself androcentric pleasure by sharing her cell. Her company costs him the work that often accompanies courting while his spinning bestows the familiarity of (the spinnstube's) gynocentric companionship. This reading may seem far-fetched after the story withstood zealous bowdlerization in serial editions. But if we return to its core its principal points cannot be obscured.

For years the tale's heady sexual implications were not just slighted but forcefully subdued as the Grimms' successive redactions sternly weighed prevailing cultural norms and gauged the probable effect on sales. That erotically corrupt culture of outward piety (Victorian-era) might relish sadistic hair-breath rescues of isolated and bereft women or the comeuppance of the dissolute—but the market would not tolerate bartered sex as wholesome entertainment. For it's the nineteenth-century veneer that must be scrubbed off in order to peer into the story's heart. We'd like to think the stories come to us from some pure fountain of authenticity but the Grimms encountered and were swayed by powerful commercial incentives that urged shifting the stories' suggestive tone increasingly from what Maria Tatar called "the realities of folk culture" that were both disturbingly brutal and unfashionably a-moral.[13] The reproachful middle-class book-buying public justified the brothers' revisions and expurgations. And decorum would not tolerate weighing the pros and cons of date rape or mildly prostituting yourself to save your life, however coquettish or playful the sex. Yet intimate bodily realities did not pass unnoticed by folk culture.

The ladies who originally told the tale were hardly squeamish about the facts of pregnancy: how it began, what it felt like, the oncoming terrors of birth. Notice of Rapunzel's swelling belly marks her story's turning point—which shows that the all-observant world of fairytales included pregnancy; omitting the pregnancy of the Miller's Daughter emphasized the Queen's moment of power over the puny man rather than recalling the physical discomforts and indignities endured while pregnant. A pregnant woman lived at her most helpless, most dependent on spouse and community, and least able to emancipate herself from Rumpelstiltskin's bargain; death in child-birth was common. The story had to take her through that moment of travail as the slightest reference fraught with birthing's torments would divert attention from the central narrative to well-founded anxiety. In the fairytale she might lose her child, but not in the birthing room. Instead of the dangerously chancy business of labor and birth, the story skips right to the resulting princeling and healthy new mother, a parent sufficiently robust to face down her oppressor, a pseudo-seducer. Substitute-seduction may represent the offense that allows the Queen to enjoy feeling no remorse. For, in many ways, their meetings resemble love-trysts.

Responding to the sobbing maiden's distress, Rumpelstiltskin comes calling at night, the romantic time for sexual congress ("as on the night before, into her room the same little man appeared"). In their relationship, the miller's daughter and Rumpelstiltskin "do it in the dark", so to speak. He works and she, passive, watches in wonder. The night hides many surprises; they meet in daylight only after her child is born: "one day he appeared suddenly in her room". And laughing in delight, with a mild curse she finally dismisses him at night as their meetings end.

Greeting Rumpelstiltskin

Men have occasionally tried to describe (or guess) a woman's initial surprise at the manifest phallus, at "the hot insulting hardness between her legs",[14] mythologized into a welcoming friend. But *exactly* what is insulting or inherently impolite about a penis?

To its playful or aggressive owner, as well as its female recipient, the penis can behave unmannerly, with a mind of its own and definite wants; it is highly indecorous, immodest, and show-offy—everlastingly performing its one attention-getting and attention-seeking trick: the one skill Rumpelstiltskin cannot perform. In modern times it embodies the obscene; in antiquity the phallus signaled fecundity. It seems both admirable, necessary, and inherently offensive while perfectly foreign to its female receiver. The woman may be confused about how to react to its arrival, its appearance, and its needs. The range of responses have been as numerous as there have been couples and occasions: pleased, proud, threatened, welcomed, annoyed, curious. But the phallus must know its place, which differentiates love-making from rape.

Unusual for a limb, this bodily member often earned its own pet name. That's not generally true for arms or legs.

As a pet-named penis, Rumpelstiltskin represents an aspect of the king's phallus allowed to invade a feminized zone forbidden to all others on pain of death. Thereby, and unexpectedly, Rumpelstiltskin's story preserves something of women's outlook by immortalizing an anti-linga, a failed erection. Once he's derisively identified with the unsuccessful penis Rumpelstiltskin's size—no longer a threat being neither torrid and cantankerous, nor rigid—could provoke gentle affection, as he's no sexual menace but a helpmate. Perhaps dubiously Freud observed that "children in dreams often stand for

FIGURE 10.1 Illustrated by Anne Anderson, 1934.

Source: The Golden Book (London: Collins).

the genitals" and, symmetrically to Rumpelstiltskin, unqualified affection for a child motivates the Queen and her minions. More reliably and less speculatively, Freud added "both men and women are in the habit of referring to their genitals affectionately as their 'little ones.'"[15] And a "tiny man", a little one, was once called Rumpelstiltskin. Such a playful name conforms to this tale's rich harvest of sexual associations. This reading might leave the story knotted in contradictions but any such disparities arise from a modern viewpoint not from within the form of the fairytale.

An amusement never intended to demonstrate formal logic the Tale of Rumpelstiltskin probes the human heart, territory awash in paradoxes—messy and illogical, complex, and not easily or truthfully reduced to maxims.

A "Dirty" Joke?

The lead character's name and actions, his appearance that amplifies background knowledge of the quandaries of marriage and kinship: taken together many of this fairytale's features raise implicitly lewd suggestions. The story neatly skirts its basic ribaldry in order to comment upon intimate relationships by round-about means. But comment it does.

It would be a grave mistake to suppose that "there is, for example, no eroticism" in fairytales.[16] It's a matter of viewpoint and gender-preferences when considering cultural and sexual-biological identity. There's plenty of eroticism but fairytales rarely purvey the explicitly bawdy graphic sex of male-begot jokes or folklore. The female variety of lewdness predominates in tales that wryly critique high-flown amorous promise and the tacit erotic bargain.[17] Discovering fairytales' eroticism means jettisoning the default male perspective to imagine what a lecherous female would enjoy mocking. And this story features gynocentric drollery.

As a last in-joke between story-telling women, the King—in the best comic tradition wherein the audience knows things the characters do not—doesn't even know that his peasant wife tricked him into the marriage by an unholy bargain with sorcery. The King doesn't know that he served as a sperm donor for a potential surrogate father. He doesn't know that his kingdom's heir was jeopardized. He doesn't know that his father-in-law's pathologically deceitful blather was only saved from disgrace because his improbable boast proved, somehow, true. But amid this humor even the King's sit-com-like mortification was topped by the ultimate male indignity of impotence. Rumpelstiltskin was condemned to emasculation before he even entered the story and at its conclusion he became the victim of a gleefully castrating woman. That detail elegantly and efficiently wove together sundry social and sexual circumstances. Yet changing times altered the lewd fairytale's situation, its reception and our understanding of it.

Despite all his faults the act of spinning rehabilitates Rumpelstiltskin. Mastering their art he sits among the spinnstube, represents their team. There's a long tradition of spinning as exculpatory evidence to counterbalance an otherwise damning personal reputation. Today it could not be entered in court. ("Your honor, despite what you have heard from the prosecution, and mighty persuasive testimony it was, my client is a fine person who spins!") But in the past. Well, that's a different matter. The story could play with all manner of lewdness if males remained the target of jest and the story glorified spinning.

Spinning That Rehabilitates Reputations

> Even great ladies, clothed in silk and thread-lace, had their toy spinning-wheels of polished oak.
>
> *George Eliot*

A witch who enchanted Odysseus' sailors when they visited her R&R isle, Circe presents an unalloyedly unsatisfactory character. She turned male guests into barnyard animals. But even her disrepute could be rescued. Homer remediated her ill fame when, in addition to her witchy crafts, she dutifully, and apparently with genuine joy, practiced women's fiber arts.

> They stood in fair-haired Circe's gateway
> and heard her sweet voice singing in the house,
> as she went back and forth before her loom,

FIGURE 10.2 *Ladies Spinning and Sewing*, 1765.

Source: *Ladies Magazine*, V&A Museum.

weaving a huge, immortal tapestry,
the sort of work which goddesses create,
finely woven, luminous, and beautiful.
(*The Odyssey*, Book V:285)

When a women's tarnished reputation needs a publicist's buffing, being shown weaving, knitting, or spinning does the trick. Through ensuing ages female rehabilitation through fiber arts issued an unfailing spring of malarkey and from this PR fountain current and recent miscreants sip, females mostly but occasionally an odd tiny man.

Unconvincingly to palace visitors who remained mute on the subject, the conniving poisoner Livia showed herself the ideal spouse, spinning and weaving the toga for her emperor-husband Augustus while Seutonius (c. 69–122 CE) reports that the emperor insisted that "In bringing up his daughter and granddaughters, he familiarized them with spinning and weaving".[18] The imperial family's lordly women pretended to competently execute domestic requirements just like everybody else. Nobody called the imperial family democrats but the symbolism of womanly spinning and weaving proved too powerful a public relations tool to jettison. Mastering fiber arts conferred the ultimate domestic accolade, a point that nighttime auditors of Rumpelstiltskin's tale understood.

Romania's first queen (Elizabeth 1894–1956) presented herself spinning while dressed in peasant garb. The outfit didn't fool anybody. No angel, Elizabeth of Romania said, "I've committed every vice in my life except murder, and I don't want to die without doing that too". A contender for Livia or Circe's odiousness like them Elizabeth presented herself spinning. In her unconvincing peasant outfit as a spinner she portrayed virtue's quintessence. The spinnstube's ladies would have understood, maybe not approved but cackled understanding as they continued to tell their tale of a woman who also pretended to spin and overpowered the men in her world to gain a kingdom.

Once married the Miller's Daughter ostensibly gave up spinning, except ostentatiously in public. It would be beneath her station. Becoming like other royals who cultivated their own history the legend of her miraculous spinning would serve her PR needs, especially as bards on her payroll repeated and embellished the miraculous story with added panegyrics. Presumably the King had enough gold but insufficient courage to order the Queen to spin again. The winking message from the spinnstube: queens don't (have to) spin. Subjects of a kingdom knew that—similar to the women of the family of the Emperor Augustus or Romania's Queen Elizabeth—royalty might spin ceremonially and publicly but, as sex functioned solely to supply a dynasty, for lofty nobility spinning was no hobby or relaxation. For royalty neither actual household spinning nor playful procreation were job-related or required. Comparable to demanded sex, the chore of spinning became optional with sufficiently high social station. Queens don't have to spin or swallow. Yet, something missing, an unsaid bit "between the lines", potently reinforces the story's editorial flavor.

FIGURE 10.3 *Queen Elizabeth of Romania Spinning*, 1882.

Source: Photograph by Franz Duschek, in *Roumania Past and Present* by James Samuelson (London: Longmans, Green & Co.)

The Politics of Rumpelstiltskin

The Tale of Rumpelstiltskin carries a fair measure of political satire aimed at the upper classes, a burlesque secreted in the story's assumptions.[i] But those clues rest exposed on the surface, no digging necessary.

Before she gave birth to a royal heir the miller's daughter spun, as all maidens learned as girls. Then she was challenged to spin supernaturally, a skill that no one learns, so she hired someone to discharge her assignment. As Queen she performed neither housework nor cooking—a liberating fantasy that appealed to the ladies of the spinnstube. But she might still be expected to spin royal fabrics as offerings to the gods or as ambassadorial presents. Such gifts were especially esteemed coming from the hands of a Queen and special fabrics engaged special creators.

The Bible recounts how, preparing to build the Tabernacle, "All the women that were wise-hearted did spin *with their own hands* [emphasis added]" (Exodus 35:25) and did not delegate the work to others. Likewise, illustrating exemplary womanhood despite her station, the *Odyssey's* Queen Penelope weaves endlessly; every night she unraveled what she composed by day. She wove a tapestry to keep her suitors at bay as Penelope claimed she would re-marry when her work was done. If she married while still weaving she would commit implicit bigamy as figuratively the episode of her continual weaving means something quite different from a literal telling. On the surface she's merely declared a kind of sensible waiting period (exactly the courtesy Queen Gertrude fails to observe and riles her son Hamlet), a time to adjust to the presumed death of Odysseus.

Were Penelope to cease (if she abandoned the work or declared her tapestry completed and signaled her readiness to marry) she would be admitting the probability of her long-absent husband's death. Finishing her work would tacitly concede that Odysseus, no longer MIA or delayed had, for her, ceased to be and was tantamount to "legally" dead. Using thread that she or her handmaidens spun Penelope kept her husband alive as long as she toiled at the fabric. She seemed to elongate the thread of his life, an earthly version of a Fate. Simultaneously, but across the sea from Penelope's palace at

---

i. Covert commentaries slipped "below the radar" of officialdom. Audiences for the *Twelfth Night* might guess that noblemen whose lives cruised above harsh reality likely misunderstood what sounded merely a silly, innocent, and an a-political amusement. As fiber-workers toiled they bandied ulterior meanings preserved in plain old songs; in addition to singing the praises of love and ancient heroes lyrics reproached the upper classes in songs known to a boy from the hinterlands.

> Duke Orsino:
> O, fellow, come, the song we had last night.
> Mark it, Cesario, it is old and plain;
> The spinsters and the knitters in the sun
> And the free maids that weave their thread with bones
> Do use to chant it: it is silly sooth,
> And dallies with the innocence of love,
> Like the old age.

(Act II scene 4)

FIGURE 10.4 Pintoricchio, *Penelope with the Suitors*, c. 1509.

Source: National Gallery of Art, London. Image supplied with permission to use by Alamy.

FIGURE 10.5 Servant with Horizontal Box Spinning Wheel (detail from Pintoricchio).

Source: National Gallery of Art, London. Image supplied with permission to use by Alamy.

Ithaca, the enchantress Circe weaves a textile while she detained Odysseus, both women weaving for his admiration and love. Thus both complete their womanliness. But that's only the ideal. "Managing a palace is one thing, but", like Penelope, "actually spinning or weaving like the slaves, even with a spindle made of gold, is another".[19] The image Homer created of her plumps as much PR as Roman emperors needed or as other celebrities invoked their adroit fiber-working.

Goddesses, queens, royal servants, nobles, and peasants ideally all spun thread and wove—and all, with one exception, were females. The spinnstube's women proposed that Rumpelstiltskin's newly created queen only qualified for her job by spinning with magical male help. Her promotion perpetrated a fraud contrary to the natural order of gender assignment. With hidden chicanery the tale violates natural expectations about sex-divided labor and tests community standards for dealing in magic although, with all this weirdness, the story withholds disapproval from the Miller's Daughter. She remains both beneficiary and victim. For good reason. The spinnstube's ladies would gladly take on her royal assignment and its benefits.

In the fairytale's circumstances any pretensions to royalty were absurd; the ladies of the evening's spinning circle were fully as capable as the Queen. That underlying assumption about the story's creators and its early reciters rings consistent with the intentions of the story's transcribers. The Grimms strongly advocated Herder's idea of the German volk, a people unified in spirit, volkgeist—from the lowest peasant to the princes of the German states. The story never questions whether a genuine Teutonic peasant women could properly execute the role of Queen; all such women possessed Herder's authentic soul of her peoplehood and were therefore competent to represent or become chieftains of German-ness. To the peasant women from among whom this story originated, the wry truth (minus the hocus-pocus of volkgeist) was that they harbored nothing but contempt for the aristocracy whose job, with all its luxuries and perks, they felt they could, and would cheerfully, step into. As did the Miller's Daughter. She apparently made the leap effortlessly once properly gowned and crowned. How fortunate she was to meet a helpful fairyland character and employ some opportunistic witchcraft. In other words, with a little magic to get through the supernatural chore, any of the spinnstube's women could have run the palace, mastered the King, overseen the kingdom, and certainly produced babies. As do several other famous fairytales of peasant girls elevated to nobility, this story caches a radical social leveling. In fairytales peasant girls become Princesses on a regular basis.

Of all the tale's messages, its social jibe reposes the least camouflaged. The story's odd twists fail to screen its editorializing nor are its assumptions disguised by a weird character: the King presents a typical and undistinguished king while an ordinary charmless peasant girl can serve as queen if only she can spin thread. Some story-tellers made the point even clearer as, "The Magyar variant of Rumpelstiltskin bears the title of 'The Lazy Spinning Girl, who became a Queen.'"[20] The spinning ladies marveled that luck provided the crucial determinant that could lift any peasant woman into the social stratosphere—and recognizing the role of luck in life (rather than assuming congenital social position expressed innate virtue and divine Providence) is a liberal and progressive idea. That notion wars with static history and ensconced aristocracy.

The tellers likely understood and savored the story's social implications as this same mechanism of a girl's ennobling occurs in so many other fairytales. (That rarely happens to a boy except when King Arthur is discovered as the True Heir, which occurs in a national legend and not a fairytale. Likewise, the de-mobbed soldier of H.C. Andersen's *The Tinder Box* gains the hand of a princess, and presumably the throne by threatening to kill everyone with his canine genies, in a story written by a man.) Along with its snide sexuality the Tale of Rumpelstiltskin elevated an otherwise crude and cruel story to piquant humor about how, unqualified except by mastering household spinning and perhaps, in her father's eyes, appearing comely, any girl can adequately function as Queen. So implied the smiling the ladies of the spinnstube. Because Rumpelstiltskin's tale was funny with so many targets to skewer and so many levels of social sarcasm it remained worth re-telling time and again. Lewd and revolutionary, because all dirty jokes are anti-establishment, its mirth supplied the essence of its appeal, but the Tale of Rumpelstiltskin is hardly funny in a modern comedic sense.

Notes

1. I recognize this note's generation-specific necessity. For many readers the reference's obviousness exceeds all fame's conspicuousness and needs no explanation. But younger readers may not know that a half-hour comedy quiz show called *You Bet Your Life* ran on radio from 1947 to 1960 and subsequently (in simultaneous broadcast in both media) on television from 1950 to 1961. The "host"—and master of supposedly improvised repartee filmed before a live audience (a first)—was Groucho Marx. (Already a slight man Groucho's comic persona walked with a stooped gait that made him appear shorter; he wore a ridiculous greasepaint moustache; he never "got the girl" in a riff that rewarded his hapless brother Harpo with the attractions of an innocent.) At the beginning of each broadcast the audience learned that a common word had been selected and if a contestant said the word a duck would descend from the ceiling carrying a $100 prize. Sometimes Groucho guided conversation toward the secret word.
2. Tatar (1987, p. 78).
3. Jean Anouilh, *Becket* (1960) Act 1.
4. There's an alternative theory (online and unattributed) which I recite here in the interests of thoroughness. According to this exceptional interpretation the tale as a lesson intended to instruct girls and young women on the gravity of playing only a supporting role in their marriage. Hence, the story of spinning straw into gold becomes a parable about the value of household skills, which it clearly is not, since nobody but an enchanted little guy can do it.
5. Alternately, Taylor's version (1823/1920) is as follows: "Now the queen lay awake all night, thinking of all the odd names that she had ever heard, and dispatched messengers all over the land to inquire after new ones" (p. 149).
6. Peasant had no choice but to engage in humiliating rituals. As female commoners the spinnstube ladies impersonated self-deprecating courtesies performed for nobility or husbands, both of whom had the right to beat them or worse. The tale implicitly critiques such manners: those forced to perform those gestures and mouthed platitudes detested what their recipients doted upon as beloved traditions devotedly bestowed. (Former slave-owners grew nostalgic about the Old South's supposed gentility; Europeans pine for the bygone days of refinement when Jews knew "their place", etc.) The spinnstube's ladies tacitly granted to

courtiers the possibility of practicing a body of debonair knowledge they themselves lacked. The spinnstuben conceived the high castes' intricate politics in a world of leisure, florid manners inaccurately visualized by peasants as they envisioned castle intrigue truly unimaginable to them. The urban/rural divide featured in high art. How much wiser appears *The Merchant of Venice*'s bucolic Portia than the urban males she bests, both Jew and gentile. That play more fully contrasts country/city life and womanly wisdom it essays Roman law, revenge, Venetian sophistication, or commerce.

7. Neither exposition nor narration, magic's pure vocalized abstract sounds supply the uttered tools to enchant (a kind of pure poetry). These actions may be heightened if accompanied with special gestures, perhaps incense, sacrifices, and so forth. In any usual sense the sounds of magic are not discursive communication. They function as mandatory signals to a parallel realm outside nature that may compel nature. Magic is not speech and magical spells perform as a sonic implement. (These sheer vocalizations—if set to a distinctive, secret tune, or necessary chant—have the power to indirectly effect the world we see.) When non-magical words alter the world they are "performative", as when a judge passes sentence or a clergyperson declares a marriage.

Most of us overlook such "performative" language, an everyday human occurrence that, although an insubstantial speech-act, truly modifies situations as much as many other things brought to bear to amend or alter our world. When a convicted prisoner hears his sentence pronounced, his world really alters for some time to come, maybe years or a lifetime. And instantly upon the declaration of marriage vows many things change (insurance coverage, tax rates, inheritance, power-of-attorney, the legal ability to withstand inquiry about a spouse and to refuse to answer). A dignitary may declare a bridge "open". These words are not magic but performative language. Believers and non-believers in magic understand that words can alter the world but disagree concerning *which* words and what *kind* of alterations are possible.

In addition to its many other manifestations magic supplied an early quasi-technology to shape circumstance and gain purchase on otherwise inexorable forces. It is (a sometimes spoken) instrument for drawing energy from some unseen place (a world outside nature) to the task at hand (within nature).

8. Bettelheim (1976, p. 226).

The Miller's Daughter had been entered in a Medieval ordeal to determine the truth of her father's boast, a kind of tournament in which her defender came forth in the shape of a little man. When the Queen learns her champion's name and thereby understands his vulnerability, she teases him although he saved her life repeatedly, won her the best possible marriage, and allowed her to renegotiate her contract.

9. Tatar (1987, p. 128).
10. Attributed to Henry Kissinger by *The New York Times*, October 28, 1973.
11. Once again, fine art parallels fairytales and folk art. Coleridge's highly suggestive and sexually charged words created a similar analogy in *Kubla Khan* (1797, published 1816), in phrases like "Caverns measureless to man".

Excerpted for its naughty parts (see following), his poem becomes as wildly and luxuriantly erotic as men's deliriums about the spinnstube's female "harem". Not limited to the grubby working class (unlettered rural types from the Lake District or its German equivalent) or small-minded Medieval aldermen—that vision fueled the poet's erotic phantasmagoria:

A stately pleasure-dome
Where . . . the sacred river, ran
Through caverns measureless to man
Down to a sunless sea. . . . fertile ground girdled round. . .
that deep romantic chasm which slanted
Down . . . A savage place! as holy and enchanted
As e'er beneath a waning moon was haunted
By woman wailing for her demon-lover!
And from this chasm, with ceaseless turmoil seething,

> As if this earth in fast thick pants were breathing,
> A mighty fountain momently was forced:
> . . . It flung up momently the sacred river.
> Then reached the caverns measureless to man,
> And sank in tumult to a lifeless ocean:
> . . . It was a miracle of rare device,
> A sunny pleasure-dome with caves of ice!

The poet seems to simultaneously describe a woman's body approaching mutual orgasm and an architectural space (and possibly an unresponsive lover, "caves of ice").

12. Rumpelstiltskin may represent a penis capable of partial erection but incapable of fertilization, hence a "friendly" penis. This distinction supposes a richly nuanced telling of the story and that complexity should be awarded the spinnstube's ladies. Generations had nothing but time to polish tale's subtlety and their understanding of it. As they spun and re-told the tale, the group functioned as both artists and critics. Un-distracted, both inventing and reciting tales supplied their principal amusement, interrupted by an occasional festival or market day. That expanse of endless work-and-talking burnished the narrative's smallest womanly details beyond even the Grimms' editing to roil.

13. Conspicuously, the tale of Rumpelstiltskin ignores the interval of the Queen's pregnancy. "Conceivably", this absence was intended to mollify middle-class readers of the Grimms' collection by expunging a physical state which Victorians never mentioned, as it visibly evidenced sexual congress. Like Rumpelstiltskin's name, pregnancy was unspoken by bourgeois book-sellers whose purchases of the Grimms' work represented many more sales than the scanty market offered by scholars. According to Maria Tatar (1997) the book trade dictated that "when faced with the realities of folk culture, the Grimms had no reservations about censoring, revising, and reworking tales so that they would conform with the notion of positive cultural values" (p. 10).

14. Southern and Hoffenberg (1958/1964, p. 41).

15. Freud, "Representation by Symbols" (1900, p. 357).

16. Rohrich (1991, p. 9).

17. To explain this mock eroticism, McGlathery created a charming and delicately elaborate construction.

    As Rumpelstiltskin bargains with the girl for his magical services in spinning flax into gold for her, he acts as though he were engaged in a game of forfeits or in extorting gifts from an older sister in exchange for doing her a favor. The erotic element of this game is indicated by the series of presents she accords him, each of which has symbolic import with regard to love and marriage. The first evening she offers him her necklace, an intimate part of a women's attire of the sort to be especially coveted as a token of romantic favor. The second evening she pays him with a ring from her finger, which under other circumstances might serve as a token of engagement to marry. The third evening, it may be said, she indirectly offers her body, as a bride does on the wedding night, when she exclaims that she has nothing left to give. (McGlathery [1991], p. 177) The supposed obliqueness by which the heroine offers her body vanishes as were the heroine asked to surrender herself to Rumpelstiltskin she might comply as her life was in peril and she readily gave everything else. What did she have to lose?

18. Gais Seutonius Tranquillius (called Seutonius), *The Lives of the Twelve Caesars*, "Augustus" § 64.

19. Barber (1994, p. 227)

20. A. W. T. and Edward Clodd (1889, p. 149). Clodd's cited *Magyar Folktales*, Kropf and Jones, p. 46.

11

A LAMENTABLE EXAMPLE OF SELF-ABUSE

Men who have trouble achieving an erection don't want the whole world to know.[1]
The New York Times (2015)

"In rage, he pulled out his left leg so hard with both hands, that he tore himself in two."

Abuse and Self-Abuse

Delusional, mad with jealousy that drives unwarranted paranoia, King Leontes charges his innocent wife with infidelity. He savagely insults her:

> My wife's a hobby-horse, deserves a name
> As rank as any flax-wench that puts to
> Before her troth-plight: say't and justify't.
> (*The Winter's Tale*, 1:2)

Aside from the thoroughly modern slang of "puts out" (that only in the 1920s replaced Shakespeare's flax-wench who "puts to" before her wedding), the play's audience instantly grasped the disreputable connotation of a stereotype: flax-workers or spinning maids suggested loose sex.[i] (The association, apparently pre-historic, was

---

i. In this late play, Shakespeare grappled with the impeached bastardy of an infant princess. Just this question had roiled the kingdom after Henry VIII's death. Questions of legitimacy colored Mary's succession followed by Elizabeth, not to mention the unfortunate Lady Jane Grey. As Shakespeare's eyes turned toward home and retirement, the citified country-boy recalled women's occupations of his rural youth; nobody in London practiced as a "flax-wench". Men imputed allegations of loose morals to the spinnstuben. To the degree that anybody now uses the term at all, it vaguely means prostitute.

already well-established when Joshua's spies entered the house of the courtesan Rahab who was retting flax on her roof while servicing her clients downstairs.) We recall that in Beham's fanciful portrayal almost nobody is spinning while riotous sex rules the spinnstube. Yet—even alone in a sealed chamber mountained with flax-straw and a girl who might die at dawn and can risk her reputation—Rumpelstiltskin never gets propositioned. Where's the immoral, licentious, rank, flax-wench now? The pit of ignominy: Rumpelstiltskin's sexually discounted by a young woman who supposedly belongs to an assembly of libertines, as Shakespeare offhandedly refers to rural fiber-workers as a depraved type. (A manifestly ancient association, the Bible's part-time flax-worker Rahab operated her one-woman-brothel.) Jilted, Rumpelstiltskin's self-esteem descends even further than when overlooked as a potential screw by a notably promiscuous partner with nothing to lose. There's yet a further degradation he must endure. In some versions of the story Rumpelstiltskin suffers public scorn after suffering sexual non-performance. Even that is not the bottom. Another humiliation befalls Rumpelstiltskin. Already victimized by female haughtiness in an alternative ending Rumpelstiltskin violently self-bifurcates.

Compared to his smooth exit on a flying spoon, in their last revision the Grimms added this barbaric conclusion. The violence seems incoherent compared to the story's other images, narrative elements that neatly join to mutually reinforce. In a story where punning words joust with hidden sexual innuendo as told from the woman's perspective meant to wreak verbal revenge, this savage finale might be disqualified on the grounds of unintelligibility. Its physical brutality seems alien, at first.

Surely its incongruent savagery indicates this ending's most prominently outlandish aspect. Although the King threatens execution the story lacks bodily violence but emphasizes emotional coercion. No muscle-flexing "action movie", Rumpelstiltskin resonates to a quieter, but not softer, sensibility. Hurtful words are one thing; inducing self-torture introduces quite another matter. This ferociously discordant motif interrupts a story of psychological states, of psychopathic lying and insecurity, of regal pride, of fear and shaming, of greed and insecurity. The furious alternate conclusion introduces an apparently foreign—and, because of its violence, disharmonious—element that might be reconciled if we can discover some basic essential unity that incorporates it into the whole. The stakes are high, as perhaps gratuitous violence threatens to render incoherent what preceded unless Rumpelstiltskin's physical harm somehow, and quite unexpectedly, attunes to the entirety. And it does.

In some versions Rumpelstiltskin disappears into the earth; in others he flies away: "Rumpelstiltskin beats a hasty retreat on a flying spoon at the end of some versions of this tale, but the Grimms seem to have favored violence over whimsy. Their Rumpelstiltskin becomes ever more infuriated by the queen's discovery of his name; in the second edition of the *Nursery and Household Tales*, he is so beside himself with rage that he tears himself in two".[2] This may be the Grimms' invention. As a confused moral resolution this outwardly stupid ferocity offers pretty thin narrative soup compared to the hearty feast that preceded. Except.

Another hidden but no less witty aside lies barely encrypted in the story, a suggestion that may explain the Grimms' preference. In the late nineteenth century Edward Clodd reprinted a version with this variant ending:

> Soon after this the mannikin appeared before the queen, who asked him if his name was Conrad or Harry? When he said "No", she said, "Perhaps your name is Rumpelstiltskin?" "The devil has told you that", cried the little man; and in his anger he plunged his right foot so deep into the earth, that his whole leg went in; then, in rage, he pulled out his left leg so hard with both hands, that he tore himself in two.[3]

Splicing this ending to the main narrative correlates aspects of spinning and weaving technology that would have been obvious to the women who worked at these tasks.

★★★

The flax plant grows tall and has few branches. It needs a short, cool, growing season with plenty of evenly distributed rainfall—otherwise the plants become woody and the fiber rough and dry. These facts would have scant bearing on our story but the original storytellers knew something else as well, a relationship that correlates to how the plant grows. To harvest fiber flax, farmers pull the plants up by the roots because cutting injures the fibers. The gesture of pulling up by the roots presages the variant ending in which Rumpelstiltskin, trying to pull his foot out of the ground, yanks himself in half, an interesting act for an impotent penis-surrogate. That gruesome motif blemished with uncharacteristic ferocity the tale's clarity but this ending gained favor as it evolved in the minds of its collectors. The self-mutilation carries sexual and anatomical analogies derived from the story's agricultural origins.

If they compiled this odd ending rather than inventing it themselves, the Grimms' variant conclusion implicates how flax is gathered from the earth. And that's just how the story states the situation: "he plunged his right foot so deep into the earth, that his whole leg went in"—Rumpelstiltskin was rooted. This ending also left Rumpelstiltskin's butchered corpse in the palace. Body parts strewn about appears less tidy a conclusion than a humiliated airborne escape, unless such self-disfigurement can be justified because it preserved a naturalistic observation, as do other elements of the fairytale.

The farmers' families had sown the seeds, cultivated, weeded, harvested, and retted the flax: a natural product that, through women's skill at spinning, became a "manmade" artifact. Within the spinnstube's sorority mockery of men's many failings awarded spinning its true worth: women's labor turned raw plant matter to the jingling gold in their husbands' purses.[ii] That idea pervaded the rural worldview. Farming's daylight

---

ii. To remind his subjects that their wealth derived from spun fiber Edward III (1327–77) commanded a wool sack placed in Parliament for the seat of the Lord Speaker of the House of Lords. Facing it an even larger wool bale, the Judges Wool Sack, on which sat the Law Lords (now the Attorney General)—a requirement practiced ever since. Raw wool cushions reminded any prone to forget that the whole kingdom's welfare rested upon trade in this fiber.

FIGURE 11.1   Illustrated by Charles Robinson, 1911.

Source: The Big Book of Fairy Tales, ed. Walter Jerrold (London: Blackie & Son).

work in the fields united in a deep cultural continuity with indoor cottage labor at night—performed by the same people: women. (Livelihoods laboriously secured from the earth represented a condition that bourgeois urbanites knew about but preferred not to dwell on: their wealth ultimately derived from peasant's unremitting toil. The facts of rural captivity to cyclical seasonal drudgery was best politely ignored but it occasionally surfaced in art, moreso as Realism won the day. Emile Zola's most sexually explicit and most brutal book *The Earth*, "La Terre" [1887], recounts the endless labors of rural women bringing fibers from raw state to thread.) The spinners were intimately familiar with every aspect of raising flax and tugging it from the ground was just one of those chores, a detail observed as they left harvested fields with rows of flax stalks lying about for retting. That image suggests the stalk-stilt comparison. Each, stilt or stalk though related, implies something slightly different.

Crucial discrepancies separate the two, now interchangeable, endings. In the first version Rumpelstiltskin flew out of a window on a cooking spoon, an object that makes considerable editorial sense. But in the Grimms' 1812 edition Rumpelstiltskin angrily fled on foot—an acceptable, if bland, description of a humiliated man. The Grimms gradually spiced the finale to match their taste for savagery. In the final 1857 edition they revised the ending so an enraged Rumpelstiltskin drove his right foot into the ground up to his waist only to grab his free left foot with both hands, tearing himself in half—an excruciating vision.[4] This ending partially confirms another aspect to his punning name as his violent straining might be the woman's-eye-view of the "pulling" of masturbation.[5] Flax is pulled from the ground; a penis (without a sexual partner) is "jerked off".[6] Infuriated to hear himself called what he really is, a sexual flop, he tries to prove the opposite by yanking at himself until, unable to demonstrate any form of competence (erection, intromission, ejaculation, withdrawal), he disappears in shame.

If, as so much of this story intimates, Rumpelstiltskin personifies an impotent penis his struggle with his own body attempts relief from the embarrassment of non-performance. Called by his true and humiliating name, he tries a kind of last-ditch effort to demonstrate potency. But he has a new problem. When, after she mastered her situation, he faces the formerly helpless girl now appearing a commanding woman of recently acquired self-confidence. (Truly, Rumpelstiltskin had been all but forgotten as "A year passed [and] The queen brought a handsome baby boy into the world [but during that time] She hardly ever thought of the little man".) Recently a peasant girl, a status the spinnstube's ladies shared, during the year of Rumpelstiltskin's absence she became a nightmarishly smirking emasculator, a dominating figure whose purchase on her situation the story-tellers implicitly admired. Of course, Rumpelstiltskin wilts before her. It doesn't help that she insults him by calling him a limp dick. When cornered, outed about his already embarrassing condition and further chagrined by the Queen's announcement of it to his face, a desperately impotent fellow like Rumpelstiltskin might try to perform solo by pulling with a gesture the story-tellers knew from flax harvesting.

Because Rumpelstiltskin can neither achieve orgasm nor concomitantly procreate a child, pulling on himself demonstrates that he is not merely sexually useless but shameful. A disappointing alternative to intercourse, his pitifully enraged performance becomes ultimately injurious when he causes himself physical damage: truly a case of self-abuse. His condition of witnessed sexual humiliation represents a reality the spinnstube's ladies noted locally, or had heard of decisions inadvertently disclosed from ecclesiastical sexual courts. The spinners knew that public demonstrations of male impotence actually took place in these courts. In front of witnesses. Just as Rumpelstiltskin was dishonored.

FIGURE 11.2   Illustrated by Magaret Evans Price, 1921.

Source: Once Upon a Time, ed. Katherine Lee Bates (Chicago: Rand McNally).

Whether or not the Grimms invented this (replacement) ending or gathered a new finale from material that circulated among their sources, they preferred a vicious degradation of male inadequacies that hardly differed from ecclesiastical courts that supplied professional sexual helpmates. But those sexual helpers attended trials as both assistants and, when unsuccessful at rousing a sleepy member, as witnesses who only exacerbated the poor man's ordeal. Those courts never aimed at supplying therapy to ameliorate the male's distress or his partner's sexual frustration and her resulting barrenness. They only convened to ascertain the truth of a miserable situation. But a fairytale could make the problem "go away" by speaking its name. As a bonus the same story demonstrated that masturbation was useless: only a woman's caresses supplied the genuine article, tenderness withheld from Rumpelstiltskin.[7] Rumpelstiltskin couldn't use the vagina anyway; it only clasps the erect penis to, as Freud suggested, ingeniously play "around" the erection.

The finale resolved the fairytale's many rich structural correspondences, metaphors that an evening's spinnstube might relish to amusingly confirm female superiority when women exercised few prerogatives. The story bundled abundant observations with the quotidian realities of women's lives and complaints and the closing motif proved consonant with facts of women's daily labors: first as spinners and secondly in their annually sequenced chores in the agricultural cycle. The story confirmed the spinnstube's shared knowledge of, and suppositions about, men. Thirdly, either conclusion made sense in a bygone world of theological-judicial practices that publicly tested male potency. The story reproduced features of all these long-vanished circumstances.

Though unlovely, self-bifurcation as an alternative corroborates the story's allegorical identification of Rumpelstiltskin as impotent along with the spinnstube's preference for flax as superior to hemp. In some sense Rumpelstiltskin *was* the flax plant. He knew the secret of how to turn golden. He was ripped up by the root(s). He personified a stunted creative force that outlived the pagan world's bountifully fertile nature. But he survived as a cripple, his fertility gone.

A supernatural being who's no devil, Rumpelstiltskin outlived his pre-Christian world as an unfortunate counter-fertility dwarf. (He confutes the pagan Garden Gnome's rebirth as a harmless accoutrement. Not really a gnome, the Garden Gnome turns out to be Rumpelstiltskin's closest living relative, both partake of a dialogue about fertility as "the pre-Disney [garden] gnome represented a link with the natural world".[8] But nobody plants Rumpelstiltskin in a garden. They might even be related on some enormous family tree as "the garden dwarf seems to have originated in the German state of Thuringia".)[9] Rumpelstiltskin's story probably formed over a long time to incorporate so many closely observed facts about agriculture's growing season and harvest. These agglomerated natural observations sound distinctly un-modern as a way to represent a state of affairs, but in this tale a country girl banishes barrenness (perhaps not from the world but certainly from her life and probably after a flax harvest). The tale editorializes about a state of affairs thrown off-kilter and then restored by a pronouncement. It's illogical but weirdly poignant in a special way. Not modern but solidly rational, the tale remains deeply evocative like the best art.

The Puzzle and a Happy Ending

He never was heard from again.

After he threw down a challenge in what seemed like a pretty safe bet, a correctly guessed riddle drove Rumpelstiltskin to self-annihilate. The spinners recognized that contest.

A standard feature of ancient (especially northern European) court entertainment, riddles amusingly tested wits. Guests were expected to bring fresh enigmas, puzzles, and word-play to acknowledge hospitality—a running theme of "Norse" myths adopted by pan-Germans. That tradition lives in the myths and also in Renaissance literature. Zany or shrewd questions served as standard fare through Elizabethan times when Shakespeare's witty fools parried and dodged rhetorical points. But in the Rumpelstiltskin story, his "naming is comic relief and points to the optimistic disposition of the tale, intended to demonstrate how the spinner can overcome obstacles and realize her desires and purpose in life".[10] Guessing the secret name turns the story to hopefulness from despair, supposedly. More accurately, the Queen and Rumpelstiltskin trade places: the confident tormentor surrenders and demolished, his self-confidence broken, he escapes leaving the newly triumphant mother to her son, her former misery transferred to her fled helper-irritant.

Rumpelstiltskin's cruel humiliation dispenses neither a sunny outcome for all parties nor universal cheer, even by outdated rural German standards of optimistic jollity. While preferable to losing her child, the ending offers neither a fair nor a just resolution. The situation might be truly laughable if we believe a wholly innocent but wronged woman regained purchase on her situation by disgracing her violator. But that does not correspond to the facts.

It's preposterous to blame Rumpelstiltskin for the girl's misery. We must also credit him with saving her life, elevating her to power, granting kingdom-wide fame, awarding a new reality of endless luxury, vindicating her father's improbable boast and likely sparing him execution. Recently a critic asserted that "the naming demonstrates the cleverness, skill, and luck of the spinner, who liberates herself and comes into her own through guessing the right name".[11] The naming contest does not demonstrate the queen's "cleverness", only the fluke of eavesdropping. (Even that's often delegated to other searchers in variants of the tale: the woodsman or maid.) She also doesn't "guess"; she knows the answer. She's rigged the game by the third day and that slim awareness of her foreknowledge introduces this tale's only modicum of "comedy". What the naming really demonstrates is her unmitigated hostility toward her benefactor.

Only for the Queen does the story end, in any sense, well. And then only if she remains utterly ungrateful, un-reflective, and conscience-less. Her situation may have offered another more equitable choice that she overlooked.

After she defeated Rumpelstiltskin in the riddle-challenge she could have, at least, asked if there was anything else he might want.[12] That is, she could have reciprocated his generosity. As the story-tellers intimated—and therefore she, their creation, might have figured out—Rumpelstiltskin lacks only one thing from the human world: the power of procreation. And he had picked her as a sexual surrogate. So, if there's any "comic relief" in this fairytale it's almost invisible to modern sensibilities.

The spinners' everyday circumstances dictated the story's moral universe. But times change and Rumpelstiltskin's subsequent reception varied with each era's ethical standards and worldview. Medieval amusement earned Ruskin's reproach that children's laughter "should not be at the weaknesses or faults of others" which, flagrantly exampled in Rumpelstiltskin, may have contributed to the story's eventually second-class status as an odd, indeed unique, addition to the Grimms' collection. No one quite knew what to make of its absent "lesson". So each generation greeted the story with its own ethical gauge to judge Rumpelstiltskin's pedagogical fitness.[13] His place in the story seems ambiguous (and that uncertainty, rare in pre-modern literature, further argues against a sole literary author as the tale's originator). In some ways he's the central active personage, a figure usually cast as the dashing if temporarily de-sexualized hero. Evicted from an ambiguously admirable, but still starring, place in the story Rumpelstiltskin's role becomes further complicated. He's not the champion but after the opening scene Rumpelstiltskin stands in the spotlight. In some ways the Miller's Daughter emerges heroic. Ultimately, though remaining the story's star, Rumpelstiltskin transforms into the victim, his ending symmetrical with how the heroine began. They trade places: the puissant and carefree Rumpelstiltskin ends powerless, the helpless girl reigns a monarch. As Ruth B. Bottigheimer noted, "he suffers the sort of dreadful fate normally reserved for witch figures". Yet he towers over the story. Although "he never was heard from again" without Rumpelstiltskin nobody would ever have heard of a miller's daughter who never became Queen.

The Mind in the Story

The story associated all abhorrent behavior to men and especially men's misconduct toward women while the Queen's cruelty *somehow* seems retaliation. (She's really engaging in a counter-offensive against slights to women that happen outside the story's bounds.) Her actions seem deserved reprisal when re-framed as all-consuming and fiercely protective motherhood. The Queen's glee reflects her relief at saving her infant to preserve the mother-child link in a custody battle and thereby she discovers in herself the mother otherwise missing from the story. In this dual accomplishment the tale generally repudiates male-kind to reveal a pristine gynocentric worldview. She achieves on her own, in spite of her father, in secret from her husband/king, and by discarding her helper—all men. The tale's justifications only make sense when so valenced; otherwise she festers an ungrateful Queen, roaming her castle, prone to malice.

★★★

Each version of the Rumpelstiltskin story confirms that some blustering men cannot be relied upon—like the girl's father, a kind of hapless Ralph Kramden or Andy Capp. Inveterate liars. The subversive tale (as it's insubordinate to male dominance) paints varieties of men as miserable losers; some men can't even get it up.[14] It should otherwise be her story but is never called the "Miller's Daughter" or the "Queen by Guile" or some other name in English as this tale relates how Rumpelstiltskin behaves, not her. Yet, once set into motion by men's misdeeds, Rumpelstiltskin's actions (his unheralded arrival, labors, indiscretion, deficiency) direct this story's course. How these themes, risible in a story but serious enough in life, are dealt with in this seemingly childish narrative, hints at shrewd adaptive mental mechanisms: survival by keeping your wits as a woman.

Fairytales' motifs often arose from expectations about real-life situations that differed from how men explained things.

Dreams, fairytales, literature—inspect human behavior and harvest the imagination while consciously constructed stories attempt to decipher the state of affairs, some from a masculine others from a feminine viewpoint. As early as 1900, Freud noted, "There can be no doubt that the connections between our typical dreams and fairytales and the material of other kinds of creative writing are neither few nor accidental".[15] The doctor did not specify the direction of influence from dream to art (inspiration) or from art to dream (obsessive preoccupation). Whatever the direction of mental flow, fairytales should not be belittled as inconsequential, backhandedly dismissed in the way the word "myth" became synonymous with falsehoods.

As a body of literature fairytales remain subject to analysis for artistic quality and psychological truth. The spinnstube's ladies, no more dimwits than a congregation of men, probed the same twilight exploration of self-understanding as any modern therapist or artist who gropes toward coherence. Centuries before science deliberated behavior the spinnstube's women, though lacking diplomas and certificates, proved to be attentive observers equal in vigilance to any white-coated lab lord with a clipboard when spotting and identifying human adaptations. That is to say, personality. (Psychology studies human behavior. And behavior is the response to stimuli. Aggregated behavior evidences personality.) Although other fairytales share this ambition, the Tale of Rumpelstiltskin emerges a pure study in psychology.

Something irritates or affects us (consciously or unconsciously) and we react. Some things that rouse us to action produce instantaneous results. If you touch a hot stove your reaction will be swift. Tap your knee in a certain spot and your leg will jump. Other responses take a while to manifest and therefore the prompt or cause may be long gone, an event back in childhood, hence invisible to others. For example, what did the Miller think when informed that his daughter *did* spin straw into gold? Unless we guess his initial motivation for the boast it's hard to imagine his reaction. Did he hold himself culpable for her plight? Was he an inveterate drunkard who allows himself the luxury of avoiding responsibility? A psychotic who really imagined his daughter could perform this alchemical feat? In his perhaps megalomaniacally lunatic mind did he imagine his wishing made the reality occur and the world followed his command? Magical thinking assumes that longing governs actuality.[iii] Was the poor miller a failure and town dimwit otherwise known for brainless swagger? Pick his motivation; depending on the supposed cause of his blurting out his boast you can paint the scene when he receives the news of his daughter's astounding three-night performance.

---

iii. Was this a kind of thinking to which the ladies of the spinnstuben were prone? They implicitly mock it. Yet, it resembles prayer. Even today in vastly altered circumstances too many young women think they will be 'rescued' by a glitteringly improbable spouse and wedding—just look at the bridal magazines. Wishful thinking never becomes anachronistic.

Then again, after her ordeal and improbable survival, how does she feel about her father putting her life in jeopardy? She might perhaps be used to mistreatment because the miller was always an irresponsible alcoholic, maybe a psychotic abuser or a ne're-do-well braggart who broke every promise. If he failed at everything he perhaps tried to turn his daughter into a loser to share his misery and prove that success was unobtainable in life? Does she forgive him and ensconce him in the palace? Perhaps she tartly suggests that hazarding her life should not be rewarded even if things did turn out well, no thanks to him. We can't hear the spinnstube's conversation after the story ended but the tellers likely expressed strong opinions on these possibilities. They talked as their hands worked the yarn.

The Story as Therapy

She hardly ever thought of the little man.

Sometimes dredging up a memory, especially an unpleasant memory, needs coaxing. Group effort helps. Another person can ask supportive questions to prompt recollection and it's especially helpful if that questioner has known the same slights and struggles, felt the same victories, honored the same goals and gods. Sympathy encourages retrieving supplementary and associated memories. The more thoroughly the questioner appreciates relevant circumstances the quicker progress moves toward answers to dig deeper into memory. Today, medical school and the accumulated literature of myriad recorded encounters prepare the professional questioner. A forerunner institution practiced pretty much the same procedures but informally. Equally useful: over a period of weeks or seasons an experienced community of trusted intimates, the spinnstube, could slowly wheedle the shy into speaking truth to the group. They were in no hurry. They had no place to go. Repeated meetings could discover contradictions or evasions to iron out of personal narratives. Finally even the reticent could say the unmentionable, recognized as truth by experienced older women.

With enough time and encouragement a reserved young lady could recall (though maybe not quickly share) forgotten unpleasantness and thereby try resolve distress using a loosely associated confederation that, while designed to enhance productivity of a useful commodity, as a by-product assembled psychological insights. These nightly sessions did not resemble men talking at the tavern. Because the discussants were not men.

The women were not consultants as no one hovered on the "outside" coolly looking in and objectively appraising the situation; they were all in the same fix and attempting mutual assistance long before any "12-Step" program thought to call them a support group. Their shared circumstances spanned generations, a condition that aided communication, encouraged wit, and accurately appraised life's predicaments gauged by elders who'd been there and done that. The spinnstube gathering offered a place to bring wordlessly intuited unease or hesitant questions of sexual perplexity conveyed however symbolically and elliptically. In the spinnstube's closed world women formed, in the words of Lévi-Strauss, "A society [that] consists of individuals and groups which communicate with one another".[16] That is, a society does not exist as a potentiality—because its members *can* or *might* communicate with one another—but because they do. By communicating they create a social organism to mutually enrich the community. But this was a special sort of community.

Now usually a hobby or artisanal refuge, pre-modern spinning did not alienate the workers from their work. The thread of life continued without end, passed from generation to generation, however wise or superstitious. No legislature, the spinnstube was not a committee with an agenda. It did not adjourn after solving a problem. It continuously offered help in coping with life while working, as there was no surcease from labor, no "getting away from it all" to clear the head. Vacation? That's what feast days offered, along with orgiastic release uncommon in modernity.

Within this community telling Rumpelstiltskin's story might encourage those whom the spinnstube sensed withheld something that needed saying—and many impediments blocked sharing sexual problems with the group: younger members were embarrassed, not realizing theirs were normal dilemmas; the reluctant or otherwise inhibited were morally disconcerted if discussing sex, or they feared disgrace while the elders knew there is no disgrace in sex, its failures, pleasures or problems. Some are preternaturally shy; others disinclined to speak about themselves except in abstractions. But the group accepted what was offered as constrained by local expectations, modesty, religion, and mores; within limits this story offered a great prompt that encouraged sharing by speaking. To discuss men. Children. Marriage. The aristocracy. Spinning. And this magical and wildly improbable story could begin to frame profoundly troubling questions about relationships, about ethics. It's easy to imagine that from time to time bringing out and re-telling the Tale of Rumpelstiltskin for the group's amusement supplied the occasion for raucous laughter at men's expense, a quieter discussion of sexual frustration, and the recitation of the centrality of children to women's identity—all to nodding agreement as the spindles turned.

Notes

1. Span (2015, p. D5).
2. Tatar (1987, p. 6).
3. A.W.T. and Edward Clodd (1889, p. 136).
4. In one telling, a leg partially substitutes for the richly symbolic cooking spoon. As Zipes pointed out, after the queen "names her exploiter", little Rumpelstiltskin "is carried away on a female utensil" (1993, p. 49).

   As many languages assign gender to nouns, the spoon became female when associated with home kitchens but this long-handled spoon—hardly female in overall shape and therefore related to a witch's broomstick—ambiguously refers to suggestive anatomy. While the shaft/handle asserts maleness, the concave spoon offers a female receptacle, doubly gendering its use in women's work, the kitchen. Its familiarity disguises the rich wit a cooking spoon contributes as an object with associations far more complex than might first appear. But, that's how the story's subversive wit operates: parading dissident social views beneath the notice of males unfamiliar with the life of females. Men didn't trouble themselves with fiber arts, child-rearing, or home cooking.

5. A popularized interpretation, targeted at an audience of girls, beclouds masturbation with menstruation, perhaps purposely shrouding all the functions "down there". In a darkly re-told paraphrase intended for teen readers (Donna Jo Napoli and Richard Tchen, 1999) the baby's father, having been transformed from a handsome boy athlete to a crippled Rumpel-stiltskin, learns that his girlfriend marries a drunken miller and dies in childbirth having borne Rumpelstiltskin's offspring; a resolution depends on guessing Rumpelstiltskin's name, which causes him to become infuriated and when he stamps his crippled leg it gets stuck in the floor so he tears away, leaving the leg behind as, running away, he bleeds from the groin. Blood oozing from the crotch is not a male trait.

6. Modern scholars lamenting how traditional academic specialties have fractured may repair to the story's final scene. Jeannine Blackwell observed (1990) that "interdisciplinary research does not necessitate tearing oneself in two, as did the furious Rumpelstiltskin when someone else mastered his secret language" (p. 112). Academics cite Rumpelstiltskin's grievance to mourn a multi-disciplinary Babel, perhaps another barren form of self-abuse.

7. One optional reading of the story's climactic final scene seems less sensibly coherent than other theories in circulation. An alternative-universe bit of science-fiction/science-popu-larization includes a discussion of the tale of Rumpelstiltskin that proposes the story as an admonition against female masturbation. Naturally, this seems highly dubious in light of the foregoing—etymological, anatomical, historical, contextual, and structural—analysis.

   In the science-fiction version, Rumpelstiltskin's foot is pushed into a crack from which he refuses to remove it (Terry Pratchett, Ian Stewart, Jack Cohen (1999). The authors sup-port their judgment by asking, "What else would you call a stilt with a rumpled skin?" Well, neither the vagina nor vulva resemble a stilt, but a penis sure does, especially a detumescent one, rumpled. Such readings try to rehabilitate the queen and demote Rumpelstiltskin. In the laudable re-appraisal of women's traditional occupations and their worth to the com-munity there's really no reason to convert Rumpelstiltskin into a culprit from a relief-worker as the story's other males are real villains while Rumpelstiltskin can't poke, impregnate, or sexually annoy a woman. Moreover, he is rendered especially harmless if you know and can say his name—if you can speak up for yourself. Yet his demotion currently veins academic fashion. It doesn't have to be a see-saw, an either/or case of Rumpelstiltskin versus elevated womanhood.

8. Campbell (2013, p. 195).

9. Campbell (2013, p. 190).

10. Zipes (1993, p. 44).

11. Zipes (1993, p. 44).

12. After prevailing in her guessing contest if the Queen made crestfallen Rumpelstiltskin a counter-offer, it might have sounded like this:

   "OK. I won. You're not going to get the Crown Prince. And I have to admit I'm really relieved. But I'm still grateful. You saved my life, for sure. Your made me Queen of, like, this whole kingdom. You probably saved my father's life and set him up in a pretty spiffy situation. But you don't have to leave this show empty-handed. I'm willing to make a new proposal. Let's go down to the royal orphanage and you can pick out some poor kid to your liking. Everybody wins. I get to keep what I've got. So does my Dad. The King will sleep soundly as ever when he's not counting his gold. Your name stays a secret with me, I promise. You get a child to raise. Some kid gets a really special Dad to take him fishing but also to teach him magic. Please don't think of this switch as a consolation prize. It's my way to show that I'm as willing to re-negotiate as you graciously did for me. How's that?" But she never allows him the chance to save face; instead, she taunts him.

13. Rumpelstiltskin's lack of a clearcut moral lesson seems to place it—like art's formalism that offers no moral lessons but a wealth of ethical models—beyond the reach of those who look

to art to teach them to how live (especially taking examples of life-lessons from novels and poems). You learn little practical about how to live from reading or hearing Rumpelstiltskin, just as you can't learn how to live from listening to Mozart, Beethoven, or reading Sappho. Many who come to art for all sorts of reasons cannot differentiate it from preachy kitsch; some take perfectly fine sensual rewards and irrelevant moral prizes from art's subjects but mistake for a schoolroom's lecture or a pulpit's instruction the urgency of art's lapel-grabbing seriousness. And that distinction proves crucial. This odd story's lack of moral preachment aligns it with a wealth of artistically ambitious material not usually recalled when thinking about fairytales, the lessons of parables, or (Aesop's or La Fontaine's) anodyne fables.

Distinguishing subject-matter from content, the occasion for art from its means, is not an exercise casually entered into and most approach art as entertainment, a distraction, a sensual respite. Yet, at their core, the fairytales had something serious to say, and they said it well. Not such a morally neutral artifact as high art neither was this tale a middlebrow entertainment for children. (Delusions, fallacies, rank idiocies are daily implanted by the authors of 'children's literature.' For example, among other falsehoods they routinely teach children the insane lesson that genuinely intractable obstacles can be overcome by trying really really hard, a notion of plucky grit and gumption that in all others spheres of adult life was extinguished by World War I. The authors of this stuff—and the parents who buy such books to indoctrinate their children—should be liable for subsequent damages, or even war crimes.) The women of the spinnstube had no such problem as they lived before psycho-therapy and modern tort law.

14. This particular mockery remains the summit of ridicule. The final insult hurled at his physician-father (played by George C. Scott) by his banished son in Paddy Chayefsky's 1971 tragicomedy *Hospital* (directed by George Hiler). The accusation of sexual insufficiency, however old, never grows old.

15. Freud, "Typical Dreams" (1900/1931; 1960/1965, volume V), p. 246.

16. Lévi-Strauss (1967, p. 288).

12

RUMPELSTILTSKIN'S COMPETITION

The Story as a Utensil

Rural-born fairytales became cryptic, even unintelligible, when recited as entertainment to hearth-gathered industrial-age families. Their allegorical content appeared merely fantastic and amusing if often spooky. Today few of these stories make sense as a practical commentaries on life. Partly, they lost lucidity when their subversive witticisms were shared with menfolk and young girls as few were intended to be heard by a company of mixed genders, ages, and relationships of blood or marriage. For good reason, modern listeners seldom ventured that tales like Rumpelstiltskin's conveyed hidden satire. Its encrypted allegory was coded to be intuited within the spinnstube while beyond the spinnstuben Rumpelstiltskin's story proved un-decipherable as a coherent whole. The tale's apparent irrationality grew more distantly bizarre with passing time that withdrew home spinning from most people's experience.

The generations that witnessed the rise of industrialization saw hordes abandon the countryside to congregate for mass-production. The landscape de-populated as workers flooded factory towns that within a single lifetime exploded into vast cities, with dire consequences to human health, spirit, and culture. The land bled fairytales along with the people who lived with the magical folk. For exploited laboring mobs, memories of farmland life faded with the agricultural calendar's forsaken rhythms; rather than create their own amusements exhausted factory laborers increasingly sated themselves with commercialized entertainments as consumerism spewed cultural merchandise not of the consumers' making. Diversions from factories' boring yet dangerous drudgery beckoned: the alienated fun of the music hall, radio, movies, sound recordings, gossip magazines, TV, and video games. All poisoned the spirit of myth, fairytales, and high art. Mass-marketing offered bulk products, eventually a worldwide junkyard of smothering kitsch, beneath which the inner logic of Rumpelstiltskin's story lay buried. Finally a wall of impenetrable amnesia rose up to block the transmission of Rumpelstiltskin's meaning. But forgetting suppresses the past in one way while different kinds of silence exert forces all their own.

Pre-modern society would hardly countenance a widely circulated story that openly attacked wealth-seeking kings (a redundancy) monarchs who ignored their subjects' painful lives. Likewise, no story would frontally assault fathers, heads of family with universally acknowledged privileges, who treat daughters as chattel to assign. (Fathers still "give away" daughters at occidental weddings and some societies commonly practice female infanticide.) Worthless husbands incapable of returning sexual satisfaction were also mostly off-limits to mainstream editorializing. Another sardonic aside recognized that a baby's arrival bestowed on the mother parity as an adult, regardless of the woman's other competencies or innate wisdom; and even a miller's daughter might capably function as a queen. Underlying these social and sexual asides, the story's core assumptions viewed the interminable work of spinning useful filaments as inherently worthwhile to the community and a personally justifiable way to spend a life. This was a skill akin to the how fortune doled out human life, and the portrayed Fates were spinners. In pre-modern times endless spinning reigned irreproachable.

Composing acid critiques that remained undetected required care and imagination. With a bit of camouflage a fairytale could hide comments on "untouchable" subjects. (The sanctity of modern commerce might be comparable. And investigators who examined the networks churning within business administration referred to stock types as appear in Rumpelstiltskin's story.[1]) Like the ladies of the spinnstube metaphors help us comprehend, describe, and perhaps accommodate to new situations.[2] Fairytales supplied a clever class of artifacts to summarize, explain, and distinguish social relationships—as do today's newspaper political cartoons. Fairytales abstracted behavioral types as they framed solutions concealed in outrageously improbable symbolism. But if a coping mechanism (a concluding moral aphorism) proved unavailable in grim circumstances a story might advise forbearance. And long suffering offered a smart personal strategy in those days before a revolutionary age swept Europe and patience could give way to rage. Rumpelstiltskin's subversive story represents one of those covert commentaries on a rickety system based on involuntary suppression of peasants, women, and anyone beneath the nobility. The tale criticized familial and caste relationships, addressed questions of fairness, personal responsibility, wealth and capital, and sexual expression or its impossibility.

As a general critique of society's once-prominent but now subtler oppression of women, it's unlikely that specific people or a particular event prompted the tale. Instead the tale credibly arose from the critique of a way-of-life and state-of-affairs associated with and based upon a distinctively gendered chore.

Calling Names

> The world from which fairy tales and folk tales emerged has largely vanished, and although it pleases us to think of these stark, simple, fantastic narratives as timeless, they aren't. Thanks to video games, computer graphics and the general awfulness of everyday life, fantasies of all kinds have had a resurgence in the past few years. But the social realities on which the original fairy tales depend are almost incomprehensibly alien to 21st-century sensibilities; they reek of feudalism. And the lessons they're supposed to teach our young don't have much force these days.[3]
>
> *Terrence Rafferty*

> Now the fantasy that prevails is the all-consuming, voraciously consumed popular culture, seemingly spawned by, of all things, freedom. The young especially live according to beliefs that are thought up for them by society's most unthinking people and the businesses least impeded by innocent ends. Ingeniously as their parents and teachers may attempt to protect the young from being drawn, to their detriment, into the moronic amusement park that is now universal, the preponderance of power is not with them.[4]
>
> *Philip Roth*

That's all true, up to a point. As a communal exercise of "stark, simple, fantastic narratives" these allegorical stories cannot really prove "timeless" when their supporting rural culture and home-centered institutions waned. Yet fairytales' useful insights about human nature endured imperishable and those buoyant truths about inspecting personalities kept them from sinking into the past. Their psychological soundness resisted dismissal although the tale's useful observations came delivered as embodied in, or accompanied by, weird supernatural creatures or animals. However improbable or outmoded, the transactions between humans and a bizarre menagerie accurately reflected how we weigh alternatives ("Jack and the Beanstalk") in decision-making and how we learn from experience ("Three Billy Goats Gruff") or anticipate challenges, patience, and reward ("The Three Little Pigs"). But their characters' memorable oddities actually helped insure the tales' survival when so much of the otherwise charmless world that created them perished without regret.

Myriad anachronisms abound in fairytales that endure despite features ripped from their native time. We still teach children to read with illustrated books of farmyard animals which most youngsters will never see, except on their dinner plate. For safety's sake childhood's adult-controlled experiences remain intentionally conservative; consequently, centuries after the sun set on feudalism the stories native to that system persist.[5]

We've been looking closely at one example of these old stories at least partly because it's well known. Emerging from the murky past's prevailing illiteracy through the printed page, Rumpelstiltskin's tale re-entered general adult consciousness. (Some have argued for a more tortuous path of re-discovery. In this view literacy among rural peasants was not that rare; they commonly entertained each other by reading from books of French and

Italian tales that had been translated into German during the preceding century.[6] From these reading sessions the stories supposedly entered general circulation but this theory, while its proponents can document traces of publication that pre-dates the Grimms, cannot rebuff the obvious: that before being transcribed into Italian, French, German, Russian, etc. the stories had been created by an illiterate peasantry.) The story of Rumpelstiltskin passed from the realm of women to the oversight of well-intentioned if naive educationalists who expunged any lingering remnant of the story's intuited phallic subtext. Schoolroom editions of the Grimms' stories omitted Rumpelstiltskin because the tale ignored "family values", the virtues of "family life, comradely relationships and the relationship between master and servant or host and guest".[7] That's for sure. This tale lacks any obvious morals. It promoted no virtues and flagrantly overlooks numerous human failings.

The story seemed nonsensical to educators for whom everything about schooling should convey a moral point in lessons that praised labor and approved extant sexual roles. Despite generations of fastidiously sanctimonious teachers its enduring relevance deserves attention as few problems that vexed the Medieval world persist into modernity.[8] Yet, this tale treats a subject as current as pharmacology and advertising can make it. So, this morsel of the past's entertainments endured despite surviving as "incomprehensibly alien to 21st-century sensibilities". Like other genuinely successful artworks, the *Tale of Rumpelstiltskin* survives against ever-renewed competition. Its rivals pour from the pens (and keyboards) of children's book authors but, despite hacks' best efforts and their publishers' excited blurbs, Rumpelstiltskin's unpleasant story thrives in its fairytale form. Because, despite its unfailingly sour disposition, it confers many rewards.

Rumpelstiltskin was never updated as a profitable amusement (by "society's most unthinking people") in any way that tapped the richness of its foundational material. Though deeply disguised as a humanly accurate essay on behavior and conventions, this folktale radically differs from the swarming commercial smarm that claims to be similar.[9] In purest flattery to it, nothing has replaced Rumpelstiltskin. Never updated, the human conflicts in Rumpelstiltskin's tale remain ageless, poignant and, generation after generation, ethically insoluble. Those conundrums persist even as the role and status of women in occidental society improved beyond the recognition of the spinnstube's ladies who would have been mighty satisfied with evolutionary feminism's progress. And, although many fairytales remain more popular than this outlier, because Rumpelstiltskin touches the nub of so much that remains vital his story lingers. It perseveres, somehow current without suffering substantial treacly modernizing, politically correct revision, or substitution by a more palatable tale. Or the addition of a conventionally 'happy' ending.

The Story Afloat in Time

Loaded with tidings from a world that no longer exists, today the tale of Rumpelstiltskin bobs into view, a sea-tossed message-in-a-bottle sent out into the world without hope of knowing its recipient(s). No spatial ocean, the story floated down through time.

Yet, in place of poll-testing or market surveys, countless children endorsed the tale's literary form and its now-esoteric references. Such confirmation, though childish, operated exactly as sophisticated criticism. No art operates democratically but upon one

FIGURE 12.1   The Brothers Grimm, Wilhelm (left) and Jacob (right).

Source: Hessian State Archives, Hamburg (HStAM Fonds 340 Grimm No B 72, Arcinsys Hessen, Germany).

audience member at a time. Rumpelstiltskin's popularity represents the generations-long willingness of innumerable young people to attend an adventure that meant little in their own lives. Its multi-part and highly gendered relationship to household fiber-work disappeared—first from industrialized cities and subsequently the post-Industrial Age. Though absent from modern childhood's everyday experience the story of spinning yet affects us as Rumpelstiltskin's story talks casually about the unmentionable, as does high art.[10] Art (not just its happenstance subjects, sometimes called "content") resembles waking dreams, with structure added. Unlike works of art, dreams have no names we can say but if a dream had a name, like a book's chapter heading, it would be impossibly dense as connotation, as compact as the name Rumpelstiltskin.

Art's essential formality is not the story's main attraction although the tale possesses an undeniable elegance and economy. As Ellen Handler Spitz points out, "Although we may profitably spend hours dwelling on form in Rembrandt, Goya, or Van Gogh, their works have survived because their content is nontrivial, because they have painted the deepest fears and wishes of mankind".[11] But deepest affect also arises from still lives and landscapes. Successful art speaks to us in a voice that we are startled to recognize as approaching from elsewhere yet already of us. That's certainly a factor in fairytales. Rumpelstiltskin's story achieved dazzling formal elegance but aside from the Grimms we really don't know who was responsible for its perfected bitter poignance. Over countless generations the story tumbled like a pebble in a stream of time as retellings smoothed it, finally compact and irreducible. Passed from one unknown reciter to equally obscure peasantry in anonymous descent Rumpelstiltskin's story's perfection reached a world audience unimaginably huge to its first tellers. Because it had something to say, enduringly so if only partially sensed.

★★★

The spinnstube's stories broke into the middle class that included Dortchen Wild whose husband, Wilhelm Grimm, captured the tales for universal circulation. Wilhelm invited his brother, Jacob, to live with him and his bride in a compact house—a definite marital obstacle to sexual spontaneity. Whether or not she bargained on this arrangement Dortchen surely noticed daily deterrents to erotic expression. While multi-generation or extended families commonly dwelled under one roof, in modern terms her situation was not enviable. Compared to a fairytale version of a loving couple nestled in a cozy home (or a castle teaming with servants to fulfill any wish) Dortchen Wild's lack of privacy and strained chasteness could have been torment . . . with somebody to blame for large or small inconveniences. With both brothers in her home to complicate or dilute her spousal identity and no children to supply maternal pride, an oddly apposite situation colored her recitation of Rumpelstiltskin's story. In a sense, Dortchen Wild was the last authentic teller of the Rumpelstiltskin story.

Dortchen Wild conceivably recited the story as disconsolately germane to her peculiar marital situation. Thereafter, Rumpelstiltskin's story was transmitted with a certain inauthenticity when splayed on the page. Yet, in books legions met Rumpelstiltskin— more than could ever have heard his story repeated with a crone's wry asides, the spinnstube's editorial replies voiced as knowing laughter or furtive glances. Speaking carefully to attentive men who scribbled her words—men with whom she had chosen enforced quotidian, if not intimate, relations in a cramped space—Dortchen Wild's husband and brother-in-law labored, obtuse to their own shortcomings though they could work marvels in their vocations.[12] That balance of traits sounds familiar. Ms. Wild's husband, Wilhelm Grimm, fathered no children. Could either brother guess to what degree they were describing themselves? Could the brothers suspect that the tale of

Rumpelstiltskin, that their editing worked to refine in various versions, portrayed their predicament of sublimation?

Scattering the Seeds

A body of materials, heretofore invisible around the house and thus considered trifling women's prattle to excite and entertain children, when published by the Grimms as *Children's and Household Fairy Tales* was instantly recognized as worth the trouble of professionals' attention. Previously, fairytales were thought "among educated males as trivial, the province of simple illiterates", that is, bumpkins and women.[13] Promoting these delightful oddities to academic notice and scholarly investigation meant snatching the stories from the control of women and passing the works to the care of highly schooled males. In the first generations of their study that was the fate of fairytales. Originally intended as part of a larger cultural effort meant to undergird German political unification the tales were not published for children but the eyes of often dreary experts driven by nationalist dogma. The printed stories dispersed becoming a global wonder. Newly literate industrial-age masses read them as children's entertainment, having forgotten that the stories had often sprung from the society of their own adult female ancestors. The circle completed when treasure retrieved from memory's attic was dictated, published, restored to its rightful owners: the industrial age's middle-class readers, themselves only a generation removed from illiteracy and superstition—the fairytale's birth matrix.

Transcribed stories sailed out on the great river of printed pages but, like a devil's bargain, the story's new-found published celebrity conceded but half the deal; there was a catch. Lost was the zesty immediacy of a parent or grandparent who told a story acquired in youth, relished it as a personal childhood memory, and felt themselves part of a living tradition. Printing also displaced the hearer's personal visual imagining. In a volume whose pages never forgot, missed, or substituted a word, and was available to everyone who could read or listen, masters of the graphic imagination illustrated the story. And Rumpelstiltskin attracted great illustrators. Their professional artistic triumphs diminished individual freedom to conceive the characters and scenes—as the price for truly memorable graphic formulations.

Removed from its native circumstance Rumpelstiltskin's Tale became an artifact gawked at, placed in a museum where strangers who wander by casually peruse what is foreign and quaint however urgent or poignant the original message. Nineteenth-century Europeans marveled at new-found strangeness from exotic settings and the Grimms' stories arrived like so many previously unseen species arrested on photographic plates. Or killed and stuffed.

Some wondrous specimens came from afar, brought back in the process of empire-building. Rumored faraway monsters contradicted nature's (European) norms. But head-shaking disbelief upon reading about a platypus only mirrored amazement at locally unearthed human equivalents. If some nineteenth-century adventurers sailed to exotic places and returned with reports of odd customs and grotesque spectacles others never left home but probed the unseen past. The distances were equivalent. You could uncover marvels right in a German pharmacist's sitting room.

Not all explorers had to navigate to the edges of the map to prospect new vistas. Savigny, the Grimms, and Freud stayed home and discovered plenty that was outlandish and wondrous.

What Does It Mean?

Is it presumptuous to assume *this* story must mean something? The problem of meaning bedevils (if we may use that word) any sanctified text, like Hebrew or Christian scripture—whose every word, exquisitely placed as stones in a mosaic, is analyzed and parsed—and Rumpelstiltskin has become a semi-canonical text. You are free to choose one of several versions of the fairytale just as the Bible exists in slightly different sectarian versions. That variety thwarts neither the reader's enthusiasm nor the text's power, for either sacred works or fairytale. Each reader, every virtuoso illustrator inventing images for the tale, and all the story's bedtime reciters, possess and control their version of Rumpelstiltskin. Yet universal acceptance does not diminish the problem of intention and denotation: presuming the story might mean something pre-determines that a meaning will likely be present. Insinuated like the X on a treasure map, once posited, hidden meaning will be found or, like a madman's raving, Rumpelstiltskin might be

> . . . a tale
> Told by an idiot, full of sound and fury,
> Signifying nothing.
> *(Macbeth V:5)*

Studded with ample fury Rumpelstiltskin may yet signify. And that significance resides in the tale irrespective of how we, individually and mentally, select, assemble, and stack up our literary images. That process cannot help but reflect something about human psychology. Humans are pattern makers. The onslaught of information coming to us from the world is sieved and organized and made coherent, whenever possible by habit for greatest efficiency. That proficiency remains our species' cardinal talent. (Even the pathologic mind exhibits characteristic regularities of thought typical of each mental "ailment".) But can we understand the outlandishly foreign in era and outlook? To some degree "yes", but not totally. Lots of stories and maxims seems senseless today because circumstances have so altered from the time and place of their composition. Consequently, inherited gems of obsolete wisdom may appear brutally lunatic. Paradoxical as it may seem, wisdom, apparently an ever-lasting category of achieved insight, can become obsolete as fundamental circumstances change and as morality evolves. So, that raises a new dilemma.

How to assign meaning even if relevance has evaporated? In this case alien concepts and unfamiliar situations may not pose a problem unsurmountable to our understanding.[14] It's easier to determine or uncover forgotten meaning in this story whose human gravity and personal implications remain current. The emotional consequences of Rumpelstiltskin's anatomical problem, which this tale likely addressed, persists, along with the relationship fallout. If we recognize Rumpelstiltskin's condition and grant the story-tellers' wit in describing that malfunction, incomprehension vanishes from the heart of the story. Instead we recognize a perfectly human tragedy. Not a tale "told by an idiot", the story frankly exceeds the candor of much political exhortation or advertising copy. Rumpelstiltskin offers a vision of a world whose defects are submitted without any suggested remedial course besides endurance, sisterhood, and speaking the truth. However unpleasant that truth.

The tale's response to stinging unfairness bridges the long interval between those who devised the remorseless story and recent times' gentler social amusements. With its veneer peeled back Rumpelstiltskin gave un-emancipated womanhood a tool for self-expression. That was then. The story bequeaths to today's reader a sense of women's contribution to great literature: fairytales that paralleled other more celebrated, and mostly male, cultural monuments. Tradition, lingering though weakened patriarchy, and other cultural impediments hinder the present interpretation and its assignment of stature to this work. Yet, many contradictions clot the present rendering of the tale's inner workings and not every element can be reconciled to the literature and scholarship surrounding the study of folktales. I know that. We have not been examining the progress of formal logic. Everything doesn't have to make sense. The fairytale, this or others, offers no self-correcting method to untie all such knots but represents a folkloric and legitimate groping toward human truths. And on that level this fairytale's quotient of valid points about how people behave offers a staggeringly rich payload. Though he surprised the Miller's Daughter and was unwelcomed by later moralistic scolds, we'd be well-advised to let Rumpelstiltskin enter the room and instruct us about the past and ourselves.

Notes

1. Dour students of business administration (who ponder regulation of the commercial climate and personnel management) repair to "a whole network of metaphor/context relationships. . . [that] need meta-metaphors", or so claim the MBAs according to Kenwyn K. Smith and Valerie M. Simmons (1983, p. 378). They continue by noting, "One possible way to think of a meta-metaphor is in terms of myths, fairy tales, and legends. In a way, these are meta-metaphoric tales that provide clues to the inner links that exist among the basic metaphors that have been mapped into existential contexts to give meaning". So, for example we might refer to: (a/the) Miller not a specific person, (a/the) King, (a/the) Daughter, (a/the) Queen, and even (a/the) Baby.

   Thus stock types form a virtual repertory company that mixes and matches parts as required by a story. Each character's capacity to handle a part competently was gauged by the tellers so as not to unduly stretch the limits of that recognizable role (not so different from the Comedia del Arte, as already mentioned). This forms a theme in Cristina Bacchilega, "An Introduction to the 'Innocent Persecuted Heroine' Fairy Tale" (1993). Inevitably, fairytales' very form conveys the ideology native to its tellers and hearers, their shared worldview that makes the stories comprehensible and politically invested.

2. Centuries later than the spinnstuben flourish earnest examinations of human relationships within closely circumscribed communities came to the same conclusions: "[I]n addition to

mapping the various interpersonal, intragroup, and intergroup dynamics as our original pur
pose dictated, we would attempt to enter, as fully as possible, the various symbols groups and
individuals chose to represent their experiences and constructions of reality. The Rumpelstiltskin organization . . . is one element of what we stumbled upon" (Kenwyn K. Smith and
Valerie M. Simmons [1983], p. 379).

3. Rafferty (2012) He continued: "Kids learn to be skeptical almost before they've been taught
anything to be skeptical of".

4. Roth (2014, p. 15)

5. If we excoriate her cowardly Dad for commodifying his daughter or chastise her king for
discounting a peasant girl's life (in a premonition of Marxist critique) this narrative proposes
a pithy, and wry, an accurate, appraisal of then-prevalent circumstances and feudal social
castes. The tale of Rumpelstiltskin that trumpeted despicably profiteering male types offered
some scholars opportunities for "formidable attempts to bring together the Marxist and New
Left critique of popular culture and Ideologiekritik with structuralist and formalist work on
folklore and with the feminist critique of socialization through popular culture" (Jeannine
Blackwell [1990], p. 107).

6. As argued by Bottigheimer (2009, p. 39).

7. Bottigheimer (1987, p. 21).

8. Despite its deathless relevance, marketplace forces yearned to supplant Rumpelstiltskin with
ersatz versions whose potential to yield (exclusive!) income streams could never be achieved
for a story in public domain. As Oscar Levant is reputed to have said, "Imitation is the sincer-
est form of plagiarism".

   The song "Sympathy for the Devil" seems to use the fairytale type 501 (Guess the Helper)
in the lyric "Pleased to meet you, hope you guess my name". And the song "Baby Got Back"
definitely alludes to Rumpelstiltskin in the lyric "Ooh rumpelsmoothskin you say you wanna
get in my benz?"

   Although I have never seen it (which is neither boasting nor snobbery) Rumpelstiltskin
appeared (played by Michael J. Anderson) in the first season's episode of *Star Trek: Deep Space
Nine*, "If Wishes Were Horses". Likewise, I have no idea what to make of the following report,
faithfully reproduced here verbatim: "In an episode of *Courage the Cowardly Dog*, Muriel is
lured to Scotland and forced to make a couple thousand kilts for a person she believed to
be her uncle. Once it's revealed he is not her uncle, Courage learns the man hates his real
name and, after discovering it, plays a game of charades in front of Muriel to help her figure
it out. After his name is revealed to be Rumpledkiltskin, Muriel suggests he should change
his name to Rumpelstiltskin. He is overjoyed to have a new name and decides to let Muriel
go". Whatever that means.

9. Maybe no successful lyrical rendition is possible. The one attempt to translate the story to
film was the 1987 version; to spare the director's (David Irving) feelings, let me only briefly
quote Leonard Maltin's *Movie Guide* that dismissed it as a "threadbare musical adaptation . . .
likely to bore even the small-fry". Rumpelstiltskin resists all such translations. In a revealing
contrast to Rumpelstiltskin's tale that defies honeyed popularization, Snow White's sticky-
sweet story enjoyed endless film treatments. It's worth noting the contrast at length to observe
that Rumpelstiltskin's sourness presents no straw man argument:
   Snow White and the Huntsman (2012), *Snow White: A Tale of Terror* (1997), *Snow White:
   A Deadly Summer* (2012), *Snow White and the Seven Dwarfs* (1937), *Snow White* (1987), *Snow
   White and the Seven Dwarfs* (1955), *Snow White: The Fairest of Them All* (2001) (TV Movie),
   Snow White and the Huntsman 2 (in development), *Grimm's Snow White* (2012) (Video), *Snow
   White* (2005), *Snow White and the Three Stooges* (1961), *Snow White Live* (1980) (TV Movie),
   White Snow (I) (2010), *Snow White* (II) (1916), *Snow White* (I) (1916), *Golden Anniversary
   of Snow White and the Seven Dwarfs* (1987) (TV Movie), *Snow White* (2014), *White as Snow*
   (2010), *Snow-White* (1933) (Short), *Snow White and Russian Red* (2009), *Snow White* (1995)
   (Video), *Snow White* (1991) (Video), *Disney's 'Snow White and the Seven Dwarfs': Still the Fairest of Them All* (2001) (Video), *Snow White and the Seven Movies* (2012) (Short), *A Snow White*

Christmas (1980) (TV Movie), *Snow White and the Seven Perverts* (1973) (Short), *Snow White and the Huntsman: The Queen* (2012), *Snow White and the Huntsman: Setting the Stage* (2012), *The Snow-White Syndrome* (2008), *Snow White and Rose Red* (1955), *Snow White and the Huntsman: Stunning Evil* (2012), *The Story of 'Snow White and the Huntsman'* (2012) *Snow White and Rose Red* (1954) (Short), *Snow White and the Huntsman: Enchanted Forest* (2012), *Snow White and the Huntsman: A Mirror Like No Other* (2012) (Video), *Snow White and the Seven Thieves* (1949), *Snow White* (1990) (Video), *The Snow White* (2010), *On the Set: Snow White and the Huntsman the First Great Battle* (Days 1 and 2) (2012), *On the Set of Snow White and the Huntsman: Fenland Village Escape* (Day 67) (2012), *On the Set of Snow White and the Huntsman: Prince William Attacks!* (Day 17) (2012), *Snow White and the Huntsman': Inside the Action* (2012) *Snow White* (1902) *On the Set of Snow White and the Huntsman: Battling the Troll* (Day 39) (2012), *Snow White and the Seven Thieves* (1973), *The Dwarves of 'Snow White and the Huntsman'* (2012), *Snow White and the Huntsman: A Look Inside—Dark Adventure* (2012), *Celebrating Walt Disney's 'Snow White and the Seven Dwarfs': The One That Started It All* (1990) (TV Movie), *On the Set of Snow White and the Huntsman: Beauty & Evil: Ravenna Speaks to the Mirror Man* (Day 7) (2012), *On the Set of Snow White and the Huntsman: Devouring Youth* (Day 12) (2012), *Snow White and the Seven Jugglers* (1962), *Snow White: The Making of a Masterpiece* (1997) (Video), *On the Set of Snow White and the Huntsman: The Drunken Huntsman* (Day 57) (2012), *Behind the Scenes on 'Snow White and the Huntsman' with Florence + the Machine* (2012), *On the Set of Snow White and the Huntsman: Death in Throne Room* (Day 11) (2012), *On the Set of Snow White and the Huntsman: Into the Sewer!* (Day 45) (2012), *Snow White and the Huntsman: The Costumes of Colleen Atwood* (2012), *Snow White* (1983) (Short), *The Legend of Snow White* (1994) (TV Series), *Snow White and the Magic Mirror* (1994) (Video), *On the Set of Snow White and the Huntsman: The Battle on the Beach* (Day 27–31) (2012), *The Legend of Snow White* (1914) (Short), *Snow White and the 7 Bachelors* (1960), *My Favorite Fairy Tales Volume 3: Sleeping Beauty / Snow White / Cinderella* (1986) (Video), *On the Set of Snow White and the Huntsman: The Huntsman Fights Finn* (Day 32) (2012), *Snow White* (1917) (Short), *As White as in Snow* (2001), *Willa: An American Snow White* (1998) (TV Movie), *Snow White* (1996) (TV Short), *Pinokyo en Little Snow White* (1972), *Snow White and the Hundredth Monkey* (1999) (Short), *Little Snow White* (1910), *Snow White: My Confidential Drawers* (2004) (Short), *Chinese Princess Snow White* (1940), *Snow White and the Huntsman, T4 Movie Special* (2012) (TV Movie), *White Snows of Fuji* (1935), *Snow White and the Gamble* (2012) (Short), *Dear Snow White* (2011) (Video), *Snow White* (1967) (TV Episode),
    Magic Mansion (1965) (TV Series), Snow White (1985) (TV Episode),
    Night Heat (1985) (TV Series), Snow White (2008) (TV Episode),
    Super Why! (2007) (TV Series), Snow White (1997) (TV Episode),
    Pantoland (1997) (TV Mini-Series), Snow White (1996) (TV Episode),
    Martin (1992) (TV Series), Snow White's Payback (2006) (TV Episode),
    Black Lagoon (2006) (TV Series), Snow White (1954) (TV Episode),
    The Spike Jones Show (1954) (TV Series), *Snow White's Meltdown* (2006) (TV Episode),
    Sesame Street (1969) (TV Series), *Snow White* (1986) (Video), *Snow White and the Seven Jockeys* (1984) (TV Episode),
    Kingswood Country (1980) (TV Series), *Snow White Bride* (2012) (TV Episode),
    My Fair Wedding (2008) (TV Series), *Snow White* (1995) (TV Episode),
    Happily Ever After: Fairy Tales for Every Child (1995) (TV Series), *Special: Snow White 2* (1981) (TV Episode),
    The Goodies (1970) (TV Series), *Snow White Elephant* (1987) (TV Episode),
    Sharon, Lois & Bram's Elephant Show (1984) (TV Series), *Snow White and the Seven Muppets* (1985) (TV Episode),
    Muppet Babies (1984) (TV Series), *On Snow White* (1975) (TV Episode),
    CBS Children's Film Festival (1967) (TV Series), *Snow White and the Juniper Tree* (2011) (TV Episode),
    Scary Tales (2011) (TV Series), *Snow White and the Seven Bradys* (1973) (TV Episode),
    The Brady Bunch (1969) (TV Series), *Red Snow, White Death* (1974) (TV Episode),

Kodiak (1974) (TV Series), *Snow White, Blood Red* (1988) (TV Episode), *Murder, She Wrote* (1984) (TV Series), *Snow White and the Seven Dorks* (1992) (TV Episode), *Saved by the Bell* (1989) (TV Series), *Snow White: Part 2* (1987) (TV Episode), *Grimm Masterpiece Theatre* (1987) (TV Series), *Case: The Snow White Affair* (1976) (TV Episode),

The Tony Randall Show (1976) (TV Series), *Snow White and the Seven Dwarfs* (1973) (TV Episode),

Festival of Family Classics (1972) (TV Series), *Curley Dimples Storybook: Snow White* (1958) (TV Episode),

Club Oasis (1957) (TV Series), *Snow White and the Seven Dwarfs* (1984) (TV Episode), *Faerie Tale Theatre* (1982) (TV Series), *Snow White: Part 3* (1988) (TV Episode), *Grimm Masterpiece Theatre* (1987) (TV Series), *Snow White and Rose Red* (1987) (TV Episode),

Grimm Masterpiece Theatre (1987) (TV Series), *Snow White: Part 1* (1987) (TV Episode),

Grimm Masterpiece Theatre (1987) (TV Series), *Snow White: Part 4* (1988) (TV Episode),

Grimm Masterpiece Theatre (1987) (TV Series), *Rugrats Tales from the Crib: Snow White* (2005) (TV Episode),

Rugrats (1991) (TV Series), *Snow White and the Seven Treasure Hunters* (1986) (TV Episode), *Yogi's Treasure Hunt* (1985) (TV Series), *Magic Mirror of Snow White Castle* (1980) (TV Episode),

Don de la mancha (1980) (TV Mini-Series), *Black Day for Snow White* (2002) (TV Episode), *Fairy Tale Police Department* (2002) (TV Series), *Snow White and the Huntsman: A New Legend* (2012) (TV Episode),

HBO First Look (1992) (TV Series), *Familiar Shorts: The Harlem Globetrotters Meet Snow White* (2010) (TV Episode),

Familiar Faces (2009) (TV Series), *Snow White and the Seven Dwarves: Diamond Edition* (2009) (TV Episode),

Leo Little's Big Show (2009) (TV Series), *Mr. Magoo's Little Snow White: Part 2* (1965) (TV Episode),

The Famous Adventures of Mr. Magoo (1964) (TV Series), *After Mamoru's Kiss! Ann's Snow White Plan* (1993) (TV Episode),

Sailor Moon R (1993) (TV Series), *Snow White and the Seven Lady Truckers: Part 2* (1979) (TV Episode),

B.J. and the Bear (1978) (TV Series), *Mr. Magoo's Little Snow White: Part 1* (1965) (TV Episode),

The Famous Adventures of Mr. Magoo (1964) (TV Series), *Snow White and the Seven Lady Truckers: Part 1* (1979) (TV Episode),

B.J. and the Bear (1978) (TV Series), *Snow White Bear/Pushy Cat/Wiki Waki Huck* (1960) (TV Episode),

The Huckleberry Hound Show (1958) (TV Series), *Snow White and the Motor City Dwarfs/ Don't Touch That Dial* (1988) (TV Episode),

Mighty Mouse, the New Adventures (1987) (TV Series), *Okami-san and a Snow White that the Poisoned Apple Didn't Work On* (2010) (TV Episode),

Okamisan (2010) (TV Series), *Snow White Ladies* (in development), *Mirror Mirror* (I) (2012), *"Mirror Mirror: The Untold Adventures of Snow White" Snow White* (1913) (Short), Snow White's Adventure (1991) (Video Game), Making Snow White and the Seven Sisters (2009), Snow White and the 7 Clever Boys (2006) (Video Game), *Snow White and Other Fabulous Fables* (1991) (Video), *Little Snow White* (1927) (Short), *White Snow* (2005) (TV Episode),

IGPX: Immortal Grand Prix (2005) (TV Series), *White Snow, Red Blood* (2013) (TV Episode),

Alaska: Ice Cold Killers (2012) (TV Series), *White Snow, Red Ice* (1964) (TV Episode),

Bob Hope Presents the Chrysler Theatre (1963) (TV Series) *Happily N' Ever After 2: Snow White and the Great Hall Game* (2008) (Video Game), *The General of Asura, Han! The Man Who Stains White Snow Into Crimson!* (1987) (TV Episode),

Hokuto no Ken 2 (1987) (TV Series), *White as Snow* (1967) (TV Episode), *Captain Scarlet and the Mysterons* (1967) (TV Series), *The Snow Walker* (2003), *You Ain't Seen Nothin' Yet* (2012), Grand Theft Auto: San Andreas (2004) (Video Game), *Happily Ever After* (1990),

"*Snow White and the Realm of Doom*" *Happily N'Ever After 2* (2009),

"*Happily N'Ever After 2: Snow White—Another Bite @ the Apple*" *My Son, My Son, What Have Ye Done* (2009), *Schneewittchen und das Geheimnis der Zwerge* (1992) (TV Movie),

"*Snow White*" *Blanche Neige, la suite* (2007),

"*Snow White: The Sequel*" *Grimm's Fairy Tales for Adults* (1969),

"*The New Adventures of Snow White*" *Branca de Neve* (2000),

"*Snow White*" *Biancaneve & Co.* (1982),

"*Snow White and 7 Wise Men*" *Yeti: Curse of the Snow Demon* (2008) (TV Movie), *The White Sun of the Desert (1970) What If God Were the Sun?* (2007) (TV Movie), *Schneewittchen* (1961),

"*Snow White and the Seven Dwarfs*" *It Was the Son* (2012), *Pamuk Prenses ve 7 cüceler* (1970),

"*Snow White and the Seven Dwarfs*" *Un homme et son chien* (2008), *A Scene at the Sea* (1991), *The Great White Trail* (1917), *They Call It Sin* (1932), *Just Seen It* (2011) (TV Series), *Queen of the Sun: What Are the Bees Telling Us?* (2010), *Séraphin: un homme et son péché* (2002), *Sonny and Jed* (1972), *Eat the Sun* (2011), *Slatko od snova* (1994), *Let It Snow* (1999), *Victoria Wood: As Seen on TV* (1985) (TV Series), *Staring at the Sun* (2005) (Short), *Shadow Zone: My Teacher Ate My Homework* (1997), *Yedi bela Hüsnü* (1982), *Sunny et l'éléphant* (2008), *Wait Till the Sun Shines, Nellie* (1952), *Belyy sneg Rossii* (1980), *What the Snow Brings* (2005), *Mabel and Fatty Viewing the World's Fair at San Francisco* (1915), *Black and White: A Portrait of Sean Combs* (2006) (TV Movie), *San jaat si hing* (2005), *The Sun Sets at Dawn* (1950), *Fatty and Mabel at the San Diego Exposition* (1915) (Short), *Hung bou yit sin ji Dai tao gwai ying* (2001), *Lumikki ja seitsemän kääpiötä* (2006) (Video),

"*Snow White and the Seven Dwarfs*" *Can't Wait for the Movies: Big Mommas Like Father Like Son* (2011) (Short), *Out of Time: Crime Scene* (2004) (Video), *Edda Ciano e il comunista* (2011) (TV Movie), Scene It? Disney Magical Moments (2010) (Video Game), *City at War: Sonny* (2012), *Let's Be Out, The Sun Is Shining* (2012), *San jaat si hing* (1984) (TV Series), *Last Seen at Angkor* (2006), *Sini ada hantu* (2011), *Claire Sweeney: Perfect Fit with Weight Watchers* (2005) (Video), *A Son at Sea* (2009), *Shin bjidai* [Zen] (1947), *Vincent mit l'âne dans un pré (et s'en vint dans l'autre)* (1975), *Between Resistance and Community: The Long Island Do It Yourself Punk Scene* (2002), *Moshi moshi choi to rinshô san watasha anata ni hôrensô Kadekaru Rinshô uta to katari* (1995), *San Francisco Rock: A Night at the Family Dog* (1970) (TV Movie), *La demoiselle et son revenant* (1952), *Oi san yat ho* (1985), *Staring at the Sun* (2002) (Short), *The Sun Came Out* (2010).

10. The success of Rumpelstiltskin's tale for children might result from its ability to approximate the mask of an event otherwise emotionally unavailable. All very well for children's entertainment, the story resonates for adults, even if not consciously. With adulthood's distractions, the lost event becomes unspeakably remote—like Rumpelstiltskin's name hidden behind a camouflage of propriety. The condition of the screen memory parallels the use of art by adults who marvel at the affective quality of `grown-up' literature or painting or music without knowing how or why it triggers such profound responses. Childhood and screen memories were inseparable; in their expressive concision, screen memories resemble dreams. Eventually Freud completed the cycle of psychology to art and back; in 1901 and 1904 the chapter "Childhood and Screen Memories" was simply called "Screen Memories" in 1907 (Sigmund Freud, "Childhood and Screen Memories", p. 43, n.1).

11. Spitz (1985, p. 22).

12. Neither the Grimms' demanding work nor the spiritual charge of a celibate calling proscribed females and sexual adventure. Like Rumpelstiltskin, work and play confuted in their lives. Johann Sebastian Bach had children by the dozen, and he was kept otherwise busy. Shakespeare fathered three children. Neither Grimm brother fathered a child.

13. Paradiz (2005, p. xiii).

14. Self-recognition animates arts like the novel that try to pilot the reader to the foreign terri tory of others' minds. Of course the truly foreign is incomprehensible. This assertion echoes Wittgenstein's observation that "If a Lion could talk we could not understand him" (1958, II, xi, p. 223). Notwithstanding many objections to Wittgenstein's position, I have already addressed the claim that successful art brings us into meaningful congress with what only seems foreign in: *Arshile Gorky: The Implications of Symbols* (1981/1991).

APPENDICES

1. Flax

An annual plant of the family Linaceae (cultivated flax is scientifically named *Linum usitatissimum*), the plant's woody stem contains long sturdy fibers that, when woven, yield linen cloth. This attractive textile has been cultivated for thousands of years—in ancient Egypt, Assyria, and Mesopotamia—as flax's long fibers make a fine cloth. Strong, durable, moisture absorbent, and highly lustrous, linen resists microorganisms and its smooth surface repels soil.

After harvesting, bundles of flax go to deseeding machines that separate the seed from the straw. (Farmers harvest seed flax with a combine that mows and threshes the seeds shipped to market as linseed used in paints, varnishes, in linoleum, oilcloth, and as a foodstuff.) After the stalks are cut, they are retted, or made to rot, so that the outer bark is more easily removed. They are either soaked in pools for water retting or left on the ground to absorb rain and dew, called dew retting. The stalks are then dried and crushed. A shaking operation completes the separation of the fiber from the woody portion.

The next major operation, scutching, extracts from the remainder of the plant the fiber loosened during retting. Various types of scutching machines have been developed, but all methods are based on two treatments of the straw. First, the woody central portion of the stem is crushed and broken into small pieces, called shives. Next, the straw is held tightly near one end while the free end is subjected to a beating and scraping action. This completes the separation of the long fiber (called line fiber) from the woody portion.

The flax line fiber from the scutching machine is usually hackled, or combed by hand to grade it and prepare it for the spinner. Hackling draws the scutched fibers over a series of coarse and fine pins to straighten them, in parallel, which removes short, tangled fibers, called flax tow. Formerly a waste product, now machines dry and clean flax tow for use in upholstery padding and coarse yarns woven into braided linen and wool, or flax, rugs. Today, Russia, Poland, and Romania are among the world's leaders in growing flax for thread, while Belgium, France, and the Netherlands produce fine quality fiber. Northern Ireland's linens are renowned while the required hand-labor in its production limits flax cultivation in the United States, which relies on cheaper imported products.

2. Hemp

Hemp's long fiber strands—exceeding 6 feet (1.8 meters)—are fairly straight, yellowish, greenish, dark brown, or grey in color. The plant is an annual herb with angular, rough stems and alternate deeply lobed leaves. It may grow to 16 feet (5 meters) tall, though plants cultivated for fiber are densely sowed and generally reach heights of only 7 to 10 feet (2 to 3 meters). Male and female flowers, small and greenish yellow flowers, grow on separate plants.

Originating in Central Asia, for millennia after hemp's importation into Europe the plant was cultivated for its strong, durable fiber. (The hemp plant's scientific name is *Cannabis sativa*, though other plant fibers used for cordage have incorrectly been called hemp.) True hemp was cultivated in China as early as 2800 BCE. Early in the Christian Era, it was grown in Europe's Mediterranean region and its cultivation spread throughout the rest of Europe during the Middle Ages. Its many uses yield twine, yarn, rope, cable, and string, artificial sponges, and coarse fabrics like sacking and canvas. Production of hemp fiber is a leading industry in India, Romania, China, Hungary, Poland, Turkey, and it is grown in North and South America. In Italy it is used to make a fabric similar to linen. The plant is also grown for its seed—used in hempseed oil, paints, soaps, varnishes, and bird feed. Only its leaves and blossoms yield the drugs marijuana and hashish; in warmer regions, hemp may be grown for the production of marijuana or hashish. The active ingredient in these drugs is present in all parts of both the male and female plants but is most concentrated in the resin in the flowering tops of the female. (Today, in the United States, the hemp plant may be cultivated only under a government permit.)

3. Another Tale: Spindle, Shuttle, and Needle[1]

Once upon a time there was a girl whose parents died when she was still a little child. Her godmother lived all alone at the end of the village in a little house, and earned her living with spinning, weaving, and sewing. The old woman took the orphaned child into service and gave her a pious upbringing.

When the girl was fifteen years old the godmother took ill, called the child to her bedside, and said, "My dear daughter, I feel that my end is near. I leave to you this little house, that will protect you from wind and weather; and also a spindle, a shuttle, and a needle, with which you can earn your living".

She then laid her hands on the girl's head and blessed her, saying, "Keep God in your heart, and it will go well with you". With that she closed her eyes. At her funeral the girl walked behind the coffin crying, and paid her last respects as she was laid to rest in the earth.

The girl now lived all alone in the little house. She was industrious. She span, wove, and sewed; and everything she did was touched by the good old woman's blessing. It was as though the flax multiplied itself in her kitchen, and whenever she wove a piece of cloth or a carpet, or sewed a shirt, she always immediately found a buyer who paid so well that she was never in need and always had something to share with others.

At this time the king's son was traveling throughout the country in search of a bride. He wanted neither a poor one nor a rich one. He said, "My wife shall be the girl who is at the same time the poorest and the richest".

When he came to the village where the girl lived he asked, as he had done everywhere, who was the richest girl and the poorest girl. First of all they named for him the richest girl, and then said that the poorest girl was the one who lived in the little house at the end of the village.

The rich girl sat in her doorway in all her finery, and when the prince approached she bowed before him. He looked at her, said not a word, and rode on.

When he arrived at the poor girl's house she was not standing in the doorway, but instead was sitting in her little kitchen. He stopped his horse and looked into the window, through which the bright sun was shining, and saw the girl, sitting at her spinning wheel and diligently spinning. She looked up, and when she saw the prince looking in she blushed all over, closed her eyes, and continued to spin. I do not know if the thread was entirely even at this time, but she continued to spin until the prince had ridden away.

Then she stepped to the window and opened it, saying, "It is so hot in the kitchen", but she continued to follow him with her eyes as long as she could recognize the white feathers on his hat.

The girl sat back down in the kitchen and continued to work at her spinning. Then a saying came to her that the old woman had sometimes said while she was at work, and she sang it thus:

> Spindle, spindle, go on out,
> And bring a suitor to my house.

What happened? The spindle immediately jumped out of her hand and out the door. Amazed, she stood up and watched it as it danced merrily across the field, pulling along a glistening golden thread behind it. Before long, it had disappeared from her eyes.

Because the girl no longer had a spindle, she picked up her shuttle, seated herself at her loom, and began to weave.

Now the spindle danced ever onward, and just as the thread came to an end it reached the prince.

"What do I see?" he cried. "Is this spindle showing me the way?"

He turned his horse around and followed the golden thread back.

The girl was seated at her work singing:

> Shuttle, shuttle, weave so fine,
> Lead a suitor here to me.

Just then the shuttle jumped from her hand and out the door. However, it began to weave a carpet before the threshold, a more beautiful one than anyone had ever seen before. At its sides blossomed roses and lilies. In its middle, against a golden background, there were rows of green upon which hares and rabbits were jumping about. In between, stags and deer stuck out their heads. Colorful birds sat above in the branches. The only thing missing was their singing. The shuttle jumped back and forth. It was as though everything was growing by itself.

Because her shuttle had run away, the girl now sat down to sew. She held her needle in her hand and sang:

> Needle, needle, sharp and fine,
> Clean up the house for the suitor of mine.

Then the needle jumped out of her fingers and flew about in the kitchen as quick as lightning. It was as though invisible spirits were at work. The table and benches were soon covered with green cloth, the chairs with velvet; and silk curtains hung at the windows.

The needle had scarcely made its last stitch when the girl looked through the window and saw the white feathers on the prince's hat. The spindle had brought him here with its golden thread. He dismounted and walked across the carpet into the house. When he stepped into the kitchen, she was standing there in her simple dress, but she was glowing in it like a rose in a bush.

"You are the poorest, but also the richest", he said to her. "Come with me. You shall be my bride".

She said nothing, but reached out her hand to him. Then he gave her a kiss and led her outside, lifted her onto his horse, and took her to the royal palace where their wedding was celebrated with great joy.

The spindle, shuttle, and needle were secured in the treasure chamber, where they were kept in great honor.

4. Another Tale: The Three Spinners[2]

There was once a girl who was idle and would not spin, and, despite all rebukes, her mother could not bring her to it. At last the mother was once so overcome with anger and impatience that she beat her, on which the girl began to weep loudly. Now at this very moment the Queen drove by, and when she heard the weeping she stopped her carriage, went into the house, and asked the mother why she was beating her daughter so that the cries could be heard out on the road. Then the woman was ashamed to reveal the laziness of her daughter and said, "I cannot get her to leave off spinning. She insists on spinning for ever and ever, and I am poor, and cannot procure the flax". Then answered the Queen, "There is nothing that I like better to hear than spinning, and I am never happier than when the wheels are humming. Let me have your daughter with me in the palace, I have flax enough, and there she shall spin as much as she likes". The mother was heartily satisfied with this, and the Queen took the girl with her.

When they had arrived at the palace, she led her up into three rooms which were filled from the bottom to the top with the finest flax. "Now spin me this flax", said she, "and when thou hast done it, thou shalt have my eldest son for a husband, even if thou art poor. I care not for that, thy indefatigable industry is dowry enough". The girl was secretly terrified, for she could not have spun the flax, no, not if she had lived till she was three hundred years old, and had sat at it every day from morning till night.

When she was alone, she began to weep, and sat thus for three days without moving a finger. On the third day came the Queen, and when she saw that nothing had been spun yet, she was surprised; but the girl excused herself by saying that she had not been able to begin because of her great distress at leaving her mother's house. The Queen was satisfied with this, but said when she was going away, "To-morrow thou must begin to work".

When the girl was alone again, she did not know what to do, and in her distress went to the window. Then she saw three women coming towards her, the first of whom had a broad flat foot, the second had such a great underlip that it hung down over her chin, and the third had a broad thumb. They remained standing before the window, looked up, and asked the girl what was amiss with her. She complained of her trouble, and then they offered her their help and said, "If thou wilt invite us to the wedding, not be ashamed of us, and wilt call us thine aunts, and likewise wilt place us at thy table, we will spin up the flax for thee, and that in a very short time". "With all my heart", she replied, "do but come in and begin the work at once". Then she let in the three strange women, and cleared a place in the first room, where they seated themselves and began their spinning.

The one drew the thread and trod the wheel, the other wetted the thread, the third twisted it, and struck the table with her finger, and as often as she struck it, a skein of thread fell to the ground that was spun in the finest manner possible. The girl concealed the three spinners from the Queen, and showed her whenever she came the great quantity of spun thread, until the latter could not praise her enough. When the first room was empty she went to the second, and at last to the third, and that too was quickly cleared. Then the three women took leave and said to the girl, "Do not forget what thou hast promised us, it will make thy fortune".

When the maiden showed the Queen the empty rooms, and the great heap of yarn, she gave orders for the wedding, and the bridegroom rejoiced that he was to have such a clever and industrious wife, and praised her mightily. "I have three aunts", said the girl, "and as they have been very kind to me, I should not like to forget them in my good fortune; allow me to invite them to the wedding, and let them sit with us at table". The Queen and the bridegroom said, "Why should we not allow that?"

Therefore when the feast began, the three women entered in strange apparel, and the bride said, "Welcome, dear aunts".

"Ah", said the bridegroom, "how comest thou by these odious friends?"

Thereupon he went to the one with the broad flat foot, and said, "How do you come by such a broad foot?" "By treading", she answered, "by treading".

Then the bridegroom went to the second, and said, "How do you come by your falling lip?" "By licking", she answered, "by licking".

Then he asked the third, "How do you come by your broad thumb?" "By twisting the thread", she answered, "by twisting the thread".

On this the King's son was alarmed and said, "Neither now nor ever shall my beautiful bride touch a spinning-wheel". And thus she got rid of the hateful flax-spinning.

5. Rumpelstiltskin and the Jews[3]

When a post-classical (occidental) text hints pejoratively of contractual obligation as "legalistic" the deathless mystery of anti-Semitism lurks. Jew-hatred may not motivate every snide aspersion to legalism but that possibility ought to be considered.[4] Sadly but inevitably the two concepts deeply entwine, perhaps inextricably, and it would be doing Rumpelstiltskin's story a disservice to ignore this unsavory undertone as insinuated in comparisons with Shakespeare's Shylock.

Orthodox Christian theologians contemptuously regard Legalism as an excessive regard for, and a reflexive self-examination of, personal conduct that follows (a priori) legal notions—that is, ordinances, jurisprudence, and precedent. Gentile antagonism arises because such regard for law(s) inhibits trust in spontaneous feelings, especially of intuitive faith in God's redemptive grace. The resulting rage at legalism often vented against that most replete legal expression: the Jewish Talmud, a work without Christian equivalent.

Accordingly, following hints laid out in the Gospels, although neither the term "legalism" nor the term "legalist" appears in Hebrew or Christian Scriptures, the charge of Legalism can indict both Jews and some fellow-Christians charged with a delusional rigor in practicing what is regarded as superficiality instead of cultivating mercy and an instinctive cognizance of God's grace. As a corollary Legalists are considered prideful by adhering to the letter of law at the expense of the spirit. Nevertheless, the word "legalistic" carries two parallel theological meanings. Mainly in Protestant usage the term refers to a disciple or promoter of the religious doctrine of "legalism": of justification by works (a position supported by some books of Christian Scripture, especially Galatians) as opposed to exclusive salvation by faith or sacraments. That is not the sense in which Rumpelstiltskin's cause appears in the fairytale. His scrupulous prosecution of his case involved no religious schism. He might have standing to pursue his defamation according to another older, and justifiably disreputable, understanding of the word.

This mainly Roman Catholic usage derives from the sense of a person, typically a Jew or specifically a Pharisee who, versed in the law, is a stickler for legality.[5] Specifically, for such a hypothetical person the law's letter supersedes mercy.[6] The basis for constructing such a hoary straw-man rests on the most venerable foundation.

In a wholly inequitable representation, propaganda really, the legalist is opposed by the moralist. On one side is posed Jesus who supposedly dismissed the structure and substance of Jewish law. His followers deemed that body of statutes and ordinances anachronistic as their messiah would offer the Hebrew Covenant's salvation universally, to all nations—even, or especially, those beyond the strictures of the Hebrew nation. To the new Christians the Jews' commandments (governing Temple sacrifices, domestic and personal conduct, hygiene, food, dress, ritual purity, business dealings and other daily regulations) were viewed as obsolete. The coming of Jesus rendered all such binding social fabrics outmoded and governance by them or appeals to their venerable operation should not be condoned. Beginning with St. Paul this intolerant doctrine (perversely described as loving though it spawned, and continues to generate, oceans of unnecessary hatred in otherwise simple hearts) remains a cornerstone of the Roman Catholic Church and derives its legitimacy from the doctrine of Apostolic Succession.

The Roman Church preaches that any appeal to Jewish statutes represents a legalism of outward observance without the underlying and apparent observance, through performance, of the moral law. The proof-text for this position comes from the Gospel of Matthew:

For where two or three are gathered together in my name, there am I in the midst of them.

Then came Peter to him, and said, Lord, how often shall my brother sin against me, and I forgive him? till seven times?

Jesus said to him, I don't say to you, Until seven times: but, Until seventy times seven.

Therefore is the kingdom of heaven compared to a certain king, who would take account of his servants.

And when he had begun to reckon, one that owed him ten thousand talents was brought to him.

But forasmuch as he could not pay, his lord commanded him, his wife, his children, and all that he had, to be sold and payment made.

The servant therefore fell down, and worshipped him, saying, Lord, have patience with me, and I will pay you all.

Then the lord of that servant was moved with compassion, and loosed him, and forgave him the debt.

But the same servant went out, and found one of his fellow servants, who owed him a hundred pence: and he laid hands on him, and took him by the throat, saying, Pay me that you owe.

And his fellow servant fell down at his feet, and entreated him, saying, Have patience with me, and I will pay thee all.

And he would not: but went and cast him into prison, till he should pay the debt.

So when his fellow servants saw what was done, they were very sorry, and came and told their lord everything that had happened.

Then, hearing the whole story, his lord called him and said to him, O you wicked servant, I forgave you all that debt, because you wanted me to;

Shouldn't you also have had compassion on your fellow servant, even as I had pity on thee?

And his lord was angry and delivered him to the tormentors, till he should pay all that was due unto him.

So likewise shall my heavenly Father do also with you, if you from your hearts forgive not every one his brother their trespasses.

(Matthew 18:20–35)

Of course, as in much of Matthew's writing, even this presentation as a parable unfairly loads the argument against the lesson's main probable objection: hurdles to full religious participation erected against some Jews by ritual purity, an entirely intra-religious matter and not a situation bearing on general morality.

What supposedly represents the essence of Jewish legalism describes Roman law.[7] The Apostle balances this mis-attribution with testimony about the new Christian ideal and that false contrast permeated Western civilization, to great woe. As we have already seen, when Shakespeare fashioned his Jewish Shylock he repaired to Roman law as he recalled Cicero's De Oratore and the Roman orator's commendation of the Twelve Tables' harsh penalty; such Roman punishment (like crucifixion) were not only unlike Jewish law in spirit but involved suffering utterly forbidden in Jewish law's proscription against inflicting gratuitous cruelty.[8] Yet, such was put into the mouth of a pitiless Shylock, perhaps the only "Jew" many English saw for centuries.

That same Christian condemnation of unbending judgement provides the foundation for Rumpelstiltskin's actions and the resulting guiltless glee with which he is punished—as would the Jew at court, as did the Jew in *The Merchant of Venice*. That, incidentally, explains why for so long the play was seen as a comedy (that drew laughs akin to the guffaws elicited by last century's black-face racial stereotypes), a sadistically funny alternative to the Globe's next-door rival of bear-baiting. Finally, several factors converge to propose a deeply rooted folk-horror that tethers Rumpelstiltskin to Jew-hatred.

1. He may be accused of Jewish avarice as opposed to a spiritually Christian other-worldliness that dismisses both the body and material goods. He bargains away the only possessions the Miller's Daughter owns in this world. While Rumpelstiltskin unquestionably did not create her life-threatening situation he is a "sharp dealer" for taking advantage of her situation rather than helping her gratis. His concern for payment aligns him with a vicious inevitability. Beginning in the late Middle Ages when the Jews were gradually driven from agriculture into finance, charges of Jewish usury became commonplace as did the associated accusations of mean-spirited and relentless pursuit of money—a self-fulfilling prophesy as, aside from banking and money-lending, one-by-one most professions were closed to them. So Rumpelstiltskin seeks and obtains recompense for his work that in other fairytales is rewarded with love (a universal emotion that Christians claimed as their exclusive boon to the world and certainly the antithesis of the gentile construct of "legalism").

2. Quintessentially he is an outsider without family or friends in the community into which he is insinuated. He travels, or appears, from place to place. Rumpelstiltskin's rootlessness binds him to another manifestation of Jew-hatred, the myth of the

"Wandering Jew": he doesn't belong in the community or indeed in the world where he materializes.[9] Consequently Rumpelstiltskin was banished from the company of gentility—the Queen, her court, and Christendom's gentile society—as he lacks all polish, knowledge of local ways and their refinements. Humiliated he goes, we know not where, for the tale identifies him with no race of supernatural creatures. Expelled in shame he is forced to leave behind the good that he did and seek comfort and welcome elsewhere.

3. Rumpelstiltskin proves himself to be a master of capital formation. He came into the human world and created more wealth than what he found. Magically, with means unknown to his witnesses, he makes them all richer, somehow. This (proto-capitalist) skillset, rather than being envied and emulated, is suspect. The pre-modern world viewed the sum of all assets a fixed quantity.

4. His short stature and cleverness combine to create the image of a figure who is not physically robust, who will not respond with force or vigorously defend himself. Dwarfish in body but mentally alert, highly skilled, he agilely adapts, not rooted being of the earth or a native culture. This cliché of the pre-Zionist ghettoized Jew as a weakling, compared to hardy gentile males, seems, and for centuries was meant to be, a repugnant and laughable figure. And in the end Rumpelstiltskin is ridiculed and laughed out of the elite company to which he aspired (to become an adoptive father of one of these shining, clear-skinned, straight-haired, tall, perhaps blue-eyed, darlings) by helping one of their own. His shortness fetches up this association when seen as part of the entire constellation of the images of Jew-hatred. That roster of hatred's emblems was later joined by the scheming capitalist (once industrial-age capitalism appeared) or the rat-like infecting vampire (after the germ theory developed and could be used as a metaphor).

5. Another and far more sinister reason suggests why Rumpelstiltskin might have wanted to obtain the child is the old Blood Libel. He intended to drain the helpless (proto-Christian) child's blood in a tale told by Christian peasants. The blood libel often (and sometimes still) erupted whenever a gentile child went missing but this time the sinister act was thwarted by a clever girl, the Miller's Daughter, hence the finale's general euphoria. Nervous relief supplies the conclusion's undertone.

6. Legalism binds these suspicions into a single flood of innuendo. Rumpelstiltskin functions in a climate without the possibility of pardoning the victim of an unsporting deal contracted under duress; neither will Rumpelstiltskin exercise clemency borne of sympathy for the girl's plight. To the nominally Christian peasant (the sort of person who first told or heard the fairytale) operating more by superstition than refined reason this seems either pagan or Jewish. And Christian Scripture heard in church sanctioned that same peasant's loathing of the Jew. Rumpelstiltskin and the Jew are best mocked, deprived of their rightful gains, and banished. Outside of folklore, the theft and humor accorded Rumpelstiltskin befalls the helpful Jewish money-lenders, Raquel and Vidas, in the poem of El Cid. The same ending resonates echoing from *The Merchant of Venice*. The reality of European history's repeated expulsions and Jew shaming feature in the tale of Rumpelstiltskin.

6. Singing Versus Talking

Worksongs for Men, Fairytales for Women

When he sets down to spin in the castle chamber, he invokes no special charm and Rumpelstiltskin resembles any accomplished artisan who believes in his own competence. Before beginning a task some people pray, solicit a god, or summon a muse's guidance but without an invocation Rumpelstiltskin spins quietly and diligently with workmanlike dispatch. He works with non-magical substances (flax or wool) and everyday tools (the commonplace spinning wheel at hand). At leisure he sings of his wondrous self and unlike magical incantation, his words change nothing. The song he sings around his fire is the worksong of a jack-of-all-trades.

> Today I bake, tomorrow brew,
> The next I'll have the young Queen's child.
> Ha! glad am I that no one knew
> That Rumpelstiltskin I am styled.[10]

Rumpelstiltskin celebrates himself a baker, a brewer, a spinner. Self-sufficient, he can get no progeny which is only strange if he is fertile and potent but if sterile or impotent he can still accomplish much, though, vexingly, he's incapable of siring the child he wants.

Unlike female camaraderie (that gently fostered discursive and empathetic bonding before "sisterhood") when early–industrial era men sought stag company they created tall tales, and work-narratives flourished but in western Europe story-telling was not cultivated in the smoking lounge, middle-class bar, pub, a fraternal hall's warmly arcane and highly structured rituals, a rowdy saloon, or the sanctum of a men's club. (Male work and play environments encouraged jokes, some at women's expense. That genre was preserved in vaudeville and Comedia del Arte's descendant sit-coms: "My wife is so dumb that . . ". or "My wife/woman is so mean that. . . ". And women gave as good as they got.) The spinnstuben did not sound like the spaces where men worked because until the moment when men arrived with fiddles or bagpipes, music contributed a small part of women's self-made diversions. Men were allowed into the spinning chamber to amuse and court a lover, sometimes with music. Subordinating music to the life of the spinning chamber created a great opportunity.

With no need to arrange the spinners' exertions into coordinated effort, the place of worksongs in male labor was occupied by chatting and stories about the world of women or domestic chores.

Worksongs

Every element of the story considered work, extolled its rewards and skills while assuming the tellers' camaraderie in shared tasks. But the story respected some trades and skills more than others. Each profession's speech features a distinct jargon—perhaps a regional accent emphasized tools and terms of a trade—preferences that may color the tale. The rhyme-scheme of Rumpelstiltskin's song melodically and rhythmically conveys a message, tuneful to him, unheard by us, as in the night forest a little man boasts of his deftness and his secret name. Readers downplay his shoptalk while emphasizing the word that dramatically unlocks the story, his name. His "work" brings him to aid the Miller's Daughter and what he sings resembles a worksong.

With unavoidable beats, worksongs pound out strong rhythms absent from spinning. Spinning delivers prose and story-telling, not the matrix from which cadenced poetry or song arises.

Hand-spinning lacks robust rhythmic emphasis but feels continuous, uniformly weak, and fluid. Its motions vary constantly with the thickness and unexpected variety of the mass of fibers, knotted or loose, from which the thread descends. A gracefully individual craft, though spinning in a group each woman adjusts her own work to a rhythm different from companions sitting right beside her. This elastic rhythm differs markedly from men's physical work where worksongs harness group power to exert maximum force on certain beats (Sea Chanteys, Railroad Songs, Fieldwork songs, etc.). Worksongs grow from the needs of organized team efforts. The spinner's endless fine manual adjustments cannot generate the recurring melodic patterns of a tune, nor do they lend themselves to rime. Spinning may inspire vocal displays, just not worksongs; it prompts speech, story-telling.

Like a mortal man, Rumpelstiltskin sings a non-magical worksong with a thumping pulse and rime. But Rumpelstiltskin works solo and worksongs conform and concentrate a working crew's breathing to match the straining energy-output needed for a task. Rumpelstiltskin shows little strain but still has a worksong.

Smoothly unbroken spinning needs no worksong so that, in a tale of two spinners, one mortal and the other magical, Rumpelstiltskin's solitary midnight singing introduces an interesting mirror-imaging of male and female work environments.

From Reality to Metaphor

There's another idiomatic fiber connection. The spinnstube's story echoes the circumstances within which it was created. The insecurity-crazed miller told a tall tale, a yarn; in this context "yarn" beckons to a male ambience.

Yarn tends to be a highly worked fiber spun for weaving, or sewing-thread, knitting, and so forth. Formerly it referred to any spun fiber of silk, hemp, cotton, wool, flax or later, sisal. Even the much thicker strands used in rope-making were called yarn and by the early seventeenth-century "spun-yarn" formed a ship's rigging. From its nautical association came the phrase "to spin a yarn", a typically long story (as rope for warships was made in lengths of 1,000+ feet). These stories were sometimes believable but often intentionally incredible, festooned with marvelous incidents (like an inherently fantastic "fish tale"). Told for amusement, a yarn was never meant as a trusted report on reality.

As fairytales arose from the female world yarns regarded males' trades or adventures (for example, Sinbad was a *sailor* whose job supplied the frame-story explaining his exotic travels).[11] Men's yarns flaunted amusing or admonitory tales while women worked yarn to the accompaniment of fables both entertaining and cautionary. Another counterpart to sexual symmetry in the expression of gender: the yarn and the fairytale probe psychological reality using similar but not identical tools. (Was the Miller telling a yarn or was he out of his mind to speak thus to his king?) By sea or land the stories came; some lived on, most were forgotten.

7. Rumpelstiltskin and Karl Marx

> It is not linen you're wearing out, But human creatures' lives.
>
> *Thomas Hood*[12]

Labor

The Millers Daughter's helplessness and, until the tale's last moment, her subordination to the wishes of everybody else, represent the rural peasantry that preceded the industrial working class. Yet, a purely Marxist reading of Rumpelstiltskin would be ludicrous (but somebody out there must already be sharpening a pencil eyes fixed on tenure). Though many girls think themselves plain how many will grasp that the Miller's Daughter, only gratuitously called beautiful by her father, appears basically unattractive aside from her supposed money-minting talent.[13] Her dubiously capitalistic father (a failed capitalist is still a capitalist) occupies the bourgeoisie's lowest rung. However they are socially defined, these two figures stand in opposition to the aristocracy, its insensate cruelty and unchallenged privilege (while the superstitious peasantry practiced its own vengeful cruelty). In addition to charting class stratification the story also captures a commercial and not strictly social dynamic.

Exactly contemporaneous with the Brothers Grimm collecting Rumpelstiltskin's story a wave of social awakening swept Europe. This stirring was neither so retrospective nor hopeful as the nationalistic and cultural edifice the Brothers represented as prime examples.

Between the last decades of the eighteenth century and the first decades of the nineteenth (especially in England but eventually throughout Europe) workers were challenged by wholesale mechanization. Newly installed devices uprooted from their employment what had been a semi-skilled class of factory laborers, specialists who tended their day's hi-tech machinery. The next generation of machines required ever fewer workers to mind them (in a process of automation that continues today). The most famous anti-industrial reaction came from the Luddites, a name that stands for rousing opposition to mechanization. But other factors also drove the factory workers' quickening to action.

Already dispossessed from their age-old ties to the land and agriculture, food shortages and the rising price of grain drove desperate factory workers to occasionally plunder granaries. Sometimes self-trained and drilled armies of workers smashed the textile finishing machines that displaced them. These fiber workers sensed they had been permanently ousted by a technology of staggering efficiency and productivity. The machines left a swath of society without hope of finding new jobs through either upgrading skills or further education, a situation that presaged the twenty-first century's first decades. If wide-frame automated looms displaced landless semi-skilled workers their unemployment foretold more than their own bleak dead-end; textile worker's newly unmarketable skills extinguished hope of apprenticing their children to eventually replace them in jobs that no longer existed. No fiber or textile craft was immune. Lacemaking, formerly the essential cottage industry, was automated, as was all manner of spinning thread, cords, string, and so forth.

The capitalist factory-owners' position was easily understood: fewer employees meant lower expenses. The mills' uncomplaining machines required no amenities (light, air, heat, lunch, or dinner breaks). Mechanics with no feeling for cloth or spun fibers became the essential employee and this early-nineteenth-century turmoil arose alongside the Grimms' work. Rumpelstiltskin was born a contemporary of the Luddites. In its last iteration, the one the Grimms recorded, his story captures a tincture of that struggle to make fiber without human hands.

He increases the king's wealth as Rumpelstiltskin's finished thread will not belong to the Millers Daughter who is alienated from her labor, work she can (indeed must) claim as her own though she never laid a hand on the product. As in a mechanized mill.

She works neither at home nor in a convivial spinnstube but is locked into a drear workplace. Her working conditions could not be worse, unless she toiled in a real nineteenth-century Manchester textile mill (as observed by Friedrich Engels), with all its dust, deafening noise, life-threatening machines that too regularly amputated their attendants' body parts (threatening a death sentence like hers), and pitifully low pay.

The allegory is complete. A fable about and against early Capitalism. Perhaps.

Management

The managerial "Rumpelstiltskin Syndrome" can infect middle managers of either sex. These miserable souls impose unreasonable workloads on subordinates and after those daunting tasks are, with super-human effort, miraculously completed, the manager inflicts equal or greater workloads. Appropriate acknowledgement of the worker's achievement or due credit within the organization is then withheld (along with suitable recompense that would threaten the insecure manager). No fairytale, the syndrome's costs highly burden the unit and the whole society suffers an upwardly distorting displacement of credit as recompense eventually lands in the plush laps of the "1 percent".

Because they never learn of their employees' labors higher ups on the company's executive ladder, or Boards of Directors, never express appreciation which, if allowed by middle management, would illuminate the real source of productivity and creativity at a lower level. Likely, the queen never confessed her inability to spin gold but reaped the rewards of her employee—whom she stiffed. Rumpelstiltskin's name clung to a workplace affliction that describes other malefactors, the miller, the King, the Queen.

Notes

1. Jacob and Wilhelm Grimm, "Spindel, Weberschiffchen und Nadel", in *Kinder-und Hausmärchen* (Children's and Household Tales, known as Grimms' Fairy Tales), as added to the Grimms' fifth edition (1843) of *Kinder-und Hausmärchen* (Berlin, 1857), no. 188. The Grimms' source seems to have been Ludwig Auerbacher, "Die Patengeschenke", *Büchlein für die Jugend* (Stuttgart and Tübingen, 1834), pp. 160–166. The text follows the translated by D. L. Ashliman, 2002 and is considered folktales type 585.
2. Jacob and Wilhelm Grimm, *Household Tales*, translated by Margaret Hunt (London: George Bell, 1884), 1:59–61.
3. See: Yolen (1993, pp. 11–13). Her notion of this relationship is quite different from what follows.
4. For completeness sake, though it does not bear on our story, mention can be made of the Chinese philosophical school called Legalism that flourished during the Warring States era (475–221 BCE). The Legalists' dour view of human nature conceived of the emerging national state's governing establishment as a response to the psychological truths of human nature and not to a high-minded ideal of civic management. Accordingly they held for broadly circulating the content of the law—something like Mosaic public readings or the Magna Carta's overall governance—contrary to Confucianism's faith in an enlightened leader. Rigorous application of law, the employment of methods for sound governance, and the feedback of accountability, all tended to enlarge the power of the state and its ruler. This school of thought laid the harsh intellectual foundations for China's first imperial dynasty, the Qin (221–207 BCE).
5. This understanding does not hold for Greek Orthodoxy and its sub-denominations which observe the Apostolic Decree promulgated at the Council of Jerusalem (c. 50) by James the Just:

   > Wherefore my sentence is, that we trouble not them, which from among the Gentiles are turned to God: But that we write to them, that they abstain from pollutions of idols, and [from] fornication, and [from] things strangled, and [from] blood. For Moses of old time did in every city them that preach him, being read in the synagogues every Sabbath day.
   > *(Acts 15:19–21)*

   So, new Christians should adhere to both Mosaic law and accept Jesus, his life, and his teachings. The unfulfilled promise of the James (the brother of Jesus) church in Jerusalem represents a great gap in occidental culture.

6. Originating from a different scriptural authorization than Greek Orthodoxy, clearly at odds with Roman Catholicism, the obscure but influential sect of postmillennialist Christian Reconstructionism conceives that Christians remain obligated to obey and implement the complete Mosaic law.
7. In contrast to the spirit of Roman law that pervades Western society, the eighteenth-century rabbi Israel ben Eliezer, universally called the Ba'al Shem Tov (Master of the Good Name), created modern Hasidism in direct opposition to prevailing scholarly Judaism. He introduced a mystical, spontaneous and personal form of Judaism whose opposite might be called "legalistic". Yet human nature prevailed in confusing even that clear-cut antagonism. Not surprisingly—exactly as happened to Zen Buddhism in Japan, a movement intended to sweep away the endless memorization and chanted recitations of Sutras in favor of a mystical, spontaneous and personal form of Buddhism—modern Hasidim quickly slid into a text-based and ultra-orthodox cluster of warring cults that have more-or-less abandoned the Ba'al Shem Tov's ecstatic, instinctive, welcoming, and unrehearsed forms of worship. Thus, two forms of Jewish piety clashed. One: a saintliness derived from unceasing meditation on the wonders of the law(s) of the Lord—social and natural, evidenced in human psychology and in the universe's physical laws—as an up-lifting source of wonder to be practiced with punctiliousness That tradition (the older version of Hasidism, meaning piety) that began at least as far back as the Hellenistic period (c. 300 BCE–c. 300 CE). The second: a more recent and ostentatious version that split off from mainstream Judaism. The Gospels refer to that older version of Hasidism, specifically to its strictures of ritual purity.

8. And more than the Jew/Gentile contest on which the modern and especially post-Holocaust intelligence fixes, the play seems principally a competition of Urban/Male versus Rural/Female, with the latter winning Shakespeare's heart as—however much or little we think or suppose we know of him—when he had the choice he expressed his preference by quitting London and retiring to the countryside. Portia is the victor.

Shakespeare would probably be surprised at the enormous recent attention directed at Shylock's Jewishness (that echoed Marlowe's *Jew of Malta* with Shakespeare's slightly kinder, but still cruelly comical, version) that to the play's author seemed incidental, merely a plot device. To the former lad of Stratford who'd been drilled in elementary Latin and who subsequently excelled with adroit language play, as an adult playwright he recalled Cicero's *De Oratore* (1.44), its praise for the "little book of the Twelve Tables [that epitomized] the fountains and sources of the laws [that may] assuredly . . . surpass the libraries of all the philosophers". For when it came time to account for Shylock's atavistically heathen rage, Stratford's lad recalled what The Twelve Tables said about debtors:

> One who has confessed a debt . . . shall have thirty days to pay it in. After that forcible seizure of his body is allowed. . . . On the third market day let [his creditors] divide his body among them. If they cut more or less than each one's share it shall be no crime.
> *(Table III: 1–2)*

9. I am decidedly *not* saying that Rumpelstiltskin is "The Wandering Jew". That well-researched figure associates with a huge network of myths that vary in details from region to region and range in seriousness from merely theologically odious to folklore's dismissible, but quaintly creepy, endless traveler apt to appear anywhere at any time. So, for example, German folk tales "describe the Wandering Jew as to clothing and general appearance; they emphasize his wandering (he is everywhere and nowhere); they describe certain taboos concerning his ability to rest" (Anderson, 1965, p. 80). While the Grimms do not equate Rumpelstiltskin with the Wandering Jew, both figures possess a sibling likeness having emerged from the same matrix of folkloric exploration and share, disturbingly to be sure, many traits native to their creators' provincial worldview.

10. *The Complete Grimm's Fairy Tales* (New York: Pantheon Books) 1994, p. 267. In Taylor's translation the basic elements are all arranged less neatly:

> Merrily the feast I'll make,
> To-day I'll brew, to-morrow bake;
> Merrily I'll dance and sing,
> For next day will a stranger bring:
> Little does my lady dream
> Rumpel-Stilts-Kin is my name!

The "stranger" is probably not the Queen's baby, but Rumpelstiltskin's next client. Although some future tomorrow is suggested (another untold and unrecorded story) in a long process, Rumpelstiltskin's various interventions in other lives never needed to be unfurled because, though limited to one episode, this wonderfully concise story is sufficient wherein Rumpelstiltskin's nature was made clear.

In the interests of completeness, and because the reader may have encountered other versions of the song, here are the alternate renditions:

> Today I'll brew, tomorrow bake;
> Merrily I'll dance and sing,
> For next day will a stranger bring.
> Little does my lady dream
> Rumpelstiltskin is my name! or:
> Tomorrow I brew, today I bake,
> And then the child away I'll take;
> For little deems my royal dame
> That Rumpelstiltskin is my name! or:
> Merrily I prance and sing,

Tomorrow will, a baby bring.
Merrily I dance and shout,
The name the queen cannot find out; Rumpelstiltskin!or:
Today I brew, today I bake,
Tomorrow the Queen's own child I take;
This guessing-game she'll never win,
For my name is Rumpelstiltskin!

11. The yarn developed as a gendered equivalent to specifically women's fairytales. Curiously, the word yarn derives from the Old English (and related Germanic languages) term for guts; hence, to spill your guts, tell a tale, meant to tell a yarn.
12. Thomas Hood (1789–1845), *The Song of the Shirt*, 1843.
13. It's possible to view the story exclusively through a Marxist lens, as serious, and mainly successful, examples of such interpretations propose that initially anodyne works contain a hidden dose of venom. In one of his more remarkable performances, Ariel Dorfman (with coauthor Armand Mallelart) issued a self-explanatory exegesis, *How to Read Donald Duck: Imperialist Ideology in the Disney Comic*, trans. David Kunzle (New York: International General) 1975, originally published in Chile (Ediciones Univarsarías de Valparaíso) 1971.

WORKS CITED

Bacchilega, Cristina, "An Introduction to the 'Innocent Persecuted Heroine' Fairy Tale", *Western Folklore*, Vol. 52, No. 1, January 1993.

Basque. "The Pretty but Idle Girl", *Basque Legends*. Wentworth Webster, p. 56. [cited by Clodd 1889].

Beckett, Samuel, Letter to Alan Schneider, 4 January 1960, quoted in *No Author Better Served: The Correspondence of Samuel Beckett and Alan Schneider*, ed. M. Harmon (Cambridge: Harvard University Press) 1998.

Bennett, Judith M., *Ale, Beer, and Brewsters in England: Women's Work in a Changing World, 1300–1600* (Oxford: Oxford University Press) 1996.

Bettelheim, Bruno, "Art: A Personal Vision", in *Art as the Measure of Man* (New York: Doubleday for the Museum of Modern Art) 1964.

Bettelheim, Bruno, *The Uses of Enchantment* (New York: Knopf) 1976.

Blackwell, Jeannine, Review Essay, "The Many Names of Rumpelstiltskin: Recent Research on the Grimms' Kinder- und Haus-Märchen, Grimms' Bad Girls and Bold Boys: The Moral and Social Vision of the Tales by Ruth B. Bottigheimer; The Brothers Grimm and Folktale by James M. McGlathery; The Hard Facts of the Grimms' Fairy Tales by Maria Tatar; The Brothers Grimm: From Enchanted Forests to the Modern World by Jack Zipes", *The German Quarterly*, Vol. 63, No. 1, Winter 1990.

Bottigheimer, Ruth B., *Grimms' Bad Girls & Bold Boys* (New Haven: Yale University Press) 1987.

Bottigheimer, Ruth B., "From Gold to Guilt: The Forces Which Reshaped Grimms' Tales", in *The Brothers Grimm and Folktale*, ed. James M. McGlathery (Urbana and Chicago: The University of Illinois Press) 1991.

Bottigheimer, Ruth B., *Fairy Tales: A New History* (Albany: Excelsior Editions, SUNY Press) 2009.

Briggs, Katherine, *An Encyclopedia of Fairies* (New York: Pantheon) 1976.

Britain (Annandale). Whuppity Stoorie. *Chambers Popular Rhymes of Scotland*, p. 76. [cited by Clodd 1889].

Britain (The Border). Habetrot. *Henderson's Folklore of the Northern Counties*, p. 258. [cited by Clodd 1889].

Britain (Suffolk), "Tom Tit Tot", *Ipswich Journal*, 15 January 1878. [cited by Clodd 1889].

Brooks, David, "Love and Gravity", *New York Times*, 21 November 2014, p. A 27.

The Burlington Magazine, "Grimm's Fairy Tales by Arthur Rackham", Vol. 16, No. 81, December 1909, pp. 171–172.

Busk, R. H., Tyrol: *The Wild Jiger and the Baroness. Household Stories from the Land of Hofer.* p. 110. [cited by Clodd 1889].

Campbell, Gordon, *The Hermit in the Garden: From Imperial Rome to Ornamental Gnome* (Oxford: Oxford University Press) 2013.

Campbell, Joseph, "Commentary", in *The Complete Grimm's Fairy Tales* (New York: Pantheon Books) 1994.

Carroll, James, *Jerusalem, Jerusalem* (New York: Houghton Mifflin Harcourt) 2011.

Clodd, A. W. T. and Edward, "The Philosophy of Rumpelstilt-Skin", *The Folk-Lore Journal*, Vol. 7, No. 2, 1889, Clodd had previously read this article as a paper delivered to the Folklore Society on 26 February 1889.

Clodd, Edward, *Tom Tit Tot: An Essay in Savage Philosophy in Folktales* (London: Duckworth and Co.) 1898.

Clodd, Edward, "What's in a Name?", *Folklore*, Vol. 1, No. 2, June 1890.

Clodd, Edward, *The Childhood of Religions* (London: Kegan Paul, Trench, Trübner & Co.) 1902.

de Santillana, Giogio and Hertha von Dechend, *Hamlet's Mill: An Essay on Myth & the Frame of Time* (Boston: Gambit) 1969.

Dorfman, Ariel and Armand Mallelart, *How to Read Donald Duck: Imperialist Ideology in the Disney Comic*, trans. David Kunzle (New York: International General) 1975, originally published in Chile (Ediciones Univarsarías de Valparaíso) 1971.

Fink, Gonther-Louis, "The Fairy Tales of the Grimms' Sergeant of Dragoons J. F. Krause as Reflecting the Needs and Wishes of the Common People", in *The Brothers Grimm and Folktale*, ed. James M. McGlathery (Urbana and Chicago: The University of Illinois Press) 1991.

Fissell, Mary E., *Vernacular Bodies: The Politics of Reproduction in Early Modern England* (Oxford: Oxford University Press) 2004.

Freud, Sigmund, "Representation by Symbols", from *The Interpretation of Dreams*, 1900, in *The Standard Edition of the Complete Works* (London: Hogarth Press) 1960.

Freud, Sigmund, "Representation by Symbols in Dreams—Some Further Typical Examples", from *The Interpretation of Dreams*, 1900/1931, ed. and trans. James Stachey (New York: Avon, Discus), 1965 volume V in *The Standard Edition of the Complete Works* (London: Hogarth Press) 1960.

Friedan, Betty, *The Feminine Mystique* (New York: W. W. Norton & Co.) 2013.

Gais Seutonius Tranquillius (called Seutonius) *The Lives of the Twelve Caesars*, "Augustus" § 64. Germany [cited by Clodd 1889].

Girouard, Mark, *Cities and People* (New Haven: Yale University Press) 1985.

Goldfarb, Michael, *Emancipation* (New York: Simon & Schuster) 2009.

Grimm, Jacob and Wilhelm, "Rumpelstilzchen", *Kinder- und Hausmärchen*, Vol. 1 (Göttingen: Verlag der Dieterichschen Buchhandlung, 1857) [Children's and Household Tales – Grimms' Fairy Tales], no. 55, pp. 281–284.

Hahn, Barbara, "A Dream of Living Together: Jewish Women in Berlin Around 1800", in *Jewish Women and Their Salons: The Power of Conversation* (New Haven: Yale University Press; New York: The Jewish Museum) 2005.

Harvard Law Review, "Rumpelstiltskin Revisited: The Inalienable Rights of Surrogate Mothers", Vol. 99, No. 8, June 1986.

Heaney, Seamus, *Beowulf: A New Verse Translation* (New York and London: Norton) 2000.

Hunt, R., Britain (Cornwall). Duffy and the Devil. *Popular Romances of the West of England*, p. 239. [cited by Clodd 1889].

Iceland. Gilitrutt. *Pen and Pencil Sketches of Faroe and Iceland*. Symington. p. 240. [cited by Clodd 1889].

Ireland. "The Idle Girl and Her Aunts", Kennedy's Fireside Stories. [cited by Clodd 1889].

Kalsched, Donald, *The Innner World of Trauma* (London: Routledge) 1996.

Kane, Bronach, *Impotence and Virginity in the Late Medieval Ecclesiastical Court of York* (York: University of York, Borthwick Paper 114) 2008.

Kohlberg, Nancy and Philip Kopper, eds., *Shetland Breeds: Ancient, Endangered and Adaptable* (Chevy Chase, MD: Posterity Press) 2003.

Köhler, Reinhard, "Tom-Tit-Tot", Letter in *Folklore*, Vol. 2, No. 2, June 1891.

Lévi-Strauss, Claude, "Social Statics of Communication Structures", in *Structural Anthropology* (New York: Anchor Books) 1967.

Maher, John C., Review Article, "The Native Speaker in Applied Linguistics by Alan Davies", *TESOL Quarterly*, Vol. 31, No. 3, Autumn, 1997. [Published by: Teachers of English to Speakers of Other Languages, Inc. (TESOL)].

McGlathery, James M., *Fairy Tale Romance* (Urbana and Chicago: University of Illinois) 1991.

McGlathery, James M., *Grimms' Fairy Tales: A History of Criticism on a Popular Classic* (Columbia, SC: Camden House) 1993.

McLaren, Angus, *Impotence: A Cultural History* (Chicago: University of Chicago Press) 2007.

McWhorter, John, *Our Magnificent Bastard Tongue: The Untold Story of English* (New York: Gotham Books) 2008.

Miller, Martin, "Poor Rumpelstiltskin", *Psychoanalytic Quarterly*, Vol. 54, 1985.

Milnes, Humphrey, Review Article, "The Grimms' German Folk Tales by Francis P. Magoun and Alexander H. Krappe", *The Modern Language Journal*, Vol. 46, No. 3, March 1962.

Murray Cuddihy, John, *The Ordeal of Civility* (New York: Basic Books) 1974.

Napoli, Jo, and Donna and Richard Tchen, *Spinners*, illustrated by Donna Diamond (New York: Dutton/Penguin Juvenile) 1999.

Olmstead, Robert, "Private Lives: War and Baked Beans", *New York Times*, Sunday Review, 6 October 2013, p. 9.

Olson, Charles, "Muthos", in *The Special View of History* (Berkeley: Oyez) 1970.

Oppen, George, "The Mind's Own Place", *Kulchur*, Vol. 3, No. 10, Spring 1963, pp. 2–8; reprinted in *Selected Prose, Daybooks, and Papers*, ed. Stephen Cope (Berkeley: University of California Press) 2007.

Ozick, Cynthia, "All the World Wants the Jews Dead", *Esquire*, November 1974, pp. 103–107; pp. 207–210.

Paradiz, Valerie, *Clever Maids: The Secret History of the Grimm Fairy Tales* (New York: Basic Books) 2005.

Patrañas, R. H. Busk, *Spain: What Ana Saw in the Sunbeam*, p. 181. [cited by Clodd 1889].

Pound, Ezra, *ABC of Reading* (New York: New Directions) 1960.

Pratchett, Terry, Ian Stewart and Jack Cohen, *The Science of Discworld* (London: Ebury Press) 1999.

Quine, W. V., *Quiddities: An Intermittently Philosophical Dictionary* (Cambridge: Belknap, Harvard University Press) 1987.

Radice, Betty, trans., *Letters of [Peter] Abelard and Heloise* (London: Penguin, Great Loves) 1994.

Rafferty, Terrence, "The Better to Entertain You With, My Dear: Mirror Mirror, Grimm and Hollywood Love for Fairy Tales", *New York Times,* 21 March 2012, p. AR1.

Rand, Harry, "Letter: Why the Israelites Ate Matzah on the Exodus", *Biblical Archaeology Review*, Vol. 37, No. 1, 2011, pp. 8–10.

Rand, Harry, "The Modes in Recent Art", *Arts*, December 1980, pp. 76-92.

Rand, Harry, *Arshile Gorky: The Implications of Symbols* (Berkeley: University of California Press) 1991.

Rand, Harry, "Who Was Rumpelstiltskin?", *International Journal of Psychoanalysis* (London), Vol. 2000, No. 81, October 2000.

Rand, Harry, "Spontaneity's Passion & the Afterlife of a Societal Memory: When Two Murders Are Better Than One", in *Thinking and Imaging—Remembering: The Afterlife of Memory* Studies in Cultural Meaning (Paris: Université Paris Ouest, Nanterre) 2012.

Rohrich, Lutz, "The Quest for Meaning in Folk Narrative Research", in *The Brothers Grimm and Folktale*, ed. James M. McGlathery (Urbana and Chicago: The University of Illinois Press) 1991.

Roth, Philip, Interview with Daniel Sandstrom (for *Svenska Dagbladet*) "My Life as a Writer", *New York Times: Book Review*, 16 March 2014, p. 14.

Rowley, Julius L., "Rumpelstiltskin in the Analytical Situation", *International Journal of Psychoanalysis*, Vol. 32, 1951.

Ruskin, John, "Introduction", in *Grimm's Popular Stories* (London: Chatto & Windus) 1920, with Edgar Taylor's 1823 translation and illustrations by George Cruikshank.

Sacks, Oliver, *Hallucinations* (New York: Knopf) 2012.

Schneider, Jane, "Rumpelstiltskin's Bargain: Folklore and the Merchant Capitalist Intensification of Linen Manufacture in Early Modern Europe", in *Cloth and Human Experience*, ed. Annette B. Weiner and Jane Schneider (Washington and London: Smithsonian Institution Press) 1989.

Schwarzenegger, Arnold, "By the Book", *The New York Times*, Sunday Book Review, 30 December 2012, pp. BR9.

Smith, Kenwyn K. and Valerie M. Simmons, "A Rumpelstiltskin Organization: Metaphors on Metaphors in Field Research", *Administrative Science Quarterly*, Vol. 28, No. 3, Organizational Culture, September 1983.

Soskice, Janet, *The Sisters of Sinai: How Two Lady Adventurers Discovered the Hidden Gospels* (New York: Knopf) 2010.

Southern, Terry and Mason Hoffenberg, *Candy* (Paris: Olympia) 1958 and subsequently (New York: G. P. Putnam's Sons) 1964.

Span, Paula, "'Sex Never Dies', but a Medicare Option for Older Men Does", *New York Times,* 4 August 2015, p. D5.

Spitz, Ellen Handler, *Art and Psyche: A Study in Psychoanalysis and Aesthetics* (New Haven: Yale University Press) 1985.

Spitz, Ellen Handler, *Image and Insight: Essays in Psychoanalysis and the Arts* (New York: Columbia University Press) 1991.

Spitz, Ellen Handler, *Museums of the Mind* (New Haven: Yale University Press) 1994.

Stewart, Alison, "Distaffs and Spindles: Sexual Misbehavior in Sebald Beham's Spinning Bee", in *Saints, Sinners, and Sisters: Gender and Northern Art in Medieval and Early Modern Europe*, ed. Jane L. Carroll and Alison Stewart (Aldershot: Ashgate) 2003.

Tatar, Maria, "Introduction", in *Grimm's Grimmest* (San Francisco: Chronicle Books) 1997.

Tatar, Maria, *The Hard Facts of the Grimms' Fairy Tales* (Princeton, NJ: Princeton University Press) 1987.

Tatar, Maria, *The Annotated Brothers Grimm* (New York: Norton) 2012.

Taylor, Edgar, ed. and trans., *Grimm's Popular Stories* (London: Chatto & Windus) 1823/1920.

Thorpe, B., "Sweden (Upland)", *The Girl Who Could Spin Gold from Clay and Long Straw: Yule-Tide Stories*, p. 168 (and see Ib. p. xi. for references to Variants). [cited by Clodd 1889].

Time-Life Books, "American Country" series, *The Needle Arts: A Social History of American Needlework* (Alexandria, VA: Time-Life Books) 1990.

van Voss, Lex Heerma, *Ashgate History of Textile Workers 1650–2000* (Farnham: Ashgate) 2013.

von Unwerth, Matthew, *Freud's Requiem* (New York: Riverhead Books) 2005.

Wayland Barber, Elizabeth, *Women's Work: The First 20,000 Years* (New York and London: W.W. Norton & Co.) 1994.

Wittgenstein, Ludwig, *Philosophical Investigations*, trans. G. E. M. Anscombe (Upper Saddle River, NJ: Prentice Hall) 1958.

Yardley, Jim and Binyamin Appelbaum, "In Fiery Speeches Francis Excoriates Global Capitalism", *New York Times,* 12 July 2015.

Yolen, Jane, "The Rumpelstiltskin Factor", *Journal of the Fantastic in the Arts,* Vol. 5, No. 2, 1993.

Zelinsky, Paul O., *Rumpelstiltskin* (New York: Dutton) 1986.

Zipes, Jack, "Spinning with Fate: Rumpelstiltskin and the Decline of Female Productivity", *Western Folklore,* Vol. 52, No. 1 (Perspectives on the Innocent Persecuted Heroine in Fairy Tales), January 1993.

NOTES ON THE ILLUSTRATIONS

Frontispiece

Figure 0.1 Detail of a bas-de-page scene of a woman at a spinning wheel being kissed by a man, from the Smithfield Decretals, Southern France, with marginal decoration added in England; last quarter of the thirteenth century or the first quarter of the fourteenth century, Royal 10 E. iv, f. This example of Canon law was created to replace the Decretum of Gratian (who has long been recognized as the 'Father of Canon Law'; he probably came from Bologna) to coalesce and codify all previous canon law up to that date.

I: The Story's History

1.1. *Clemens Brentano* (1778–1842), from *Meyers Konversations-Lexikon*, (1905–1909), 6th ed, (Leipzig und Wein: Verlag des Bibliographischen Instituts).

1.2. *Friedrich Karl von Savigny* (1779–1861), Lithograph by E. Winderhalder after a chalk drawing by Louise Claude Henry.

II: Meaning Is Purpose

2.1. George Cruikshank (1792–1878) in Jacob & Wilhelm Grimm, *German Popular Stories*, Edward Taylor (trans.), (London, 1823). Cruikshank was an English caricaturist and cartoonist, famed for his political satire and his extensive illustrations of the works of Charles Dickens.

2.2. *The Sublime Moment*, Salvador Dali, (1938), oil on canvas, 47 × 38 cm, Staatsgalerie, Stuttgart, Germany.

2.3. "Vaudoises or Waldenssians as Witches" (1451) by Martin Le Franc (1410–1461) in *Champion Des Dames* 'Les Champion des Dames,' a prose poem by Martin le Franc, in which the poet acts as a champion or defender of virtuous women, citing many historical examples of women who are remembered for their valor, heroism, and wisdom, like Joan of Arc and the Virgin Mary.

    This work is part of a wider discussion surrounding women, femininity, and romance, best exemplified by Jean de Meung's "Romance of the Rose". In reference to the illustration, this drawing has been labelled as depicting Vaudoises or Waldensians. The Waldensians were a pre-Reformation sect founded in the late twelfth century. Their beliefs, amongst others, allowed for the free interpretation of the Bible, and for anyone, including women, to consecrate sacraments. As such, the sect was proclaimed heretical by the Roman Catholic Church at the 4th Lateran Council of 1215. The Waldensians were thus considered to be outcasts and endured much persecution and suspicion, which could explain the two witches being depicted as 'Vaudoises.'

2.4. *Flying Green Monster Penis*, in Decretum Gratiani, with commentary of Bartolomeo de Brescia, Italy 1340–45 Lyon, Bibliotheque Municipale Ms 5128 fol. 100r (Gratian of Bologne, d. 1170?, the "Father of Canon Law").

2.5. *Women Spinning*. The Brygos Painter (c. 490–470 BC), Athens, White Ground, 21.59 cm, British Museum. Little is known about the Brygos Painter. He was one of the most prolific artists of ancient Greece. He produced over 200 vases and vessels and was active in the mid to late fifth century BC.

2.6. *Young Woman Spinning with Servant*, Susa, Iran (8th–6th centuries BCE), elamite period, Bitumen, 3.5 × 5.1 in (9 × 13 cm), photo credit Franck Raux, Musée du Louvre

2.7. *Tomb stele, woman with distaff and child*, late Hittite, eighth to seventh century BCE. Photo by Erich Lessing, Adana Archaeology Museum, Turkey

2.8. *Hercules and Omphale*, 201–225 CE. Mosaic, Madrid National Archaeological Museum, Spain

2.9. *Hercules and the Maids of Omphales* [tying a woman's wimple on his head] (1537), Lucas Cranach the Elder (1472–1553), oil on beech wood, 32.3 × 46.8 in (82 × 118.9 cm), Herzog Anton Ulrich-Museum, Braunschweig, Germany. The writing in the background reads:
    'HERCVLEIS MANIBVS DANT LYDAE PENSA PVELLAE/ IMPERIVM DOMINAE FERT DEVS ILLE SVAE./SIC CAPIT INGENTIS ANIMOS DAMNOSA VOLVPTAS/FORTIAQVE ENERVAT PECTORA MOLLIS AMOR.'
    The inscription points toward the emasculating dangers of love. In Greek mythology, the partridge was linked to Aphrodite, the goddess of love and beauty. It could signal both pure love and evil lust

2.10. Lovestruck (male) Cupid. Daniël Heinsius, *Ambacht van Cupido* (1613), in *Nederduytsche poemata*, Leiden University Library, Shelf no. 20643 E 32. Web, Emblem Project Utrecht.

This illustration is derived from *Ambacht van Cupido* (1613), or the Craft of Cupid, by Daniël Heinsius. This book was published as a sequel to Heinsius' earlier *Emblemata amatoria*. Both works contained love emblems, a new innovation, that were accompanied by short poems or morals. It is striking that Heinsius wrote these works in Dutch, as the standard would have been to produce works in Latin. Thus, this work greatly influenced the development of Dutch poetry. In these works, Cupid has come to the Netherlands to learn the ways of love. The original Caption Reads: oordat ik een vrouw vereer, word ik een vrouw [By honouring a women, I shall become one] also: Non ego turpe putem deducere mollia fila: Vidimus Herculeas pensa decere manus; I should not feel any shame spinning threads like a woman. We have seen Hercules' hands working on some nice threads as well.

2.11. 'Woman Beating a Man (Her Husband?) with a Distaff,' *Luttrell Psalter*, (1320–1340), add. 42130, f.60, British Library.

This Psalter was commissioned by Sir Geoffrey Luttrell (1276–1345) sometime between 1320 and 1340. It is famed for its depictions of daily life in England as well as its animal-monster hybrids rather than the more typical Biblical images.

2.12. *The Spinner*, Gerard ter Borch (1617–1681), oil on panel, c. 1652, 13.39 × 10.63 in (34 × 27 cm), Museum Boijmans Van Beuningen. The model for this work was the artist's stepmother, Wiesken Matthys

2.13. *The Spinner, Goatherd of the Auvergne* (1868–1869). Jean-François Millet (1814–1875), oil on canvas, 92.5 × 73.5 cm, photo credit: Hervé Lewandowski, Musée D'Orsay, Paris [spinning while walking and tending flocks].

III: Rumpelstiltskin's Author

3.1. 'Women Spinning Wool,' *Ovide Moralise*, attributed to Chretien Logouais, 14th C, Vellum, Bibliothèque municipale de Rouen (Ms O 4).

This work is an adaptation of Ovid's 'Metamorphoses.' As well as recounting mythology, this work adapts the Classical stories into the realm of Christian ethics. It may have been commissioned by Jeanne de Bourgogne, wife of Philippe V. References to the Papal Schism, when Clement V established residence at Avignon, date the manuscript to around 1316–1328.

3.2. *"Les Veilles", Evening Work, or The Night Workers* (a spinnstube) (1888), Léon Lhermitte (1884–1925), Oil on canvas, 93.3 × 122 cm, Kelvingrove Museum, Glasgow, UK.

Modern can visualize the spinners' situation based on an image of a "Spinnstube" painted by Leon Augustin Lhermitte (1844–1926), his *Evening Working* (1888) (Glasgow Museums, Kelvingrove Museum, Glasgow, Scotland catalogue #2140, o/c 93.5 × 112 cm). The artist witnessed the last generation of western-European women who practiced this dusk-to-midnight occupation. The spinnstube proceeded as long as it fared unchallenged by popular home entertainments like the phonograph and the even more invasive radio that brought the outside world's norms into isolated villages.

3.3. *The Four Conditions of Society: Work* (c. 1505–1510), Jean Bourdichon (1457–1521), Vellum, Bibliotheque de l'Ecole des Beaux-Arts, Paris, France. Jean Bourdichon was an official court painter to four French Kings: Louis XI, Charles VIII, Louis XII, and François I. This image is a part of a series of four depicting poverty, work, nobility, and the wild state of man (man outside the realms of society).

3.4. *The Spinnstube*, 1524. (Hans) Sebald Beham, (1500–1550) woodcut, Ashmolean Museum of Art and Archaeology, Oxford. The first graphic record of the spinnstube sadly derives only from pedestrian copyists' lackluster woodcuts, copies of Sebald Beham's print that "is the first surviving example of a spinning bee in visual art" (Alison Stewart [2003] p. 127). But, notwithstanding its nominal subject, in Beham's riotous print of imagined debauchery, only two women spin while the rest cavort or fend off frisky advances. Clearly, this illustrates no real spinnstube but a pornographer's idea.

3.5. *Theseus and Athena with Minotaur*, Kylix, attributed to Aison (420 BC), Fired and painted clay, Attica (Greece), Madrid Archaeological Museum, Spain. A Kylix is a drinking vessel—normally used for wine.

3.6. 'Frigga Spinning the Clouds,' by John Charles Dollman (1851–1934), in Guerber, H. A., *Myths of the Norsemen from the Eddas and Sagas*. (London: George G Harrap & Co.) 1909, p. 43. John C. Dollman was a member of the Royal Academy in London, specializing in watercolors. His more famed works were centered on literature: particularly Norse mythology as well as illustrating scenes from *Robinson Crusoe* and the *Jungle Book*.

3.7. *Time and the Fates Sundial*, Paul Manship (1885–1966), (1938), bronze on marble base, 14 × 8½ in (35.5 × 21.6 cm), Smithsonian American Art Museum, Smithsonian Institution.

IV: The Spinner's Libido

4.1. Rumpelstiltskin, 1921 Margaret Evans Price (188–1973), in *Once Upon a Time*, Katherine Lee Bates (ed.) (Chicago: Rand McNally). Professionally known as Margaret Evans, Price was one of the founders of the Fisher-Price toy company.

V: Fairytale Contracts and Commerce

5.1. Rumpelstiltskin, Charles Robinson (1870–1937) in *The Big Book of Fairy Tales*, Walter Jerrold (ed.) (London: Blackie & Son) 1911. Charles Robinson was a British illustrator; the most famed of his works include his illustrations for Robert Louis Stevenson's *A Child's Garden of Verses* and Frances Hodgson Burnett's *The Secret Garden*.

5.2. Rumpelstiltskin, John B. Gruelle (1880–1938), in *Grimm's Fairy Tales*, Margaret Hunt trans. (New York: Cupples & Leon) 1914. Gruelle is better known for creating Raggedy Ann and Raggedy Andy.

VI: Supernatural Zoology

6.1. Gnome (1555) woodcut by Olaus Magnus [Olof Månsson] (1490–1557) and Cornelius Grapheus in *Historiae de gentibus septentrionalibus* (Rome: 1555), p. 74. Olaus Magnus was the Archbishop if Uppsala. In 1555 he published a work *Historiae de gentibus septentrionalibus* (the History of the Northern Peoples) in Rome, which, when translated into many European languages, became the main authority on Sweden and its folklore and customs.

VII: The Talking Cure

7.1. Ecclesiastical Court Examining a Husband for Impotence, from Gratian's *Decretum*, Walters Collection, Baltimore, Ms. W.133 Fol. 277.

VIII: The Devil versus Motherhood

8.1. *Rumpelstiltskin*, 11 March 1946, artist Dik Browne (1917–1989). Richard Arthur Allan Browne, creator of the comic strip *Hagar the Horrible*.

8.2. *Rumpelstiltskin*, 1882, by George R. Halkett (1865–1918). Grimm, Jacob and Wilhelm, *Rumpelstiltskin*, George R. Halkett (illustrated and translated) (London: Thos de la Rue & Co.) 1882.

8.3. *Rumpelstiltskin* (1889), by Henry Justice Ford (1860–1941) in Andrew Lang (ed), *Blue Fairy Book* (New York, 1965, originally published in 1889).

8.4. *The Huntsman Spies Rumpelstiltskin* (1906), illustration by Herbert Cole in Ernest Rhys, *Fairy Gold: A Book of Old English Fairy Tales* (London: J. M. Dent & Sons) 1906.

X: A Bad Reputation, Unearned

10.1. *Rumpelstiltskin Enters* (1934), by Anne Anderson (1874–1952), *The Golden Book* (London: Collins).

10.2. *Ladies Spinning and Sewing* (1765), from *Ladies Magazine*, V&A Museum.

10.3. *Queen Elizabeth of Romania Spinning*. Elizabeth of Wied (1843–1916), Pauline Elisabeth Ottilie Luise zu Wied, who wrote under the name "Carmen Sylva", 'Queen of Roumania in the National Costume,' photograph by Franz Duschek, in *Roumania Past and Present* by James Samuelson, (London: Longmans, Green & Co.) 1882.

10.4. *Penelope & Her Suitors* (c.1509), Bernardino di Betto, called Pintoricchio (1454–1513), fresco, detached and mounted on canvas, 125.5 × 152 cm, National Gallery of Art, London.

10.5. Detail of 10.4: seated maidservant with horizontal box spinning wheel.

XI: A Lamentable Example of Self-Abuse

11.1. Illustration by Charles Robinson (1870–1937) in *The Big Book of Fairy Tales*, ed. Walter Jerrold (London: Blackie & Son).

11.2. *Rumpelstiltskin* (1921) Margaret Evans Price (188–1973), in *Once Upon a Time*, ed. Katherine Lee Bates (Chicago: Rand McNally). Price was one of the founders of Fisher-Price toy company.

XII: Rumpelstiltskin's Competition

12.1. *Wilhelm and Jacob Grimm* (1858). The Brothers Grimm: Wilhelm (l); Jacob (r) by Hermann Biow (1800–1850), Daguerreotype, Hessian State Archives, Hamburg (HStAM Fonds 340 Grimm No B 72, Arcinsys Hessen, Germany).

ACKNOWLEDGMENTS

Thanks are humbly offered in varying degree and for varying services to the project:

Jennifer Gibson and Leah Rand
Madelyn Shaw
Jennifer Abbott
Nikola Zerber
Maurice Varanian
Autumn Spalding

They each know the inestimable value of their contributions, herein acknowledged with a gratitude that cannot adequately repay advice, patience, kindness, and encouragement.

INDEX

Note: Page numbers in *italics* indicate pictures or illustrations.